CRITICAL INSIGHTS

The Sun Also Rises

by Ernest Hemingway

CRITICAL
INSIGHTS

The Sun Also Rises

by Ernest Hemingway

Editor
Keith Newlin
University of North Carolina Wilmington

Salem Press

Pasadena, California   Hackensack, New Jersey

Cover photo: AP/Wide World Photos

Published by Salem Press

© 2011 by EBSCO Publishing
Editor's text © 2011 by Keith Newlin
"The *Paris Review* Perspective" © 2011 by Petrina Crockford for *The Paris Review*

∞ The paper used in these volumes conforms to the American National Standard for Permanence of Paper for Printed Library Materials, Z39.48-1992 (R1997).

Library of Congress Cataloging-in-Publication Data
The sun also rises, by Ernest Hemingway / editor, Keith Newlin.
    p. cm. — (Critical insights)
Includes bibliographical references and index.
ISBN 978-1-58765-713-9 (alk. paper)
    1. Hemingway, Ernest, 1899-1961. Sun also rises. I. Newlin, Keith.
PS3515.E37S9288 2010
813'.52—dc22
                                                      2010029211

PRINTED IN CANADA

Contents

About This Volume, Keith Newlin   vii

The Book and Author

On *The Sun Also Rises*, Keith Newlin   3
Biography of Ernest Hemingway, Stanley Archer   12
The *Paris Review* Perspective, Petrina Crockford for *The Paris Review*   17

Critical Contexts

An American in Paris: Hemingway and the Expatriate Life,
    Matthew J. Bolton   23
Gender Identity and the Modern Condition in *The Sun Also Rises*,
    Jennifer Banach   36
The Art of Friction: Ernest Hemingway and William Faulkner,
    Lorie Watkins Fulton   49
The Critical History of *The Sun Also Rises*, Laurence W. Mazzeno   65

Critical Readings

The Wastelanders, Carlos Baker   87
The Death of Love in *The Sun Also Rises*, Mark Spilka   107
Cabestro and *Vaquilla*: The Symbolic Structure of
    The Sun Also Rises, Dewey Ganzel   123
The Sun Also Rises: The Wounded Anti-Hero, Delbert E. Wylder   145
The Sun Also Rises: A Reconsideration, Donald T. Torchiana   175
Hemingway's Morality of Compensation, Scott Donaldson   202
Love and Friendship/Man and Woman in *The Sun Also Rises*,
    Sibbie O'Sullivan   227
Performance Art: Jake Barnes and "Masculine" Signification
    in *The Sun Also Rises*, Ira Elliott   249
Reading Around Jake's Narration: Brett Ashley and
    The Sun Also Rises, Lorie Watkins Fulton   270
The "Whine" of Jewish Manhood: Rereading Hemingway's
    Anti-Semitism, Reimagining Robert Cohn, Jeremy Kaye   294

The Pedagogy of *The Sun Also Rises*, Donald A. Daiker   314
Life Unworthy of Life? Masculinity, Disability, and Guilt
   in *The Sun Also Rises*, Dana Fore   331

Resources_____

Chronology of Ernest Hemingway's Life   351
Works by Ernest Hemingway   354
Bibliography   356

About the Editor   363
About *The Paris Review*   363
Contributors   365
Acknowledgments   368
Index   370

About This Volume

Keith Newlin

This collection of essays contains a diverse selection of criticism on *The Sun Also Rises*, the novel that launched Ernest Hemingway's reputation and that is still central to understanding the nature of his artistic achievement. The volume is divided into two parts. The first, which provides a series of essays specifically commissioned for this collection, presents an overview of the novel's critical history as well as discussions of the context in which Hemingway composed his first novel and its influence. The second consists of reprinted essays that are not only interesting and revealing studies in their own right but also reflect the trajectory of criticism over the years. In addition, the volume includes a brief biography by Stanley Archer, and Petrina Crockford, writing for *The Paris Review*, offers a writer's perspective on the novel; I also supply an introduction that provides a brief account of the novel's origins, composition, and revision.

In the "Critical Contexts" section that begins the collection, Matthew J. Bolton discusses the ways in which Hemingway fictionalized his experiences in Paris to form a mythic representation of expatriate life within the novel. Jennifer Banach provides an enlightening discussion of the novel's redefinition of masculinity and femininity in which "androgyny becomes a symbol of the modern condition." Lorie Watkins Fulton argues that Hemingway's long competition with William Faulkner for public acclaim is anticipated in Jake Barnes's rivalry with Robert Cohn. Finally, Laurence W. Mazzeno surveys the shifting trends in scholarship on the novel.

The essays reprinted in the "Critical Readings" section offer a representative selection of a variety of critical and theoretical perspectives, beginning with a series of influential essays concerning the nature of the Hemingway hero. Hemingway's first biographer, Carlos Baker, draws on his detailed knowledge of Hemingway's life to illuminate the novel's compositional context and major themes. In an important essay, Mark Spilka argues that the novel functions as a parable in which its central characters are psychically wounded by war and from which Pedro Romero emerges as "the final moral touchstone, the man whose code gives meaning to a world where love and religion are defunct." Dewey Ganzel suggests that the novel offers not a parable in which characters are "anguished creatures of a perverse fate" but an elaborate and more affirmative analogy to the corrida—the running of the bulls—in which each character has a counterpart in the ritual: Jake is a *cabestro,* a "working steer," who manages and controls the action of others until he attains "self-recognition and resolution." Delbert E. Wylder examines more specifically the nature of the novel's antiheroism as reflected in each of its major characters. Donald T. Torchiana takes issue specifically with Baker and Ganzel, arguing that the novel does not depict a symbolic wasteland but instead "celebrates this enduring earth"; for him, the novel's structural analogy to the bullfight reveals that Jake functions less as a steer and more as a matador who dominates the action. Scott Donaldson examines the novel in terms of the trope of compensation, in which "money and its uses form the metaphor by which the moral responsibility of Jake, Bill, and Pedro is measured against the carelessness of Brett, Mike, and Robert."

Reflecting the changing critical preoccupations of recent years, other essays consider the novel in terms of its engagement with notions of masculinity, femininity, and gender. Sibbie O'Sullivan examines Brett and Jake's relationship and finds it offering "the cautious belief in the survival of the two most basic components of any human relationship: love and friendship." Ira Elliott discusses the novel's cultural construction of gender and Jake's performance of masculinity. Lorie Watkins Fulton offers a reassessment of Brett's character by treating Jake as an unreliable narrator, and Jeremy Kaye finds Robert Cohn to be an agent of Jewish manhood—"the novel's figure of hyper-masculinity"—who disrupts traditional notions of masculinity. Donald A. Daiker explores the novel's patterns of teaching and learning, examining the effects of the various lessons on Jake as a learner. Finally, in a provocative reading, Dana Fore analyzes the novel from the perspective of disability studies, arguing that Jake accepts a "worldview that equates disability with pathology and that forces disabled people continually to 'prove' to the world at large that they are completely 'cured' and therefore 'normal.'" A chronology of Hemingway's life, a list of his works, and a bibliography conclude the volume.

THE BOOK
AND
AUTHOR

On *The Sun Also Rises*

Keith Newlin

Today, more than eighty years after it was published, *The Sun Also Rises* has attained the status of a classic American novel. The themes it introduced—the need to create meaning in a world that does not seem to have any inherent values, the necessity to attain some measure of dignity in the face of despair, the destructive nature of romantic illusions— resonated with readers when it was published as they still resonate with readers today. The novel has been read as the statement of a generation unhinged by war and struggling to find meaning within chaos, and it has been seen as the first major artistic achievement of a writer who later attained mythic proportions as the foremost craftsman in the art of implication through understatement, irony, and indirection.

For Hemingway, however, his first novel did not come easily. When he began the novel, in July 1925, he had been living in Paris since 1922 as part of a group of remarkable writers who were then in the process of writing the poems, stories, novels, and plays of what scholars would later call modernism. Within this group meeting at Sylvia Beach's bookstore, Shakespeare and Company, and in the cafés that dotted the Latin Quarter, Hemingway counted among his friends James Joyce, Ezra Pound, Gertrude Stein, and F. Scott Fitzgerald. Hemingway had always been competitive by nature, and the company of such innovative artists only encouraged his desire to excel. He had come to Paris determined to achieve distinction as a writer, and he had spent the past three years paring his prose of superfluous adjectives, subordination, and rhetorical embellishments in order to craft a new manner of suggesting the larger truth lying beneath the surface. His first commercial book, *In Our Time*, had achieved a measure of acclaim for its conveyance of scene and action through a startling economy of language devoid of syntactical flourishes, but Hemingway knew that to achieve the acclaim he craved, he would need to publish a novel.

For a writer who specialized in brevity, writing a novel was no easy task. His first book, *Three Stories and Ten Poems*, had been published in 1923 by a small avant-garde press in a fifty-eight-page edition of only three hundred copies. Hemingway had then turned to honing his craft by creating what he would call "Unwritten Stories," a series of vignettes characterized by extreme compression of action, description, and dialogue in which he experimented with depicting a brutal and violent world through irony and indirection. As befitting a book of experimental prose, the thirty-eight-page collection of eighteen untitled chapters appeared in 1924 as *in our time* in an edition of 170 copies. The next year he recycled sixteen of these chapters, revised and rearranged them, and interspersed them with fourteen short stories to make up *In Our Time*, a thin volume published by Boni & Liveright that contained nearly everything he had written up to that point; of the fourteen short stories, two were former untitled vignettes, now presented as fiction, and eight had been previously published in magazines. Only the final story, presented in two parts—"Big Two-Hearted River"—occupied more than a few pages, and Hemingway was daunted not only by the prospect of branching out into a full-length novel but also by the task of embarking on entirely new material.

When he began writing what would become *The Sun Also Rises* in July 1925, he was baffled by how to begin his story of a group of expatriate writers and their drinking companions arriving at Pamplona to take part in the annual festival of San Fermin. As with much of his fiction, Hemingway began with a memorable experience from his own life, a trip to Pamplona he had taken earlier that summer with his wife, Hadley, and his friends Bill Smith, Donald Ogden Stewart, Harold Loeb, Pat Guthrie, and Duff Twysden to witness the annual running of the bulls and the accompanying corridas. As Hemingway's biographers have amply documented, the festivities soon erupted into a series of drunken squabbles and rivalries, at the center of which was Hemingway's jealousy over Loeb's affair with Duff Twysden. On reflection, he was struck by the contrast between the petty jealousies and vanities of his friends and the more serious matter of a matador's confrontation of danger in the ritual of the corrida: here, he realized, was a proper subject for fiction.

Hemingway began his story as a journalistic account of the corruption of the bullfighter Cayetano Ordoñez, nicknamed Niño de la Palma, in Pamplona, opening with the lines, "I saw him for the first time in his room in the Hotel Quintana in Pamplona. We met Quintana on the stairs as Bill and I were comeing [*sic*] up to the room to get the wine bag to take to the bull fight. 'Come on,' said Quintana. 'Would you like to meet Niño de la Palma?'" (Svoboda 6). In this draft, Hemingway's account of the events is largely autobiographical—he uses the real names of the people involved, and the story is told through the first-person perspective of "Hem." As William Balassi has observed, the conflicts in this opening chapter reveal "not the potential ruination of Niño, as later developed in the novel, but the conflicts and turmoil within Hem as he tries—unsuccessfully—to resolve the tensions and contradictory values of two mutually exclusive worlds: the *aficionado* world he preferred and the expatriate world he inhabited" (67). As Hemingway developed the characters, he soon began to shift to fictionalized names, expanding and departing from the real-life prototypes: Harold Loeb became Gerald Loeb, then Gerald Cohn, before Hemingway settled on Robert Cohn; Bill Smith and Donald Stewart became Bill Gorton; and "Hem" became first Rafael and then Jacob Barnes, while Duff remained "Duff" throughout the manuscript, and Niño de la Palma did not become Pedro Romero until the revision stage (Reynolds 120).

In this early stage of composition, Hemingway was still defining the sort of story he would tell. On the day he changed his narrator from "Hem" to "Jake," he devoted a number of pages to exploring Jake's boyhood by recounting Jake's first awareness of the meaning of death as he attends a favorite uncle's funeral and listens to his pious mother lecture him about avoiding the vices his uncle supposedly pursued: "There were several things my mother said she would rather see me in my grave than do. They were quite unimportant things such as smoking cigarettes, gambling, and drinking and the last two were quite un-thought of and far off sins" (Svoboda 12). The point of the anecdote is to dramatize Jake's awareness of the disjunction between what a person says and means, for if his mother literally means what she says, as Frederic Joseph Svoboda explains, then "she is a monster; if, as is far more likely, she means something very different from her literal statement, she is guilty of falsification or foolish confusion" (14). Hemingway apparently wrote the anecdote as a means of working through his thinking about a major motif of the novel: the disparity between what characters say and what their actions mean.

At this point, Hemingway embarked on one of many digressions in which he mused about the purpose and method of his writing:

> Probably any amount of this does not seem to have anything to do with the story and perhaps it has not. I am sick of these ones with their clear re-strained writing and I am going to try to get in the whole business and to do that there has to be things that seem as though they had nothing to do with it just as in life. In life people are not conscious of these special moments that novelists build their whole structures on. That is most people are not. That surely has nothing to do with the story but you can not tell until you finish it because none of the significant things are going to have any literary signs marking them. You have to figure them out by yourself.
>
> Now when my friends read this they will say it is awful; it is not what they had hoped or expected from me. Gertrude Stein once told me that remarks are not literature. All right, let it go at that. Only this time all the remarks are going in and if it is not literature who claimed it was anyway. (Svoboda 37)

Such comments reveal Hemingway working through his ambitions and intentions as he experimented with developing character and establishing scene; he seems to have worried about his initial journalistic impulse—to set down the events as they actually happened—while also realizing that fiction necessarily requires the writer to select events and scenes to shape the significance of the story. At this point, he resisted selection, determined to "try to get in the whole business," while he was also equally determined to continue writing in the restrained understatement, devoid of "literary signs," that had marked his earlier short fiction.

As he reflected on his intentions, Hemingway realized he needed to provide background for his characters, so he began the second manuscript chapter with "To understand what happened in Pamplona you must understand the quarter in Paris" (Reynolds 123), and he proceeded to sketch Jake's movements amid the nightlife of Paris, devoting much attention to Jake's interactions with Gerald Cohn to develop the contrast between Jake's hard-boiled acceptance of life and Cohn's romantic illusions. He worried about who would be the hero of his developing story, having Jake comment: "Now you can see. I looked as though I were trying to get to be the hero of this story. But that was all wrong. Gerald Cohn is the hero. When I bring myself in it is only to clear up something. Or maybe Duff is the hero. Or Niño de la Palma. He never really had a chance to be the hero. Or maybe there is not any hero at all. Maybe a story is better without any hero" (Svoboda 32). As his story unfolded, Hemingway gradually realized that it would not contain a conventional hero, a character who stood as the novel's moral center, but rather a series of characters whose interactions illustrate the alienation of the post-World War I generation.

After he completed a draft of the novel, Hemingway embarked on what he later called "the most difficult job of rewriting I have ever done . . . when I had to take the first draft of *The Sun Also Rises* which I had written in one sprint of six weeks, and make it into a novel" (*Moveable Feast* 202). He excised all of the reflective passages in which he mused on the purpose of his writing, tightened up and repaired gaps in the narration, and pared down overwritten passages that went into too much detail and thereby diminished the effectiveness of key scenes. For example, at the beginning of chapter 14 of *Sun*, an intoxicated Jake goes to bed, listens to Brett and Cohn come up the stairs, and tries to read to keep his mind from dwelling on Brett. The second paragraph concludes, "I could shut my eyes without getting the wheeling sensation. But I could not sleep. There is no reason why because it is dark you should look at things differently from when it is light. The hell there isn't!" (151). In the typescript Jake reflects for four paragraphs on his relationship with Brett, the opening paragraph beginning as follows:

> And the conversation of all day kept coming back in a sort of regurgitation. I felt pretty well through with Brett. In life you tried to go along with out [*sic*] criticizing the actions of other people but sometimes they offended you in spite of yourself. Brett had lost something. Since she had gone to San Sebastian with Cohn she seemed to have lost that quality in her that had never been touched before. All this talking now about former lovers to make this seem quite ordinary. She was ashamed. Really ashamed. She had never been ashamed before. It made her vulgar where before she had been simply going by her own rules. She had wanted to kill off something in her and the killing had gotten out of her control. Well she had killed it off in me. That was a good thing. I did not want to be in love with any woman. I did not want to have any grand passion that I could never do anything about. I was glad it was gone. The hell I was. (Svoboda 20-21)

In the following paragraphs, Jake goes on to dwell on his love for Brett and his efforts to kill it off by picturing her with other men and concludes that she can hurt him no longer, though the interior monologue instead reveals that he is lying to himself about no longer loving her. When he revised, Hemingway cut these reflections because they were unnecessary: Jake's actions have already demonstrated Brett's effect on him, particularly his inability to cut her loose.

After Hemingway completed revisions and sent the typescript to Scribner's, his editor, Maxwell Perkins, sent a carbon copy to F. Scott Fitzgerald, who had earlier been instrumental in bringing Hemingway to the firm, while also having the manuscript set in galley proof. Fitzgerald was aghast at the opening chapters, the first of which began, "This is a novel about a lady. Her name is Lady Ashley and when the story begins she is living in Paris and it is Spring. That should be a good setting for a romantic but highly moral story. As every one knows, Paris is a very romantic place. Spring in Paris is a very happy and romantic time. Autumn in Paris, although very beautiful, might give a note of sadness or melancholy that we shall try to keep out of this story" ("Unpublished" 7). Jake goes on to describe Brett Ashley's and Mike Campbell's background, how they came to be together, and their unplanned affair (they found themselves at a hotel with only one available room, and that with a double bed), with considerable discussion of why they drink so much. We learn that Brett's favorite term for being drunk—being "blind"—is not just metaphorical but describes the literal effects of her drinking: she "first lost her power of speech and just sat and listened, then she lost her sight and saw nothing that went on, and finally she ceased to hear" ("Unpublished" 9). In the second chapter Jake defends his use of first person: "I did not want to tell this story in the first person but I find that I must. I wanted to stay well outside the story so that I would not be touched by it in any way, and to handle all the people in it with that irony and pity that are so essential to good writing" ("Unpublished" 10). He recounts his own history before moving on to discuss the Latin Quarter as a state of mind and then to introduce Robert Cohn.

"I think parts of *Sun Also* are careless + ineffectual," Fitzgerald wrote Hemingway in a ten-page critique. "I find in you the same tendency to envelope or (and as it usually turns out) to *embalm* in mere wordiness an anecdote or joke thats casually appealed to you, that I find in myself in trying to preserve a piece of 'fine writing.' Your first chapter contains about 10 such things and it gives a feeling of condescending *casuallness*" (Bruccoli 64). Fitzgerald proceeded to catalog the faults of the opening two chapters: "I think there are about 24 sneers, superiorities and nose-thumbings-at-nothing that mar the whole narrative up to p. 29 where (after a false start on the introduction of

Cohn) it really gets going" (Bruccoli 65). Fitzgerald quite rightly identified the sort of posturing and self-absorption that Hemingway had mostly cut from his first draft, and he concluded by suggesting, "Why not cut the inessentials in Cohens [*sic*] biography? . . . From here   Or rather from p. 30 I began to like the novel but Ernest I can't tell you the sense of disappointment that beginning with its elephantine facetiousness gave me" (Bruccoli 66).

Hemingway took Fitzgerald's comments to heart, for he wanted to make a ten-strike with his first novel and not alienate readers. Then, too, he had made his reputation by crafting stories that showcased the art of omission, and Fitzgerald's comments made him realize he had failed to omit the nonessential. Most of the elaborations of the opening were given later in the novel, and more indirectly. He tried condensing and drafted several new openings but eventually decided to cut the first chapter entirely and half of the second, beginning the novel with a line that appeared midway: "Robert Cohn was middleweight boxing champion of Princeton." In explaining the cuts, he wrote to Perkins, "There is nothing in those first sixteen pages that does not come out, or is explained, or re-stated in the rest of the book—or is unnecessary to state. I think it will move much faster from the start that way" (*Selected Letters* 208). To Fitzgerald, he explained, "I believe that the book is really better starting as it does now directly with Cohn and omitting any preliminary warming up. After all if I'm trying to write books without any extra words I might as well stick to it" (*Selected Letters* 215). Time proved Hemingway right: *The Sun Also Rises* contains no "extra words" and remains a masterpiece of implication.

Works Cited

Balassi, William. "The Writing of the Manuscript of *The Sun Also Rises*, with a Chart of Its Session-by-Session Development." *The Hemingway Review* 6.1 (1986): 65-78.

Bruccoli, Matthew J. *Fitzgerald and Hemingway, A Dangerous Friendship*. New York: Carroll & Graf, 1994.

Hemingway, Ernest. *A Moveable Feast*. 1964. New York: Charles Scribner's Sons, 1996.

_____. *Selected Letters, 1917-1961*. Ed. Carlos Baker. New York: Charles Scribner's Sons, 1981.

_____. *The Sun Also Rises*. 1926. New York: Charles Scribner's Sons, 1954.

_____. "The Unpublished Opening of *The Sun Also Rises*." *Antaeus* 33 (1979): 7-14.

Reynolds, Michael S. "False Dawn: A Preliminary Analysis of *The Sun Also Rises* Manuscript." *Hemingway: A Revaluation*. Ed. Donald R. Noble. Troy, NY: Whitston, 1983. 115-34.

Svoboda, Frederic Joseph. *Hemingway and "The Sun Also Rises": The Crafting of a Style*. Lawrence: UP of Kansas, 1983.

Biography of Ernest Hemingway_____
Stanley Archer

Because of his compelling prose style and his vision of heroism, Ernest Miller Hemingway holds a secure place among the leading fiction writers of the twentieth century. Born in the Chicago suburb of Oak Park, Illinois, Hemingway was the second child of Clarence "Ed" Hemingway, a physician, and his wife, Grace Hall, a voice teacher. Though reared in a strict home, as a youth Hemingway developed the energetic lifestyle for which he later became known. He participated in competitive sports—football, boxing, swimming—and enjoyed hunting and fishing trips with his father. During high school, he wrote poems and short stories, and following graduation he became a reporter for the *Kansas City Star*. During World War I, he was an ambulance driver on the Italian front and suffered severe shrapnel wounds. Sent to a military hospital, he fell in love with his nurse, who ended their affair after he returned to Oak Park. Because he was intent on becoming a writer, Hemingway found a position with the *Toronto Star*. In 1921, he married Hadley Richardson, eight years his senior, and they moved to Paris, where Hemingway studied his craft and found stimulation in the company of Gertrude Stein and other expatriates of the Left Bank.

The Paris experience laid a firm foundation for Hemingway's literary career. There, he wrote the autobiographical Nick Adams stories of *In Our Time* (1925), in which critics have discerned the basic themes of his later fiction, and his first novel, *The Torrents of Spring* (1926), which parodied the prose of his friend Sherwood Anderson. During this time, he also wrote *The Sun Also Rises* (1926), which is based on his experiences in Paris, and introduced what critics would come to call "the Hemingway hero" through the novel's protagonist, Jake Barnes, a veteran wounded during World War I. The novel includes a galaxy of characters that represent the "lost generation" in Paris.

Following his Paris years, Hemingway lived in Key West, Florida, in Cuba, and in Ketchum, Idaho, and frequently traveled to other parts of the world, including Africa for safaris. In 1927, he divorced Hadley Richardson and married her friend Pauline Pfeiffer; that marriage lasted until 1940, when he married Martha Gellhorn, a war correspondent and writer. After their divorce in 1945, he married Mary Welsh, to whom he remained married until his death.

Three years after *The Sun Also Rises* made him famous, Hemingway published a novel set during World War I, *A Farewell to Arms*, which narrates the story of Frederic Henry, a soldier who is wounded on the Italian front, falls in love with his nurse, and flees with her from the war. *To Have and Have Not* (1937) features the Hemingway hero as a gunrunner and smuggler. Like other heroes, Harry Morgan is defeated after a courageous fight in which he adheres to his personal code. In *For Whom the Bell Tolls* (1940), Robert Jordan, an American expatriate volunteer, undertakes a dangerous mission for the Loyalist side in the Spanish Civil War. He finds love amid danger and loses his life for a cause he values, demonstrating another quality of the Hemingway hero: "grace under pressure."

During World War II, Hemingway participated as a reporter and became involved in fighting in France. The episodes that he witnessed formed the background for *Across the River and into the Trees* (1950), which is generally regarded as his least significant novel. Its hero, Richard Cantwell, an introspective colonel in his early fifties, finds romance in Venice while suffering from heart disease.

The Old Man and the Sea (1952), which is essentially a novella, introduces the hero as an old man, Santiago the fisherman, who catches a marlin larger than his boat but is unable to protect it from sharks. According to his own understanding, he went out too far and was defeated attempting what no one else could have done. For this book, Hemingway received the 1953 Pulitzer Prize, and the work was influential in securing for him the Nobel Prize in Literature in the following year. After the publication of *The Old Man and the Sea*, Hemingway's health gradually declined, aggravated by injuries sustained in two plane crashes in Africa. He suffered depression, paranoia, and hypertension, among other afflictions, and committed suicide at his home in Ketchum, Idaho, on July 2, 1961.

From three thousand pages of unpublished manuscripts, editors have produced several posthumous publications. *Islands in the Stream* (1970) portrays the life of a hero grieving for the deaths of his sons and throwing his energy into a campaign against German submarines in the Caribbean Sea. *The Garden of Eden* (1986), set in the 1920's and based on the author's relationships with his first two wives, depicts its writer-hero undergoing divorce and remarrying with a more suitable woman. *True at First Light* (1999), edited by his son Patrick, is a fictionalized memoir of Hemingway's last visit to Africa between 1953 and 1954.

All of Hemingway's fiction has strong autobiographical elements; in each of his novels, the hero's age is approximately that of the author's. His works, which have often been the basis for successful films, retain their appeal for a large reading public and for students of literature. The most pervasive element of Hemingway's writing is his development of a hero whose values are clear, who lives by a code, and who is doomed to defeat despite his efforts. A wounded man cut off from conventional society, he seeks adventure, prizes courage, faces danger, and courts death. He is sensitive and chivalrous toward women, but though he easily recognizes the presence of an ethical code in others, he lacks close friends. Having lost the innocence of youth, he struggles to wrest meaning from life. The hero assumes mythical proportions, as does the author himself, who lived as much of his myth as possible.

A second striking feature of Hemingway's fiction is its style. Deceptively simple, it conveys deep emotion. Hemingway relies on the exact word, on understatement, and on the "iceberg principle"—the omission of everything that is not absolutely essential to the narrative. The result is clear, crisp, and often hard-hitting prose, with terse, pithy, direct dialogue.

From *Cyclopedia of World Authors, Fourth Revised Edition* (Pasadena, CA: Salem Press). Copyright © 2004 by Salem Press, Inc.

Bibliography

Benson, Jackson J., ed. *New Critical Approaches to the Short Stories of Ernest Hemingway*. Durham, N.C.: Duke University Press, 1990. Section 1 covers critical approaches to Hemingway's most important long fiction; section 2 concentrates on story techniques and themes; section 3 focuses on critical interpretations of the most important stories; section 4 provides an overview of Hemingway criticism; section 5 contains a comprehensive checklist of Hemingway short fiction criticism from 1975 to 1989.

Berman, Ronald. *Fitzgerald, Hemingway, and the Twenties*. Tuscaloosa: University of Alabama Press, 2001. Offers an explication of the cultural context of the era and discusses how the works of these two American writers are imbued with the attitudes and icons of their day.

_____. "Vaudeville Philosophers: 'The Killers.'" *Twentieth Century Literature* 45 (Spring, 1999): 79-93. Discusses the influence of the modernist reevaluation of vaudeville on Ernest Hemingway's short story; notes that Hemingway's interest in vaudeville resulted from its pervasive presence in society and its acceptance in the intellectual world; argues that vaudeville scripts inspired Hemingway's interest in the juxtaposition of urban sophistication and rural idiocy.

Bloom, Harold, ed. *Ernest Hemingway*. Broomall, Pa.: Chelsea House, 2000. Includes articles by a variety of critics who treat topics such as Hemingway's style, his visual techniques, and the unifying devices in his works.

Burgess, Anthony. *Ernest Hemingway*. New York: Thames and Hudson, 1999. Concise introduction to Hemingway was published originally in 1978 as *Ernest Hemingway and His World*. Includes photographs.

Dubus, Andre. "A Hemingway Story." *Kenyon Review*, n.s. 19 (Spring, 1997): 141-147. Dubus, a respected short-story writer, discusses Hemingway's "In Another Country." States that, whereas he once thought the story was about the futility of cures, since becoming disabled he has come to understand that it is about healing.

Flora, Joseph M. *Ernest Hemingway: A Study of the Short Fiction*. Boston: Twayne, 1989. An introduction to Hemingway's short fiction that focuses on the importance of reading the stories within the literary context Hemingway creates for them in the collections *In Our Time*, *Winner Take Nothing*, and *Men Without Women*. Argues that Hemingway devises an echo effect in which one story reflects another.

Hays, Peter L. *Ernest Hemingway*. New York: Continuum, 1990. Presents a brief but instructive overview of Hemingway's life and his achievement as a writer. Offers brief critical summaries of the novels and many short stories. Contains a useful chronology.

Hotchner, A. E. *Papa Hemingway: A Personal Memoir*. New ed. New York: Carroll & Graf, 1999. Written by one of Hemingway's close friends, an editor, novelist, playwright, and biographer. Originally published in 1966, this Hemingway Centennial Edition features a new introduction.

Lamb, Robert Paul. "The Love Song of Harold Krebs: Form, Argument, and Meaning in Hemingway's 'Soldier's Home.'" *The Hemingway Review* 14 (Spring,

1995): 18-36. Claims that the story concerns both war trauma and a conflict between mother and son. Discusses the structure of the story; argues that by ignoring the story's form, one misses the manner of Hemingway's narrative argument and the considerable art that underlies it.

Leonard, John. "'A Man of the World' and 'A Clean, Well-Lighted Place': Hemingway's Unified View of Old Age." *The Hemingway Review* 13 (Spring, 1994): 62-73. Compares the two Hemingway stories in terms of the theme of age. Notes also the themes of aloneness, consolation of light, loss of sexuality and physical prowess, depression, violence, and the need for dignity.

Mellow, James R. *Hemingway: A Life Without Consequences*. Boston: Houghton Mifflin, 1992. A well-informed, sensitive handling of Hemingway's life and work by a seasoned biographer.

Nolan, Charles J., Jr. "Hemingway's Complicated Enquiry in *Men Without Women*." *Studies in Short Fiction* 32 (Spring, 1995): 217-222. Examines the theme of homosexuality in "A Simple Enquiry" from Hemingway's *Men Without Women*. Argues that the characters in the story are enigmatic, revealing their complexity only after one has looked carefully at what they do and say.

Reynolds, Michael. *The Young Hemingway*. New York: Basil Blackwell, 1986.
_____. *Hemingway: The Paris Years*. New York: Basil Blackwell, 1989.
_____. *Hemingway: The American Homecoming*. New York: W. W. Norton, 1992.
_____. *Hemingway: The 1930's*. New York: W. W. Norton, 1997.
_____. *Hemingway: The Final Years*. New York: W. W. Norton, 1999. Reynolds's five-volume, painstaking biography is devoted to the evolution of Hemingway's life and writing.

Tetlow, Wendolyn. E. *Hemingway's "In Our Time": Lyrical Dimensions*. Lewisburg, Pa.: Bucknell University Press, 1992. Argues that the collection is a "coherent, integral work" unified by such elements as the character Nick Adams, image patterns, symbols, and recurrent themes. Claims the book is analogous to a poetic sequence, a group of works that tend to interact as an organic whole. Discusses the lyrical elements in Hemingway's self-conscious juxtaposition of stories and interchapters.

Wagner-Martin, Linda. *Ernest Hemingway: A Literary Life*. New York: Palgrave Macmillan, 2007. Examines Hemingway's life, especially his troubled relationship with his parents. Wagner-Martin makes insightful connections among the author's personal life, his emotions, and his writing.

_____, ed. *Ernest Hemingway: Seven Decades of Criticism*. East Lansing: Michigan State University Press, 1998. A collection of essays ranging from Gertrude Stein's 1923 review of Hemingway's stories to responses to *The Garden of Eden*. Includes essays on "Indian Camp," "Hills Like White Elephants," and *In Our Time* as self-begetting fiction.

Weber, Ronald. *Hemingway's Art of Non-Fiction*. New York: St. Martin's Press, 1990. Provides systematic critical analysis of Hemingway's major nonfiction works, including those published posthumously, to assess the author's achievement in this genre.

the PARIS
REVIEW

The *Paris Review* Perspective

Petrina Crockford for *The Paris Review*

The Sun Also Rises has become required reading for anyone interested in the course of American literature. The standard curriculum has
us read Hemingway's novel in sociological terms, as a relic of the "lost
generation" and the post-Great War world. Never mind that Hemingway was never comfortable with the attention given to his choice of
Gertrude Stein's "you are all a lost generation" as an epigraph; in a letter to his editor, Maxwell Perkins, about a review of the book, Hemingway wrote, "It was refreshing to see someone have some doubts that I
took the Gertrude Stein thing very seriously—I meant to play off
against that splendid bombast. . . . Nobody knows about the generation
that follows them and certainly has no right to judge." And never mind
that the book's cultural influence in some ways ran counter to the author's intentions to write "a damn tragedy": Malcolm Cowley observed that after the novel's 1926 publication, young girls from Smith
came to New York "modeling themselves after Lady Brett" and "hundreds of bright young men from the Middle West were trying to be
Hemingway heroes, talking in tough understatements from the sides of
their mouths." Despite these difficulties there is value in reading the
novel as an artistic record of a moment, but this reading risks missing a
larger and more valuable point. Perhaps more so than any of Hemingway's other books, *The Sun Also Rises* stands out as a testament to what
Hemingway was and would become: complexly gifted, influential to
the point of parody, romantic and tragic in his art as well as in his life.
　　Hemingway wrote *The Sun Also Rises* early in his career, and it is
electric with a young writer's exuberance. It is the product of a gifted

young writer forging his own methodology, and the seams sometimes show: its weaknesses are closely tied to its strengths. "He was unquestionably a genius," E. L. Doctorow has written, "but of the kind that advertises its limits." *The Sun Also Rises* is the most stylized of the Hemingway canon: the sentences are shorn of adjectives and adverbs, dialogue is short and clipped, and words and phrases repeat themselves—the Hemingway typography, Ralph Ellison called it. Together these function as an emotional synecdoche, providing the parts from which we make revelations about a whole not wholly present. The sentences can be clean to the point of being antiseptic, and when characters speak, they are almost always being evasive. "I've never felt such a bitch," Lady Brett Ashley repeats several times in the novel, "I've never felt such a bitch." The pattern of her words is an attempt to evoke the sentiment behind the words—her confession evokes her indifference and the indifference of the people Hemingway saw around him—but her words risk becoming less evocative of emotion than of a literary style: this is where Hemingway falls open to parody.

The Sun Also Rises also gives us our first extended look at the characters that Hemingway would return to again and again—archetypes that in the hands of other writers would become stereotypes. The quintessentially tough narrator Jake Barnes, who stoically accepts the lot fate has handed him, would be reincarnated as Robert Jordan in *For Whom the Bell Tolls*, as Thomas Hudson in *Islands in the Stream*, as any number of men who face their eventual defeat in the final pages with hard-edged bravado. The female protagonist, Lady Brett Ashley, is elusive in her motives and prey to narrative—another character model Hemingway would write and rewrite throughout his life. Lady Brett Ashley might not be as completely drawn as Jake Barnes, but she is undeniably vivid, a victim of joie de vivre even as it sustains her through the pain of unattainable love. People who are heroic in their acceptance of the inevitable, who nobly accept failure and defeat— these are the Hemingway men and women. And if redemption is possible, it is not achieved through religion, heroism, or success, but through the acceptance of the natural order, over which the sun always rises. The search for this redemption is the struggle that animates Hemingway's entire body of work.

If *The Sun Also Rises* offers a way into Hemingway's art, it also offers a way into Hemingway himself. This was a writer who had gone from mimicking Ring Lardner in Oak Park, Illinois, to creating an artistic method in Paris that would change the way Americans think about writing. Hemingway forged a new path for American fiction with his ruthless devotion to his craft and his obsession with this creative vision. He spawned a generation of acolytes. The good ones understood the finer points of what Hemingway did; the bad ones operated from the same misunderstanding as the parodists. *The Sun Also Rises* gives us all of this: the good, the bad, and the misunderstood. It gives us Hemingway himself, who ultimately had, to return to Ellison, "that which is most enduring in the human enterprise: the power of man to define himself against the ravages of time through artistic style."

Works Cited

Cowley, Malcolm. *Exile's Return: A Literary Odyssey of the 1920s*. New York: Penguin Classics, 1994.

Doctorow, E. L. "Braver Than We Thought." Rev. of *The Garden of Eden*, by Ernest Hemingway. *The New York Times Book Review* 18 May 1986.

Ellison, Ralph. *Living with Music*. Ed. Robert G. O'Meally. New York: Modern Library, 2002.

Ellison, Ralph, and James Alan McPherson. "Indivisible Man." *The Atlantic Monthly* Dec. 1970: 45-60.

Hemingway, Ernest. *The Sun Also Rises*. 1926. New York: Collier Books, 1986.

_____. "To Maxwell Perkins." 19 November 1926. *Selected Letters, 1917-1961*. Ed. Carlos Baker. New York: Charles Scribner's Sons, 1981. 229.

CRITICAL CONTEXTS

An American in Paris:
Hemingway and the Expatriate Life_____

Matthew J. Bolton

Paris has long held a totemic place in American culture as the ideal city in which to lead the artist's life. In the Paris of the popular imagination, one leaves behind the conventionality, materialism, and petty moralizing of American culture and instead pursues a bohemian life of the mind. Perhaps no single work has more powerfully shaped American conceptions of the city than Ernest Hemingway's 1926 novel *The Sun Also Rises*, the definitive representation of the floating world of café life and expatriate culture. Jake Barnes, Hemingway's stoic and solitary journalist, remains a writerly ideal, a man who lives the sort of free and self-directed life an American nine-to-fiver can only dream of. Hemingway's 1964 posthumous memoir, *A Moveable Feast*, amplifies his vision of Paris as the spiritual home of the artist and writer. Barnes is a journalist rather than a novelist, and so the artist's life is only tangentially represented in *The Sun Also Rises*; in his memoir, on the other hand, Hemingway talks explicitly and lyrically of being a writer in the city. In the opening chapter, "A Good Café on the Place St.-Michel," Hemingway invokes a sepia-toned vision of the expatriate writer at work:

> It was a pleasant café, warm and clean and friendly, and I hung up my old waterproof on the coat rack to dry and put my worn and weathered felt hat on the rack above the bench and ordered a *café au lait*. The waiter brought it and I took out a notebook from the pocket of the coat and a pencil and started to write. (7)

This is the sort of creative life that countless Americans imagine Paris will offer them. Although Paris was home to a thriving Anglo-American literary scene, Hemingway presents the expatriate writer as a radically independent figure, an incarnation of the American archetype of the rugged individualist. Paris, in Hemingway's imagination, becomes a last frontier through which the writer or artist must blaze his own path. One way to understand Hemingway's work in the larger context of the Paris expatriate scene is to compare his actual experience in Paris with his representation of it in *The Sun Also Rises*. In the gap between the two, one can see how Hemingway transformed the materials of his own life into a great novel and how, in so doing, he cultivated the image of the expatriate as an autonomous figure.

When Hemingway arrived in Paris in 1922—that remarkable year in which both James Joyce's *Ulysses* and T. S. Eliot's *The Waste Land* were published—he found a city that was already the site of a large Anglo-American expatriate community and a center of literary production. To list the members of the city's expatriate literary community is to catalog the major forces in modernism. At different points in the 1910s and 1920s, Paris was home to James Joyce, Ford Madox Ford, E. E. Cummings, Gertrude Stein, T. S. Eliot, Ezra Pound, William Faulkner, F. Scott Fitzgerald, and, eventually, Ernest Hemingway himself. It was another seminal writer, Sherwood Anderson, who first encouraged Hemingway to go to Paris and who furnished him with letters of introduction to Pound, Stein, and others who would prove important mentors. For his part, Anderson had already served as a mentor to Hemingway while the two men were living in Chicago. Hemingway, who had been a volunteer with the Red Cross in Italy during World War I, confided in Anderson that he wanted to return to that country with his new wife. Anderson suggested Paris instead, making a persuasive argument about the low exchange rate and its effect on the standard of living, and offered to introduce Hemingway to the literary friends and acquaintances he had in the city. Hemingway was not shy about drawing on Anderson's connections: at the older writer's prompting, he met with Sylvia Beach, proprietor of Shakespeare and Company, as well as with Stein and Pound. As a point of reference, Anderson would within two years furnish another young novelist with similar letters to Pound and company. But William Faulkner, on his own journey through Italy and France, was too shy to approach these luminaries. Hemingway's assertiveness served him well: on moving to Paris, he immediately introduced himself to the established writers who lived there. The relationships with Stein and Pound were valuable in themselves and also led to Hemingway's meeting more and more of the important writers of his day. From the start, then, Hemingway benefited from the mentorship of more seasoned artists, and Paris offered him not merely a good café in which to write but also a community of writers who were willing to help him in his craft.

Why had this community of English-speaking writers and artists blossomed in Paris? In the wake of World War I, a combination of cultural and economic factors conspired to make the city an attractive destination for footloose Americans. The United States' involvement in the war meant that some five million young men had been exposed to life in Europe. With the war over, some of these veterans found that France held far more attraction for them than did their American hometowns. As a popular song of 1918 went, "How ya gonna keep 'em down on the farm (after they've seen Paree)?" The song seems to express the country's fear that it had won the war but lost the generation that had fought it. The young veterans had seen too much of the world to be able to return to their old lives. The 1920s may be remembered as the roaring jazz age—an era of flappers and socialites—but this facet of postwar culture must be understood in the larger context of a reactionary decade. Prohibition, America's "noble experiment" in outlawing the manufacture and sale of alcohol, had gone into effect in January of 1920. Mainstream American culture, and the legal apparatus that supported it, was resolutely bent on reintegrating the veterans of the Great War into a life of temperance, family values, and the Protestant work ethic.

Someone of Hemingway's disposition therefore had many reasons for choosing Paris over his native Chicago. Hemingway had grown up in the Chicago suburb of Oak Park, a dry town where godliness, propriety, and respectability were of paramount importance. Hemingway would always have a conflicted relationship with the Protestant tradition in which he had been raised and which was epitomized by the pieties of Oak Park. In some respects, Prohibition represented the triumph of Oak Park over Chicago: the value system of the well-regulated and well-heeled town was being extended to a national front. An aspiring artist therefore had two reasons to move abroad: Prohibition and reactionary politics were pushing him out of America, while artistic and intellectual freedom—not to mention the allure of having a legal drink at a streetside café—were pulling him toward Paris. In Paris, one could live a life that was far freer than American cultural mores would allow, and the favorable rate of exchange between the dollar and the franc made the expatriate life possible. Hemingway described the dollar's buying power in an article he sent back to the *Toronto Star*, the newspaper for which he was a foreign correspondent: "An American or Canadian can live comfortably, eat at attractive restaurants and find amusement for a total expenditure of two and one half to three dollars a day" (Reynolds 5). A man who would have to work steadily and live modestly in the United States could instead use his dollar's buying power to live comfortably in Paris—and therefore to devote his time to the arts.

Moreover, Paris was arguably the intellectual and artistic capital of the world. In art, it was a city of "isms": the birthplace of Impressionism, post-Impressionism, Fauvism, and cubism. In music, Claude Debussy was still composing, while Igor Stravinsky over the preceding decade had premiered works such as *The Firebird Suite* and *The Rite of Spring*. In the second half of the nineteenth century, Paris had been home to novelists such as Gustave Flaubert and poets like the symbolists—Charles Baudelaire, Arthur Rimbaud, and Paul Verlaine among them. In Hemingway's time it was home to André Gide and to Marcel Proust, who beginning in 1909 and continuing throughout the 1920s was releasing his monumental *Remembrance of Things Past*. The life of the arts and letters could be lived on any level, it seemed: from the ancient halls of the Sorbonne and the Academy to the café tables on the Left Bank of the Seine. Paris offered a life of art and culture that no American city could rival.

Interestingly enough, however, the expatriate community was not particularly concerned with Parisian culture or society in a broader sense. The English and Americans had their own social circles, their own literary presses and journals, and their own English-language bookstores. There was enough of a critical mass of English and American writers and artists living in Paris for them to have a vibrant literary community. The relative insulation of this community is reflected in *The Sun Also Rises*. Little of French history, culture, or society makes its way into Hemingway's novel. Instead, the work is bound up with the lives of the American expatriates themselves; Barnes and his contemporaries make up a separate subculture that has no interest in assimilating with the native Parisians. The overwhelming majority of the characters' interactions are with each other or with French people providing services—among them waiters, hoteliers, and prostitutes. The English speakers' relationships with the French themselves are primarily transactional in nature. Compare this insularity with the relationships between Americans and Europeans in the novels of Henry James, where the plots often revolve around delicate social interactions across languages and cultures. The Jamesian motif of the innocent abroad would have little resonance in a Hemingway novel. Not only are Hemingway's Americans not innocent, but they also have no meaningful relationships with the Europeans they encounter abroad.

Gertrude Stein identified this insularity as one of the factors that had made Paris so important to her own development as an artist. She wrote: "One of the things that I have liked all these years is to be surrounded by people who know no English. It has left me more intensely alone with my eyes and my English" (Kennedy 72). Hemingway may well have sympathized with this sentiment. It is telling that so many of the short stories that he wrote in Paris are set not in that city but in Michigan. Paris may have served as a retreat from America, but America remained the subject of Hemingway's early work. From Paris, he had the proper perspective from which to tell stories about American life. In *The Sun Also Rises*, America may no longer be Hemingway's setting, but in many ways it is still his theme. Though Jake and his friends live in Paris and visit Spain, none of them has truly assimilated to European culture. Instead, the European backdrop often serves to offset the characters' distinctly American qualities. These uprooted Americans are "lost," to use Stein's term, in a way that their Parisian or Spanish counterparts are not.

Here, then, is the prototypical expatriate story. The veteran of World War I, finding that he no longer is at ease in his own country, trades Illinois for Paris. A true bohemian, he lives in a garret, writes and drinks in the cafés, and mingles with the best minds of his generation. In America, he would have been pressured into cultivating a career, getting married, and raising a family. In Paris, however, he can be himself and is free to undertake the great artistic work that his own countrymen do not have the capacity to value. Yet despite his exile, he remains an American, and his ingrained Protestant work ethic leads him to hone his craft and to stand by his values. His subject matter, too, may well center on what it means to be an American and what it means to be at home neither in his native country nor in his adopted one. If this story is familiar, it is in no small part because Hemingway's *The Sun Also Rises* has made it so.

Jake Barnes, the definitive American expatriate, shares elements of Hemingway's own biography. While it would be a mistake to associate the character too closely with the author who created him, one could read Jake as Hemingway's idealized version of himself. In creating Jake, Hemingway seems to have written large some of the formative experiences of his own life, casting them into a heroic and tragic vein. Whereas Hemingway was wounded while delivering chocolates and cigarettes as a Red Cross volunteer, Barnes was profoundly maimed while fighting for the Italian army. Barnes speaks fluent French and Spanish; Hemingway was far less proficient with the two languages. Hemingway lived with his wife, Hadley, and was supported during their time in Paris in large part by the interest on her trust fund. Barnes, on the other hand, is entirely self-sufficient, earning his living through journalism. Through Jake Barnes, and through later protagonists such as Frederic Henry of *A Farewell to Arms* and Robert Jordan of *For Whom the Bell Tolls*, Hemingway set the mold for a certain kind of American expatriate.

Hemingway and his protagonist have both broken with America, settling in Paris on a permanent basis. If one associates Barnes with Hemingway too closely, however, one runs the risk of overlooking those aspects of Hemingway's time in Paris that do not make their way into the text of *The Sun Also Rises*. By making Barnes a journalist rather than a novelist or poet, Hemingway downplays the importance of the larger Anglo-American literary community to his own time in Paris. To understand fully the cultural and historical context in which Hemingway wrote *The Sun Also Rises*, one ought to pay attention to an aspect of expatriate life that the novel tends to occlude: the concentration of great American writers who gathered there in the decade before and after the war. Hemingway's memoir and letters, as well as biographies such as Michael Reynolds's excellent *Hemingway: The Paris Years*, reveal the depth and complexity of a literary community that Hemingway tends to denigrate or ignore in *The Sun Also Rises*.

Hemingway may, like Jake, have been a foreign correspondent, but his real goal always was to be a poet and novelist. In Paris he apprenticed himself to some of the best writers of his generation. He paid his famous visits to Gertrude Stein, edited Ford Madox Ford's literary journal *the transatlantic*, and submitted his work to Ezra Pound to be edited and revised. Hemingway's apprenticeships bore fruit: he grew as a writer and his work was published. It was Pound, for example, who first arranged for a volume of Hemingway's poems and short stories to be published. At the time, Hemingway was quite ready to acknowledge his debt to the poet. In 1922, Hemingway described Pound as "a great guy and a wonderful editor" (Baker 8) and said of their relationship, "I'm teaching Pound how to box and he's helping me with my writing" (8). Hadley Hemingway recalled her husband's uncharacteristic adulation of the poet: "Ernest listened at E.P.'s feet, as to an oracle, and I believe some of the ideas lasted all through his life" (Reynolds 22). As a new arrival in Paris, Hemingway benefited greatly from the mentorship of more established writers.

F. Scott Fitzgerald, whom Hemingway befriended in 1925, was another important friend and mentor to Hemingway. Fitzgerald made a series of suggestions regarding *The Sun Also Rises* that led Hemingway to cut away the novel's first fifteen pages. Fitzgerald, unlike Hemingway, had already published two novels and two collections of short stories. He was able to draw on his considerable experience in advising Hemingway. It is interesting to think about whether Fitzgerald and Hemingway's friendship would have taken seed had they met in America rather than in Paris. They were certainly from strikingly different backgrounds: Fitzgerald was a Princeton graduate, whereas Hemingway had not attended college. At times, Hemingway was painfully sensitive about not having gone to college and was acutely aware of differences in class, money, and privilege. Yet exiles have a way of transcending these kinds of divisions, and in Paris Hemingway mixed with people whom he might not have encountered in America.

Hemingway lived a sort of *Künstlerroman* during the first half of the 1920s: it was a time in which he came of age as an artist. Yet very little of this intellectual ferment appears in *The Sun Also Rises*. Jakes Barnes is on a different trajectory from Hemingway, one that does not involve the artist's life in any meaningful way. Because he does not share Hemingway's literary ambitions, Barnes is independent in a way that Hemingway was not. *The Sun Also Rises* therefore covers its own tracks. The novel is a product of the years Hemingway spent learning how to write among the great writers of Paris's Left Bank, yet it makes no mention of this learning process. In making Barnes a journalist rather than a novelist or poet, Hemingway downplays the literary character of the expatriate community. The novelists who appear in *The Sun Also Rises* are clownish: Ford Madox Ford makes an appearance as the buffoonish Braddocks (which rhymes with Madox, of course), who fails to understand that Jake's companion is a prostitute. Robert Cohn has published two novels, but he is a child in the world, one who has gotten his ideas about Paris and Spain "out of a book" (12). Jake has some measure of integrity, but the writers and artists around him do not.

Because Hemingway's authorial stand-in is not himself an artist, he can hold himself aloof from this community of writers. After meeting Braddocks and Cohn, for example, Barnes and the prostitute Georgette discuss them:

> "Who are your friends?" Georgette asked.
> "Writers and artists."
> "There are lots of those on this side of the river."
> "Too many." (17)

The Sun Also Rises therefore has a conflicted, contradictory relationship not only with the milieu in which Hemingway wrote but also with the role of the novelist. As much as it may critique the expatriate community—and in particular the expatriate *literary* community—the novel nevertheless cannot help but glorify it. After all, no one who has dreamed of living in Paris imagines living like Robert Cohn or Braddocks. Rather, it is Barnes who is living out the fantasy, and behind Barnes, Hemingway himself, the expatriate novelist working in the one city in which he can be wholly free. Ironically, *The Sun Also Rises* is in many respects a product of the literary community that it works to minimize. In occluding the importance of other writers to his own development as a novelist, Hemingway gives the impression that it is the city of Paris itself that has licensed his work. This impression is only amplified by Hemingway's memoir. J. Gerald Kennedy puts it this way:

> The Paris of *A Moveable Feast* is an imaginary city, a mythical scene evoked to explain the magical transformation of an obscure, Midwestern journalist into a brilliant modern author. Almost every aspect of the city contributes to the making of the artist. (128)

All Hemingway really needed, the novel and memoir seem to imply, was to be left alone with his notebook in a good café on the Place St.-Michel.

Hemingway's treatment of the Anglo-American literary community in *The Sun Also Rises* and in *A Moveable Feast* is characteristic of the author's tendency to denigrate those who had once been of help to him. His treatment of Sherwood Anderson demonstrates the suddenness with which Hemingway could turn on a former mentor. In 1926, Hemingway published a short novel called *The Torrents of Spring*, written as a parody of Sherwood Anderson's style and themes. Anderson had been nothing but helpful to Hemingway; it is no exaggeration to say that were it not for Anderson, Hemingway might never have gone to Paris in the first place. Yet the younger author's response was to write a book designed to ridicule his mentor. Hemingway had several motives for writing *The Torrents of Spring*. For one, he was frustrated at having some of his own stories—notably "My Old Man"—compared to Anderson's. *The Torrents of Spring* may have been an attempt to repudiate Anderson's influence and to show once and for all that his own work was not derivative. Furthermore, Hemingway used the book to break his contract with Boni & Liveright, which would not publish a manuscript that so clearly targeted Anderson, who was one of the publishing company's own authors. Horace Liveright himself said, "It would be in extremely rotten taste, to say nothing of being horribly cruel, should we want to publish it" (Meyers 169). Yet undergirding all of these motives may have been a primal, cruel desire to lash out at Anderson. In a letter to Anderson, Hemingway wrote, "when a man like yourself who can write very great things writes something that seems to me . . . rotten, I ought to tell you so" (170). As if the novel were not betrayal enough, Hemingway felt a need to justify himself in a letter that only underscores the contempt he now held for Anderson's work.

Hemingway would eventually fall out with most of his other mentors as well. He ran a fiercely critical and sarcastic piece in *the transatlantic* that forced Ford Madox Ford to relieve him of his duties as editor. In *A Moveable Feast*, he lampoons Stein and Fitzgerald alike, and even thirty years later there is a surprising vitriol to his treatment of these two artists. With the possible exception of Pound, Hemingway seemed unable to maintain cordial relations with any writer who had been of aid to him. As Fitzgerald once remarked, "Ernest would always give a helping hand to a man on a ledge a little higher up" (Mellow 176). Again and again, he rejected those who were once his teachers.

Hemingway's representation of the Anglo-American literary community in *The Sun Also Rises* is therefore part and parcel of his tendency to reject those to whom he is indebted. But where does this tendency itself come from, and is it particular to Hemingway or indicative of some larger cultural phenomenon? One could take a psychoanalytic approach to the question, noting that Hemingway some years before had precipitated a confrontation with his mother, a figure of moral probity and propriety. The move to Paris itself might be read as a further rejection of his mother's value system. Hemingway would repeat this pattern throughout his life, behaving badly so as to force wives, friends, and mentors to separate themselves from him. Yet Hemingway's need to reject those who had helped him may also have its roots in a particularly American notion: it is the author's enactment of the rugged individualist's credo.

Hemingway had grown up with the archetype of the rugged individualist, for he was born only two years before Teddy Roosevelt became president of the United States. In fact, the vigorous president may serve as the "pattern in the carpet" of Hemingway's work and of his conception of what it means to be a man. Roosevelt embodied many of the values that Hemingway would later adopt as his own: he was a prolific writer, an accomplished soldier, an active outdoorsman, a hunter, and a sportsman. Like Hemingway, Roosevelt came from an established, white-collar society family, yet left the security of his gentrified upbringing to explore the frontier. As Hemingway grew older, his activities often put him in Roosevelt's orbit. Going on safari in Africa, for example, meant following in the big-game hunter's footsteps—especially since Hemingway employed the same guide that the president had used twenty-five years before. One might even see Roosevelt's maxim of "speak softly and carry a big stick" (Miller 337) as connecting with the laconic nature of so many of Hemingway's characters, as well as with Hemingway's own injunctions about a good writer being able to "omit things that he knows" (*Death in the Afternoon* 192). Like his quondam role model, Hemingway felt that a person with real authority could use fewer words.

Perhaps it is in the spirit of Roosevelt, a larger-than-life embodiment of the American as rugged individualist, that Hemingway felt a need to present his success in Paris as wholly his own. By rejecting his teachers and by writing the literary community itself out of *The Sun Also Rises*, Hemingway makes the writer autonomous. Jake Barnes does not need anybody else's help, nor does Hemingway's romanticized version of his younger self in *A Moveable Feast*. Hemingway may have encountered Stein, Pound, and other great writers in Paris, but these encounters do not contribute to his eventual success. Instead, it is the city of Paris itself that is responsible for the birth of the artist. Yet Hemingway's impulse to reject those who helped him might even extend to his feelings about the city, for ultimately Hemingway will reject Paris as a home and as a subject. With the dissolution of his first marriage, Hemingway would leave Paris for Key West. Jake Barnes shares some of his creator's growing antipathy toward the city. Pamplona and the Spanish countryside offer Jake a way of life that seems pure and authentic; by comparison, Paris is a site of modern neuroses and moral bankruptcy. Jake may end the novel back in Paris, but his return to the city partakes more of defeat and resignation than of victory or homecoming. In Hemingway's life and art, he had already begun to repudiate the city that had been the site of his artistic coming-of-age. His representation of the city and of the expatriate lifestyle is therefore fundamentally conflicted, for he views them with both gratitude and resentment.

There is a temptation to take Hemingway's representation of the expatriate life at face value. Somewhere along the blurred line between Hemingway the novelist and Jake Barnes the journalist lies the perfect image of the radically free American in Paris. Yet as Hemingway himself wrote in *A Moveable Feast*, "There is never any ending to Paris and the memory of each person who has lived in it differs from that of any other" (211). The radical independence of Hemingway's Jake Barnes is so appealing precisely because it is a private fantasy made public. Through the character of Barnes, Hemingway rewrites his own experiences in Paris to minimize the importance of other writers to his own artistic coming-of-age. The Paris of *The Sun Also Rises* is not the same city that Joyce, Eliot, Pound, Faulkner, and dozens of other important modernists called home at some point in their lives. Instead, this Paris is uniquely Hemingway's, and Hemingway's vision of the city holds out the promise that readers who make their way to Paris will likewise find a city that makes them its sole protagonist.

Works Cited

Baker, Carlos. *Hemingway: The Writer as Artist*. Princeton, NJ: Princeton UP, 1952.

Hemingway, Ernest. *Death in the Afternoon*. New York: Charles Scribner's Sons, 1932.

_____. *A Moveable Feast*. New York: Charles Scribner's Sons, 1964.

_____. *Selected Letters, 1917-1961*. Ed. Carlos Baker. New York: Charles Scribner's Sons, 1981.

_____. *The Sun Also Rises*. New York: Charles Scribner's Sons, 1926.

Kennedy, J. Gerald. *Imagining Paris: Exile, Writing, and American Identity*. New Haven, CT: Yale UP, 1993.

Mellow, James R. *Hemingway: A Life Without Consequences*. New York: Da Capo Press, 1992.

Meyers, Jeffrey. *Hemingway: A Biography*. 1985. New York: Da Capo Press, 1999.

Miller, Nathan. *Theodore Roosevelt: A Life*. New York: HarperCollins, 1993.

Reynolds, Michael. *Hemingway: The Paris Years*. 1989. New York: W. W. Norton, 1999.

Gender Identity and the Modern Condition in *The Sun Also Rises*_____

Jennifer Banach

Following his literary debut in Paris with the publication of *Three Stories and Ten Poems* and his subsequent introduction to American audiences with the short-story collection *In Our Time*, Ernest Hemingway published his first novel, *The Sun Also Rises*, in 1926. The book, which presented an intense portrait of the modern world through an emotionally disfigured group of American expatriates living in France and Spain during the years immediately following World War I, met with immediate success and propelled its author to literary stardom. Chronicling the deepest psychological effects of the war and presenting a hauntingly candid look at a society struggling to redefine itself and reconsider its values in the conflict's unsettling aftermath, Hemingway was able to present a fictional drama of a uniquely personal nature, using his characters to yield deeply complex insights into the human condition. More than eighty years later, *The Sun Also Rises* remains one of Hemingway's most significant novels and is also recognized as one of the most important works within the canon of American literature.

Examining the reasons for the novel's lasting success, one is compelled to consider first its extraordinary characters: they seem infinitely complex and haunt the reader long after the book is set down. In fact, despite the revolutionary style of *The Sun Also Rises*, which has commanded the attention of scholars and critics with its lean, precise prose, the deepest and most significant concerns of the novel begin with Hemingway's treatment of character. Through its dynamic characters, such as Jake Barnes, Robert Cohn, and Lady Brett Ashley, Hemingway is able to demonstrate the enormity of the effects of World War I. The book presents a startling discourse on gender roles in modern times alongside considerations of topics such as modern sexuality, androgyny, and the endurance (or extinction) of traditional models of romance in the postwar world. It raises questions about identity, challenging conventional definitions of manhood and womanhood, and ruminates on the bounds of human nature, asking which parts of oneself, if any, may remain unchanged and how loss can affect one's core identity. Through its exploration of these topics, the novel is also able to speak about the complexity of modern relationships, both sexual and platonic, utilizing Jake's impotence as an allegory of the condition of the modern world.

World War I and the staggering amount of injury, death, and loss it inflicted on the generation that fought in it threw into question traditional notions of love and romance, challenged religious faith, and raised moral issues. An entire generation underwent an overwhelming loss of innocence, making it impossible for them to continue living as they had before the war. The changes were of such great significance that they were manifested in people's everyday behavior and appearance, with the war affecting the very way that people identified themselves. The issue of gender identity and its correlation to the greater human condition, which could no longer be denied, became a key focus for Hemingway in *The Sun Also Rises*.

Within the novel, one finds that traditional gender roles are often overturned and definitions of gender blurred, making the characters representative of an androgyny that extends beyond the sexual. In other words, the sexual androgyny represented by the characters in the novel has its basis in gender—women act and even dress in a masculine manner, and men possess characteristics typically identified as feminine—and their androgyny performs as an allegorical representation of a larger cultural condition tangled up in the postwar spirit of uncertainty. This androgyny, defined by scholar Mark Spilka in his book *Hemingway's Quarrel with Androgyny* as "a mixture or exchange of traditionally male and female traits, roles, activities, and sexual positions," was the symptom of an existential crisis born of the postwar world in which old values were no longer functional and even those most basic parts of human nature had to be reevaluated. As Spilka points out, Hemingway would continue to grapple with the notion of androgyny throughout the entirety of his career, but in *The Sun Also Rises* "his interest in the androgynous makeup of men and women had begun" with the "mannish Lady Brett Ashley" and the "unmanned Jake Barnes" (1). In this novel Hemingway first presented androgyny as "an edenic garden that a man must lose or leave" (4). Indeed, Spilka demonstrates, the strangely worded "damned good time" that Brett and Jake cannot attain is not the kind of "damned good time" one might associate with the debauchery of the Jazz Age, but rather romantic love itself (2). While Spilka speculates that Hemingway's interest in androgyny may have, at least in part, been formed as a result of his own androgynous upbringing and Victorian forebears, he also recognizes the evolution of androgyny as a societal condition—a "wounding condition" or "bedeviling condition"—a side effect brought about by the postwar extinction of the romantic love that Brett and Jake crave and the death of old conceptions of masculine and feminine (3).

Indeed, as androgyny becomes a symbol of the modern condition, so too do the characters of the novel take on allegorical roles. Despite these roles, the men and women who inhabit *The Sun Also Rises* are remarkably complex characters who bring to life questions of how the most basic parts of an individual's nature may be altered by war and loss. They embody the shifts in gender roles that were exhibited in real life throughout the 1920s and reinforce the significance of modern problems such as the expiration of traditional notions of masculinity and femininity and the uncertainty of human nature.

In fact, Hemingway chose to open the book with a powerful reference to gender—specifically, an image of masculinity. The story begins with Jake Barnes introducing Robert Cohn, a former "middleweight boxing champion of Princeton" (11). However, this initial image of masculinity is promptly undercut when Jake suggests that Cohn adopted his masculine qualities as a survival device, as protection against the emotional injury of being tormented for his Jewish heritage. Jake tells us, "He cared nothing for boxing, in fact he disliked it, but he learned it painfully and thoroughly to counteract the feeling of inferiority and shyness he had felt on being treated as a Jew at Princeton" (11). From the opening lines of the novel, then, it is suggested that in the modern world masculinity is not rooted solely in mere biology. Rather, it is something that can be learned and performed, its definition alterable in accordance with circumstances. Thus Hemingway chooses to begin with a description that registers the uncertainty of what it means to be a man in the world Cohn and Jake inhabit, and this description becomes a powerful reminder of the myth of gender in modern times. Robert Cohn is the image of machismo shattered, and readers are prompted to read the book questioning the most basic assumptions about what it means to be a man.

As Hemingway further develops the character, we learn that Cohn's wife has left him and that he is now having an affair with a commanding woman who only wishes to take care of herself. He is denigrated by the other men and allows himself to be taken advantage of. He lacks the strength and assertiveness normally associated with a strong male, and, therefore, he does not fit within the bounds of traditional notions of masculinity. However, Cohn still seeks love and romance, asking Jake, for instance, to travel with him to South America because he read about it in a book. Jake tells us:

He had been reading W. H. Hudson. That sounds like an innocent occupation, but Cohn had read and reread "The Purple Land." "The Purple Land" is a very sinister book if read too late in life. It recounts splendid imaginary amorous adventures of a perfect English gentleman in an intensely romantic land, the scenery of which is very well-described. For a man to take it at thirty-four as a guide-book to what life holds is about as safe as it would be for a man of the same age to enter Wall Street direct from a French convent. . . . Cohn, I believe, took every word of "The Purple Land" as literally as though it had been an R. G. Dun report. . . . It was all that was needed to set him off. (17)

As with all of the male characters in the novel, the ambiguity of Cohn's masculinity can be seen as a metaphor for a greater human condition. Unlike the other male characters, however, Cohn reminds readers of a passion that is absent in the other characters. In fact, Spilka proposes that Cohn represents a romanticism that has been lost in the postwar world, that it is this sensibility that provokes a negative response from the other male characters, most of whom have resigned themselves to the absence of love and romance as a fact of existence in modern times. In his essay "The Death of Love in *The Sun Also Rises*" Spilka explains:

> Cohn still upholds a romantic view of life, and since he affirms it with stubborn persistence, he acts like a goad upon his wiser contemporaries. . . .
> . . . [Cohn] is the last chivalric hero, the last defender of an outworn faith, and his function is to illustrate its present folly. (108-9)

Like Cohn, the narrator Jake Barnes also fails to fit within a traditional mold of masculinity, and he functions somewhat symbiotically with Cohn, serving as a constant reminder of the romance that is impossible in the new modern world. Rendered impotent by a war injury, he is unable to consummate a sexual relationship and, it is implied, is therefore not wholly a man. The war has literally interfered with his manhood. However, in light of his physical impotence, it becomes critical to note that while Jake cannot be intimate with a woman, by being enlisted as narrator, he is made capable of intimacy through the revelation of his thoughts, feelings, and observations. In other words, his character suggests that intimacy may also be, or must be, redefined in the modern world as more than mere sexuality. Of equal importance is Jake's sensitivity, or, more specifically, his role as a sensitive man. We find evidence of his sensitivity not only in the way that he interacts with Brett but also in his attention to detail, such as the overwhelming attention that he pays to his natural surroundings. For instance, in chapter 6, Jake observes the barges of the Seine:

Crossing the Seine I saw a string of barges being towed down the current, riding high, the bargemen at the sweeps as they came toward the bridge. The river looked nice. It was always pleasant crossing the bridge in Paris. (48)

He pays equal attention to the landscape when he goes fishing with Bill. This interest in what is around him, which he has been able to maintain despite the effects of the war, provides important evidence that Jake is, despite his injury, still a passionate person. While the other male characters are, perhaps, too psychically injured themselves to recognize Jake's passion, the bullfighting aficionados, who are depicted as powerful, virile men, are able to recognize that Jake has true passion or "aficion."

Robert Cohn and Jake Barnes have a second commonality: their unrequited love for another androgynous character, Lady Brett Ashley. Just as Cohn and Jake introduce us to atypical modern male characters, so too the introduction of Brett compels us to reevaluate our assumptions about femininity in modern society. Though she is a woman, Brett has a man's name and refers to herself as "a chap," as if she were one of the men. In fact, throughout the course of the story, all of her companions seem to be men. She flicks her cigarette ashes on the floor and drinks more excessively than any male character. Although we know that she wears skirts and still possesses an air of femininity, as Jake notes by describing her curves, Jake also tells us that her hair is cut like a boy's and later reveals that she does not wear stockings. And while the men worry that Brett may become upset if the bullfights are gory, it is not Brett but Cohn who is nauseated by the spectacle of the bullring. Finally, unlike other women in the novel who seem to seek out romance as a means to marriage, we also discover that Brett is unable or unwilling to commit to any of the men interested in her.

Further, Hemingway is careful to present plenty of examples to show that Brett's androgyny is genuine and something she has freely chosen. Commenting on her masculine haircut, Jake observes that, rather than following a preexisting trend, "she started all that" (30), and when the bullfighter Pedro Romero attempts to feminize her, asking her to grow out her hair so she will look more like a woman and expressing an interest in marrying her so that she will settle down, she refuses.

While characters such as Cohn, Jake, and Brett command our attention, the minor characters of the novel also impart meaningful information about gender identity as a reflection of the modern condition. Robert Cohn's new partner, Frances Clyne, while immensely different from Brett, also fails to fulfill traditional notions of womanhood. She is hard and outspoken, as evidenced in the scene in which she unreservedly confronts Cohn in front of Jake. In chapter 6, we learn that she does not like children but figures that she will have children "and then like them" (54). Her motivations for wanting to marry Cohn seem to be based more on a desire for financial and social stability than on actual love and respect for him, thereby subverting the traditional feminine ideals of domesticity and motherhood. Likewise, the prostitute Georgette, who appears only briefly in the book, also helps to dispel traditional concepts of femininity and womanhood. Her profession represents the opposite of the romantic ideal, but Hemingway is also careful to draw a link between Georgette's own condition and the state in which the modern woman at large finds herself. When she orders a pernod and Jake suggests that there may be more feminine drinks, Georgette responds, "It doesn't make any difference with me. It doesn't make any difference with a woman" (24)—a statement that reveals a kind of sad camaraderie in the shaken-up state of modern womanhood and a resignation that is characteristic of women's new role. Georgette's presence reinforces the notion of the impossibility of romance, for Jake confesses flatly that he "had picked her up because of a vague sentimental idea that it would be nice to eat with some one" (24), and Georgette's attempt to stroke Jake's crotch draws our attention to a more literal obstacle to romantic love: his impotence.

Hemingway employs minor male characters, such as Brett's fiancé,

Michael Campbell, and Count Mippipopolous in similar ways, using them as symbols of a postwar manhood that consists primarily of what scholar Thomas Strychacz calls a "theater of masculinity." In other words, with the impossibility of romantic love and the death of glorified notions of the hero, such characters provide evidence that masculinity can no longer be considered something inherent; rather, it is the effect of a kind of self-consciousness that depends on the presence of an audience. Aware of their inadequacy as men, they enact the kind of posturing now demanded by postwar manhood, a posturing that relies not on inherent maleness but on the obtainment or proffering of the illusion of wealth, success, and popularity. Their role as men is dependent on others accepting this illusion as truth. In this way, Campbell and the count serve as counterpoints to each other, with Campbell possessing too few of these things and the count possessing too many. Campbell speaks about not having any medals and going bankrupt because of "false friends" (141). The count, meanwhile, seems to possess unlimited funds, believing that he can buy whatever he wants. He offers to pay Brett to accompany him in his travels, and has no problem leaving her alone with another man while he fetches champagne. Together, the characters create a sense of the absurd as it relates to new definitions of maleness.

There are also several instances in the novel in which minor characters provide a contrast to those characters who have been directly affected by the war. The family that Bill and Jake meet on the train contrasts with other models of gender in the book. The woman is referred to not by her name but rather as "Mother" and, as such, is defined by her role within her family, not by her individuality. She provides a counterpoint to the other female characters, seeming to possess a mind of her own, but she also displays a willingness to please her husband. Likewise, the other travelers on the train, who are on a religious pilgrimage and who, it is implied, have been able to maintain their faith, are referred to disdainfully by Bill as "Puritans." The allegorical presentation of family and the faithful creates a strong sense of other, a contrast that only heightens our awareness of the failure of family and faith in the modern world as presented to us by the major characters of the novel. Finally, there are the bullfighters. Of particular note, Pedro Romero symbolizes passion and power, and his presence suggests a triumph of faith and the endurance of the heroic. Although Hemingway began his first draft with Romero as the protagonist, he later shifted the bullfight section to the center of the novel; some critics, however, recognize that Romero remains the central character even in the final text. Spilka, for instance, argues that

> Pedro is the real hero of the parable, the man whose code gives meaning to a world where love and religion are defunct, where the proofs of manhood are difficult and scarce, and where every man must learn to define his own moral conditions and then live up to them. ("Death" 118)

Aside from the topical portraits of the characters, their complex interactions illustrate an astounding range of representations of love and romance—or, perhaps more accurately, suggestions of the impossibility of traditional, prewar love and romance. Brett has relationships with several men throughout the story but is unable to commit to any one man. While we know that she is in love with Jake, because of his injury the two are unable to consummate their love, suggesting again the impossibility of romantic love in the postwar age. Furthermore, there are the empty relationships between Jake and Georgette, Brett and the count, and Robert Cohn and Frances. The overwhelming number of failed romances in the novel should serve as a signal that they are deliberate and significant. The relationships that the characters cannot consummate, either literally or figuratively, and that cannot be defined as romantic are as significant as the romantic relationships typically depicted throughout literature. Novelist, poet, and literary critic Robert Penn Warren reminds us of the major significance of these relationships and the choices faced by the characters:

It is important to remember . . . that the sinking into nature, even at the level of drinking and mere sexuality, is a self-conscious act. It is not the random gratification of appetite. We see this quite clearly in *The Sun Also Rises* in the contrast between Cohn, who is merely a random dabbler in the world of sensation . . . and . . . Jake and Brett, who are aware of the nada at the center of things. (46)

The empty relationships that we witness and the characters' responses to these relationships are emblematic of the modern condition in which the characters find themselves unwillingly entangled. With traditional notions of romance no longer viable, the characters are forced to seek out other kinds of relationships, such as friendship or the camaraderie born of shared failures and present obstacles. In fact, the men often seem to have closer relationships with one another than with any single woman in the story. One might consider the scenes between Jake and Bill, for example, as an instance of the kind of camaraderie shared between men in the absence of women. Meanwhile, the androgynous Brett seems most comfortable among homosexuals and other men to whom she need not commit.

Perhaps the greatest achievement of the novel lies in its ability to move these issues beyond straightforward characterization, further revealing them in other formal elements of the text. For instance, while Hemingway uses symbolism sparingly, a handful of major symbols contained in the book parallel and reflect the characters' condition. First, the bullfights are an undeniable allegory, a symbol both of the new theater of gender to which the characters are subjected—enacted not only in the gender of the animals and their corresponding roles but also in the death that occurs in the ring—and a reminder of the endurance of old ideals of faith, love, and the heroic. "In the bullring," Strychacz aptly observes, "men are made or unmanned" (53). The performance of masculinity that has become necessary in the postwar age is reflected by the arena and its audience, whose "function is to appraise rituals of manhood and bestow praise or condemnation on the protagonist—a particularly important role," Strychacz points out, "if we take the matador's actions as somehow representative of masculine codes of behavior" (54). The bullfights reflect the "wounded condition" that manifests itself in androgyny (Spilka, *Quarrel* 3). They are purposefully described with sexually suggestive language, and Jake draws parallels between himself and the steers, or castrated cattle, that are used to calm the fertile bulls as they enter the ring and that are killed as part of the bullfight ritual.

Second, through his narrator, Hemingway creates a character who pays close attention to his natural surroundings. Despite the gloom that seems to haunt the characters, the natural world remains beautiful, seemingly unchanged despite the war. This tactic of juxtaposing the modern world with the natural one enhances the reader's awareness of the enormity of the shift the war has created. The very title of the book, taken from a passage in the biblical book of Ecclesiastes, reinforces this notion of nature as a constant:

> The sun also ariseth, and the sun goeth down, and hasteth to the place where he arose. . . . The wind goeth toward the south, and turneth about unto the north; it whirleth about continually, and the wind returneth again according to his circuits. . . . All the rivers run into the sea; yet the sea is not full; unto the place from whence the rivers come, thither they return again. (8)

The sun continues to rise and the wind continues to blow, even though society and humanity change. Though people may struggle, the world goes on.

Hemingway uses both of these major symbols—bullfighting and nature—to draw our attention to the contrasting notions of impotence and fertility, wherein questions of inadequacy and strength begin to surface. Of course Hemingway provides us with the literal example of Jake's impotence; however, like other writers of this time period, Hemingway also uses his character's disability to illuminate the flaws of the modern world and as a symbol of the emotional impotence those flaws have caused. Again, this symbolic impotence becomes more visible when paired with images of nature, reminders of the sexuality of other characters, and the always pervasive reminders of love that cannot be consummated.

Finally, the language and style that Hemingway employs—perhaps the most well-known elements of *The Sun Also Rises*—are also instrumental in facilitating this dialogue about gender and identity. In his article "Melancholy Modernism: Gender and the Politics of Mourning in *The Sun Also Rises*," Greg Forter explains that Hemingway's

> style defends against yet keeps alive the dual loss of sentiment and potency by serving as a kind of monument that ceaselessly speaks of the losses its erection seeks to silence. Style allows Hemingway and his characters neither openly to embrace lost affect nor to do without it, neither to lay claims to a hard masculinity nor really to renounce it. (33)

The style and language, in other words, mimic the characters' androgyny and ambiguity, with the clean, hard sentences possessing a masculine quality while their emotional suggestiveness offers a countering feminine balance.

Ultimately, Hemingway's study of gender and associated models of love and romance became a symbol of a new, modernist sensibility. As a movement, modernism, among other things, abandoned Victorian notions of masculinity and femininity, sought to redefine romance and spirituality, and recognized the emergence of a new, postwar morality. As Spilka illuminates, these traits in Hemingway's fiction serve as "part of a larger study of the taboo on tenderness in modern fiction, whereby the old Victorian quarrel with sexuality has been replaced by our modern quarrel with the softer sentiments" (*Quarrel* 5). *The Sun Also Rises* remains relevant not only because it so aptly captures a period of American history and culture but also, more important, because through its exploration of gender it presents an existential discourse that transcends geographic boundaries and triumphs against the passage of time. Although gender connects us to the characters specifically, it is a topic that opens doors to a broader discourse about humanity, culture, loss, and love. In *Ernest Hemingway*, Gerry Brenner and Earl Rovit describe the characters as "sensitive recorders of the shock they have suffered" (140). More accurately, the characters can be described as sensitive recorders of a collectively suffered shock, and the book and its reflections on gender and romance should be remembered as a record of the truth of human nature and a significant commentary on adaptation and resilience in the face of loss.

Works Cited

Brenner, Gerry, and Earl Rovit. *Ernest Hemingway*. Boston: G. K. Hall, 1986.

Forter, Greg. "Melancholy Modernism: Gender and the Politics of Mourning in *The Sun Also Rises*." *The Hemingway Review* 21.1 (2001): 22-37.

Hemingway, Ernest. *The Sun Also Rises*. 1926. New York: Charles Scribner's Sons, 2006.

Spilka, Mark. "The Death of Love in *The Sun Also Rises*." *Ernest Hemingway*. Ed. Harold Bloom. New York: Chelsea House, 1985. 107-18.

_____. *Hemingway's Quarrel with Androgyny*. Lincoln: U of Nebraska P, 1990.

Strychacz, Thomas. *Hemingway's Theaters of Masculinity*. Baton Rouge: Louisiana State UP, 2003.

Warren, Robert Penn. "Ernest Hemingway." *Ernest Hemingway*. Ed. Harold Bloom. New York: Chelsea House, 1985. 35-62.

The Art of Friction:
Ernest Hemingway and William Faulkner_____

Lorie Watkins Fulton

During the first half of the twentieth century, American modernism produced an astounding array of talented writers who, in wildly varying styles, explored the condition of modern man. Surely no two styles differed more, however, than those of Ernest Hemingway and William Faulkner. In *Death in the Afternoon*, Hemingway invokes the image of an iceberg to describe his style:

> If a writer of a prose knows enough about what he is writing about he may omit things that he knows and the reader, if the writer is writing truly enough, will have a feeling of those things as strongly as though the writer had stated them. The dignity of movement of an ice-berg is due to only one-eighth of it being above water. A writer who omits things because he does not know them only makes hollow places in his writing. (192)

Thus Hemingway's style is based on the exclusion of extraneous information and words, and as a result his prose is lean, spare, and seemingly straightforward, deriving its power and meaning from what is not explicitly said. Faulkner, on the other hand, writes lush, syntactically difficult prose that challenges its reader with its vocabulary and sheer volume.

The two writers' lives differed as much as their literary styles. For example, although both longed to participate in World War I but could not register for active duty, Hemingway actually saw combat as a volunteer ambulance driver for the Red Cross, whereas the war ended before Faulkner completed training with the Canadian Royal Air Force. Hemingway later covered the Spanish Civil War and World War II as a news correspondent and went on to become the sportsman of the famed Hemingway legend by boxing, hunting for big game on safari in Africa, fishing in the Gulf Stream, and, of course, displaying his enthusiasm for the artistry of the bullfight. He filled his life with adventure, and his life seems as expansive as his prose seems narrow. The opposite seems to hold true for the relationship between Faulkner's life and his work. Although Faulkner traveled extensively overseas for the U.S. State Department during the 1950s and spent extended periods of time in Hollywood writing for Metro-Goldwyn-Mayer and Warner Bros., he primarily confined himself to his "little postage stamp of native soil" in Oxford, Mississippi, for most of his life. Despite, or perhaps because of, their differences, these two writers shared a lifelong rivalry that emerges often in their letters and sometimes in their fiction; in fact, their hostility is even anticipated by Hemingway's depiction of the rivalry between Jake Barnes and Robert Cohn in his early novel *The Sun Also Rises*.

* * *

Given their personal and artistic differences, it is not surprising that Hemingway and Faulkner moved in separate social circles. In fact, they met only once, if at all. In a letter to reviewer Harvey Breit dated July 4, 1952, Hemingway mentions meeting Faulkner, but he does not provide specific information about the encounter. This meeting, if it indeed occurred, appears to have been the only face-to-face one between the two men. Semipublic exchanges instead replaced personal interaction and defined the most notorious literary professional rivalry of the modernist period. Faulkner voiced the more positive opinion from the start, telling Phil Stone, a friend and Oxford attorney, in 1925 that Hemingway "is so far the greatest American fictionist" (Blotner 448). In contrast, Hemingway offered mixed comments on Faulkner's work as early as 1931. When Milwaukee bookstore owner Paul Romaine collected some of Faulkner's early works for *Salmagundi*, he contacted Hemingway and asked permission to reproduce one of his early poems, "Ultimately," on the back cover (Baker 227). "Ultimately" had appeared in a 1922 issue of the New Orleans *Double Dealer* alongside

Faulkner's work (204). Hemingway agreed, but "privately told his bibliographer, Captain Cohn, that the early poem was bad enough to fit perfectly into a collection of Faulkner's 'early shit.'" Of Faulkner's more recent work at that time, Hemingway told novelist Owen Wister that he enjoyed *As I Lay Dying* but *Sanctuary* seemed "pretty phony." Hemingway nevertheless sent "his best wishes by way of Romaine, adding that he seemed to be going well as a writer and that he sounded like 'a good skate'" (Baker 227).

Maxwell Perkins, meanwhile, considered trying to lure Faulkner to Scribner's but decided against it. Fellow Scribner's editor John Hall Wheelock thought that Perkins "was afraid of arousing Hemingway's jealousy" and added, "in Hemingway's mind, there was no more room in Max's life for another power so threatening as William Faulkner" (Berg 181). Hemingway first shows the public face of such sentiment in *Death in the Afternoon* (1932), where he writes, "My operatives tell me that through the fine work of Mr. William Faulkner publishers now will publish anything rather than try to get you to delete the better portions of your works." Hemingway presumably refers to *Sanctuary* when he adds, "I look forward to writing of those days of my youth which were spent in the finest whorehouses in the land." He also advises, "You can't go wrong on Faulkner. He's prolific too. By the time you get them ordered there'll be new ones out" (173). At least one reviewer, Robert Coates, objected to Hemingway's "bitterness" in his "gibes at William Faulkner, who has done him no harm save to come under his influence" (Lynn 397). Hemingway protested in a letter to Coates, "I'm damned if I wrote any petulant jibes against Faulkner and the hell with you for telling citizens that I did" (*Letters* 369). Nevertheless, some twelve years later Hemingway admitted to philosopher and novelist Jean-Paul Sartre that he thought Faulkner the better writer (Baker 439), and he wrote of Faulkner to editor Malcolm Cowley in a letter dated October 17, 1945:

He has the most talent of anybody and he just needs a sort of conscience that isn't there. Certainly if no nation can exist half free and half slave no man can write half whore and half straight. But he will write absolutely perfectly straight and then go on and on and not be able to end it. I wish the christ I owned him like you'd own a horse and train him like a horse and race him like a horse—only in writing. How beautifully he can write and as simple and as complicated as autumn or as spring. (*Letters* 604)

Interestingly enough, Faulkner used a similarly competitive metaphor when he responded to Cowley's suggestion that Hemingway write the preface for Viking's *The Portable Faulkner*: "I am opposed to asking Hemingway to write the preface. It seems to me in bad taste to ask him to write a preface to my stuff. It's like asking one race horse in the middle of a race to broadcast a blurb on another horse in the same running field" (Blotner 1209).

This figurative race began indeed when Faulkner contracted to meet with a series of six literature classes at the University of Mississippi in April 1947. As Joseph Blotner describes the lectures, Faulkner "never approached a public meeting without some trepidation, but he was determined to do as good a job as he could and to give the university its money's worth. And he could relax somewhat, since it had been specified and agreed that no notes would be taken" (1230). Over the course of the six classes some students did take notes, however, and the university's director of public relations, Marvin Black, issued a press release containing the highlights of Faulkner's sessions. Hemingway later saw excerpts from that release reprinted in the *New York Herald Tribune*'s book section and took offense at two of Faulkner's comments (1234). First, Faulkner ranked his literary contemporaries (including himself, upon the students' insistence) according to "the splendor of the failure" of each to "achieve the dream." The list, in Faulkner's original order, named Thomas Wolfe, Faulkner himself, John Dos Passos, Hemingway, and John Steinbeck (1232). Faulkner offered a further critique of Hemingway: "He has no courage, has never climbed out on a limb. He has never used a word where the reader might check his usage by a dictionary" (1233). The low ranking surely offended Hemingway, and Faulkner's challenge of Hemingway's courage drew a strong reaction from the author known for his depictions of characters facing tests of their courage as well as for his brittle combativeness. He felt that Faulkner had "called him a coward" and he "sent the newspaper clipping to General [Buck] Lanham and asked him to write Faulkner the truth about his behavior under fire in 1944" (Baker 461). Lanham did so, speaking of Hemingway's physical and moral courage, and concluded that the novelist was "the most courageous man I have ever known, both in war and peace" (Baker 461). Faulkner insisted that his own statement "had no reference whatever to Hemingway as a man: only to his craftsmanship as a writer" (Blotner 1235). He wrote immediately to Lanham and sent a copy of the letter to Hemingway along with a note that said:

> I'm sorry of this damn stupid thing. I was just making $250.00, I thought informally, not for publication, or I would have insisted on looking at the stuff before it was released. I have believed for years that the human voice has caused all human ills and I thought I had broken myself of talking. Maybe this will be my valedictory lesson. (Blotner 1235)

Hemingway seemed satisfied and cordial in the initial section of his reply to Faulkner, dated July 23. He began with the salutation "Dear Bill" and continued:

> Awfully glad to hear from you and glad to have made contact. Your letter came tonight and please throw all the other stuff away, the misunderstanding, or will have to come up and we can both trompel on it. There isn't any at all. I was sore and Buck [Lanham] was sore and we were instantly unsore the minute we knew the score. (*Letters* 623)

However, it soon became clear that Hemingway wasn't "unsore" at all. He went on to disagree with Faulkner's ranking of Wolfe and Dos

---

Passos, and even referred to Dos Passos as a "snob," a "bastard," and "a 2nd rate writer on acct. no ear" (623). Hemingway also defended *For Whom the Bell Tolls* against Faulkner's charges and added, "Probably bore the shit out of you to re-read but as a brother would like to know what you think." Hemingway then warned Faulkner, "You shouldn't read the shit about living writers," and encouraged him to write his "best against dead writers that we know what stature (not stature: evocative power) that they have and beat them one by one" (624). In taking care to define "stature" for Faulkner, Hemingway also seemed to illustrate what he saw as Faulkner's fundamental misreading of Hemingway's work as simplistic. Hemingway ended the letter on a strange, perhaps even passive-aggressive note: "Excuse chickenshit letter. Have much regard for you. Would like to keep on writing" (625).

Although this proposed correspondence did not ensue, Hemingway did tell Harvey Breit that he sent a cable to Faulkner as soon as he heard that Faulkner had won the Nobel Prize in Literature. Of course, Hemingway added that if he ever won it, he would "be strongly tempted to thank them politely and then refuse to appear for the ceremony" (Baker 489). Faulkner instigated the next skirmish in the competition between the two authors. In a June 1952 letter to Harvey Breit, Faulkner responded to the critical panning of *Across the River and into the Trees*:

> A few years ago, I forget what the occasion was, Hemingway said that writers should stick together just as doctors and lawyers and wolves do. I think there is more wit in that than truth or necessity either, at least in Hemingway's case, since the sort of writers who need to band together willy nilly or perish, resemble the wolves who are wolves only in pack, and, singly, are just another dog.

Faulkner then appeared to defend Hemingway against this assertion when he suggested that "the man who wrote the MEN WITHOUT WOMEN pieces and THE SUN ALSO RISES and A FAREWELL TO

ARMS and FOR WHOM THE BELL TOLLS and most of the African stuff and most of all the rest of it, is not one of these, and needs no pack protection" (Faulkner, *Letters* 333-34).

Breit passed the letter on to Hemingway, "telling him that he planned to use it in a piece he was writing. To his dismay, the letter made Hemingway furious, for he concluded that Faulkner was calling him 'just another dog'" (Faulkner, *Letters* 334). Hemingway responded with two letters to Breit, dated June 27 and June 29, expressing his confusion over Faulkner's statement: "It really does sound as though he considered that he had been asked to speak well of something worthless by someone who could no longer write and he was, instead, making just as noble a statement about the poor chap as his conscience would allow" (*Letters* 771). Hemingway thought that Faulkner's making "statements *without* reading it is chicken," and the four-page-long rant contains personal attacks, including charges that Faulkner could "be better than anyone if he knew how to finish a book" and of writing "on corn" (770, 772). Hemingway implored Breit not to "speak about any of this to Faulkner" because he did "not want any quarrels." He also admitted, "I'm sure I am too hard on Faulkner. But I know I am not as hard on him as I am on myself" (770). Unaware of Hemingway's criticisms, Faulkner wrote the following cable upon reading *The Old Man and the Sea*: "Splendid news. stop not that quote the old man unquote needs more accolade than it already has from us who know the anguish it took and have tried to do it too" (Faulkner, *Letters* 348).

That very novel played a central role in the authors' next and final major quarrel. Faulkner wrote a review of *The Old Man and the Sea* for Washington and Lee University's literary journal, *Shenandoah*. The review began, "His best. Time may show it to be the best single piece of any of us, I mean of his and my contemporaries." Faulkner's continuing praise, however, also contained implicit criticism, for he suggested that Hemingway had finally discovered God, a Creator. Until now, his men and women had made themselves, shaped themselves out of their own clay; their victories and defeats were at the hands of each other, just to prove to themselves or one another how tough they could be. But this time, he wrote about pity; about something somewhere that made them all . . . made them all and loved them all and pitied them all.

Faulkner concluded, "Praise God that whatever made and loves and pities Hemingway and me kept him from touching it any further" (Blotner 1428-29). Hemingway, obviously disgusted, wrote to journalist Lillian Ross soon afterward, "I cannot help out very much with the true dope on God as I have never played footy-footy with him; nor been a cane brake God hopper; nor won the Nobel Prize. It would be best to get the true word on God from Mr. Faulkner." As for himself, Hemingway claimed to "know the same amount about God as you do." In a snide reference aligning Faulkner with *The Sound and the Fury*'s Benjy, Hemingway continued, "Have not been vouchsafed any revelations. It's quite possible that Mr. Faulkner sits at the table with him each night and that the deity comforts him if he has a bad dream and wipes his mouth and helps him eat his corn pone or hominy grits or wheaties in the morning." In another reference to Faulkner's earlier "dog" comment, Hemingway told Ross that he believed that what Faulkner "means is that he is spooked to die and is moving in on the side of the strongest battalions. We will fight it out here and if there are no reserves it is too Faulking bad and they will find what is left of Dog company on that hill" (*Letters* 807).

Fight it out they did. Hemingway continued to hurl primarily private insults in his darker moods, and Faulkner continued to speak about the infamous list when an interviewer or audience member raised the subject. Faulkner outlived Hemingway and thus got the last word by virtue of surviving him. Interestingly, in speaking of Hemingway's death, Faulkner turned back to the subject of courage. He told Joseph Blotner, "Hemingway was obviously sick, but there was something unmanly about what he had done." However, the remark may have had more to do with Faulkner's own life than with Hemingway's death, for Faulkner curiously added to his comment to Blotner, "It's bad when a man does something like that. It's like saying death is better than living with my wife" (1790).

* * *

Despite this rivalry, the novelists' works share a "host of common themes—among them hunting, troubled gender relationships, the interconnection of people and place, and . . . war" (Fruscione, "One Tale" 279). Their lives also shared uncanny similarities, including connections to Hollywood, run-ins with Sherwood Anderson, alcoholism, depression, and penchants for younger women. The result, a "remarkable psycho-competitive influence over each other," spawned a "textual dialectic between Faulkner and Hemingway in which they explored the style, themes, and direction of American Modernism" (280). Joseph Fruscione writes of this influence:

> Throughout their careers, Hemingway and Faulkner influenced each other in ways that were directly psychological, indirectly artistic. Psychologically, each was driven to outshine the other and anxiously felt the other's sway; artistically, their texts and aesthetic sensibilities embodied (and were partly shaped by) their rivalry. Their efforts to surpass each other pushed them to innovate—each knew that his adversary was worthy and often responded to, riffed on, or took chances because of him. ("*Mano a Mano*" 71)

Many critics have already explored the dimensions of this textual dialectic.[1] Hemingway offered his most direct criticism of Faulkner in the fictionalized conversation with the "old lady" in *Death in the Afternoon*. Faulkner's *If I Forget Thee, Jerusalem* stands as Faulkner's most obvious jab at Hemingway, a parodic response to the criticism in *Death in the Afternoon*. As Fruscione notes:

In *Death in the Afternoon*, Hemingway took Faulkner to task for his vast productivity and "prolific" nature. Faulkner fired back in each of *If I Forget Thee, Jerusalem*'s two stories: "The Wild Palms" recasts much of Hemingway's work in Faulknerian form, while "Old Man" refers to the main character as a *matador* and his subservient backwoods companions as *aficionados*. In short, each story of *If I Forget Thee, Jerusalem* symbolizes Hemingway and Faulkner, respectively, and the allusion to Hemingway in "Old Man" implies—part-jokingly, part-seriously—Faulkner's artistic superiority to Hemingway, as one cannot write *matador* and *aficionados* without calling Hemingway's *The Sun Also Rises* (1926), *Death in the Afternoon*, and physically-active masculine persona to mind—Faulkner, as well as his readers, undoubtedly knew this. ("One Tale" 298)

The troubled relationship seems firmly rooted in Hemingway's competitive nature and attendant fears of inferiority. As Earl Rovit and Arthur Waldhorn note, "In their several semi-public exchanges, usually incited by misunderstandings of reported comments, it is the ostentatiously self-confident Hemingway who is quick to take umbrage and strike back at what he believed were Faulkner's criticisms of him and his work" (158). Their competition, for Hemingway, also "held a certain creative value: artists attempting to 'equal or surpass' their rivals could improve their own work" (Fruscione, "*Mano a Mano*" 68). The "public face of Hemingway's jealousy began in 1932" with the publication of *Death in the Afternoon* (Monteiro 75), but *The Sun Also Rises* also anticipates the contentious relationship in its depiction of the authorial rivalry between Jake Barnes and Robert Cohn.[2] Admittedly, Hemingway's novel appeared in 1926, long before the majority of the literary fallout from his rivalry with Faulkner, but it nonetheless foreshadows the later friction between the two modernist giants. In this roman à clef, Jake Barnes, like Hemingway, is a newspaperman and an injured veteran.[3] Hemingway bases much of the novel on a trip he took with friends to Spain in 1925, and his depiction of Cohn, based on the novelist Harold Loeb, likely also served as a deliberate attempt to "get"

Loeb for engaging in an affair with Lady Duff Twysden, the real-life counterpart for Brett Ashley (Lynn 295-96).

The novel begins with a description of Cohn, a former middleweight boxing champion whom Jake calls his "tennis friend" (13). As is true of all the characters in the novel, circumstance largely defines Cohn's life; in fact, he did not even care for boxing but "learned it painfully and thoroughly to counteract the feeling of inferiority and shyness he had felt on being treated as a Jew at Princeton" (11). In the first chapter, readers learn that Cohn "was married by the first girl who was nice to him," divorced her when she left him, moved to California, and "fell among literary people" (12). Cohn soon finds himself editing a literary review and "taken in hand by a lady who hoped to rise with the magazine" (13). When the magazine fails, Cohn turns to writing and produces a novel that Jake deems "not really such a bad novel as the critics later called it, although it was a very poor novel" (13). Poor novel or not, a "fairly good publisher" accepts it. Cohn travels to New York and comes back "quite changed" because the publisher "praised his novel pretty highly and," in Jake's opinion, "it rather went to his head" (16).

Jake narrates *The Sun Also Rises*, and his perceptions of Cohn necessarily color his depiction of him. In chapter 6, Jake even warns readers that he cannot speak of Cohn objectively when he writes, "Somehow I feel I have not shown Robert Cohn clearly." His narrative bias lies in his jealousy of Cohn's ability to express his love for Brett in a sexual relationship.[4] Jake reflects, "The reason is that until he fell in love with Brett, I never heard him make one remark that would, in any way, detach him from other people" (52). Later, Jake admits, "I certainly did hate him" (105). Kenneth S. Lynn points out that Hemingway committed basically the same crime in real life; his construction of Loeb as Cohn made Loeb "look even worse" (295). While Lynn suggests that Hemingway "took sadistic delight in degrading the fictional stand-in for Harold Loeb," he adds that Hemingway became "ashamed of himself in the process and ambivalently sympathetic with Cohn as a result" (296). In retrospect, it is easy to see some of the same ambivalence that would lead Hemingway to praise Faulkner on one hand while criticizing him on the other.

Another scene later in the novel illustrates the principles of "irony and pity" that Jake deems "so essential to good writing" in the excised material cut from the beginning of the novel ("Beginning" 133).[5] In the scene, Jake and Bill Gorton riff and pun on the terms that, according to H. R. Stoneback, constituted "the literary catchphrase of the hour," as per Anatole France's formula (202). After bandying about the terms for almost two pages, Bill tells Jake, "You don't understand irony. You have no pity. Say something pitiful." Jake responds, "Robert Cohn," and Bill replies, "Not so bad. That's better. Now why is Cohn pitiful? Be ironic." Jake declines, saying, "Aw, hell! . . . It's too early in the morning," and Bill, still joking, rejoins, "And you claim you want to be a writer, too. You're only a newspaper man. . . . You ought to be ironical the minute you get out of bed. You ought to wake up with your mouth full of pity" (119).

In the excised material, however, Jake rejects the methods that irony and pity require when he admits, "I did not want to tell this story in the first person but I find that I must. I wanted to stay well outside the story so that I would not be touched by it in any way, and handle all the people in it with that irony and pity that are so essential to good writing" ("Beginning" 133). Jake continues, "I made the unfortunate mistake, for a writer, of first having been Mr. Jake Barnes. So it is not going to be splendid and cool and detached after all. 'What a pity!' as Brett used to say" (133-34). Jake says that he tells his story a bit differently from other writers:

> I am writing the story, not as I believe is usual in these cases, from a desire for confession, because being a Roman Catholic I am spared that Protestant urge to literary production, nor to set things all out the way they happened for the good of some future generation, nor any of the usual high moral urges, but because I believe it is a good story. (134)

Jake draws further distinction between himself and the other writers that he seems to fear becoming when he reflects, "Like all newspaper men I have always wanted to write a novel, and I suppose, now that I am doing it, the novel will have that awful taking-the-pen-in-hand quality that afflicts newspaper men when they start to write on their own" (134). Here again, readers can anticipate Hemingway's charges of artifice against Faulkner, claims that he "cons himself" and his readers ("The Art of the Short Story" 97, in Hemingway, *Letters* 770).

While Jake writes his own story, one from which he cannot distance himself, Cohn writes a novel with "a great deal of fantasy in it" ("Beginning" 135). Jake—and, for that matter, every other character in *The Sun Also Rises*—rejects Cohn and his fantasies by the conclusion of the novel. Cohn disappears, and no one in the group knows what has happened to him; they only speculate that he'll "pick up with his old girl, probably" (226). Yet Jake envies Cohn, too, and covets his experience with Brett and likely his simpler outlook on life. Cohn seems a romantic type basically untouched by war. Mark Spilka aptly describes him as "the last chivalric hero, the last defender of an outworn faith" (109). Jake, ostensibly searching to learn "how to live in" the world, suspects, "Maybe if you found out how to live in it you learned from that what it was all about" (152). Cohn seems to have found the peace Jake seeks, and Jake surely envies him that as well.

Jake even figuratively tries on Cohn's identity, however briefly, in chapter 15, when he cannot find the key to his own room and falls asleep "on one of the beds in Cohn's room" (163). After Jake awakens from a heavy sleep, feeling that he is "too late," he puts on one of Cohn's coats and walks "out on the balcony" (164). Jake watches the festivities below for a few minutes and then goes back to sleep. Cohn wakes him when he returns and begins undressing to go to sleep himself (164). As Cohn undresses, Jake takes leave of him and his dreams, and readers are again reminded of Hemingway's admiration for, and perhaps envy of, the perceived ease of Faulkner's simpler life. After all, while Hemingway made fun of "Anomatopeoio [Yoknapatawpha] county" (*Letters* 770), he strikes a wistful note in his July 1947 letter to Faulkner: "Difference with us guys is I always lived out of country (as mercenary or patriot) since kid. My own country gone. Trees cut down, Nothing left but gas stations, sub-divisions where we hunted snipe on the prairie, etc." (624).

Does all this mean that Hemingway had Faulkner in mind when he constructed the character of Robert Cohn? Of course not, but it does suggest a pattern of antagonistic competition, one that Hemingway seems to have thrived on.[6] Regardless of how he felt personally about Faulkner, he consistently defined himself against Faulkner as an artist, and from this friction came some of the most powerful fiction of the twentieth century. Frederick R. Karl writes of Faulkner's reaction to Hemingway's suicide:

> Faulkner saw something ominous in Hemingway's death, since the two had become famous together, the twins of American fiction from 1930 to 1950 or so. . . . The two were intertwined, and it may not be too conjectural to assert that Faulkner saw in the other's death something of his own. It was not only the death of Hemingway, however, but the end of an era in American writing: the few great ones had passed. Faulkner felt there was no one to replace them. (1037)

That is one assessment, at any rate, with which Hemingway would certainly have agreed.

Notes

1. See George Monteiro's "The Faulkner-Hemingway Rivalry" for an extensive discussion of critical work concerning these textual exchanges. For a comprehensive discussion of the rivalry, as well as evaluations and remarks from the authors' contemporaries, see Earl Rovit and Arthur Waldhorn's *Hemingway and Faulkner in Their Time*.

2. See Thomas L. McHaney's *William Faulkner's "The Wild Palms": A Study* for

an insightful analysis of the connections between the two novels. McHaney points to specific parallel scenes in "The Wild Palms" section of *If I Forget Thee, Jerusalem* and *The Sun Also Rises* that employ imaginary and stuffed dogs, respectively, as symbols (80-81).

3. In *Hemingway: A Biography*, Jeffrey Meyers suggests that Jake's wound "derived from Hemingway's imaginative extension of his *own* wound at Fossalta and his convalescence at the hospital in Milan." Meyers quotes Hemingway on Jake's wound: "It came from a personal experience in that when I had been wounded at one time there had been an infection from pieces of wool cloth being driven into the scrotum. Because of this I got to know other kids who had genito urinary wounds and I wondered what a man's life would have been like after that if his penis had been lost and his testicles and spermatic cord remained intact" (190).

4. Jake does not begrudge Cohn the sex alone, or he would hate Mike Campbell equally; Jake must resent Cohn because he can both love Brett and have sex with her, something Jake knows he can never do.

5. This material, cut from the galleys at the last minute, informed Hemingway's composition of the novel. His deletion of the crucial information contained therein, as Linda W. Wagner notes in "'Proud and Friendly and Gently,'" actually encouraged misinterpretation because it "left readers too little direction" (242). While not a part of Hemingway's published text, the discarded material nevertheless sheds valuable light on many aspects of the novel.

6. See Joseph Fruscione's "'One Tale, One Telling'" for a discussion of how the anxiety of influence drove each author.

Works Cited

Baker, Carlos. *Ernest Hemingway: A Life Story*. New York: Charles Scribner's Sons, 1969.

Berg, A. Scott. *Maxwell Perkins: Editor of Genius*. New York: Dutton, 1978.

Blotner, Joseph. *Faulkner: A Biography*. 2 vols. New York: Random House, 1974.

Faulkner, William. *Selected Letters of William Faulkner*. Ed. Joseph Blotner. New York: Random House, 1977.

Fruscione, Joseph. "*Mano a Mano* Rivalries in Spain and America: Hemingway vs. Faulkner in *The Dangerous Summer*." *The Hemingway Review* 28.1 (2008): 68-88.

_____. "'One Tale, One Telling': Parallelism, Influence, and Exchange Between Faulkner's *The Unvanquished* and Hemingway's *For Whom the Bell Tolls*." *War, Literature, and the Arts* 18.1-2 (2006): 279-300.

Hemingway, Ernest. "The Beginning Cut from the Galleys." *Hemingway and "The Sun Also Rises": The Crafting of a Style*. Frederic Joseph Svoboda. Lawrence: UP of Kansas, 1983. 131-37.

_____. *Death in the Afternoon*. New York: Charles Scribner's Sons, 1932.

_____. Letter to Harvey Breit. 4 July 1952. Hemingway Collection, John F. Kennedy Library, Boston.

_____. *Selected Letters, 1917-1961*. Ed. Carlos Baker. New York: Charles Scribner's Sons, 1981.

_____. *The Sun Also Rises*. New York: Charles Scribner's Sons, 1926.

Karl, Frederick R. *William Faulkner: American Writer*. New York: Weidenfield & Nicolson, 1989.

Lynn, Kenneth S. *Hemingway*. New York: Simon & Schuster, 1987.

McHaney, Thomas L. *William Faulkner's "The Wild Palms": A Study*. Jackson: UP of Mississippi, 1975.

Meyers, Jeffrey. *Hemingway: A Biography*. New York: Harper & Row, 1985.

Monteiro, George. "The Faulkner-Hemingway Rivalry." *Faulkner and His Contemporaries*. Ed. Joseph R. Urgo and Ann J. Abadie. Jackson: UP of Mississippi, 2004. 74-92.

Rovit, Earl, and Arthur Waldhorn. *Hemingway and Faulkner in Their Time*. New York: Continuum, 2006.

Spilka, Mark. "The Death of Love in *The Sun Also Rises*." *Ernest Hemingway*. Ed. Harold Bloom. New York: Chelsea House, 1985. 107-18.

Stoneback, H. R. *Reading Hemingway's "The Sun Also Rises": Glossary and Commentary*. Kent, OH: Kent State UP, 2007.

Wagner, Linda W. "'Proud and Friendly and Gently': Women in Hemingway's Early Fiction." *College Literature* 7 (1980): 239-47.

The Critical History of *The Sun Also Rises*_____

Laurence W. Mazzeno

With the publication of *The Sun Also Rises* in 1926, Ernest Hemingway announced to the world that he had completed his apprenticeship in fiction and was ready to take his place among the major new voices of the postwar generation. More than eighty years after its appearance, the novel continues to prove the strength of its author's claim. It has gradually taken on iconic status, not only among Hemingway's work but in the American literary canon as well. It has worn well with critics and students alike, and the novel continues to appear on high school and college reading lists.

More critical commentary has been published on *The Sun Also Rises* than on any other work by Hemingway. Virtually every book about Hemingway contains significant commentary on the novel, and several have it as their exclusive focus. Journal articles number in the hundreds. Additionally, most studies of twentieth-century American fiction include analyses of the novel and its impact on succeeding generations of writers. In her 1977 reference guide, Linda Wagner (now Wagner-Martin) lists seventy-five entries for books and articles devoted specifically to discussion of *The Sun Also Rises*. Kelli Larson's 1991 extension of Wagner-Martin's work cites nearly two hundred additional publications, and annual bibliographies in *The Hemingway Review* routinely provide dozens of new citations. Hence a complete critique of the novel's critical history could fill a fairly thick volume.

Criticism of *The Sun Also Rises* has followed what might be described as a predictable trajectory. The first reviews concentrated on the contemporary aspects of the work, hailing it as a masterful depiction of the "lost generation" that Hemingway knew so well. In some circles the novel prompted a kind of parlor game in which readers guessed the identities of the real people Hemingway had lightly disguised in this roman à clef. Gradually, critics trained in formalism discovered more universal themes in the book, viewing it as a depiction of humankind's struggle to find meaning in a world without prescribed values. The explosion of new critical theories in the closing decades of the twentieth century led to new interpretations influenced by deconstruction and cultural studies. The novel became a particular favorite of feminists and gender studies critics, whose revisionist readings led to a new, more nuanced understanding of Hemingway's achievement. By the end of the century, *The Sun Also Rises* ranked beside F. Scott Fitzgerald's *The Great Gatsby* as one of the two most widely read and frequently taught modern American novels.

Initial Reception and Criticism, 1926-1970

Hemingway intended *The Sun Also Rises* to be a popular novel as well as a critical success, and by virtually any measure he succeeded on both counts. Charles Scribner's Sons' first printing of just over five thousand copies was followed by six reprints within a year. Even more significant was the impact the novel had on the generation it purported to describe. Writing retrospectively, James Nagel has noted that after its publication "nothing was ever the same" (87). Hemingway went from aspiring writer to international celebrity and spokesman for the postwar generation. The Hemingway style became a model for fiction and journalism alike, and young people began "imitating its characters and lifestyle" (87). In fact, within a year of its publication, satirist and critic Dorothy Parker reported that it was impossible to go anywhere and not hear people talking about the novel. As Parker observed, some critics were calling it the greatest American novel, while others derided it with equal fervor (108-9).[1]

Michael Reynolds describes the early reviewers as falling into "three camps: the repulsed, the anti-expatriates, and the effusive" (*Novel of the Twenties* 9). A sampling of the reviews shows the *Chicago Daily Tribune* reviewer expressing outrage at Hemingway's "utterly degraded people" ("Hemingway Seems" 4) and faulting him for sensationalizing trivial matters, *Time*'s reviewer finding the book pseudoromantic ("Sad" 4), and Allen Tate, an admirer of Hemingway's early short stories, lamenting that the author achieved a popular following for his first novel by sacrificing artistic integrity and complaining that the characters are little more than caricatures (94-95). Edwin Muir agreed; ultimately one feels that Hemingway's characters do not matter, he stated, and as a result there is "a lack of artistic significance" in the novel (96). Virginia Woolf wrote that Hemingway's claim to being "modern" derived only from his choice of subject matter, not from "any fundamental novelty in his conception of the art of fiction" (105).

In contrast, the reviewer for the *The New York Times Book Review* celebrated Hemingway's "magnificent writing" ("Marital Tragedy" 36). In the *Saturday Review*, Cleveland Chase described the novel as having a "sense of unbounded vigor and enthusiasm coolly repressed and controlled" and declared it a "triumph of style over matter" (41-42). Herbert Gorman argued in the *New York Book World* that the novel firmly established Hemingway in "the first rank of that younger group from whom we may expect so much" (93). André Maurois admitted that, while the plot of the novel is slight, "any plot will do when a novelist knows how to create live human beings, and Hemingway's characters are alive" (Rev. 97). In the *New Republic*, Edmund Wilson, an early admirer of Hemingway, wrote that the novel's hero is "highly civilized" and possesses a "rather complex temperament and extreme sensibility" ("Sportsman's Tragedy" 46).

For the next forty years critical commentary on the novel was dominated by discussions of the postwar loss of values, Hemingway's new, spare style and characterization techniques, and his creation of a new kind of hero. Formalists took great pains to detect artistic unity and to describe Hemingway's craftsmanship, while humanists focused on the novel's moral vision. Meanwhile, new works by Hemingway were invariably compared (often unfavorably) to *The Sun Also Rises*. In a perceptive critique published in 1943, the novelist James Farrell observed that the novel "struck deep chords in the youth of the Twenties" (5) because it reflected the social conditions among those of the postwar generation who did *not* fight in the war. "The best of Ernest Hemingway is still to be found in *The Sun Also Rises*," Farrell wrote; it "remains one of the best American novels of the Twenties" (6). Not everyone was convinced of its enduring value, however. André Maurois, who had reviewed the book favorably when it first appeared, dismissed it in two paragraphs in his *Revue de Paris* retrospective, finding that it celebrated a kind of "silent romanticism drowned in cocktails and champagne" ("Emergence" 44).

Beneath the "cocktails and champagne," however, critics had begun to discover and describe the "Hemingway code" and the "Hemingway hero" that play such a large role in the author's first novel. Edmund Wilson, who had become increasingly disaffected with Hemingway's work by the 1940s, begrudgingly admitted that "one can catch hold of a code in all the drunkenness and the social chaos" (*Wound* 219). The hero and his code—the gendered reference is intentional—are the principal subject of Philip Young's *Ernest Hemingway* (1952). Young categorizes the Hemingway code, which Hemingway himself described as "grace under pressure," as being made up of "the controls of honor and courage" that a man uses to set himself apart from the masses of people who act simply on impulse (63). Those who follow the code act deliberately, shaping their own value systems in a world where there are no moral absolutes. The code hero is one who has already internalized these virtues and lives by high standards he has set for himself. The Hemingway hero, on the other hand, is a figure who has been wounded, sometimes physically and almost always psychically, by some early experience. He must learn to employ courage and honor in governing his own actions, often by observing the behavior of code heroes. In *The Sun Also Rises*, Jake Barnes is the Hemingway hero, while the bullfighter Pedro Romero represents the code hero. Unfortunately, Young suggests, while Jake may learn how he should live, for most of the people in the novel, life is futile, and "their motions, like the motions of the sun in the title," are "endless, circular, and unavailing" (87).

In *Hemingway: The Writer as Artist* (1952) Carlos Baker provides a considerably more optimistic judgment of the novel's hero. Baker says Hemingway managed to "dissociate himself from the very idea of lostness" (81) he describes in the novel. Jake is not "lost" either, but instead is the "moral norm" (82) against which the dissipated members of the lost generation are measured and found wanting. Baker is also among the first to provide a systematic, albeit brief, description of Hemingway's "special 'mythological' methods" (87), an idea expounded upon in greater detail by critics such as Philip Young, Richard Adams, Leslie Fiedler, and Robert W. Lewis during the subsequent decades.

Critics of this period often made much of the Hemingway hero at the expense of the novelist's female characters, particularly Lady Brett Ashley. Described variously as temptress, seductress, man-eater, manipulator, and dissipated hedonist, Brett is characterized by Baker (borrowing Robert Cohn's description of her in the novel) as a Circe-figure who lures men into her orbit and turns them into swine. Leslie Fiedler goes even further in vilifying her, claiming she is "the most satisfactory female character in all of Hemingway" principally *because* she is presented "quite audaciously as a goddess, the bitch-goddess with the boyish smile" (319). Witness, he says, the way the Spaniards recognize her as an evil presence who will eventually ruin the chaste and heroic young bullfighter Pedro Romero. The same rather traditionalist (now considered patriarchal) view of men's and women's natures and social roles serves as the basis of Robert Lewis's view of Jake and Brett in *Hemingway on Love* (1965). Traditional love is denied them, of course, partly because of Jake's wound and partly because Brett refuses to conform to traditional expectations for women. Lewis views the two as eventually coming to some understanding of their own flawed natures and of their mutual dependency.

By the 1960s, critical opinion had gelled around the notion of an almost monolithic Hemingway hero whose code of behavior closely follows the pattern described by Young in his seminal study. In *Heming-*

way's Heroes (1969) Delbert E. Wylder refutes this position, insisting that the fictional heroes in Hemingway's novels differ from each other in important ways. Wylder sees *The Sun Also Rises* as a kind of bildungsroman in which Jake, the wounded hero, tries to learn how to live in a world without prescribed and agreed-upon values. Jackson J. Benson's reading of the novel in *Hemingway: The Writer's Art of Self-Defense* (1969) also stresses the importance of its hero's developing a value system. However, Benson's insistence that Hemingway's portrayal of sexual identity conforms to traditional notions of sexuality provided the kind of ammunition a new generation of critics would use to attack Hemingway and his masculine code of conduct.

A sense of how critics not specifically focused on explicating the Hemingway code were approaching his work during the middle decades of the century can be found in Richard P. Adams's "Sunrise out of the Waste Land" (1959) and Mark Spilka's "The Death of Love in *The Sun Also Rises*" (1958). Adams espouses a mythical interpretation of the novel, tracing in detail Hemingway's debt to T. S. Eliot's *The Waste Land* (1922). He goes so far as to draw comparisons between its major characters and figures in the medieval Grail legend. The importance of this kind of criticism, Adams suggests, is to demonstrate that "as a literary artist" Hemingway is "not an isolated phenomenon" but instead "has the usual ties with other writers and with a tradition" (62). Spilka asserts that Hemingway, better than any other writer, captures the theme of "the death of love in World War I" (238). Repeatedly, he writes, the novel provides images of integrity against which Jake and his generation are tested and found wanting. If there is a hero in *The Sun Also Rises*, it is the abiding earth described in the novel's epigraph, or the bullfighter Pedro Romero, who becomes the moral touchstone in a world in which everyone has to define his or her own moral standards. Spilka's analysis prompted several rebuttals, notably one by Robert Lewis, who says in *Hemingway on Love* that Hemingway considers romantic love not dead but simply a kind of sickness. Richard B. Hovey is even more direct in attacking Spilka, claiming in *Heming-*

way: The Inward Terrain (1968) that love remains alive both in Paris and in Spain.

The critical debates carried on by Hemingway scholars at midcentury are adeptly summarized for students by Earl Rovit in his 1963 volume in the Twayne United States Authors series. Rovit reads the novel as a moral commentary that explores traditional value systems brought into question by the war, but he finds that it also contains a mythic dimension that allows it to transcend its immediate social setting. Positive assessments of Hemingway's novel were commonplace through the 1960s, although some complained that the novelist's code was morally suspect, if not bankrupt. Within the constraints of critical practice current at the time, some revision was under way. For example, Donald T. Torchiana's "*The Sun Also Rises*: A Reconsideration" (1970) argues for a more optimistic reading of the social and moral climate, suggesting that the novel is carefully structured along the lines of the bullfight to show Jake emerging victorious from his struggle to find a modus vivendi amid the chaos he finds about him. Scott Donaldson's "Hemingway's Morality of Compensation" (1970) essentially takes an opposing view, reading the novel through the lens of what might be called the economy of morality and finding that anyone who obtains happiness within the novel pays for it, often with corresponding pain. By 1970, however, there were signs on the horizon that Hemingway's reputation was about to undergo serious revaluation; not even *The Sun Also Rises* would escape the scrutiny of a new generation of critics not enamored of traditional modes of critical inquiry or traditional attitudes about morality and gender relations.

Revaluations, 1970-Present

Melvin Friedman aptly describes the dramatic change in critical approaches to Hemingway in a 1973 essay. "We are in the midst of a serious reappraisal and stocktaking of Hemingway's reputation" he notes, "with the personal myth being punctured and deflated while the work gets vigorous new readings" (392-93). Critics employing new methodologies—deconstruction, narratology, post-Freudian psychology, cultural and new historical analysis, and especially feminist and gender studies—began raising serious questions about Hemingway's accomplishments both as an artist and as a social critic.

In the vanguard of this more critical reassessment were the feminist critics. It is certainly true, as Jamie Barlowe notes in "Re-reading Women II: The Example of Brett, Hadley, Duff, and Women's Scholarship," that women have often provided new perspectives on *The Sun Also Rises* because their "rereading[s] rest on a different set of assumptions about literature, culture, author/reader relationships, gender, sexuality, identity, subjectivity, and integrity" (26). But for a decade or more, many feminist scholars were highly critical of Hemingway, describing his work as outmoded and patriarchal. Complaints ranged from mild reproofs, such as Rosalind Miles's dismissal of his work as antifeminist, to more serious ones, such as Mary Allen's assertion that Hemingway is misogynistic.

As one might expect, feminist criticism of *The Sun Also Rises* centers on Hemingway's portrayal of Brett Ashley. Where earlier critics characterized Brett as the villain of the novel, feminists characterized Hemingway as a villain for making Brett out to be a monster. However, by the 1980s the portrait of Brett as bitch-goddess gradually gave way to more complex interpretations, largely as a result of the application of new approaches grounded in feminist perspectives of literature but lacking the vitriol that characterized earlier critiques. The range of these assessments is made apparent in the forty-plus essays collected by Harold Bloom in the *Brett Ashley* volume of Bloom's Major Literary Characters series (1991).

Among Brett's defenders is Roger Whitlow, whose *Cassandra's Daughters: The Women in Hemingway* (1984) is intended as a counterpunch thrown at "the most recent crop of Ph.D. candidates treating Hemingway's women in their dissertations" (xii). Brett is actually "better than she wants to think herself," he insists, and "in no legitimate way can she be interpreted as a bitch" (58). Wendy Martin's "Brett Ashley as the New Woman in *The Sun Also Rises*" (1987) proposes that as the "new woman" Brett poses a "radical challenge to the traditional social structure" (68). Martin claims Hemingway intended her to be perceived as Jake's equal and that the novel is actually an exploration of the possibility of finding "new kinds of relationships for women and men in the twentieth century" (81).

Similarly, Linda Patterson Miller's "Brett Ashley: The Beauty of It All" (1995) counters earlier criticism of Brett as a destructive force, suggesting that she is instead a complex character whose "stunning beauty" is a positive quality in a novel in which she plays an "intricate role" (170). Kathy G. Willingham suggests in "The Sun Hasn't Set Yet: Brett Ashley and the Code Hero Debate" (2002) that most unfavorable interpretations of Brett emerge from "arbitrary social conventions and prejudices as well as rigid, modernist definitions or understandings" of gender roles (52). Applying theoretical principles developed by Georges Bataille, Willingham discovers that Brett provides for readers "a model no less significant, important, or romantic than any of the male code heroes who have inspired or influenced countless readers" (34). By 2004, opinion of Brett had shifted so radically that Lorie Watkins Fulton could write that, far from being a stereotyped bitch-goddess, Brett is an "intriguing mix of femininity and masculinity, strength and vulnerability, morality and dissolution" (116) who possesses "an appealing generosity of spirit" and "subtle wit" (121).

Closely allied to feminist scholars' work of revealing new dimensions of Hemingway's novel has been that of gender studies critics. Although Gerry Brenner's *Concealments in Hemingway's Works* (1983) is not intended primarily as a study of gender in Hemingway's novels, Brenner's comments on *The Sun Also Rises* in the volume initially raised some eyebrows because Brenner contends that among the things Hemingway sought to conceal in *The Sun Also Rises* was his personal bent toward homoeroticism, a theme pursued by a number of critics during the 1980s and 1990s.

Another outgrowth of the influence of gender studies on readings of Hemingway has been a new focus on the subject of androgyny. The most prominent of such studies, and to date the most influential, is Mark Spilka's *Hemingway's Quarrel with Androgyny* (1990), in which Spilka opens his discussion with the observation that Hemingway's interest in the androgynous makeup of men and women "had its origin in *The Sun Also Rises*" (1). In *Alchemy in "The Sun Also Rises"* (1992) Wolfgang E. H. Rudat, author of a 1990 book describing Hemingway's use of literary allusion and mythology, develops an analysis similar to Spilka's, focusing on Hemingway's "concern with sexual identity, sexual crossover, and androgyny" (3). Also following up on Spilka, Nancy R. Comley and Robert Scholes argue in *Hemingway's Genders: Rereading the Hemingway Text* (1994) that Brett's appeal lies in Hemingway's portrayal of her as a strong character who is also a strong woman, androgynous by design. Carl P. Eby's psychoanalytic study *Hemingway's Fetishism: Psychoanalysis and the Mirror of Manhood* (1999) contains scattered comments about the characters in *The Sun Also Rises* throughout its examination of Hemingway's ideas about the nature of sexuality and gender. Debra A. Moddelmog's Lacanian reinterpretation of Hemingway, *Reading Desire: In Pursuit of Ernest Hemingway* (1999), traces the way *The Sun Also Rises* brings the "traditional significance of gender and sexuality into conflict" to expose "the intellectual limitations that result when 'gender' and 'sexuality' are read as innocent acts of nature and as fixed boundaries" (93).

Another important result of new gender studies has been a renewed interest in, and reinterpretation of, Hemingway's concept of masculinity. Thomas Strychacz's chapter "Dramatizations of Manhood in Hemingway's *In Our Time* and *The Sun Also Rises*," in his *Hemingway's Theaters of Masculinity* (2003), applies performance theory in an assessment of gender formation to explain how Jake Barnes "employs some of the functions of gazing within a theatrical representation of manhood" (79). Men are forced constantly to perform for others, Strychacz says, in order to assert their claims to masculinity. Also typical of examinations motivated by recent developments in gender studies is Ira Elliott's "Performance Art: Jake Barnes and 'Masculine' Signification in *The Sun Also Rises*" (1995), in which Elliott explores themes of homosexuality present in the novel; these, he says, help reveal "the extent to which sexual categories and gender roles are cultural constructions" (64). Although Jake cannot perform like a man, "inasmuch as Jake considers himself to be heterosexual, the novel posits the site of sexuality in gendered desire rather than sexual behavior" (71). Richard Fantina's discussion of *The Sun Also Rises* in *Ernest Hemingway: Machismo and Masochism* (2005) examines the novel "in the tradition of literary machismo and the responses to it" (2). Viewing "male masochism's subversive potential" as a "threat to patriarchal notions of gender relations" (8), Fantina argues that "the humiliation of the subject" (57)—namely, Jake—is a central component of the novel. However, Hemingway seems less interested in glorifying degradation for its own sake than in explaining how this kind of behavior can "lead to a renewed masculine awareness" (57).

Finally, Amy Strong's rather aggressive attack on earlier critics in *Race and Identity in Hemingway's Fiction* (2008) is used to bolster her argument that their focus on themes of courage and masculinity has long drowned out much-needed discussion of neglected issues such as race and sexual identity in the novel. The diversity of opinion represented in the volumes noted above demonstrates just how much ideas about Hemingway's treatment of gender issues have shifted in a mere three decades.

While it would be fair to say that feminist and gender studies have provided the most fertile grounds for revisionist readings of the Hemingway canon in general and *The Sun Also Rises* in particular, a number of critics have employed other new critical approaches with notable results, while others have continued to use more traditional methods of textual analysis and to explore relationships between Hemingway's life and art, especially in work written for a wide readership. For example, Arthur Waldhorn's 1972 volume *A Reader's Guide to Ernest Hem-*

ingway focuses on the novel's structure, themes, and social dimensions. Michael Reynolds's *The Sun Also Rises: A Novel of the Twenties* (1988) offers its primary audience, high school and college students, a traditional formalist-humanist examination of the novel's structural unity, the role of the narrator, and the significance of the novel's historical background. A special issue of *The Hemingway Review* published in 1986 provides several revaluations of *The Sun Also Rises* based on studies of the manuscripts recently made available to scholars. Frederic Joseph Svoboda's *Hemingway and "The Sun Also Rises": The Crafting of a Style* (1983) offers an even more scrupulous analysis of the development of the work from the original drafts through the many revisions Hemingway made before its publication in 1926. Svoboda's study provides a clear record of how Hemingway transposed his personal experiences in France and Spain into a novel that transcends time and place.

Svoboda's line of argument highlights one of the continuing problems critics have faced in writing about *The Sun Also Rises*. The earliest readers knew the novel to be in part a roman à clef, and many took great delight in reading it as true-life chronicle rather than as fiction. For decades, critics writing for popular highbrow magazines, whose readership might be as interested in the novelist as in his work, frequently offered tantalizing comparisons between Hemingway's characters and their real-life counterparts. As late as 1983, Andrew Hook found it necessary to argue in "Life and Art in *The Sun Also Rises*" that, to understand the novel, one must somehow get beyond biography (49), since Hemingway's flamboyant lifestyle had often overshadowed and obscured his dedication to his craft. Nearly every biographer has been faced with the "fact versus fiction" dilemma. Carlos Baker (1969), Kenneth S. Lynn (1987), Michael Reynolds (1989), and James R. Mellow (1992) all devote attention to this question, and all end up providing some evidence to suggest that Hemingway's Jake is not simply the author himself in disguise. Bertram D. Sarason addresses the relationship between real life and fiction exhaustively in *Hemingway and the*

Sun Set (1972). Sarason's book includes lengthy interviews with a number of individuals who crossed paths with Hemingway in the 1920s, several of whom figure prominently in the novel.

The Sun Also Rises has not escaped the critical eye of poststructuralists or late-century structuralists, either. Cathy Davidson and Arnold Davidson suggest in "Decoding the Hemingway Hero in *The Sun Also Rises*" (1987) that the novel "should be particularly appreciated by deconstructionists" (84). They caution that earlier readings that reduce the novel to a simple inscription of the Hemingway code do not do justice to the richness of the text, which is a welter of contradictions and inconsistencies. Eugene Kanjo's "Signs Are Taken for Nothing in *The Sun Also Rises*" (1990) also employs deconstructive techniques to demonstrate that the novel is a collection of signs that ultimately point nowhere outside themselves. On the other hand, in his discussion of *The Sun Also Rises* in his volume *New Readings of the American Novel: Narrative Theory and Its Application* (1990), Peter Messent conducts a structuralist analysis of the novel, examining it "against the background of the literary system of which it is a part" (2) to discover that "the notion of autonomous individuality is a myth" (128). Messent continues this line of analysis in his *Ernest Hemingway* (1992), in which he examines "the theme of damaged subjectivity" (52) in the novel.

New studies stressing the importance of the cultural context of *The Sun Also Rises* have also helped to reshape ideas about Hemingway's achievement. J. Gerald Kennedy's commentary in *Imagining Paris: Exile, Writing, and American Identity* (1993), emerging from his discussion of Hemingway's experiences in Paris in the 1920s, suggests that Jake's circular journey from Paris to Pamplona and back again is intended to dramatize "the circular inferno of inextinguishable desire" (118). Marc Baldwin's *Reading "The Sun Also Rises": Hemingway's Political Unconscious* (1997) is an extended Marxist analysis of the novel. Baldwin points out how Hemingway suppresses uncomfortable socioeconomic issues that, if made apparent to his initial readers, might have damaged the best-seller status of the book. Baldwin exposes these hidden substrata in the text, stressing the capitalist values that motivate the characters and drive their actions. Echoes of Darwinism permeate Deirdre Ann Pettipiece's analysis of the novel in *Sex Theories and the Shaping of Two Moderns: Hemingway and HD* (2002), a work that analyzes characters by applying theories of the evolution of sexuality and sexual differences.

Ronald Berman examines the changing critical opinions regarding Hemingway's anti-Semitism and his focus on "the outsider" in *Fitzgerald, Hemingway, and the Twenties* (2001). Berman argues that recent attempts to explain away Hemingway's anti-Semitism are misguided. Convinced that Judaism represents a false, even pernicious value system, Hemingway intended his portrait of Cohn to be an attack on all Jews. Cohn is especially contemptible in Hemingway's eyes, Berman says, because he has attempted to assimilate into the larger culture by becoming an "imitation Protestant" (88). In a similar vein, Keith Gandal begins his analysis of the novel in *The Gun and the Pen: Hemingway, Fitzgerald, Faulkner, and the Fiction of Mobilization* (2008) with the rather startling central premise that Hemingway, Faulkner, and Fitzgerald were all motivated to write great novels in the 1920s "not so much, as the story goes, by their experiences of the horrors of World War I but rather by their inability to have those experiences" (5). It was not alienation from traditional values but "personal rejection by the U.S. Army" (5) that made Hemingway feel like an outsider. *The Sun Also Rises*, Gandal says, is about outsiders and rivalries; in it Hemingway dramatizes "the new and uncomfortable Anglo male sense of sexual and social rivalry with ethnic Americans" (132).

Evidence of Enduring Reputation

In 2000, the Gale publishing conglomerate commissioned three books on Hemingway: Michael Reynolds's *Ernest Hemingway* in the Literary Masters series, Albert J. DeFazio III's *The Sun Also Rises* in the Literary Masterpieces series, and Kirk Curnutt's *Ernest Heming-*

way and the Expatriate Modernist Movement, which traces Hemingway's links with important expatriate figures living in Europe after the war. These three are but the tip of the iceberg, so to speak, in a movement to make the novel continually accessible to a new generation of readers. Lisa Tyler's *Student Companion to Ernest Hemingway* (2001) contains a chapter designed to assist readers in understanding the novel's themes, literary devices, and historical context. Peter L. Hays's *Teaching Hemingway's "The Sun Also Rises"* (2003) is designed to help teachers provide students information about the background to the text, dispel some of the myths about Hemingway that might cause them to reject the work out of hand, and examine the work from a variety of critical perspectives. In 2007, Kent State University Press inaugurated its new Reading Hemingway series with the publication of H. R. Stoneback's *Reading Hemingway's "The Sun Also Rises": Glossary and Commentary*. Dedria Bryfonski's *Male and Female Roles in Hemingway's "The Sun Also Rises"* (2008) collects essays that examine major social issues reflected in the novel and essays that provide students with background information to help them understand its historical, cultural, and sociological context. All of these guidebooks approach the novelist and his work from the premise that Hemingway's reputation as a major figure in American literature is undisputed and that *The Sun Also Rises* is his most important and in some ways most representative work.

As Albert DeFazio has observed, "Each generation arrives at its own reading of *The Sun Also Rises*" (106), and it is likely that succeeding generations, armed with new critical tools not yet fashioned, will revise our understanding of this book. Whether renewed interest in biographical studies or new emphasis on what are now considered traditional approaches to critical study or some new wave of "theory" prompts another flurry of interest in the Hemingway canon, it seems certain that devoted scholars will continue to apply their talents to enriching readers' understanding of one of America's most insightful and influential works of fiction.

Note

1. Many early reviews of *The Sun Also Rises* appeared in popular magazines or journals no longer in print, posing problems for readers interested in finding these materials. The same might be said of essays published in journals available only in major research libraries. Fortunately, a representative sample of important commentary has been made available in a number of anthologies. Whenever possible, I have cited publication information on such reprints along with original publication information to facilitate readers' ability to locate these materials.

Works Cited

Adams, Richard P. "Sunrise Out of the Waste Land." *Critical Essays on Ernest Hemingway's "The Sun Also Rises."* Ed. James Nagel. New York: G. K. Hall, 1995. 53-62. Reprinted from *Tulane Studies in English* 9 (1959): 119-31.

Allen, Mary. *The Necessary Blankness: Women in Major American Fiction of the Sixties*. Urbana: U of Illinois P, 1976.

Baker, Carlos. *Ernest Hemingway: A Life Story*. New York: Charles Scribner's Sons, 1969.

_____. *Hemingway: The Writer as Artist*. 1952. Rev. ed., Princeton, NJ: Princeton UP, 1972.

Baldwin, Marc. *Reading "The Sun Also Rises": Hemingway's Political Unconscious*. New York: Peter Lang, 1997.

Barlowe, Jamie. "Re-reading Women II: The Example of Brett, Hadley, Duff, and Women's Scholarship." *Hemingway and Women: Female Critics and the Female Voice*. Ed. Lawrence R. Broer and Gloria Holland. Tuscaloosa: U of Alabama P, 2002. 23-32.

Benson, Jackson J. *Hemingway: The Writer's Art of Self-Defense*. Minneapolis: U of Minnesota P, 1969.

Berman, Ronald. *Fitzgerald, Hemingway, and the Twenties*. Tuscaloosa: U of Alabama P, 2001.

Bloom, Harold, ed. *Brett Ashley*. New York: Chelsea House, 1991.

Brenner, Gerry. *Concealments in Hemingway's Works*. Columbus: Ohio State UP, 1983.

Bryfonski, Dedria, ed. *Male and Female Roles in Hemingway's "The Sun Also Rises."* Detroit: Greenhaven Press, 2008.

Chase, Cleveland. "Out of Little, Much." *Ernest Hemingway: The Critical Reception*. Ed. Robert O. Stephens. New York: Burt Franklin, 1977. 41-42. Reprinted from *Saturday Review of Literature* 3 (11 Dec. 1926): 420-21.

Comley, Nancy R., and Robert Scholes. *Hemingway's Genders: Rereading the Hemingway Text*. New Haven, CT: Yale UP, 1994.

Curnutt, Kirk. *Ernest Hemingway and the Expatriate Modernist Movement*. Detroit: Gale, 2000.

Davidson, Cathy, and Arnold Davidson. "Decoding the Hemingway Hero in *The Sun Also Rises*." *New Essays on "The Sun Also Rises."* Ed. Linda Wagner-Martin. New York: Cambridge UP, 1987. 83-107.

DeFazio, Albert J., III. *The Sun Also Rises*. Literary Masterpieces. Detroit: Gale, 2000.

Donaldson, Scott, "Hemingway's Morality of Compensation." *American Literature* 43 (1971): 399-420.

Eby, Carl P. *Hemingway's Fetishism: Psychoanalysis and the Mirror of Manhood*. Albany: State U of New York P, 1999.

Elliott, Ira. "Performance Art: Jake Barnes and 'Masculine' Signification in *The Sun Also Rises*." *Ernest Hemingway's "The Sun Also Rises": A Casebook*. Ed. Linda Wagner-Martin. New York: Oxford UP, 2002. 63-80. Reprinted from *American Literature* 67.1 (Mar. 1995): 77-94.

Fantina, Richard. *Ernest Hemingway: Machismo and Masochism*. New York: Palgrave Macmillan, 2005.

Farrell, James T. "Ernest Hemingway, Apostle of a 'Lost Generation.'" *Ernest Hemingway: Critiques of Four Major Novels*. Ed. Carlos Baker. New York: Charles Scribner's Sons, 1962. 4-6. Reprinted from *The New York Times Book Review* 1 Aug. 1943: 6, 14.

Fiedler, Leslie. *Love and Death in the American Novel*. New York: Criterion, 1960.

Friedman, Melvin. "Ernest Hemingway: Supplement." *Sixteen Modern American Authors: A Survey of Research and Criticism*. Ed. Jackson Bryer. Durham, NC: Duke UP, 1973. 392-416.

Fulton, Lorie Watkins. "The Nurturing Nature of Lady Brett Ashley." *Male and Female Roles in Hemingway's "The Sun Also Rises."* Ed. Dedria Bryfonski. Detroit: Greenhaven Press, 2008. 115-28. Reprinted from "Reading Around Jake's Narration: Brett Ashley and *The Sun Also Rises*," *The Hemingway Review* 24.1 (Fall 2004): 61-80.

Gandal, Keith. *The Gun and the Pen: Hemingway, Fitzgerald, Faulkner, and the Fiction of Mobilization*. New York: Oxford UP, 2008.

Gorman, Herbert. Rev. of *The Sun Also Rises*, by Ernest Hemingway. *Ernest Hemingway: The Critical Heritage*. Ed. Jeffrey Meyers. New York: Routledge, 1982. 92-93. Reprinted from *New York Book World* 14 Nov. 1926: 10M.

Hays, Peter L., ed. *Teaching Hemingway's "The Sun Also Rises."* Moscow: U of Idaho P, 2003.

"Hemingway Seems Out of Focus in 'The Sun Also Rises.'" *Ernest Hemingway: A Reference Guide*. Linda W. Wagner. Boston: G. K. Hall, 1977. 4. Reprinted from *Chicago Daily Tribune* 27 Nov. 1926: 13.

Hook, Andrew. "Life and Art in *The Sun Also Rises*." *Ernest Hemingway: New Critical Essays*. Ed. A. Robert Lee. Totowa, NJ: Barnes & Noble, 1983. 49-63.

Hovey, Richard B. *Hemingway: The Inward Terrain*. Seattle: U of Washington P, 1968.

Kanjo, Eugene. "Signs are Taken for Nothing in *The Sun Also Rises*." *Hemingway in Italy and Other Essays*. Ed. Robert W. Lewis. New York: Praeger, 1990. 85-97.

Kennedy, J. Gerald. *Imagining Paris: Exile, Writing, and American Identity*. New Haven, CT: Yale UP, 1993.

Larson, Kelli. *Ernest Hemingway: A Reference Guide, 1974-1989*. Boston: G. K. Hall, 1991.

Lewis, Robert W. *Hemingway on Love*. Austin: U of Texas P, 1965.

Lynn, Kenneth S. *Hemingway*. New York: Simon & Schuster, 1987.

"Marital Tragedy." *Critical Essays on Ernest Hemingway's "The Sun Also Rises."* Ed. James Nagel. New York: G. K. Hall, 1995. 35-36. Reprinted from *The New York Times Book Review* 31 Oct. 1926: 7.

Martin, Wendy. "Brett Ashley as the New Woman in *The Sun Also Rises*." *New Essays on "The Sun Also Rises."* Ed. Linda Wagner-Martin. New York: Cambridge UP, 1987. 65-82.

Maurois, André. "Emergence of Ernest Hemingway." *Hemingway and His Critics: An International Anthology*. Ed. Carlos Baker. New York: Hill & Wang, 1961. 38-54. Reprinted from *Revue de Paris* 62 (Mar.1955): 3-16.

_____. Rev. of *The Sun Also Rises*, by Ernest Hemingway. *Ernest Hemingway: The Critical Heritage*. Ed. Jeffrey Meyers. New York: Routledge, 1982. 97-100. Reprinted from *This Quarter* 2 (1929): 212-15.

Mellow, James R. *Hemingway: A Life Without Consequences*. Boston: Houghton Mifflin, 1992.

Messent, Peter. *Ernest Hemingway*. New York: St. Martin's Press, 1992.

_____. *New Readings of the American Novel: Narrative Theory and Its Application*. New York: Macmillan, 1990.

Miles, Rosalind. *The Fiction of Sex: Theme and Function of Sex Difference in the Modern Novel*. London: Vision, 1974.

Miller, Linda Patterson. "Brett Ashley: The Beauty of It All." *Critical Essays on Ernest Hemingway's "The Sun Also Rises."* Ed. James Nagel. New York: G. K. Hall, 1995. 170-84.

Moddelmog, Debra A. *Reading Desire: In Pursuit of Ernest Hemingway*. Ithaca, NY: Cornell UP, 1999.

Muir, Edwin. "*The Sun Also Rises*." *Ernest Hemingway: The Critical Heritage*. Ed. Jeffrey Meyers. New York: Routledge, 1982. 96. Reprinted from *Nation & Athenaeum* 2 July 1927: 450, 452.

Nagel, James. "Brett and the Other Women in *The Sun Also Rises*." *The Cambridge Companion to Hemingway*. Ed. Scott Donaldson. New York: Cambridge UP, 1996. 87-108.

Parker, Dorothy. "A Book of Great Short Stories." *Ernest Hemingway: The Critical Heritage*. Ed. Jeffrey Meyers. New York: Routledge, 1982. 107-10. Reprinted from *The New Yorker* 29 Oct. 1927: 92-94.

Pettipiece, Deirdre Ann. *Sex Theories and the Shaping of Two Moderns: Hemingway and HD*. New York: Routledge, 2002.

Reynolds, Michael. *Ernest Hemingway*. Detroit: Gale, 2000.

_____. *Hemingway: The Paris Years*. New York: Basil Blackwell, 1989.

_____. *"The Sun Also Rises": A Novel of the Twenties*. Boston: Twayne, 1988.

Rovit, Earl. *Ernest Hemingway*. Boston: Twayne, 1963.

Rudat, Wolfgang E. H. *Alchemy in "The Sun Also Rises": Hidden Gold in Hemingway's Narrative*. Lewiston, NY: Edwin Mellen Press, 1992.

_____. *A Rotten Way to Be Wounded: The Tragicomedy of "The Sun Also Rises."* New York: Peter Lang, 1990.

"Sad Young Men." *Ernest Hemingway: A Reference Guide.* Linda W. Wagner. Boston: G. K. Hall, 1977. 4. Reprinted from *Time* 1 Nov. 1926: 28.

Sarason, Bertram D. *Hemingway and the Sun Set.* Washington, DC: NCR/ Microcard Editions, 1972.

Spilka, Mark. "The Death of Love in *The Sun Also Rises*." *Twelve Original Essays on Great American Novels.* Ed. Charles Shapiro. Detroit: Wayne State UP, 1958. 238-56.

_____. *Hemingway's Quarrel with Androgyny.* Lincoln: U of Nebraska P, 1990.

Stoneback, H. R. *Reading Hemingway's "The Sun Also Rises": Glossary and Commentary.* Kent, OH: Kent State UP, 2007.

Strong, Amy. *Race and Identity in Hemingway's Fiction.* New York: Palgrave Macmillan, 2008.

Strychacz, Thomas. *Hemingway's Theaters of Masculinity.* Baton Rouge: Louisiana State UP, 2003.

Svoboda, Frederic Joseph. *Hemingway and "The Sun Also Rises": The Crafting of a Style.* Lawrence: UP of Kansas, 1983.

Tate, Allen. "Hard-Boiled." *Ernest Hemingway: The Critical Heritage.* Ed. Jeffrey Meyers. New York: Routledge, 1982. 93-95. Reprinted from *The Nation* 123 (15 Dec. 1926): 642-44.

Torchiana, Donald T. "*The Sun Also Rises*: A Reconsideration." *Fitzgerald/ Hemingway Annual 1969.* Dayton, OH: NCR Microcard, 1970. 77-103.

Tyler, Lisa. *Student Companion to Ernest Hemingway.* Westport, CT: Greenwood Press, 2001.

Wagner, Linda W. *Ernest Hemingway: A Reference Guide.* Boston: G. K. Hall, 1977.

Waldhorn, Arthur. *A Reader's Guide to Ernest Hemingway.* New York: Octagon Books, 1972.

Whitlow, Roger. *Cassandra's Daughters: The Women in Hemingway.* Westport, CT: Greenwood Press, 1984.

Willingham, Kathy G. "The Sun Hasn't Set Yet: Brett Ashley and the Code Hero Debate." *Hemingway's Women: Female Critics and the Female Voice.* Ed. Lawrence R. Broer and Gloria Holland. Tuscaloosa: U of Alabama P, 2002. 33-53.

Wilson, Edmund. "The Sportsman's Tragedy." *Critical Essays on Ernest Hemingway's "The Sun Also Rises."* Ed. James Nagel. New York: G. K. Hall, 1995. 46. Reprinted from *New Republic* 53 (14 Dec. 1927): 102-3.

_____. *The Wound and the Bow: Seven Studies in Literature.* Boston: Houghton Mifflin, 1941.

Woolf, Virginia. Review of *Men Without Women*, by Ernest Hemingway. *Ernest Hemingway: The Critical Heritage.* Ed. Jeffrey Meyers. New York: Routledge, 1982. 101-7. Reprinted from *New York Herald Tribune Books* 9 Oct. 1927: 1, 8.

Wylder, Delbert E. *Hemingway's Heroes.* Albuquerque: U of New Mexico P, 1969.

Young, Philip. *Ernest Hemingway.* New York: Rinehart, 1952. Rev. ed. published as *Ernest Hemingway: A Reconsideration.* University Park: Pennsylvania State UP, 1966.

CRITICAL
READINGS

The Wastelanders_____

Carlos Baker

> It is the mark of the true novelist that in searching the meaning of his own unsought experience, he comes on the moral history of his time.
>
> —John Peale Bishop[1]

I. Beat-Up, Not Lost

"Hemingway's first novel might rock the country," wrote Alfred Harcourt to Louis Bromfield one day in 1925.[2] The prediction was sound. A year had not gone by before Hemingway awoke one autumn morning in Paris to find that the sun had also risen.

He had labored long and hard to give his first novel (really his third if you counted the one that was stolen and *The Torrents of Spring*) the solid structure and the freshness of texture which have since sustained it. "I started *The Sun Also Rises* on the 21st of July, my [26th] birthday, in Valencia," he wrote. Work on the first draft was continued through the last ten days of July and the month of August in Valencia, Madrid, St. Sebastian, and Hendaye, and the complete run-through was finished in Paris on September 21, 1925.[3]

"There is only one thing to do with a novel," he once told Fitzgerald, "and that is to go straight on through to the end of the damned thing."[4] The remark was perhaps designed as an exhortation to Fitzgerald, whose dilatory habits in the completion of novels occasioned some pain to a friend who wished him well. The first draft of *The Sun Also Rises* was set down in approximately forty-eight writing days, but Hemingway nearly killed himself in the process. "I knew nothing about writing a novel when I started it," he recalled in 1948, "and so wrote too fast and each day to the point of complete exhaustion. So the first draft was very bad . . . I had to rewrite it completely. But in the rewriting I learned much."[5]

Following a rest period during which he produced *The Torrents of*

The Wastelanders   **87**

Spring and gave his first draft a chance to settle and objectify itself, he went down to Schruns in the Voralberg in mid-December. Here he spent the period before Christmas in skiing and revising his book. A trip to New York in mid-February provided a brief interlude in the concentrated labors of rewriting. These filled January, part of February, and the month of March. By April first the book was ready for the typist. Heavy cuts in the original opening and elsewhere had now reduced a much longer novel to about 90,000 words. The completed typescript was mailed to Maxwell Perkins on April 24, 1926. The total operation had covered nine months of extremely hard work.[6]

The result justified the effort. If there had been any suspicion that Hemingway's skills were limited to short fiction, the publication of the first novel on October 22, 1926, dispelled it. The book showed, said a pleased reviewer, that he could state a theme dramatically and develop it to book length, a problem not previously attacked except for purposes of travesty in the book on Anderson. Three years later, on September 27, 1929, Hemingway proved with *A Farewell to Arms* that he could do it again. The interim publication of *Men Without Women* (October 14, 1927) indicated that the novelist had not killed the short-story writer. But the books which elevated him to fame, and established him firmly on that eminence, were a pair of remarkable novels.

"Famous at twenty-five; thirty a master" was MacLeish's summary of the record. In their respective ways *The Sun Also Rises* and *A Farewell to Arms* also summarized a record. In reverse chronological order, they represented the essence of that densely packed period in Hemingway's life between 1918 and 1925. They struck a total for the meaning of his own experience, both sought and unsought, and became in effect two long chapters in the moral history of the nineteen-twenties.

No book is inevitable, though every good book comes out of a strong internal compulsion. Given a man of Hemingway's talents and experience, both books happened naturally. They were done not only for reasons of normal artistic compulsion but also as a means of trying-out the moral essence of seven years. If *The Torrents of Spring* was a declaration of esthetic independence, *The Sun Also Rises* was the means Hemingway chose to declare himself out of the alleged "lost-ness" of a generation whose vagaries he chronicled. In 1922 he had recorded his humorous scorn for the artistic scum of Montparnasse. Now, through Jake Barnes, he withdrew to the position of a detached observer looking on at aimless revels which at once amused him and left him sick at heart. For it is one view of Jake that he is an imperturbable and damaged Hamlet. By talking thus and thus at the court of the Duchess of the Dome, he rids himself of a deep-seated disgust for the oppressions of his environment and the people who make it oppressive. In somewhat the same fashion, *A Farewell to Arms* meant the shunting-off of the old war, writing it out, getting rid of it by setting it down in all its true intermixture of humor and horror—until, thirty years after, the rude ceremonial of Colonel Cantwell on a grassed-over Italian battleground could bury it forever.

There was much more to these first two novels, of course, than an act of personal exorcism, however complicated. For to destroy by embodying is also to create by arranging. The artist's special blessing exists in the impulse to destroy an aspect of the thing he creates, and to render permanent what for him, in another and internal dimension, must be permanently destroyed. By 1929, Hemingway had done both tasks. With the attainment, at age thirty, of his majority as a writer, he became what he had not been so completely before—the free man who had served his apprenticeship to an art and fulfilled (in quite another way) his obligations to society. From that date on he moved off on another tack, and one began to catch echoes of one of his favored maxims: "Don't do anything too bloody long."

Of *The Sun Also Rises*, Robert Littell brightly remarked that it "won the *succès de scandale* of a *roman à clef* floated on *vin ordinaire*."[7] An immediate cause of its success was that if one knew something about the Montparnassians who frequented the Dome, the Rotonde, the Select, the Deux Magots, the Napolitain, the Dingo Bar, or Zelli's during the period 1923-1925, one likewise possessed a key which would admit the bearer to the "real" identities of the fictional people. As Model-T jokes helped early Fords to fame, so the international guessing-game of who was who in *The Sun Also Rises* assisted with the word-of-mouth promotion of the book. The prototypes of Robert Cohn, Lady Brett Ashley, and Mike Campbell were all familiarly known in the Latin Quarter. Though Pedro Romero bore the name of an eighteenth-century matador, he was clearly a projection of Niño de la Palma in his great period before a series of bad horn-wounds damaged his nerve. Wielders of the key could, of course, unlock the identities of Bill Gorton, Mr. and Mrs. Braddocks, Count Mippipopoulos, Wilson-Harris the Englishman at Burguete, or Robert Prentiss, the American novelist with the cultivated Oxford accent. For a time after the book was published, Paris gossip asserted that its title should have been *Six Characters in Search of an Author—With a Gun Apiece*. Still, as Hemingway pointed out to Fitzgerald, "no bullets whistled."[8] When the *scandale* had run its course, the wise ones turned to a new topic of absorbing interest: which author had Hemingway imitated when he wrote *The Sun Also Rises*, Fitzgerald in *This Side of Paradise* or Michael Arlen in *The Green Hat*?[9]

Littell had observed that many of the people had been "practically kidnapped" into Hemingway's novel. Such kidnapping, if that was the best descriptive term, was hardly a new experiment. Sherwood Anderson, starting with the actual residents of his Chicago boarding-house and allowing his mind to play freely over their supposed frustrations, had evolved a population for his *Winesburg, Ohio*. Lewis's *Main Street*, Fitzgerald's *This Side of Paradise*, or a little later Bravig Imbs' *The Professor's Wife* all had recognizable real-life sources. Among the poets, Frost, Robinson, and Masters invented in terms of people they knew. Yeats in the holy land of Ireland praised Maud Gonne into public property. People knew the background of Douglas' *South Wind*, Huxley's *Antic Hay*, and Joyce's *Portrait of the Artist as a Young Man*. It was, in fact, an age of indirect or direct "transcription," when the perfectly sound esthetic theory was that the author must invent out of his own experience or run the risk of making hollow men of his characters.

Hemingway shared in the belief (which has been called behaviorist) that any group of living people, placed under the microscope and candidly watched for typical or idiosyncratic conduct, can be made to provide the groundwork of a novel.

The question with any such novel is always whether it has the power to survive the immediate moment when its possible real-life origins are being gossiped about. Unless the *clef* of a *roman à clef* is finally irrelevant, the novel can have no more just claim on the interest of posterity than the society pages or racing forms from last year's newspaper. The *succès de scandale* of 1926 could not possibly explain the rapidity and assurance with which *The Sun Also Rises* became, as it has remained, one of the genuine classics of modern American fiction.

Hemingway did not at all intend to have his novel construed as a text-book of lost-generationism. But the "Lost Generation" catch-phrase, facing the title page, seemed to sum up for many people an aspect of the social history of the nineteen-twenties. Ernest Boyd said that Hemingway had triumphantly added a new chapter to the story Fitzgerald began in *This Side of Paradise*.[10] The feeling was that both books, though in far different ways, helped to anatomize the desperate gaiety with which the Jazz Age covered its melancholia. And there can be no doubt that, with his brilliant dramatization of the moral predicament of a small group of Jazz Age D. P.'s, Hemingway offered a "myth" whose extension in social space far outreached the novel's national boundaries of France and Spain. What he had done could be regarded as dramatized social history. But it was not intended to be the social history of a lost generation.

Towards the materials of his book Hemingway's attitude was more complex than has since been generally understood. Because he quite properly refused to explain his position in other than dramatic terms, and because, in his dramatization, he would not consent to oversimplify, he was often taken for the sentimental and mournful singer of an empty day, or, quite as erroneously, as the hardshelled and disillusioned chronicler of social disintegration.

One illustration of the extent of the misunderstanding is the contrast which Hemingway intended to draw by giving the book its two epigraphs, one from Gertrude Stein and the other from Ecclesiastes. The remark there attributed to "Gertrude Stein in conversation" did not represent the position of Hemingway. According to his testimony, she said it in French, and it was supposed to have been said to her by "a garage-keeper in the Midi describing his mechanics, the young ones: *une génération perdue.*" Gertrude Stein sought to extend the application of the remark from the young French mechanics (with their marked ineptitudes in the proper use of screwdrivers) to all the sad young men whom the late war and the high cost of living had cast up on the shores of France.[11]

As Hemingway explained to Perkins on November 19, 1926, he regarded the "lost generation" comment as a piece of "splendid bombast" and was very skeptical of "Gertrude's assumption of prophetic roles."[12] He could not agree with her at all. He himself did not feel lost. His reason for adding the quotation from Ecclesiastes was to indicate his own belief that "there was no such thing as a lost generation."

"I thought [he said in 1951] beat-up, maybe, [deleted] in many ways. But damned if we were lost except for deads, *gueules cassées*, and certified crazies. Lost, no. And Criqui, who was a real *gueule cassée*, won the featherweight championship of the world. We were a very solid generation though without education (some of us). But you could always get it."[13]

In order to write his book it had been necessary for Hemingway to dissociate himself in a moral sense from the very idea of lostness. He might tell Fitzgerald that *The Sun Also Rises* was "a hell of a sad story" whose only instruction was "how people go to hell."[14] But the point of the book for him, as he wrote Perkins, was "that the earth abideth forever." He had "a great deal of fondness and admiration for the earth, and not a hell of a lot for my generation," and he cared "little about vanities." The book was not meant to be "a hollow or bitter satire, but a damn tragedy with the earth abiding forever as the hero."[15]

The reading public in general did not appear to understand the point or the degree of dissociation between the artist and his characters. One heard that Jake Barnes was a modified self-portrait of Hemingway, dripping with self-pity, when in fact Hemingway was facing the hazards of *la vie humaine* with courage and a reasonably light heart, as, for that matter, was Jake Barnes. "There really is, to me anyway, very great glamour in life—and places and all sorts of things and I would like sometime to get it into the stuff," he wrote to Maxwell Perkins. "I've known some very wonderful people who even though they were going directly to the grave (which is what makes any story a tragedy if carried out until the end) managed to put up a very fine performance en route."[16] It ought to have been plain to discerning readers that Jake Barnes, Bill Gorton, and Pedro Romero were solid—if slightly beat-up—citizens of the republic. They were not lost. They refused to surrender to neuroses like those which beset Robert Cohn, Brett Ashley, and Mike Campbell. And three lost neurotics do not make a lost generation.

It was one of the ironies that Hemingway, having rejected the lost-generation tag both for himself and for his generation, should find his first book widely accepted as Exhibit A of "lost-generationism." Another conspicuous irony was that most readers found Brett and her little circle of drinking-companions so fascinating as to overshadow the idea of the abiding earth as the true hero of the book. Hemingway's love and admiration for the natural earth was certainly quite clearly projected. Any beat-up Antaeus who could gain strength and sanity from contact with the earth was a kind of hero in his eyes, as one saw in the portraits of Barnes and Gorton and Romero. Yet all eyes were drawn towards Brett—possibly by the odd mixture of irony and pity, of condemnation and admiration, with which she was treated.

II. Counterpoint

Hemingway had told Perkins that he cared little about the vanities. *The Sun Also Rises* was one of the proofs of that statement. The title comes from the first chapter of Ecclesiastes. It is useful to recognize the strong probability that the moral of the novel is derived from the same book: "All is vanity and vexation of spirit." All is vanity, at any rate, along the Vanity Fair of the Boulevard Montparnasse where the novelist introduces his people and completes his preliminary exposition. "Everybody's sick," says Jake's little *poule* in the Parisian horse-cab. The novel goes on to prove that if you concentrate on a certain segment of expatriated society, she is very nearly right. All is vanity at the Pamplona fiesta when Cohn and Campbell, moody and sullen among the empty bottles, bicker over Brett while she makes off with the matador. All is vanity when Jake concludes this little chapter of social history in a taxi on the Gran Via of Madrid. "Oh, Jake," cries Brett, "we could have had such a damned good time together." "Yes," Jake answers, closing the volume. "Isn't it pretty to think so?"

The novel contains, however, enough bright metal to bring out by contrast the special darkness of the sullen ground. We are meant to understand that all is vanity—except the things that are not vain The moral norm of the book is a healthy and almost boyish innocence of spirit, and it is carried by Jake Barnes, Bill Gorton, and Pedro Romero. Against this norm, in the central antithesis of the novel, is ranged the sick abnormal "vanity" of the Ashley-Campbell-Cohn triangle.

Long before the middle of the book, a reader who is reasonably sensitive to changes in tone may discover that he has been silently forced into a choice between two sets of moral and emotional atmospheres. Something tarnished is opposed to something bright; vanity is challenged by sanity; a world of mean and snarled disorder is set off against a world clear of entangling alliances. The whole mood of the novel brightens, for example, when the men-without-women, Jake Barnes and Bill Gorton, climb to the roof of the bus which will take them to Burguete in the Pyrenees. This bright mood has passed through certain preliminary stages. One is the pleasant dinner which the two friends have shared at Madame Lecomte's in Paris. Another comes when Bill and Jake entrain at the Gare d'Orsay for Bayonne. Almost immediately they are in the well-known eighteenth-century situation where every prospect pleases and only man is vile. Vile is hardly the word, of course, for all the people they meet. Certain fellow-travelers on the train, and later on the bus, admirably sustain their holiday mood. But their delight in "the country" and its quiet beauties, as seen from the train-windows, anticipates the Burguete experience.

If the reader performs the experiment of watching the country over the shoulders of the travelers, he is likely to be struck by the way in which the references to natural beauty are used to document the feeling of holiday (a holiday from the company of Brett and her friends) which Jake and Bill share. An otherwise unforgivable compression of the train-ride chapter will illustrate the point.[17]

"It was a lovely day, not too hot, and the country was beautiful from the start. We went back to the diner and had breakfast. . . . [Later] we ate the sandwiches and drank the Chablis and watched the country out of the window. The grain was just beginning to ripen and the fields were full of poppies. The pastureland was green, and there were fine trees, and sometimes big rivers and chateaux off in the trees. . . . About seven-thirty we had dinner and watched the country through the open window of the diner. . . . It got dark and we could feel the country hot and sandy and dark outside of the window, and about nine o'clock we got into Bayonne. . . . It was a nice hotel, and the people at the desk were very cheerful, and we each had a good small room. . . . Bayonne is a nice town. It is like a very clean Spanish town and it is on a big river. . . ."

The chapter carefully establishes the beauty of the countryside and the healthy male companionship between Jake and Bill. What makes them happiest, though they do not say so, is their freedom from the petty and noxious tribulations of Robert Cohn and company.

Although they meet Cohn in Bayonne and drive with him to Pamplona, Bill and Jake have already established between them an unspoken camaraderie into which Cohn and his troubles do not greatly intrude. Across the Spanish frontier, for example, they come upon a handsome vista. "The road went on, very white and straight ahead, and then lifted to a little rise, and off on the left was a hill with an old castle, with buildings close around it and a field of grain going right up to the walls and shifting in the wind." Jake, who is riding in the front seat with the driver, turns around as if to comment on the scene. "Robert Cohn was asleep, but Bill looked and nodded his head." No word is spoken, but the friendly shared reaction of Jake and Bill is silently and strongly affirmed. Cohn is asleep and out of it.

Being so much involved in his dream of Brett, Robert Cohn, the man not free of woman, refuses to take the Burguete bus with the good companions. Instead, by way of preparation for Brett's imminent arrival, he bathes carefully, gets a shave and haircut, has a shampoo and an application of pomade, fumes petulantly over Brett's failure to reach Pamplona on schedule (she has drunk too much somewhere to the north), and watches Bill and Jake depart for their fishing-trip without the pleasure of his company.

In Burguete, for five memorable days, all is gold. At that elevation the air is cool and bracing. The good companions walk happily over the uplands among the sturdy beech-trees, fish the clear brown streams, and recline in the lap of real country. This is what they were admiring, and silently longing for, during the train-trip from Paris to Bayonne. Jake digs for worms in the grassy bank; they catch trout; they eat rustic lunches of wine and sandwiches in the good air. At night they play three-handed bridge with the English sportsman Wilson-Harris. There is much playful and boy-like badinage. The landscape smiles, as healthful and vitalizing as ever the English Lake-district was in Wordsworth. Somewhere in the remote background, out of sight and as far out of mind as possible, is the Ashley-Campbell-Cohn triangle. The comrades are not troubled. For a brief but golden age there is "no word from Robert Cohn nor from Brett and Mike."[18]

Hemingway's careful contrast of emotional and social climates makes the prefatory quotation from Ecclesiastes directly relevant. "One generation passeth away," says the preacher, "and another generation cometh; but the earth abideth for ever." Wherever they go, Brett and her little coterie (the truly "lost" part of that otherwise unlost generation) carry along with them the neuroses of Montparnasse. But the earth fortunately abides. The sun rises and sets over the fields and woods of France and Spain. The fresh winds blow; the rivers run in the valleys; the white roads ascend the mountains. For those who will look at it, all this is available. But the wastelanders pass away and out of the picture, and there is no health in them.

This pleasurable contrapuntal method, with its subtly marked contrast of emotional and moral climates, continues into the climactic phase of the novel. Now, however, there is a new image to take the place of Burguete. When the Pamplona fiesta begins, the light (and the lightheartedness) which the fishermen have known in the Pyrenees grows dim and comes very near to going out. All the sullen jealousies and cross-purposes which Brett's presence causes are released among the vacationers. Outward signs of the venom which works within are Jake's obvious disgust at Cohn's fawning over Brett; Mike's relentless verbal bludgeoning of Cohn; and Cohn's physical bludgeoning of Mike and Jake. As if Brett's own neurosis were somehow communicable, her semi-voluntary victims writhe and snarl. All is vanity at Pamplona as it was in the Montparnasse cafés before the trip was undertaken.

For the Pamplona episodes the contrasting bright metal is not nature but rather a natural man, the brave matador Romero. He is used as a force of antithesis, manly, incorruptible, healthy, courageous, of complete integrity and self-possession. Beside him Mike seems a poor player indeed, and he conspicuously embodies the qualities which Cohn lacks. His control accents Cohn's emotionalism; his courage, Cohn's essential cowardice; his self-reliance, Cohn's miserable fawning dependence; his dignity, Cohn's self-pity; his natural courtesy, Cohn's basic rudeness and egotism.

The enmity between the bullfighter and the boxer—for the very nature of Romero abhors the moral vacuum in Cohn—reaches its climax when Cohn invades Romero's room and finds Brett there. In a bed-room fist-fight the boxer has every advantage over the bullfighter except in those internal qualities which fists cannot touch. Though he is knocked down fifteen times, Romero will not lose consciousness, give up, shake hands, or stop trying to hit Cohn for as long as he can see him. Afterwards, like a Greek chorus, Bill and Mike close the chronicle-history of Robert Cohn, the pomaded sulker in the tent, and Romero, the manly and unspoiled warrior.[19] "That's quite a kid," says Bill. "He ruined Cohn," says Mike. Cohn presently leaves Pamplona under the cloud of his own ruination. Romero's face may be cut up, but his moral qualities have triumphed, as they do again in the bullring the day following the brawl. He has been "beat-up" like many other members of his generation. But not "lost."

Maxwell Perkins, a good and perceptive editor, understood the intent of the novel perfectly. He admiringly called it "a healthy book, with marked satirical implications upon novels which are not—sentimentalized, subjective novels, marked by sloppy hazy thought."[20] Its morality, like its esthetics, was notably healthy. Against the background of international self-seekers like Cohn, the true moral norm of the book (Bill and Jake at Burguete, Romero at Pamplona) stood out in high and shining relief.

III. Circe and Company

Hemingway's first novel provides an important insight into the special "mythological" methods which he was to employ with increasing assurance and success in the rest of his major writing. It is necessary to distinguish Hemingway's method from such "mythologizing" as that of Joyce in *Ulysses*, or Eliot in *The Waste Land*. For Hemingway early devised and subsequently developed a mythologizing tendency of his own which does not depend on antecedent literatures, learned foot-notes, or the recognition of spot passages. *The Sun Also Rises* is a first case in point.

It might be jocularly argued, for example, that there is much more to the portrait of Lady Brett Ashley than meets the non-Homeric eye. It is very pleasant to think of the Pallas Athena, sitting among the statuary in one of her temples like Gertrude Stein among the Picassos in the rue de Fleurus, and murmuring to the Achaeans, homeward bound from the battle of Troy: "You are all a lost generation." As for Brett, Robert Cohn calls her Circe. "He claims she turns men into swine," says Mike Campbell. "Damn good. I wish I were one of these literary chaps."[21] If Hemingway had been writing about brilliant literary chaps in the manner, say, of Aldous Huxley in *Chrome Yellow*, he might have undertaken to develop Cohn's parallel. It would not have been farther-fetched than Joyce's use of the Daedalus legend in *A Portrait of the Artist* or Eliot's kidnapping of Homeric Tiresias to watch over the mean little seductions of *The Waste Land*.

Was not Brett Ashley, on her low-lying island in the Seine, just such a fascinating peril as Circe on Aeaea? Did she not open her doors to all the modern Achaean chaps? When they drank her special potion of French applejack or Spanish wine, did they not become as swine, or in the modern idiom, wolves? Did not Jake Barnes, that wily Odysseus, resist the shameful doom which befell certain of his less wary comrades who became snarling beasts?

There are even parallel passages. Says Jake Barnes, thinking of Brett: "I lay awake thinking and my mind jumping around. . . . Then all of a sudden I started to cry. Then after a while it was better . . . and then I went to sleep." Says Ulysses on Aeaea: "My spirit was broken within me and I wept as I sat on the bed. . . . But when I had my fill of weeping and writhing, I made answer." Or what shall be made of Robert Cohn, quietly and classically asleep on the winecasks in the back room of a Pamplona tavern, wreathed with twisted garlics and dead to the world while Brett and the others carouse in the room beyond? "There was one named Elpenor," says the *Odyssey*, "the youngest of all; not very valiant in war nor sound of understanding, who had laid him down apart from his comrades in the sacred house of Circe, seeking the cool air, for he was heavy with wine. He heard the noise and bustle of his comrades as they moved about."

If he had wished to follow the mythological method of Eliot's *Waste Land* or Joyce's *Ulysses*, Hemingway could obviously have done so. But his own esthetic opinions carried him away from the literary kind of myth-adaptation and over into that deeper area of psychological symbol-building which does not require special literary equipment to be interpreted. One needs only sympathy and a few degrees of heightened emotional awareness. The special virtue of this approach to the problem of literary communication is that it can be grasped by all men and women because they are human beings. None of the best writers are without it. It might even be described as the residuum of "natural knowledge" and belief, visible in every artist after the traditional elements have been siphoned off. This is perhaps roughly what Keats meant by saying that Shakespeare led a life of allegory, his works being the comments on it. Thoreau's phrase for the same thing, as R. L. Cook has pointed out, is "dusky knowledge." Pilar, the Cumaean sybil of *For Whom the Bell Tolls*, moves regularly in this half-subliminal area. She inherits her skill and discernment from Hemingway.

Under the matter-of-factness of the account of the feria of San Fermin a sabidurian symbolism is at work. It does not become formally apparent until the party has assembled to prepare for the festival. Then, in several ways, it develops as a dialectical struggle between paganism and Christian orthodoxy—a natural and brilliant use of the fact that the fiesta is both secular and religious, and that the *riau-riau* dancers unabashedly follow the procession which bears the patron saint through the streets of Pamplona.

The contrast is admirably dramatized through Jake and Brett. Without apology or explanation, Jake Barnes is a religious man. As a professing Catholic, he attends masses at the cathedral before and during fiesta week. On the Saturday before the festival opens, Brett accompanies him. "She said she wanted to hear me go to confession," says Jake, "but I told her that not only was it impossible but it was not as interesting as it sounded, and, besides, it would be in a language she did not know." Jake's remark can be taken doubly. The language Brett does not know is Latin; it is also Spanish; but it is especially the language of the Christian religion. When she goes soon afterwards to have her fortune told at a gypsy camp, Brett presumably hears language that she *can* understand.[22]

Her true symbolic colors are broken out on Sunday afternoon. She is in the streets with Jake watching the religious procession in which the image of San Fermin is translated from one church to another. Ahead of the formal procession and behind it are the *riau-riau* dancers. When Jake and Brett try to enter the chapel they are stopped at the door, ostensibly because she has no hat. But for one sufficiently awake to the ulterior meaning of the incident it strikingly resembles the attempt of a witch to gain entry into a Christian sanctum. Brett's witch-hood is immediately underscored. Back in the street she is encircled by the chanting pagan dancers who prevent her from joining their figure: "They wanted her as an image to dance around." When the song ends, she is rushed to a wineshop and seated on an up-ended wine-cask. The shop is dark and full of men singing,—"hard-voiced singing."[23]

The intent of this episode is quite plain. Brett would not understand the language used in Christian confessional. She is forbidden to follow the religious procession into the chapel. The dancers adopt her as a pagan image. She is perfectly at home on the wine-cask amidst the hard-voiced singing of the non-religious celebrants. Later in fiesta week the point is reemphasized. Jake and Brett enter the San Fermin chapel so that Brett can pray for Romero's success in the final bullfight of the celebration. "After a little," says Jake, "I felt Brett stiffen beside me, and saw she was looking straight ahead." Outside the chapel Brett explains what Jake has already guessed: "I'm damned bad for a religious atmosphere. I've got the wrong type of face."[24]

She has, indeed. Her face belongs in wide-eyed concentration over the Tarot pack of Madame Sosostris, or any equivalent soothsayer in the gypsy camp outside Pamplona. It is perfectly at home in the center of the knot of dancers in the street or in the tavern gloom above the wine-cask. For Brett in her own way is a lamia with a British accent, a Morgan le Fay of Paris and Pamplona, the reigning queen of a paganized wasteland with a wounded fisher-king as her half-cynical squire. She is, rolled into one, the *femme fatale de trente ans damnée*. Yet she is always and conspicuously herself. The other designations are purely arbitrary labels which could be multiplied as long as one's list of enchantresses could be made to last. They are not necessary to the full symbolic meaning which Brett has in her own right and by virtue (if that is the word) of what she is made to do in the book.

Although Hemingway carefully skirts the moralistic, as his artistic beliefs require, the moral drift of the symbolic story is unmistakable. Shortly after *The Sun Also Rises* appeared, he remarked, as he had never overtly done in the book, that "people aren't all as bad as some writers find them or as hollowed out and exhausted emotionally as some of the *Sun* generation."[25] The restriction was conspicuous. He did not say, "the lost generation." He said rather, "some of the *Sun* generation." His indictment, put into dramatic terms, was directed against those who allowed themselves to flounder in an emulsion of ennui and alcohol when there was so much else to be done, whether one was a championship-winning *gueule cassée* like Criqui or an ordinary citizen like Jake, engaged in readjusting himself to peace-time living. In contrast to the "hollow men" who went off the stage with something resembling a whimper, Hemingway presented another set of men who kept their mouths shut and took life as it came.

The emotional exhaustion of "some of the *Sun* generation" is accentuated by the oppositions Hemingway provides. Obviously no accidental intruder in the book is Romero, standing out in youthful dignity and strength against the background of displaced wastrels among whom Jake moves. The same is true of the interlude at Burguete, with Jake and Bill happily disentangled from the wastelanders, as if in wordless echo of Eliot's line: "In the mountains, there you feel free." However fascinating Brett and Cohn and Mike may be as free-wheeling international adventurers, the book's implicit attitude is one of quizzical condemnation towards these and all their kind.

Despite this fact, one finds in the presentation of Brett Ashley an almost Jamesian ambiguity. It is as if the objective view of Brett were intentionally relieved by that kind of chivalry which is never wholly missing from the work of Hemingway. On the straight narrative plane the book appears to offer a study of a war-frustrated love affair between Brett and Jake. Brett's Circean characteristics are only partly responsible for the sympathy with which she is treated, though all enchantresses from Spenser's Acrasia to Coleridge's Geraldine are literally fascinating and Brett is no exception. Whenever Jake takes a long objective view of Lady Ashley, however, he is too honest not to see her for what she objectively is, an alcoholic nymphomaniac. To Cohn's prying questions about her, early in the book, Jake flatly answers: "She's a drunk."[26]

There is, nevertheless, a short history behind her alcoholism and her constant restless shifting from male to male. During the war she was an assistant nurse; her own true love died; she married a psychotic British baronet who maltreated her; and at the time of the book she is waiting for a divorce decree in order to marry the playboy Mike Campbell. Furthermore—and this fact calls forth whatever chivalry one finds— she is in love with Jake, though both of them realize the hopelessness of the situation. She has not, as her fiancé observes, had an absolutely happy life, and Jake is prepared to take this into account when he judges her character. "Don't you know about Irony and Pity?" asks Bill Gorton during a verbal bout at Burguete. Jake knows all about them. They are the combination he uses whenever he thinks about Brett.[27]

One of the ironies in the portrait of Brett is her ability to appreciate quality in the circle of her admirers. After the trip to San Sebastian with Robert Cohn she quickly rejects him. She does not do so sluttishly, merely in order to take up with another man, but rather for what to her is the moral reason that he is unmanly. Towards her fiancé Mike Camp-

bell the attitude is somewhere in the middle ground of amused acceptance. He is Brett's sort, a good drinking companion living on an in-
come nearly sufficient to allow him a perpetual holiday. "He's so
damned nice and he's so awful," says Brett. "He's my sort of thing."
Even though Brett can be both nice and awful with her special brand of
ambiguity, she does save her unambiguous reverence for two men. One
is the truly masculine Jake, whose total sexual disability has not destroyed his manhood. The other is Romero, whose sexual ability is obviously a recommendation but is by no means his only claim to admiration. It is finally to Brett's credit, and the measure of her appreciation
of quality, that she sends Romero back to the bullring instead of destroying him as she might have done. This is no *belle dame sans merci*.
She shows mercy both to her victim and to the remaining shreds of her
self-respect.

The Heloisa-Abelard relationship of Brett and Jake is Hemingway's
earliest engagement of an ancient formula—the sacrifice of Venus on
the altar of Mars. In one way or another, the tragic fact of war or the
after-effects of social disruption tend to inhibit and betray the normal
course of love, not only in *The Sun Also Rises* but also in *A Farewell to
Arms*, *To Have and Have Not*, *The Fifth Column*, *For Whom the Bell
Tolls*, and *Across the River and into the Trees*. Brett, the first of the victims, is a kind of dark Venus. If she had not lost her "true love" in the
late war, or if Jake's wound had not permanently destroyed his ability
to replace the lost lover, Brett's progressive self-destruction would not
have become the inevitable course it now appears to be.

Much of the continuing power of *The Sun Also Rises* comes from its
sturdy moral backbone. The portraits of Brett Ashley and Robert Cohn,
like that of their antithesis Romero, are fully and memorably drawn. A
further and deep-lying cause of the novel's solidity is the subtle opera-
tive contrast between vanity and sanity, between paganism and orthodoxy, between the health and humor of Burguete and the sick neuroses
of the Montparnassian ne'er-do-wells. Other readers can value the
book for the still-fresh representation of "the way it was" in Paris and

Pamplona, Bayonne and Burguete, during the now nostalgically remembered middle Twenties. Yet much of the final strength of *The Sun Also Rises* may be attributed to the complicated interplay between the two points of view which it embodies. According to one of them, the novel is a romantic study in sexual and ultimately in spiritual frustration. Beside this more or less orthodox view, however, must be placed the idea that it is a qualitative study of varying degrees of physical and spiritual manhood, projected against a background of ennui and emotional exhaustion which is everywhere implicitly condemned.[28]

Notes

Hemingway's letters to the author are indicated by the abbreviation *EH to CB*, with date. His letters to or from Maxwell Perkins and Fitzgerald are indicated by *EH to MP* and *EH to FSF*, or the reverse, with date or approximate date. Other letters employed are cited and dated for the record.

Full titles are used for a few of Hemingway's books. As a space-saving device, the following abbreviations have been generally used: *FTA* for *A Farewell to Arms* and *SAR* for *The Sun Also Rises*.

References, unless otherwise indicated, are to the first American editions of Hemingway's books.

1. John Peale Bishop, "The Missing All," *Virginia Quarterly Review* 13 (Winter 1937), p. 118. Also in McCaffery, *op. cit.*, pp. 292-307.

2. Quoted in EH to FSF, 12/31/25.

3. EH to CB, 4/1/51.

4. EH to FSF, 9/13/29. Also EH to FSF, 5/4/26.

5. *FTA*, illustrated edition of 1948, introd., p. viii.

6. EH to CB, 4/1/51. This paragraph is based on the following additional letters: MP to EH, 2/15/26, 3/15/26; EII to MP, 3/10/26, 4/1/26, 4/19/26, 4/24/26. According to a letter from EH to MP, 11/19/26, he cut 40,000 words from the original first draft.

7. *New Republic* 51 (August 10, 1927), pp. 303-306.

8. EH to FSF, 3/31/27. Cf. also *Esquire* 2 (August 1934), pp. 42-43.

9. Although those who had been members of the group which went to the fiesta of San Fermin in 1925 all knew that *The Sun Also Rises* had a base in actuality, they carefully avoided saying so in print. It was not until Harold Loeb's *The Way It Was* ap-

peared in 1959 that names were finally named. See further below, footnote 28, at the end of this chapter.

10. *Independent* 117 (November 20, 1926), p. 594. About this date Hemingway was writing to Perkins (11/16/26): "It's funny to write a book that seems as tragic as that and have them take it for a jazz superficial story."

11. EH to CB, Easter Sunday, 1951.

12. EH to MP, 11/19/26.

13. EH to CB, Easter Sunday, 1951.

14. EH to FSF, [probably summer], 1926.

15. EH to MP, 11/19/26.

16. EH to MP, 12/7/26. A part of this letter was published by Perkins in a short commentary on Hemingway in *Scribner's Magazine* 81 (March 1927), p. 4.

17. *SAR*, Chapter Nine.

18. *SAR*, p. 129.

19. *SAR*, pp. 210-211.

20. Quoted in R. Burlingame, *Of Making Many Books*, p. 87.

21. *SAR*, p. 149. For *Odyssey* parallels, cf. *SAR*, p. 32 and *Odyssey x*, 490-500; and cf. *SAR*, p. 164 and *Odyssey x*, 552-560.

22. *SAR*, p. 156.

23. *SAR*, p. 160.

24. *SAR*, p. 216.

25. EH to MP, 12/7/26.

26. *SAR*, p. 39. Cf. also pp. 211-212.

27. *SAR*, p. 117.

28. Harold Loeb's version of the events on which Hemingway drew for the story in *The Sun Also Rises* does not specifically identify any actual person with the fictional characters. Yet it is clear from his narrative that he associates Lady Duff Twysden with Brett Ashley, Pat Swazey with Mike Campbell, Hemingway with Jake Barnes, himself (remotely) with Robert Cohn, and either Donald Ogden Stewart or Bill Smith with Bill Gorton. While Hemingway followed the broad outlines of what happened, he freely invented fictional episodes. Duff, for example, had no affair with Niño de la Palma, nor was there any fist-fight between the matador and Harold Loeb. Further details on the actual events which Hemingway made over into fiction appear in Carlos Baker, *Ernest Hemingway: A Life Story*, New York, 1969, pp. 144-154.

The Death of Love in *The Sun Also Rises*_____

Mark Spilka

> She turns and looks a moment in the glass,
> Hardly aware of her departed lover;
> Her brain allows one half-formed thought to pass:
> "Well now that's done: and I'm glad it's over."
> When lovely woman stoops to folly and
> Paces about her room again, alone,
> She smoothes her hair with automatic hand,
> And puts a record on the gramophone.
>
> —T. S. Eliot, *The Waste Land*

One of the most persistent themes of the twenties was the death of love in World War I. All the major writers recorded it, often in piecemeal fashion, as part of the larger postwar scene; but only Hemingway seems to have caught it whole and delivered it in lasting fictional form. His intellectual grasp of the theme might account for this. Where D. H. Lawrence settles for the shock of war on the Phallic Consciousness, or where Eliot presents assorted glimpses of sterility, Hemingway seems to design an extensive parable. Thus, in *The Sun Also Rises*, his protagonists are deliberately shaped as allegorical figures: Jake Barnes and Brett Ashley are two lovers desexed by the war; Robert Cohn is the false knight who challenges their despair; while Romero, the stalwart bullfighter, personifies the good life which will survive their failure. Of course, these characters are not abstractions in the text; they are realized through the most concrete style in American fiction, and their larger meaning is implied only by their response to immediate situations. But the implications are there, the parable is at work in every scene, and its presence lends unity and depth to the whole novel.

Barnes himself is a fine example of this technique. Cut off from love by a shell wound, he seems to suffer from an undeserved misfortune. But as most readers agree, his condition represents a peculiar form of emotional impotence. It does not involve distaste for the flesh, as with Lawrence's crippled veteran, Clifford Chatterley; instead Barnes lacks the power to control love's strength and durability. His sexual wound, the result of an unpreventable "accident" in the war, points to another realm where accidents can always happen and where Barnes is equally powerless to prevent them. In Book II of the novel he makes this same comparison while describing one of the dinners at Pamplona: "It was like certain dinners I remember from the war. There was much wine, an ignored tension, and a feeling of things coming that you could not prevent happening." This fear of emotional consequences is the key to Barnes' condition. Like so many Hemingway heroes, he has no way to handle subjective complications, and his wound is a token for this kind of impotence.

It serves the same purpose for the expatriate crowd in Paris. In some figurative manner these artists, writers, and derelicts have all been rendered impotent by the war. Thus, as Barnes presents them, they pass before us like a parade of sexual cripples, and we are able to measure them against his own forbearance in the face of a common problem. Whoever bears his sickness well is akin to Barnes; whoever adopts false postures, or willfully hurts others, falls short of his example. This is the organizing principle in Book I, this alignment of characters by their stoic qualities. But stoic or not, they are all incapable of love, and in their sober moments they seem to know it.

For this reason they feel especially upset whenever Robert Cohn appears. Cohn still upholds a romantic view of life, and since he affirms it with stubborn persistence, he acts like a goad upon his wiser contemporaries. As the narrator, Barnes must account for the challenge he presents them and the decisive turn it takes in later chapters. Accordingly, he begins the book with a review of Cohn's boxing career at Princeton. Though he has no taste for it, college boxing means a lot to Cohn. For one thing, it helps to compensate for anti-Semitic treatment from his classmates. More subtly, it turns him into an armed romantic, a man who can damage others in defense of his own beliefs. He also loves the pose of manhood which it affords him and seems strangely pleased when his nose is flattened in the ring. Soon other tokens of virility delight him, and he often confuses them with actual manliness. He likes the idea of a mistress more than he likes his actual mistress; or he likes the authority of editing and the prestige of writing, though he is a bad editor and a poor novelist. In other words, he always looks for internal strength in outward signs and sources. On leaving Princeton, he marries "on the rebound from the rotten time . . . in college." But in five years the marriage falls through, and he rebounds again to his present mistress, the forceful Frances Clyne. Then, to escape her dominance and his own disquiet, he begins to look for romance in far-off countries. As with most of his views, the source of this idea is an exotic book:

> He had been reading W. H. Hudson. That sounds like an innocent occupation, but Cohn had read and reread "The Purple Land." "The Purple Land" is a very sinister book if read too late in life. It recounts splendid imaginary amorous adventures of a perfect English gentleman in an intensely romantic land, the scenery of which is very well described. For a man to take it at thirty-four as a guidebook to what life holds is about as safe as it would be for a man of the same age to enter Wall Street direct from a French convent, equipped with a complete set of the more practical Alger books. Cohn, I believe, took every word of "The Purple Land" as literally as though it had been an R. G. Dun report.

Cohn's romanticism explains his key position in the parable. He is the last chivalric hero, the last defender of an outworn faith, and his function is to illustrate its present folly—to show us, through the absurdity of his behavior, that romantic love is dead, that one of the great guiding codes of the past no longer operates. "You're getting damned romantic," says Brett to Jake at one point in the novel. "No, bored," he replies, because for this generation boredom has become more plausible than love. As a foil to his contemporaries, Cohn helps to reveal why this is so.

Of course, there is much that is traditional in the satire on Cohn. Like the many victims of romantic literature, from Don Quixote to Tom Sawyer, he lives by what he reads and neglects reality at his own and others' peril. But Barnes and his friends have no alternative to Cohn's beliefs. There is nothing here, for example, like the neat balance between sense and sensibility in Jane Austen's world. Granted that Barnes is sensible enough, that he sees life clearly and that we are meant to contrast his private grief with Cohn's public suffering, his self-restraint with Cohn's deliberate self-exposure. Yet, emasculation aside, Barnes has no way to measure or control the state of love; and though he recognizes this with his mind and tries to act accordingly, he seems no different from Cohn in his deepest feelings. When he is alone with Brett, he wants to live with her in the country, to go with her to San Sebastian, to go up to her room, to keep her in his own room, or to keep on kissing her—though he can never really act upon such sentiments. Nor are they merely the yearnings of a tragically impotent man, for eventually they will lead Barnes to betray his own principles and to abandon self-respect, all for the sake of Lady Ashley. No, at best he is a restrained romantic, a man who carries himself well in the face of love's impossibilities, but who seems to share with Cohn a common (if hidden) weakness.

The sexual parade continues through the early chapters. Besides Cohn and his possessive mistress, there is the prostitute Georgette, whom Barnes picks up one day "because of a vague sentimental idea that it would be nice to eat with some one." Barnes introduces her to his friends as his fiancée, and as his private joke affirms, the two have much in common. Georgette is sick and sterile, having reduced love to a simple monetary exchange; but like Barnes, she manages to be frank and forthright and to keep an even keel among the drifters of Paris. Together they form a pair of honest cripples, in contrast with the various pretenders whom they meet along the Left Bank. Among the latter are Cohn and Frances Clyne, the writer Braddocks and his wife, and Robert Prentiss, a rising young novelist who seems to verbalize their phoniness: "Oh, how charmingly you get angry," he tells Barnes. "I wish I had that faculty." Barnes' honest anger has been aroused by the appearance of a band of homosexuals, accompanied by Brett Ashley. When one of the band spies Georgette, he decides to dance with her; then one by one the rest follow suit, in deliberate parody of normal love. Brett herself provides a key to the dizzy sexual medley. With a man's felt hat on her boyish bob, and with her familiar reference to men as fellow "chaps," she completes the distortion of sexual roles which seems to characterize the period. For the war, which has unmanned Barnes and his contemporaries, has turned Brett into the freewheeling equal of any man. It has taken her first sweetheart's life through dysentery and has sent her present husband home in a dangerous state of shock. For Brett these blows are the equivalent of Jake's emasculation; they seem to release her from her womanly nature and expose her to the male prerogatives of drink and promiscuity. Once she claims these rights as her own, she becomes an early but more honest version of Catherine Barkley, the English nurse in Hemingway's next important novel, *A Farewell to Arms*. Like Catherine, Brett has been a nurse on the Italian front and has lost a sweetheart in the war; but for her there is no saving interlude of love with a wounded patient, no rigged and timely escape through death in childbirth. Instead she survives the colossal violence, the disruption of her personal life, and the exposure to mass promiscuity, to confront a moral and emotional vacuum among her postwar lovers. With this evidence of male default all around her, she steps off the romantic pedestal, moves freely through the bars of Paris, and stands confidently there beside her newfound equals. Ironically, her most recent conquest, Robert Cohn, fails to see the bearing of such changes on romantic love. He still believes that Brett is womanly and therefore deeply serious about intimate matters. After their first meeting, he describes her as "absolutely fine and straight" and nearly strikes Barnes for thinking otherwise; and a bit later, after their brief affair in the country, he remains unconvinced "that it didn't mean anything." But when men no longer command respect, and women replace their natural warmth with masculine freedom and mobility, there can be no serious love.

Brett does have some respect for Barnes, even a little tenderness, though her actions scarcely show abiding love. At best she can affirm his worth and share his standards and perceptions. When in public, she knows how to keep her essential misery to herself; when alone with Barnes, she will express her feelings, admit her faults, and even display good judgment. Thus her friend, Count Mippipopolous, is introduced to Barnes as "one of us." The count qualifies by virtue of his war wounds, his invariable calmness, and his curious system of values. He appreciates good food, good wine, and a quiet place in which to enjoy them. Love also has a place in his system, but since he is "always in love," the place seems rather shaky. Like Jake and Brett and perhaps Georgette, he simply bears himself well among the postwar ruins.

The count completes the list of cripples who appear in Book I. In a broader sense, they are all disaffiliates, all men and women who have cut themselves off from conventional society and who have made Paris their permanent playground. Jake Barnes has introduced them, and we have been able to test them against his stoic attitudes toward life in a moral wasteland. Yet such life is finally unbearable, as we have also seen whenever Jake and Brett are alone together, or whenever Jake is alone with his thoughts. He needs a healthier code to live by, and for this reason the movement in Book II is away from Paris to the trout stream at Burguete and the bull ring at Pamplona. Here a more vital testing process occurs, and with the appearance of Bill Gorton, we get our first inkling of its nature.

Gorton is a successful writer who shares with Barnes a love for boxing and other sports. In Vienna he has helped to rescue a splendid Negro boxer from an angry and intolerant crowd. The incident has spoiled Vienna for him, and as his reaction suggests, the sports world will provide the terms of moral judgment from this point onward in the novel. Or more accurately, Jake Barnes' feelings about sports will shape the rest of the novel. For with Hemingway, the great outdoors is chiefly a state of mind, a projection of moral and emotional attitudes onto physical arenas, so that a clear account of surface action will reproduce these attitudes in the reader. In "Big Two-Hearted River," for example, he describes Nick Adams' fishing and camping activities along a trout stream in Michigan. His descriptions run to considerable length, and they are all carefully detailed, almost as if they were meant for a fishing manual. Yet the details themselves have strong emotional connotations for Nick Adams. He thinks of his camp as "the good place," the place where none of his previous troubles can touch him. He has left society behind him, and as the story begins, there is even a burnt town at his back, to signify his disaffiliation. He has also walked miles to reach an arbitrary campsite, and this is one of the ways in which he sets his own conditions for happiness and then lives up to them. He finds extraordinary pleasure, moreover, in the techniques of making coffee and pitching camp, or in his responses to fishing and eating. In fact, his sensations have become so valuable that he doesn't want to rush them: they bring health, pleasure, beauty, and a sense of order which is sorely missing in his civilized experience; they are part of a healing process, a private and imaginative means of "wiping out the damages of civilized life." When this process is described with elaborate attention to surface detail, the effect on the reader is decidedly subjective.

The same holds true, of course, for the fishing trip in *The Sun Also Rises*. As Barnes and Gorton approach "the good place," each item in the landscape is singled out and given its own importance. Later the techniques of fishing are treated with the same reverence for detail. For like Nick Adams, these men have left the wasteland for the green plains of health; they have traveled miles, by train and on foot, to reach a particular trout stream. The fishing there is good, the talk free and easy, and even Barnes is able to sleep well after lunch, though he is usually an insomniac. The meal itself is handled like a mock religious ceremony: "Let us rejoice in our blessings," says Gorton. "Let us utilize the fowls of the air. Let us utilize the produce of the vine. Will you utilize a little, brother?" A few days later, when they visit the old monastery at Roncesvalles, this combination of fishing, drinking, and male camaraderie is given an edge over religion itself. With their English friend, Harris, they honor the monastery as a remarkable place, but decide that "it isn't the same as fishing"; then all agree to "utilize" a little pub across the way. At the trout stream, moreover, romantic love is given the same comparative treatment and seems sadly foolish before the immediate joys of fishing:

> It was a little past noon and there was not much shade, but I sat against the trunk of two of the trees that grew together, and read. The book was something by A. E. W. Mason, and I was reading a wonderful story about a man who had been frozen in the Alps and then fallen into a glacier and disappeared, and his bride was going to wait twenty-four years exactly for his body to come out on the moraine, while her true love waited too, and they were still waiting when Bill came up [with four trout in his bag]. . . . His face was sweaty and happy.

As these comparisons show, the fishing trip has been invested with unique importance. By sticking closely to the surface action, Barnes has evoked the deeper attitudes which underlie it and which make it a therapeutic process for him. He describes himself now as a "rotten Catholic" and speaks briefly of his thwarted love for Brett; but with religion defunct and love no longer possible, he can at least find happiness through private and imaginative means. Thus he now constructs a more positive code to follow: as with Nick Adams, it brings him health, pleasure, beauty and order, and helps to wipe out the damage of his troubled life in Paris.

Yet somehow the code lacks depth and substance. To gain these advantages, Barnes must move to Pamplona, which stands roughly to Burguete as the swamp in "Big Two-Hearted River" stands to the trout stream. In the latter story, Nick Adams prefers the clear portion of the river to its second and more congested heart:

In the swamp the banks were bare, the big cedars came together overhead, the sun did not come through, except in patches; in the fast deep water, in the half light, the fishing would be tragic. In the swamp fishing was a tragic adventure. Nick did not want it. . . . There were plenty of days coming when he could fish the swamp.

The fishing is tragic here because it involves the risk of death. Nick is not yet ready for that challenge, but plainly it will test his manhood when he comes to face it. In *The Sun Also Rises* Barnes makes no such demands upon himself; but he is strongly attracted to the young bull-fighter, Pedro Romero, whose courage before death lends moral weight to the sportsman's code.[1]

So Pamplona is an extension of Burguete for Barnes: gayer and more festive on the surface, but essentially more serious. The spoilers from Paris have arrived, but (Cohn excepted) they are soon swept up by the fiesta: their mood is jubilant, they are surrounded by dancers, and they sing, drink and shout with the peasant crowd. Barnes himself is among fellow *aficionados*; he gains "real emotion" from the bull-fights and feels truly elated afterwards. Even his friends seem like "such nice people," though he begins to feel uneasy when an argument breaks out between them. The tension is created by Brett's fiancé, Mike Campbell, who is aware of her numerous infidelities and who seems to accept them with amoral tolerance. Actually he resents them, so that Cohn (the perennial Jewish scapegoat) provides him with a convenient outlet for his feelings. He begins to bait him for following Brett around like a sick steer.

Mike's description is accurate enough. Cohn is always willing to suffer in public and to absorb insults for the sake of true love. On the other hand, he is also "ready to do battle for his lady," and when the chance finally comes, he knocks his rivals down like a genuine knight-errant. With Jake and Mike he has no trouble, but when he charges into Pedro's room to rescue Brett, the results are disastrous: Brett tells him off, the bullfighter refuses to stay knocked down, and no one will shake hands with him at the end, in accord with prep-school custom. When Brett remains with Pedro, Cohn retires to his room, alone and friendless.

This last encounter is the high point of the parable, for in the Code Hero, the Romantic Hero has finally met his match. As the clash between them shows, there is a difference between physical and moral victory, between chivalric stubbornness and real self-respect. Thus Pedro fights to repair an affront to his dignity; though he is badly beaten, his spirit is untouched by his opponent, whereas Cohn's spirit is completely smashed. From the beginning Cohn has based his manhood on skill at boxing, or upon a woman's love, never upon internal strength; but now, when neither skill nor love supports him, he has bludgeoned his way to his own emptiness. Compare his conduct with Romero's, on the following day, as the younger man performs for Brett in the bull ring:

> Everything of which he could control the locality he did in front of her all that afternoon. Never once did he look up. . . . Because he did not look up to ask if it pleased he did it all for himself inside, and it strengthened him, and yet he did it for her, too. But he did not do it for her at any loss to himself. He gained by it all through the afternoon.

Thus, where Cohn expends and degrades himself for his beloved, Romero pays tribute without self-loss. His manhood is a thing independent of women, and for this reason he holds special attractions for Jake Barnes.

By now it seems apparent that Cohn and Pedro are extremes for which Barnes is the unhappy medium. His resemblance to Pedro is clear enough: they share the same code, they both believe that a man's dignity depends on his own resources. His resemblance to Cohn is more subtle, but at this stage of the book it becomes grossly evident. Appropriately enough, the exposure comes through the knockout blow from Cohn, which dredges up a strange prewar experience:

Walking across the square to the hotel everything looked new and changed. . . . I felt as I felt once coming home from an out-of-town football game. I was carrying a suitcase with my football things in it, and I walked up the street from the station in the town I had lived in all my life and it was all new. They were raking the lawns and burning leaves in the road, and I stopped for a long time and watched. It was all strange. Then I went on, and my feet seemed to be a long way off, and everything seemed to come from a long way off, and I could hear my feet walking a great distance away. I had been kicked in the head early in the game. It was like that crossing the square. It was like that going up the stairs in the hotel. Going up the stairs took a long time, and I had the feeling that I was carrying my suitcase.

Barnes seems to have regressed here to his youthful football days. As he moves on up the stairs to see Cohn, who has been asking for him, he still carries his "phantom suitcase" with him; and when he enters Cohn's room, he even sets it down. Cohn himself has just returned from the fight with Romero: "There he was, face down on the bed, crying. He had on a white polo shirt, the kind he'd worn at Princeton." In other words, Cohn has also regressed to his abject college days: they are both emotional adolescents, about the same age as the nineteen-year-old Romero, who is the only real man among them. Of course, these facts are not spelled out for us, except through the polo shirt and the phantom suitcase, which remind us (inadvertently) of one of those dreamlike fantasies by the Czech genius, Franz Kafka, in which trunks and youthful clothes are symbols of arrested development. Yet there has already been some helpful spelling out in Book I, during a curious (and otherwise pointless) exchange between Cohn and another expatriate, the drunkard Harvey Stone. After first calling Cohn a moron, Harvey asks him to say, without thinking about it, what he would rather do if he could do anything he wanted. Cohn is again urged to say what comes into his head first, and soon replies, "I think I'd rather play football again with what I know about handling myself, now." To which

Harvey responds: "I misjudged you. . . . You're not a moron. You're only a case of arrested development."

The first thought to enter Cohn's mind here has been suppressed by Barnes for a long time, but in Book II the knockout blow releases it: more than anything else, he too would like to "play football again," to prevent that kick to his head from happening, or that smash to the jaw from Cohn, or that sexual wound which explains either blow. For the truth about Barnes seems obvious now: he has always been an emotional adolescent. Like Nick Adams, he has grown up in a society which has little use for manliness; as an expression of that society, the war has robbed him of his dignity as a man and has thus exposed him to indignities with women. We must understand here that the war, the early football game, and the fight with Cohn have this in common: they all involve ugly, senseless, or impersonal forms of violence, in which a man has little chance to set the terms of his own integrity. Hence for Hemingway they represent the kinds of degradation which can occur at any point in modern society—and the violence at Pamplona is our current sample of such degradation. Indeed, the whole confluence of events now points to the social meaning of Jake's wound, for just as Cohn has reduced him to a dazed adolescent, so has Brett reduced him to a slavish pimp. When she asks for his help in her affair with Pedro, Barnes has no integrity to rely on; he can only serve her as Cohn has served her, like a sick romantic steer. Thus, for love's sake, he will allow her to use him as a go-between, to disgrace him with his friend, Montoya, to corrupt Romero, and so strip the whole fiesta of significance. In the next book he will even run to her rescue in Madrid, though by then he can at least recognize his folly and supply his own indictment: "That was it. Send a girl off with one man. Introduce her to another to go off with him. Now go and bring her back. And sign the wire with love. That was it all right." It seems plain, then, that Cohn and Brett have given us a peacetime demonstration, postwar style, of the meaning of Jake's shell wound.

At Pamplona the demonstration continues. Brett strolls through the fiesta with her head high, "as though [it] were being staged in her honor, and she found it pleasant and amusing." When Romero presents her with a bull's ear "cut by popular acclamation," she carries it off to her hotel, stuffs it far back in the drawer of the bed-table, and forgets about it. The ear was taken, however, from the same bull which had killed one of the crowd a few days before, during the dangerous bull-run through the streets; later the entire town attended the man's funeral, along with drinking and dancing societies from nearby communities. For the crowd, the death of this bull was a communal triumph and his ear a token of communal strength; for Brett the ear is a private trophy. In effect, she has robbed the community of its triumph, as she will now rob it of its hero. As an *aficionado*, Barnes understands this threat too well. These are decadent times in the bull ring, marred by false aesthetics; Romero alone has "the old thing," the old "purity of line through the maximum of exposure": his corruption by Brett will complete the decadence. But mainly the young fighter means something more personal to Barnes. In the bull ring he combines grace, control and sincerity with manliness; in the fight with Cohn he proves his integrity where skill is lacking. His values are exactly those of the hunter in "Francis Macomber," or of the fisherman in *The Old Man and the Sea*. As one of these few remaining images of independent manhood, he offers Barnes the comfort of vicarious redemption. Brett seems to smash this as she leaves with Pedro for Madrid. To ward off depression, Barnes can only get drunk and retire to bed; the fiesta goes on outside, but it means nothing now: the "good place" has been ruined.

As Book III begins, Barnes tries to reclaim his dignity and to cleanse himself of the damage at Pamplona. He goes to San Sebastian and sits quietly there in a café, listening to band concerts; or he goes swimming there alone, diving deep in the green waters. Then a telegram from Brett arrives, calling him to Madrid to help her out of trouble. At once he is like Cohn again, ready to serve his lady at the expense of self-respect. Yet in Madrid he learns to accept, emotionally, what he has always faintly understood. As he listens to Brett, he begins to drink heavily, as if her story has driven home a painful lesson. Brett herself feels "rather good" about sending Pedro away: she has at least been able to avoid being "one of these bitches that ruins children." This is a moral triumph for her, as Barnes agrees; but he can scarcely ignore its implications for himself. For when Brett refuses to let her hair grow long for Pedro, it means that her role in life is fixed: she can no longer reclaim her lost womanhood; she can no longer live with a fine man without destroying him. This seems to kill the illusion which is behind Jake's suffering throughout the novel: namely, that if he hadn't been wounded, if he had somehow survived the war with his manhood intact, then he and Brett would have become true lovers. The closing lines confirm his total disillusionment:

"Oh, Jake," Brett said, "we could have had such a damned good time together."
Ahead was a mounted policeman in khaki directing traffic. He raised his baton. The car slowed suddenly pressing Brett against me.
"Yes," I said. "Isn't it pretty to think so?"

"Pretty" is a romantic word which means here "foolish to consider what could *never* have happened," and not "what can't happen now." The signal for this interpretation comes from the policeman who directs traffic between Brett's speech and Barnes' reply. With his khaki clothes and his preventive baton, he stands for the war and the society which made it, for the force which stops the lovers' car, and which robs them of their normal sexual roles. As Barnes now sees, love itself is dead for their generation. Even without his wound, he would still be unmanly, and Brett unable to let her hair grow long.

Yet according to the opening epigraphs, if one generation is lost and another comes, the earth abides forever; and according to Hemingway himself, the abiding earth is the novel's hero. Perhaps he is wrong on this point, or at least misleading. There are no joyous hymns to the seasons in this novel, no celebrations of fertility and change. The scenic descriptions are accurate enough, but rather flat; there is no deep feeling in them, only fondness, for the author takes less delight in nature than in outdoor sports. He is more concerned, that is, with baiting hooks and catching trout than with the Irati River and more pleased with the grace and skill of the bull-fighter than with the bull's magnificence. In fact, it is the bullfighter who seems to abide in the novel, for surely the bulls are dead like the trout before them, having fulfilled their roles as beloved opponents. But Romero is very much alive as the novel ends. When he leaves the hotel in Madrid, he "pays the bill" for his affair with Brett, which means that he has earned all its benefits. He also dominates the final conversation between the lovers, and so dominates the closing section. We learn here that his sexual initiation has been completed and his independence assured. From now on, he can work out his life alone, moving again and again through his passes in the ring, gaining strength, order, and purpose as he meets his own conditions. He provides no literal prescription to follow here, no call to bullfighting as the answer to Barnes' problems; but he does provide an image of integrity, against which Barnes and his generation are weighed and found wanting. In this sense, Pedro is the real hero of the parable, the final moral touchstone, the man whose code gives meaning to a world where love and religion are defunct, where the proofs of manhood are difficult and scarce, and where every man must learn to define his own moral conditions and then live up to them.

From *Twelve Original Essays on Great American Novels* (1958), pp. 238-256, edited by Charles Shapiro. Copyright © 1958 by Wayne State University Press. Reprinted with the permission of Wayne State University Press.

Note

1. Hemingway's preoccupation with death has been explained in various ways: by his desire to write about simple, fundamental things; by his "sado-masochism"; or more fairly and accurately, by his need to efface an actual war wound, or to supplant the ugly, senseless violence of war with ordered, graceful violence. Yet chiefly the risk

of death lends moral seriousness to a private code which lacks it. The risk is arbitrary; when a man elects to meet it, his beliefs take on subjective weight and he is able to give meaning to his private life. In this sense, he moves forever on a kind of imaginative frontier, where the opposition is always Nature, in some token form, where the stakes are always manliness and self-respect, and where death invests the scene with tragic implications. In *The Sun Also Rises*, Romero lives on such a frontier, and for Barnes and his friends he provides an example of just these values.

Cabestro and *Vaquilla*:
The Symbolic Structure of *The Sun Also Rises*_____

Dewey Ganzel

When *The Sun Also Rises* was published in 1926, it was immediately interpreted as a study of disillusionment, the straightforward representation of a dissolute and aimless generation. Forty years later this misconception is still the dominant critical assumption about the novel. Although several critics have argued that this interpretation is too narrow and although Hemingway himself disavowed such an intention in writing the book, it persists even among the best of Hemingway's commentators, who interpret the action of the novel as a paradigm of spiritual failure, and its characters as anguished creatures of a perverse fate, incapable of love or meaningful action. This seems to me a misreading of the novel and a denial of Hemingway's intention and control. It derives from a failure to view the novel in the symbolic context which it everywhere suggests. I refer not to the incidental motifs which have been discovered in the book and used to justify a "waste land" interpretation, but rather to the symbolic analogy which patterns the novel as a whole, the analogy to the bullfight or, to be more exact, to the *corrida*—"the running of bulls", not merely the fight between the *torero* and the bull, but the whole of the ritual. All the major characters of *The Sun Also Rises* have symbolic counterparts in the *corrida*, and their interaction within this symbolic context delineates the structure of the book and reveals it to be the tragic novel Hemingway thought he had written.

These symbolic implications become apparent if the novel is read in conjunction with *Death in the Afternoon*, Hemingway's non-fiction work on the *corrida*, which describes virtually every phase of the bullfight procedures from the breeding, selection, and care of fighting bulls, through the training of *toreros*, to the execution of the bullfight ritual itself. Most of the information in this work is extraneous to *The Sun Also Rises*, which Hemingway had written six years before, but some of its details illuminate the novel. In particular, his descriptions of the *cabestro* or trained "working" steer, the fighting bull, and the *vaquilla* or female of the fighting bull give information which is essential to our understanding of the symbolic pattern of the earlier book.

In chapter eleven of *Death in the Afternoon* Hemingway describes the precautions taken to protect a fighting bull before it enters the ring and the function of the *cabestro* in these precautions. The bullfight is possible because the fighting bull "if detached from the herd, will charge instantly and repeatedly anything, man, horse, or any moving object, vehicle or otherwise, until he is killed", and he must, therefore, be kept from such isolation until he is placed in the ring with the bullfighter. It is the function of the *cabestro* to manage the bulls until that time comes, to keep them from dangerous behavior when they are temporarily isolated and from injuring or killing one another when they are in a group. The *cabestro* is able to control the bull because as a steer it is sexually passive, and because it has learned how to buffer the younger, less experienced and more aggressive bull. Indeed, the *cabestro* becomes increasingly valuable as it becomes older and more adept in manoeuvering the bulls. "It is one of the most interesting of all phases of bullfighting," Hemingway wrote, "to see the steers work in the operations of loading, separating, putting the bulls into the runways that lead to the shipping cages and in all the many operations connected with the raising, transporting and unloading of fighting bulls." The *cabestro* is in constant danger from the violence of the bulls, but unlike the beef steer or the fighting bull itself, it is not bred to be killed.

That Jake's wound has made him the sexual equivalent of a steer has been much remarked, but always to suggest his sterility: incapable of procreation he is less a man, the symbol of a sterile generation. This emphasis upon sterility (and, by implication, death) has led critics of the novel away from his function in the action of the book. Without the larger symbolic context which the *cabestro* suggests, this interpretation is a likely one; with it, the interpretation is seen to be much too narrow. Jake is not a "steer"—he is a *cabestro*; his significant characteristic is not impotence but caution and control, attributes which he maintains with "grace under pressure". Throughout the novel Jake is the peacemaker, the go-between, the general friend, and, like the *cabestro*'s, his attitude is directly the result of his wound. "I try and play it along and just not make trouble for people," he says when he contemplates his wound. His manner is accepting but not gullible, undemanding and protective to virtually all the other characters. He knows Harvey Stone is a vulgar, lying drunk, but, nevertheless, without hesitation he gives him money; he can accept without distaste the ugly smile of Georgette, the sick prostitute; he shows no irritation at being excluded from the dining car on the train; he is sensitive to the feelings of the Basques on the bus and to the sensibilities of the Spanish *aficionados* at Montoya's hotel; he wants to make others happy and finds an ironic pleasure in France where tipping can produce this happiness so easily; rather than offend the bicycle team manager in San Sebastian he pretends he will get up to see them off. Throughout the book there is no instance of Jake's assuming a belligerent attitude toward anyone. "I never mean it when I say nasty things," he says at one point, and there are many instances in which his careful consideration of others averts violence or palliates the effects of cruelty in others.

This quality is most particularly shown in his relationship with Cohn. As Cohn says, Jake is the only friend he has, and Jake consistently treats Cohn with deference and care even though he admits he "hates" him. Jake is always available to Cohn; although Jake has "a boat train to catch with a week's mail stories, and only half of them written" when Cohn interrupts his work, he tries to free himself with a "graceful exit" and, when his manoeuver is unsuccessful, he assents to Cohn's request to stay.

Jake's function as *cabestro* to Cohn is made particularly emphatic in the scene of the *desencajonada*, the unloading of the bulls. Prior to that scene, Jake describes the process to Bill Gorton.

'They let the bulls out of the cages one at a time, and they have steers in the corral to receive them and keep them from fighting, and the bulls tear in at the steers and the steers run around like old maids trying to quiet them down.'

'Do they ever gore the steers?'

'Sure. Sometimes they go right after them and kill them.'

'Can't the steers do anything?'

'No. They're trying to make friends.'

'What do they have them in for?'

'To quiet down the bulls and keep them from breaking their horns against the stone walls, or goring each other.'

'Must be swell being a steer.'

Later the unloading itself is described in detail: the two steers "backed away against the wall, their heads sunken, their eyes watching the bull"; when a bull attacked they "turned sideways to take the shock, and the bull drove into one of the steers". The unwounded steer later "came up to [the bull] and made as though to nose at him and the bull hooked perfunctorily. The next time he nosed at the steer and then the two of them trotted over to the other bull. . . . The steer who had been gored had gotten to his feet and stood against the stone wall. None of the bulls came near him, and he did not attempt to join the herd."

Jake's treatment of Cohn is the symbolic equivalent of this action. Like the *cabestro* he is continually watchful of Cohn and protective of him. When Cohn is angrily sulking upstairs at the hotel in Pamplona, it is Jake who "had to go up and bring Robert Cohn down". When Cohn is missing during the fiesta, it is Jake who shows concern for his where-abouts, searches for him, and finally finds him. His protective vigilance extends to the bullfight itself: "Several times during the bullfight I looked up at Mike and Brett and Cohn, with the glasses. They seemed to be all right." When Mike threatens to hit Cohn, it is Jake who "grabs" Mike and takes him away. When Cohn is angered by Harvey Stone, Jake quiets him. ("'He always gets me sore,' Cohn said. 'I can't stand him.' 'I like him,' I said. 'I'm fond of him. You don't want to get sore at him.'") Furthermore, this proprietary function is recognized by others. When Cohn is particularly obnoxious at Pamplona, Mike asks Jake to tell Cohn to behave and Jake answers, "He'll behave. I'll tell him. . . . it would be nice for me to tell him."

As the *cabestro* is attacked by the bull in the scene of the unloading, so Jake is attacked by Cohn: Cohn not only knocks Jake down; he hits him twice before Jake can regain his feet. ("I went down backward under a table. I tried to get up and felt I did not have any legs.") Jake is, in fact, in the same position as the wounded steer of the earlier scene. ("The steer was down now, his neck stretched out, his head twisted, he lay the way he had fallen.") The concluding isolation of the wounded steer is also figured in Jake's solitude at San Sebastian—like the steer, Jake does "not attempt to join the herd" in Paris; it would, he says, "have meant more fiesta-ing. I was through with fiestas for a while. It would be quiet in San Sebastian."

The special nature of Jake's protection of Cohn is revealed indirectly in another context. The one character against whom Jake cannot protect Cohn is Frances Clyne, and this is because her attack is not one which Jake can fend off. It is only against other men—i.e., bulls—that Jake feels any responsibility to protect Cohn. In Cohn's differences with Frances and Brett, Jake is of no use, but his sympathy for Cohn is nevertheless present:

> I do not know how people could say such terrible things to Robert Cohn [he says of Frances's attack]. There are people to whom you could not say insulting things. They give you a feeling that the world would be destroyed, would actually be destroyed before your eyes, if you said certain things. But here was Cohn taking it all. Here it was, all going on right before me, and I did not even feel an impulse to try and stop it.

That he felt no such impulse is significant; it qualifies his *cabestro* interest.

As I have implied, Jake as *cabestro* reveals Cohn as fighting bull. Here the symbolic comparison is explicit. The first sentence announces that "Robert Cohn was once middleweight boxing champion of Princeton," and later, during the unloading of the bulls, Jake makes the analogy between boxers and bulls: "He's got a left and a right," he says of one bull, "just like a boxer." As the bull is the focus of interest in the *corrida*, so Cohn is of first importance to the sequence of events in the novel. It is no accident that he is the first character described and that this description is so detailed. The three determining factors in the "making of a bull" as Hemingway describes them in *Death in the Afternoon* are breeding, condition, and age. The pedigree of the bull is of prime significance in determining the quality of the *corrida*, and Cohn's pedigree is given in remarkable detail. We know next to nothing about the previous lives of the other characters—even Jake has only a fragmentary background but concerning Cohn we are given, with great specificity, the facts of his parentage, early life, college career, first marriage and divorce, writing career, and, finally, his affair with Frances. As the pedigree of the bull suggests how he may fight in the ring, so Cohn's responses to his earlier experiences suggest his manner of facing up to his conflict over Brett. Cohn's condition is described: "He was nice to watch on the tennis-court, he had a good body, and he kept it in shape," and he shows a particular fondness for going to the barber-shop to keep himself groomed. His age is significant. In *Death in the Afternoon* Hemingway notes:

> A bull is not mature until after his fourth year. It is true that after his third year he looks mature, but he is not. Maturity brings strength, resistance, but above all, knowledge. Now the knowledge of a bull consists principally in his memory of experience, he forgets nothing, and in his knowledge of, and ability to use, his horns.

Cohn has acquired such knowledge and remembers it. His experience in the ring had revealed his boxing prowess and its limitations: he was a "middleweight champion" but, "overmatched", he had his "nose permanently flattened"—a salutary experience, for his nose was "certainly improved" and, as his fights with Jake and Romero suggest, he did not forget how to use his fists. His knowledge of women increases, too. When he went to New York "several women were nice to him . . . and when he came back he was quite changed. . . . he was not so simple, and he was not so nice. . . . his horizons had all shifted." As a result he gets rid of Frances and takes up with Brett.

Hemingway further describes the "three phases of the bull's condition in the fight . . . *levantado, parado*, and *aplomado*".

> He is called levantado, or lofty, when he first comes out, carries his head high, charges without fixing any object closely and, in general, tries, confident in his power, to sweep the ring clear of his enemies. It is at this time that the bull is least dangerous to the bullfighter. . . . When the bull is *parado* he is slowed and at bay. At this time he no longer charges freely and wildly in the general direction of any movement or disturbance; he is disillusioned about his power to destroy or drive out of the ring anything that seems to challenge him and, his initial ardor calmed, he recognizes his enemy. . . . When he is aplomado he has been made heavy, he is like lead; he has usually lost his wind, and while his strength is still intact, his speed is gone. He no longer carries his head high; he will charge if provoked. . . . in this state the bull does not want to charge unless he is sure of his objective, since he has obviously been beaten, to himself as well as the spectator, in everything he had attempted up to that time. . . .

These three phases can be recognized in Cohn's behaviour: he has great initial confidence in his relationship with Brett, and this confidence projects itself in his superior manner with Jake and Bill when he first arrives at Pamplona. His *parado* stage is brought about by the repeated attacks against which he must defend himself as the fiesta gets under way; he is no longer sure of his relationship with Brett and becomes disillusioned about her appetite for him and his ability to dislodge Mike in her affections. His *aplomado* stage is brought on by Brett's affair with Romero—he has obviously been beaten, but he is provoked enough to charge first Jake and then Romero himself. And at the hands of Romero he is "ruined".

The character of Cohn, therefore, directs the larger symbolic action of the novel and this function is supported by symbolic analogies in the other major characters. The *cabestro*-bull relationship of Jake and Cohn is repeated in Bill Gorton's manner with Mike. Unlike Jake, Bill is not, so far as we know, sexually impotent, but it is, perhaps, significant that of all the men in the novel he alone does not fancy himself Brett's lover. Although he does not share Jake's physical trauma, he shares many other characteristics with him—enough to suggest that they are symbolic equivalents of some kind. Alone among the characters in the novel they are wholly compatible, as *cabestros* would be. They are the only characters who work; they have professional responsibilities which, like those of the *cabestros*, demand expertise, and they meet these responsibilities regularly. Of all the characters they alone have seen bullfights before; they are the *aficionados* who, like *cabestros*, initiate the rest of the group to the ritual, and like *cabestros*, too, they find the experience exhausting: "Bill was tired after the bullfight. So was I. We both took a bull-fight very hard."

Even apart from his associations with Jake, Bill has psychological and emotional predilections which dearly indicate his *cabestro*-like functions in the novel. He, too, protects a boxer, who because he is a Negro might be considered the equivalent of the black fighting bull to which Hemingway refers in *Death in the Afternoon*. And his chief function in the novel is to act toward Mike in the same capacity in which Jake acts toward Cohn. At the unloading of the bulls, while Jake explains the procedure to Brett, Bill accompanies Mike, and shortly thereafter the analogy to the bull-*cabestro* relationship is made explicit when, in the context of Jake's description of the violence of the isolated bull, Bill tells Mike, "Don't you ever detach me from the herd." In the ensuing conflicts, it is usually Bill who quiets Mike or protects him. On one occasion, when Mike begins to attack Cohn, "Bill got Mike started on something else than Cohn." On another, when a fight between Mike and Cohn is imminent, Bill takes Cohn away. It is Bill who amuses Mike by buying shoeshine after shoeshine for him, just as it is Bill who finally pays for Mike's drinks at the end of the novel. Jake notes that Bill and Mike "were good together" but like Jake *vis-à-vis* Cohn, Bill is not particularly fond of Mike, and sometimes he shows his exasperation: "Nobody has any business to talk like Mike," he says at one point. But when Mike is attacked, Bill defends him even to strangers. "I had a hell of a row about him last night," he tells Jake. "Nobody ought to have a right to say things about Mike. . . . They oughtn't to have any right. I wish to hell they didn't have any right." This is an echo of Jake's response to Frances Clyne's attack on Cohn.

Just as Bill in his function suggests an analogy to Jake as *cabestro*, so Mike suggests an analogy to Cohn as fighting bull. Like Cohn's, his sexuality is his determining motive; his conflict with Cohn is derived from an animalistic desire to control Brett. This parallel is the overriding one, but it is qualified and intensified by incidental comparisons and contrasts which appear several times in the book. For example, in Cohn's introduction we are told he had his nose permanently flattened, and when Mike is introduced he has blood on his; or again, their handshakes are contrasted: "Mike had a way of getting an intensity of feeling into shaking hands," Jake reports. "Robert Cohn shook hands because we were back." Bill describes Cohn ("The funny thing is he's nice, too. I like him. But he's just so awful.") using words which Brett echoes later in speaking of Mike ("I'm going back to Mike. . . . He's so damned nice and he's so awful. He's my sort of thing.")—an echo which has the effect of reinforcing the parallel between the two. Mike, however, is not the bull to be sacrificed, and in his symbolic role therefore acts primarily as foil to Cohn.

Through the character of Romero, the bullfighter, the symbolic pattern is brought into focus with the representational one: the representational action of the Pamplona fiesta climaxes in Romero's ritual defeat of the fighting bull in the ring; the symbolic action climaxes in his ritual defeat of Cohn (as bull) in the room at Montoya's hotel. We are to believe that he defeats Cohn brilliantly ("He ruined Cohn . . . I don't think Cohn will ever want to knock people about again."), and the irony of the scene derives from this assumption, for although Romero is clearly the more injured, Cohn, crying in his bedroom, is the more destroyed. The circumstances confining this irony are more coherent in the context of the symbolic action. Here again *Death in the Afternoon* suggests the justification for believing Romero the victor in the fight. There are, as Hemingway describes, two ways of killing a bull in the ring:

> either the bull must come to and pass the man, cited, drawn on, controlled and going out and away from the man by a movement of the muleta while the sword is being inserted between his shoulders; or else the man must fix the bull in position. . . . When the man awaits the charge of the bull it is called killing recibiendo. When the man goes in on the bull it is called a volapié or flying with the feet.

Of the two, the killing of the bull *recibiendo* is by far the more dangerous since if the *torero* is not successful he will be gored in the chest, probably fatally, whereas if he is unsuccessful in killing *volapié*, he will be gored in the thigh.

> The killing of a bull recibiendo [Hemingway goes on] . . . is the most arrogant dealing of death and is one of the finest things you can see in bullfighting. You may never see it because the volapié, dangerous enough when properly executed, is so much less dangerous than the suerte de recibir that only very rarely does a fighter ever receive a bull in our times. I have seen it properly completed only four times in over fifteen hundred bulls I have seen killed.

Romero's method of "ruining" Cohn is essentially that of *recibiendo*: the bull comes to the bullfighter. Romero, we are told, had

'been knocked down about fifteen times, and he wanted to fight some more. . . . He was weak, but Brett couldn't hold him, and he got up. Then Cohn said he wouldn't hit him again. Said he couldn't do it. Said it would be wicked. So the bull-fighter chap sort of rather staggered over to him. Cohn went back against the wall.

'"So you won't hit me?"

'"No," said Cohn. "I'd be ashamed to."

'So the bull-fighter fellow hit him just as hard as he could in the face, and then sat down on the floor. He couldn't get up. . . . He was waiting to get strength enough to hit Cohn again. . . . Then Cohn leaned down to shake hands with the bull-fighter fellow. No hard feelings, you know. All for forgiveness. And the bull-fighter chap hit him in the face again.'

'That's quite a kid,' Bill said.

'He ruined Cohn,' Mike said.

The essential action of the bullfight is the charging of the *torero* by the bull until, exhausted and confused, he will attack no more and the *torero* kills him. Cohn's repeated attack against Romero and his final refusal to attack further is the symbolic equivalent of this procedure; so too is Romero's continuing willingness to expose himself to Cohn's attack. As in the bullfight itself, there is no question of which is physically the stronger—it is a test of will and stamina, and in this regard Romero is clearly the victor. But it is more significant that the final blow which ends the encounter is delivered by Romero after Cohn has come to *him*. This is the symbolic equivalent of *recibiendo* and as such worthy of particular praise.

The *cabestro*-bull-*torero* relationship has even greater meaning as it relates to the character of Brett. Her symbolic role is that of the *vaquilla*, the fighting cow, the mate of the fighting bull. Hemingway discusses the use of the *vaquilla* in *Death in the Afternoon*:

Either a bull calf or a cow calf, if passed a few times with cape or muleta, learns all about it, remembers, and, if it is a bull, becomes consequently useless for a formal bullfight where everything is built on the basis of this being the bull's first encounter with a dismounted man.

Fighting bulls cannot, therefore, be used in training bullfighters, but *vaquillas* can be. Like its male counterpart, the *vaquilla* will charge in isolation, but unlike the bull, the *vaquilla* is never used in professional bullfights and it can, therefore, be used to train bullfighters without losing a valuable animal for the bullring. Female calves

> since they are never to appear in the ring in normal fights and since there is no objection to their becoming completely educated in all the phases of bullfighting, are used exclusively for the bullfighters to train on with cape and muleta.

Like the *cabestro*, therefore, the *vaquilla* is a companion to the bull which is trained to be of use to the bullfighter.

Brett's symbolic analogy to the *vaquilla* is clear from a comparison of Hemingway's description of her in the novel and his description of the *vaquilla* in *Death in the Afternoon*:

> The female of the fighting bull is not as heavily built as the male; has a smaller head; shorter and thinner horns; a longer neck, a less pronounced dewlap under the jaw; is not as wide through the chest, and has no visible udder. I have frequently seen these cows in the ring in the amateur fights in Pamplona charging like bulls, tossing the amateurs about and they were invariably spoken of by the visiting foreigners as steers, since they showed no visible signs of their cowhood and gave no evidence of femininity. It is in the female of the fighting bull that you see most plainly the difference between the savage and domestic animal.

Both in physical description and in function Brett is the equivalent. It is perhaps an overstatement that she has "no evidence of femininity"—at least twice Jake notes the sexuality of her figure—but that she has assumed the habiliment of the male is clear. Her hair is short and "brushed back like a boy's", and she always wears a man's hat. The masculine manner is apparent in her speech (she calls herself a "chap"), and in the assertive way she has adopted the freedom of the male in her drinking and in her sexual amorality. She is first seen in the company of homosexuals ("she was very much with them," Jake notes), and in this context the homosexuals are the symbolic equivalent of ordinary steers. Jake, the *cabestro*, is infuriated by them, the more so because Brett has deliberately assumed their identity and dress (she, like them, wears a jersey and mannish tweeds), which underscores the superficial confusion of the steer and the *vaquilla* that Hemingway noted. The analogy is made the more emphatic by the fact that the only named homosexual is called Lett. Brett's superficial masculinity is suggested elsewhere in the novel. Jake informs Mike of her social class by saying she is "in the stud-book and everything", and on occasion Jake includes her among the men ("'Hello, men,' I said. 'Hello, gents!' said Brett.").

But the superficial masculinity of the *vaquilla* does not indicate any lack of basic sexual attractiveness or appetite. She is the mate of the fighting bulls, and as such an object of desire and contention among them. Her presence does not quiet the bulls but arouses them. Although she is dominated by them, she has the fighting vigor to oppose them. Hemingway indicates this spirit in his description in *Death in the Afternoon*:

> When a bull is first turned loose with the cows no one knows how he will act. . . . [S]ometimes a bull will have nothing to do with them nor they with him and they will fight savagely with their horns making a clatter of horn on horn you can hear across the field.

Brett's character has an analogy here: her relations with Cohn and Mike are apparently of a rather elemental sexual kind and of short duration. She is fully compatible with neither; she quarrels with both with vigor, has no compunction when she discards each in turn, and feels no pangs of conscience later when she recalls her actions. It is, in fact, her sexuality which creates both her bond to and her isolation from Jake. Their thwarted sexual desire for each other is transmuted into their affection for the bulls and the bullfighter. For her they are a presumed substitute; for him, an idealized self-conception. On both the representational and the symbolic level, therefore, it is logical for Jake to introduce Brett to Cohn, the bull, in the first instance, and to Romero, the bullfighter, in the second.

It is in their symbolic rôles that the affair of Brett and Romero becomes most coherent. Brett's appetite for the bullfighter has symbolic parallels: even before she has any knowledge of the bullfight ritual, she is attracted to Romero's style—she knows instinctively why he is good. "She saw," Jake tells us, "why she liked Romero's cape-work and why she did not like the others." Like a *vaquilla*, Brett initiates Romero, the novice bull-fighter, to sex ("He'd only been with two women before," she tells Jake), but she recognizes the limitations of her function as initiator. When Jake asks her, "Why didn't you keep him?", she answers, "It isn't the sort of thing one does. I don't think I hurt him any." She knows she could not marry him—the initiator must not hurt the initiate—and her recognition of this limitation is revealed in her determination not to be "one of these bitches that ruins children".

The sexuality of the relationship of the bullfighter and the bull is implied in Hemingway's description of Romero's fight with the penultimate bull whose defective vision made it necessary for him "to make the bull consent with his body . . . offering the body, offering it again a little closer, . . . then so close that the bull thought he had him, offering again and finally drawing the charge . . .". Ultimately "Romero's left hand dropped the muleta over the bull's muzzle to blind him, his left shoulder went forward between the horns as the sword went in, and for just an instant he and the bull were one. . . ." The sexual implications of the act are more emphatic when the bullfighter's opponent is a *vaquilla* rather than a fighting bull. That Brett sees herself in this role with Romero is made clear in her reply to his statement that the bulls are his best friends: "You kill your friends?" she asks, and he answers, "Always. . . . So they don't kill me." Her question indicates her identification; his answer symbolizes its result, for ultimately their relationship would have demanded that one or the other of them be "killed", so changed as to be no longer himself. If Brett were not to "ruin" Romero she would have had to be "more womanly"—an impossibility for her. ("He wanted me to grow my hair out. Me, with long hair. I'd look so like hell.") Or, if she were not to change, he would be destroyed as a bullfighter. It is Brett's role as *vaquilla*, however, which demands that she give him up. ("You know I'd have lived with him if I hadn't seen it was bad for him. We got along damned well.") Only she as *vaquilla* can avoid the disaster for them both, and through the force of will she does so.

The symbolic analogy I have been describing is particularly useful in delineating the relationship of Brett and Jake—the central conflict of the novel. In the purely representational context the attraction-separation motif that exists between them is sharply articulated—they love each other, but Jake's impotence on the one hand and Brett's nymphomania on the other make sexual fulfillment of their love impossible. Significantly, this fulfillment is not something they have been deprived of; they have loved only after each has suffered his wound, and it is made clear, at least on Brett's part, that love is inspired by the wound ("I suppose she only wanted what she couldn't have."). They are attracted not by differences but by affinities. It is in their symbolic roles as *cabestro* and *vaquilla* that these affinities are most clearly revealed: they are both adjuncts to the central activity of the *corrida*—one as the pacifying companion of the bull, the other as the initiating companion of the bullfighter. While either might be injured in fulfilling his role, neither faces death directly as do the bull and bullfighter. Their functions are supplementary and continuing ones. They presumably will be needed by other bulls and bullfighters. Their symbolic roles therefore suggest the similarities which explain their representational attraction for each other.

But though Jake and Brett are similar and mutually attractive in their functions as *cabestro* and *vaquilla*, they differ in the ways in which they recognize these functions and respond to their demands. This difference is made clear in the Christian-pagan associations which recur in the novel. The Pamplona fiesta itself is the composite of these two attitudes. It is at once the Christian Feast of San Fermin and the pagan rite of blood sacrifice in the bullring. This dual function is shown in the procession of the icon to the Church and the running of the bulls through the streets to the ring with the *riau-riau* dancers accompanying each. Jake is associated with both attitudes, but he has special affinities for the Christian. "Are you really a Catholic?" Bill asks him; and he answers, "Technically." That is, the formal attitudes of the Church are his, but they are not conclusively so. He is at once a Catholic communicant (significantly, he makes a confession during the fiesta) and an *aficionado* of the ritual of the bullring—a ritual which is essentially un-Christian in its prideful denial of death in the act of taking it. That Hemingway was aware of this duality is clear in a passage in *Death in the Afternoon* in which he describes the act:

> Once you accept the rule of death thou shalt not kill is an easily and naturally obeyed commandment. But when a man is still in rebellion against death he has pleasure in taking to himself one of the Godlike attributes; that of giving it. This is one of the most profound feelings in those men who enjoy killing. These things are done in pride and pride, of course, is a Christian sin, and a pagan virtue. But it is pride which makes the bullfight and true enjoyment of killing which makes the great matador.

Jake, however, can combine both attitudes—he can, for example, go to the church and pray

---

that the bull-fights would be good, and that it would be a fine fiesta. . . . I was a little ashamed, and regretted that I was such a rotten Catholic, but realized there was nothing I could do about it, at least for a while, and maybe never, but that anyway it was a grand religion, and I only wished I felt religious and maybe I would the next time. . . .

Jake recognizes a responsibility to a revealed discipline not of his own making—as well as his failure to meet that responsibility consistently. This responsibility is the intellectual counterpart to his *cabestro* function.

Brett on the other hand is the complete pagan, a fact shown symbolically throughout the fiesta sequence in which a direct contrast is made between her and San Fermin. Cohn calls her Circe and, like that pagan goddess, her function is to captivate, initiate, and, perhaps, degrade. Christian doctrine is unintelligible to her: she wants to go with Jake to his confession "but I told her that not only was it impossible but it was not as interesting as it sounded, and, besides, it would be in a language she did not know", and instead she goes to a gypsy camp and has her fortune told—a pagan equivalent. She is stopped from entering the Church (she has no hat) and instead, as she stands in the street, "some dancers formed a circle around Brett and started to dance. They wore big wreaths of white garlics around their necks. . . . They wanted her as an image to dance around." The icon of San Fermin was "translated" at the head of the procession and Bill suggests thereafter that they "translate" Brett to the hotel. Later Brett is seen "walking, her head up, as though the fiesta were being staged in her honor". By this subtle analogy to San Fermin, Brett is placed in brilliant contrast to Jake, a juxtaposition which qualifies and extends the symbolic pattern of the novel: as Jake and Brett are drawn together by their affinities as *cabestro* and *vaquilla*, so they are separated by their differences as Christian and pagan.

This pattern is particularly significant in the context of the central question which the book poses: "How does one continue to live though wounded?" This is the dominating question both in Brett's life and in Jake's, and, in fact, Jake addresses himself to it directly. "I did not care what it was all about," he says of the world: "All I wanted to know was how to live in it. Maybe if you found out how to live in it you learned from that what it was all about." The differing answers to the question of how one lives are projected symbolically in the contrasts between the functions of Jake as *cabestro* and Brett as *vaquilla*. In such a contrast it is not difficult to see the *cabestro*'s function as an essentially Christian pastoral one—preservation by leading aright, by self-abnegation. Speaking of his wound he says: "The Catholic Church had an awfully good way of handling all that. Good advice, anyway. Not to think about it. Oh, it was swell advice. Try and take it sometime. Try and take it." But, though it was difficult for Jake himself to follow, he nevertheless administered essentially the same advice to others: for example, to Cohn wishing to forget his affair with Brett, and to Brett trying to get over her affair with Romero. It is release through self-denial, giving up a part of one's self to secure something better, without, as he says, any "idea of retribution or punishment. Just exchange of values. You gave up something and got something else. Or you worked for something. You paid some way for everything that was any good. . . . Either you paid by learning about them, or by experience, or by taking chances, or by money." Some kind of sacrifice was demanded—giving up the lesser value to insure the greater. In his role as *cabestro* Jake introduces Brett to Romero and in return he is attacked by Cohn and loses his friendship with Montoya; he will never be able to return to Pamplona under the same aegis. But after action there is absolution. The last book of the novel reveals this symbolic intention in the recurring water images, a traditional archetypal motif of absolution and renewal: "A waiter . . . with a bucket of water and a cloth . . . commenced to tear down the notices, pulling the paper off in strips and washing and rubbing away the paper that stuck to the stone. The fiesta was over." In Bayonne, after leaving Mike and Bill, Jake washes; he goes to San Sebastian where "the streets feel as though they had just been sprinkled." Again he showers before lunch; he swims in the late afternoon, diving "deep once, swimming down to the bottom. I swam with my eyes open and it was green and dark." Back in the bathing cabin he "sloshed" himself with "fresh water". The next day he swims again; this time "in the quiet water I turned and floated. Floating I saw only the sky, and felt the drop and lift of the swells. . . . The water was buoyant and cold. It felt as though you could never sink." In this recurring symbol, Jake finds a cleansing release from the ritual of the fiesta and what it had demanded from him. But his symbolic function is not over; it never can be. When Brett's wire comes he supposes "vaguely, I had expected something of the sort." His *cabestro* function extends to Brett, and we have in his encounter with her in Madrid one of the sequence of priest-like consultations he has throughout the book with Brett, Cohn, Stone, Frances, and Mike. How does one live? By dedication to one's responsibilities.

Brett's answer to the question is necessarily different, just as her symbolic function as *vaquilla* is different. For her the action demanded is initiation and purgation. Confronted with her passion for Romero she tells Jake: "I'm a goner. It's tearing me all up inside. . . . I can't help it. I've never been able to help anything. . . . I've got to do something. I've got to do something I really want to do. I've lost my self-respect. . . . I don't say it's right. It is right though for me. God knows, I've never felt such a bitch." This state of mind is, in part, the result of her affair with Cohn. However, after she has spent the night with Romero she assumes the stature of a pagan goddess, "her head up, as though the fiesta were being staged in her honor". As Jake notes: "Brett was radiant. She was happy. The sun was out and the day was bright." She is more completely her pagan self, and when she and Jake enter the chapel of San Fermin she admits that she is "damned bad for a religious atmosphere. . . . I've the wrong type of face." She has immersed herself in the destructive element and it has purged her of her degradation with Cohn. As Jake says, "It was the first time I had seen her in the old happy, careless way since before she went off with Cohn." Later, having forced Romero to leave her in Madrid, she tells Jake that she is "all right again. He's wiped out that damned Cohn." She is safe in the knowledge that she is "not going to be one of these bitches". One can see in this sequence a pagan counterpart to Jake's process: for Jake's preservation she offers initiation; where he finds absolution in isolation, she finds purgation in action. But for each the procedure has culminated in an act of self-denial—of shaping one's self to a responsibility imposed from outside one's self. Jake, in fulfilling his function as *cabestro*, has denied himself the full enjoyment of his own pleasures in the bullfight in the present and, in the loss of Montoya's friendship, has effectively cut himself off from such pleasures in the future. Brett, for her part, finally denies her passion for Romero by sending him away, as the *vaquilla* must if she is not to destroy the bullfighter. What they have found is not release but constraint; each is ultimately restricted by the recognition of his function and the limitations which that function places upon him. And this recognition must necessarily govern their lives *together*, as the last lines imply:

> 'Oh, Jake,' Brett said, 'we could have had such a damned good time together.'
> Ahead was a mounted policeman in khaki directing traffic. He raised his baton. The car slowed suddenly pressing Brett against me.
> 'Yes,' I said. 'Isn't it pretty to think so?'

Between Brett's assertion and Jake's essential denial there is the symbol of external control and recollected responsibility. The response to that rule of law will continue to "press" Brett against Jake, but he will not allow himself hereafter to confuse contiguity with unity.

It is in this context that the novel's elusive phrase "one of us" is to be defined: to have a particular incapacity, a lack of full freedom, which has been inflicted by forces beyond one's control, but an incapacity nevertheless coupled with expertise which demands a responsibility to others. This is the source of Jake's responsibility for Cohn, Mike,

Harvey Stone, *et al.*; his knowledge is greater than theirs precisely because he is not capable of being the "whole man", and with this knowledge comes his responsibility as *cabestro* to protect them as he can. Brett, too, has such a role and the pattern of the novel can be seen in her discovery of her function as *vaquilla*: we are to agree with Jake that Brett was "probably damn good" for Romero, but her value to him was possible only if she recognized her own incapacity and her concurrent responsibility not to destroy him because of it. Her function is to initiate, but with restraint, and it is this restraint which she learns—and uses for the first time—in the course of the book.

Jake, too, has learned restraint. Early in the novel his passion for Brett, the antithesis of his function as *cabestro*, is not in control: "Couldn't we live together, Brett? Couldn't we just live together?" The answer, of course, is no, but it is not an answer which Jake apparently can accept at the outset of the novel; control with Cohn and company he has, but not control with Brett. But by the end of the novel he has that control, and the last line of the book shows how consummate it is. The irony is obvious: it is *not*, strictly speaking, "pretty" to think about what he has lost; his sleepless nights of frustration have proved that. It is, rather, "pretty", of idle fancy only, to think that they could be what they are not, and this awareness suggests a mind attuned to reality, accepting its function in a larger pattern, a new awareness of control. Just as Brett has found it in herself to make Romero leave her against her own passionate desires, so Jake is able, finally, to give up his passionate imagination of a sexual life with Brett.

But though their sacrifices are comparable, the assumptions on which these sacrifices are made are not, as their conversation at the end of the novel makes clear:

'You know it makes one feel rather good deciding not to be a bitch.'
'Yes.'
'It's sort of what we have instead of God.'
'Some people have God,' I said. 'Quite a lot.'

Not being a bitch-goddess is Brett's salvation; having God—even though the having is incomplete and not entirely salutary—is Jake's. Their resolutions are equivalent but their essential isolation from each other remains.

As this exegesis might suggest, the novel is not nihilistic in intention, execution, nor effect. Taken in this symbolic context its structure is remarkably complex and concentrated—and brilliantly sustained. Here is not "motion which goes no place" but rather the concerted movement of character into self-recognition and resolution. Neither is Jake a paradigm of sterility and despair, "an emotional adolescent" for whom "love itself is dead". As the progress of the book describes his recognition of function in society, so its conclusion suggests the value of this function. The book is what Hemingway declared it to be, not "a hollow or bitter satire, but a damn tragedy with the earth abiding forever as the hero". It is in the symbolic pattern of return which the title announces and the action describes that the earth "abides", and the novel implies that by recognizing that pattern and his place in it—and accepting the tragic demands it makes upon him—man, too, can abide.

From the *Sewanee Review* 76, no. 1 (Winter 1968): 26-48. Copyright © 1968 by the *Sewanee Review*. Reprinted with the permission of the editor.

The Sun Also Rises:
The Wounded Anti-Hero

Delbert E. Wylder

Hemingway chose to present *The Sun Also Rises* from the first-person narrative perspective, to have Jake Barnes tell his own story of his experiences in post-World War I France and Spain. The result is a very successful novel, and at least part of the success is attributable to the method of telling. As Hemingway is reported to have told A. E. Hotchner, "it was easier to write in the first person because you could involve the reader immediately. . . ."[1] Unfortunately for the critic, however, this narrative perspective also frequently disarms the reader. Especially is this true if the reader has a tendency to associate the narrator with Ernest Hemingway or to see the story as being told by a slightly older Nick Adams character. Jake Barnes is a specific character in a specific situation, and it seems to me highly important in any analysis of *The Sun Also Rises* to examine closely Jake's personality and the situation in which he finds himself. He is no traditional hero; that is clear. As the wounded man he is unable to perform as hero, even though he has the opportunity. He is, however, both the protagonist and the narrator of the novel and thus deserves the closest scrutiny.

Much of the pejorative early criticism of *The Sun Also Rises*—especially the moral criticism—makes little distinction between Jake and the other characters. Jake is frequently assumed to be one of the expatriates like Harvey Stone, Mike Campbell and Lady Brett Ashley.[2] The truth, however, is that Jake is not one of them. He is a working journalist who does, on occasion, take almost ritualistic vacation trips to Spain. Before the trip to Spain that forms the basis for this novel, he tells us that he feels very much a part of the working world: "All along the people were going to work. It felt pleasant to be going to work. I walked across the avenue and turned into my office."[3] Further, his discussions of newspaper work in the early chapters clearly indicate his competence in the field, and it is obvious that the other journalists respect him. His life is rather carefully and uncomplicatedly scheduled, and he seems to be a nucleus around which the more "restless" characters revolve. From this central position he can observe, report, and judge the activities of others and then describe the effects of the activities on him.

The most significant aspect in any consideration of Jake as a character is, of course, his impotence. F. Scott Fitzgerald, not long after the publication of *The Sun Also Rises*, wrote to Maxwell Perkins that he liked the novel but had some reservations about it.

> The fiesta, the fishing trip, the minor characters were fine. The lady I didn't like, perhaps because I don't like the original. In the mutilated man I thought Ernest bit off more than can be chewn between the covers of a book, then lost his nerve a little and edited the more vitalizing details out. He has since told me that something like this happened.[4]

Fitzgerald was perhaps alluding to the problem of censorship, but there are artistic problems as well that he must have perceived. The narrative perspective in both Fitzgerald's *The Great Gatsby* and Hemingway's *The Sun Also Rises* is much the same. Nick Carraway, although not physically mutilated, is an extremely passive individual. As a representative of the "West"[5] his commentary on the East and its effect on the other Westerners and himself is central to an understanding of the novel. Nick's passivity is an especially important aspect of his personality and roughly parallels the passivity of Jake Barnes in Hemingway's novel. Both narrators are also primarily concerned with reporting the amours of other characters, although Jake is obviously the more involved of the two.

With both novels it is necessary to examine the narrator, his personality, his truthfulness, and his attitudes, since all of the action recorded is selected and arranged in terms of the writer's concept of the narrating character. What we are concerned with in *The Sun Also Rises* is a story told by a wounded—not whole—man. Thus we can not really hope for any complete solution to the problems posed by Jake.

Jake is wounded physically much as Captain Ahab's loss of leg can be seen symbolically in *Moby Dick*; both are cases of mutilation rather than castration. But, with the romantic hero passé for the naturalists, and in a novel primarily concerned with the postwar materialistic society, an Ahabian hero would be incongruous. Unlike either Ahab or his own Biblical namesake, Jacob, Jake Barnes has not been symbolically wounded by wrestling with God—he has been physically wounded in a war. Jake Barnes bears a much closer resemblance to Ishmael than to Ahab, much less concerned with trying to break through the inscrutable unreasoning mask than with trying to find a way to live in the world.

Perhaps the most important aspect of Jake's character is that, despite much critical opinion to the contrary, he is intelligent. His main purpose appears to be an attempt to come to grips with life, especially in the area of the emotions. Like many of the Nick Adams short stories which deal with Nick's discoveries about life, *The Sun Also Rises* is primarily concerned with the "education" of Jake Barnes. One of the main differences, however, between young Nick Adams and Jake Barnes is that, in most cases, Nick merely reacts emotionally to experience.[6] Things happen to him, and he suddenly becomes aware of evil or complexity, but he does not think about the concepts of good and evil. He merely reacts. Jake Barnes, in contrast, makes a conscious effort to learn about life. As he says, "Perhaps as you went along you did learn something. I did not care what it was all about. All I wanted to know was how to live in it. Maybe if you found out how to live in it you learned from that what it was all about."[7]

This passage has often been interpreted as a statement of anti-intellectualism, of the failure of the Hemingway hero to be interested in philosophical questions. Although Jake's attitude may limit his philosophical approach, it certainly does not indicate a lack either of insight or intellectual curiosity. Jake, like Nick Carraway, reports and at the same time analyzes the experiential world and the people with whom he becomes involved. His words are more faintly reminiscent of Henry David Thoreau's statement of purpose for living at Walden.

> I went to the woods because I wished to live deliberately, to front only the essential facts of life, and see if I could not learn what it had to teach, and not, when I came to die, discover that I had not lived. I did not wish to live what was not life, living is so dear; nor did I wish to practice resignation, unless it was quite necessary.[8]

There are differences, obviously. Thoreau goes on to discuss his concept of simplicity; Barnes attempts to live in the world of nature and the world of society. But both men are vitally concerned with learning about life and finding the meaning of life through living in it. Essentially, Jake Barnes observes people and society much as Thoreau observes nature. In nature Barnes finds solace rather than meaning. For meaning he looks to the statements and actions of people.

Jake examines the world initially from a rather restricted viewpoint. At the beginning of the novel he seems to have accepted a philosophy which is particularly American in its pragmatism.

> You paid some way for everything that was any good. I paid my way into enough things that I liked, so that I had a good time. Either you paid by learning about them, or by experience, or by taking chances, or by money. Enjoying living was learning to get your money's worth and knowing when you had it.[9]

When Jake says that you pay for everything, he is using "pay" much in the sense that William James uses it.[10] Everything has its "cash value," and one determines what to do on the basis of how much "good" one can expect to gain by believing and acting in a certain manner. But there is also a strain of epicureanism mixed with the pragmatism; the "good" seems to be closely related to enjoyment or pleasure. This is also evident in Jake's commentary on morality. "That was morality; things that made you disgusted afterward. No, that must be immorality."[11] This statement sounds very much like the one Hemingway makes in *Death in the Afternoon.* "So far about morals, I know only that what is moral is what you feel good after and what is immoral is what you feel bad after. . . ."[12]

This appears to be an extremely simplistic treatment of morality, but the emphasis is clearly upon an individualistic and highly relative concept. Stressed are the physical and emotional responses to phenomena; feeling "good" becomes pleasure in a physical and psychological sense.[13]

But Jake Barnes is *not* Ernest Hemingway, and Jake is more than a trifle skeptical about his own philosophy. He recognizes that this philosophy might prove to be as silly in the next five years as all the "other fine philosophies" he has had. He follows his statement on morality with, "That was a large statement. What a lot of bilge I could think up at night."[14] For most of the novel Jake apparently operates from this "cash nexus" type of philosophy, but I think it important that he is essentially unsure of the validity of the position, that he constantly tests it, and that he finally finds it unsatisfactory because it does not explain everything, especially in one's relationships with people.

Jake is extremely sensitive to his natural surroundings; he is also extremely sensitive to human relationships. But he is very much different from the Andersonian protagonists in *Many Marriages* and *Dark Laughter* who concentrate all of their attention upon themselves. Jake Barnes is interested in people. He is capable of having close friendships with various types of people, and he admires a number of types, from the peasants to the Count and Montoya, from Harvey Stone to Mike Campbell. But he is also aware, or becomes very much aware, that people when they are together may not get along well with one another. Perhaps the most satisfactory relationship in the novel is between Jake, Bill, and their English friend Harris on the fishing trip. In isolation, and doing what they all like to do, and without sex to complicate the relationships, the three are happy. No complex situations arise in which some people want to do things that the others do not, or in which individuals compete with one another for the satisfaction of their own needs, or where different points of view conflict. As they get on the bus Bill and Jake discuss their friend.

> "Say, wasn't that Harris nice?" Bill said.
> "I think he really did have a good time."
> "Harris? You bet he did."
> "I wish he'd come to Pamplona."[15]

But Bill seems to recognize the impossibility of transplanting the friendship to another environment. He says, "He wanted to fish." And Jake then makes an important qualification: "Yes. You couldn't tell how English would mix with each other, anyway."[16]

Part of the awareness the reader has of Jake's sensitivity results from another important aspect of his character, an extremely important one in terms of his role as narrator: Jake is almost completely honest. It is partly this honesty of Jake's, his ability to discuss the reasons for his actions that makes the reader accept his narrative. But unfortunately the reader then sometimes fails to find beneath the surface of the story as Jake tells it a double dichotomy that is part of the very structure of the novel. There is a physical or geographical emphasis which allows a contrast between the countries of France and Spain and there is a psychological emphasis which stresses significant contrasts between the characters.

The geographical dichotomy is made especially clear in Book III, which functions essentially as an epilogue. Book I (roughly sixty-seven pages) had been set in France; Book II (roughly 155 pages), primarily in Spain, and the action of Book III (twenty pages) shifts between the two countries. In the epilogue Jake reflects on his experiences in a rather conscious summing up and emphasizes the contrast between the two nations; they then become symbolic of two attitudes toward life: one essentially materialistic and sterile, the other more primitive and more virile—in a sense, almost romantic. Neither country provides an easy answer to the problem of living one's life, as Jake Barnes discovers. Life in Spain, however, finally has a more lasting effect on him.

The materialistic world of France is the easier to live in. As Jake comments,

> The waiter seemed a little offended about the flowers of the Pyrenees, so I overtipped him. That made him happy. It felt comfortable to be in a country where it is so simple to make people happy. You can never tell whether a Spanish waiter will thank you. Everything is on such a clear financial basis in France. It is the simplest country to live in. No one makes things complicated by becoming your friend for any obscure reason. If you want people to like you, you have only to spend a little money. I spent a little money and the waiter liked me. He appreciated my valuable qualities. He would be glad to see me back. I would dine there again some time and he would be glad to see me, and would want me at his table. It would be a sincere liking because it would have a sound basis. I was back in France.[17]

Within the passage is a direct contrast between the waiters of France and Spain and an implied contrast between the two countries. The French waiter operates materialistically, objectively, and predictably. The Spanish waiter, it is suggested, is motivated by "obscure" reasons that make human relationships extremely difficult. Life is less complicated in France because the value systems are materialistically defined. There are no problems of abstract values and emotional responses that confuse relationships. There is irony, of course, in Jake's remark, for the important point has been developed throughout the novel that France is sterile, and this statement of contrast in the epilogue makes clear a dichotomy that has existed beneath the surface of the novel.

Jake's value system is very much like that of Count Mippipopolous, the high priest of materialism in the novel. Count Mippipopolous has a rigid system of values, and he states that the "secret" is getting to know the values. Wine and women have a strong place in his values, and he pays for his enjoyment. Love does not complicate his life because he is always in love without being emotionally involved. But Brett sagely identifies his state of being. "You haven't any values," she says. "You're dead, that's all."[18] Brett is right. Unlike the bullfighters, who live their lives "all the way up," Count Mippipopolous has quit living. It is ironically symbolic that Book I ends with a highly emotional scene between Brett and Jake, and that before going up to bed, Jake is driven home by the Count's chauffeur. Jake has just unhappily said goodbye to Brett. He has lost in his emotional life, but he receives deference from the chauffeur because he tips him. "I gave him twenty francs and he touched his cap and said: 'Good night, sir,' and drove off."[19]

The sterility of France and of both Jake's and the Count's value systems is made quite clear in a scene between Jake and Bill Gorton just after the latter has arrived in Paris.

"Here's a taxidermist's," Bill said. "Want to buy anything? Nice stuffed dog?"

"Come on," I said. "You're pie-eyed."

"Pretty nice stuffed dogs," Bill said. "Certainly brighten up your flat."

"Come on."

"Just one stuffed dog. I can take 'em or leave 'em alone. But listen, Jake. Just one stuffed dog."

"Come on."

"Mean everything in the world to you after you bought it. Simple exchange of values. You give them money. They give you a stuffed dog."[20]

One pays money for a stuffed rather than live animal. It is a simple, but meaningless, exchange of values. One notes, too, that France is the country of statues, men in stone, and most of them in some act of waving flags or raising swords. In contrast, Spain is the country of live animals—of bulls, of horses, of fish in the streams. And the men who posture with baton or sword are alive—Romero or Belmonte profiling to kill, or the policeman raising his baton in the last paragraph of the novel. This difference between countries is made even more explicit in the characterization and the description of customs.

Jake's concierge in Paris is an example of the materialistic Parisian.

> Her life-work lay in the pelouse, but she kept an eye on the people of the pesage, and she took great pride in telling me which of my guests were well brought up, which were of good family, who were sportsmen, a French word pronounced with the accent on the men. The only trouble was that people who did not fall into any of these three categories were very liable to be told there was no one home, chez Barnes.[21]

It is this concierge, as a matter of fact, who, very much like the French waiter already discussed, judges Brett Ashley by the type of tip she leaves. Lady Brett alienates the concierge on her first visit to Jake's apartment, but the latter is reconciled when Brett gives her far too much of the Count's money. After the tip, the concierge says, "It was the one who was here last night. In the end I find she is very nice."[22]

In Spain, during the bus trip to the fishing location, Bill and Jake stop for a rest at a *posada*. They go inside for a drink, and then encounter the contrasting rural Spanish attitude toward tipping. "We each had an aguardiente and paid forty centimes for the two drinks. I gave the woman fifty centimes to make a tip, and she gave me back the copper piece, thinking I had misunderstood the price."[23]

Almost all of the people in France operate on the cash-value materialistic principle. This is seen especially in those people who have anything to do with the American tourists. As Jake reports,

> We ate dinner at Madame Lecomte's restaurant on the far side of the island. It was crowded with Americans and we had to stand up and wait for a place. Some one had put it in the American Women's Club list as a quaint

restaurant on the Paris quais as yet untouched by Americans, so we had to wait forty-five minutes for a table. Bill had eaten at the restaurant in 1918, and right after the armistice, and Madame Lecomte made a great fuss over seeing him.

"Doesn't get us a table, though," Bill said. "Grand woman, though."[24]

This kind of treatment, as contrasted to that given Jake and Bill by the hotel-keeper Montoya in Spain, emphasizes the basic satiric contrast between the two countries. Bill's recognition that the earlier friendship with Madame Lecomte has not helped at all in getting them fed is contrasted to Montoya's carefully reserving Jake's usual rooms.

From the very beginning of their journey into Spain, Jake and Bill encounter friendly people. They, as American tourists, are treated with friendliness and hospitality by the peasants on the bus. The peasants insist that the two drink from the Spanish winebags. Even commercial people are friendly. During the fiesta Jake leaves a bar to buy some wineskins. When the salesman discovers that Jake wants to use them for the purpose for which they were made, and not to sell in France, he is very considerate.

"What are you going to do? Sell them in Bayonne?"

"No. Drink out of them."

He slapped me on the back.

"Good man. Eight pesetas for the two. The lowest price."

The man who was stencilling the new ones and tossing them into a pile stopped.

"It's true," he said. "Eight pesetas is cheap."[25]

Spain is a country where materialism has not yet penetrated—at least not in certain areas. Where it has been introduced, symbolized by modern plumbing, things are beginning to change. But even in these places, the Spaniards feel guilty about their materialism.

I went out to find the woman and ask her how much the room and board was. She put her hands under her apron and looked away from me.

"Twelve pesetas."

"Why, we only paid that in Pamplona."

She did not say anything, just took off her glasses and wiped them on her apron.

"That's too much," I said. "We didn't pay more than that at a big hotel."

"We've put in a bathroom."[26]

If Count Mippipopolous is the high priest of materialism, Montoya is the high priest of the world of "obscure" values in Spain. He has a strong sense of loyalty to those who have *aficion*, to those who have a "passion" or subjective feeling about bullfighting. As Jake says, "Those who were aficionados could always get rooms even when the hotel was full."[27] Jake also describes how Montoya is careful to hang in his office only the pictures of bullfighters who have *aficion*. He can forgive them any human weaknesses if they have the "feeling." Pictures of bullfighters without *aficion* go into his drawer and finally into the wastebasket, no matter how flattering the inscriptions. The subjective or emotional area of this relationship is indicated in Jake's description of the examination and "touching" ceremony.

When they saw that I had aficion, and there was no password, no set questions that could bring it out, rather it was a sort of oral spiritual examination with the questions always a little on the defensive and never apparent, there was this same embarrassed putting the hand on the shoulder, or a "Buen hombre." But nearly always there was the actual touching. It seemed as though they wanted to touch you to make it certain.[28]

Montoya, as one of the "touchers," represents this traditional and subjective area of experience, and he is in direct contrast to Count Mippipopolous and the rest of the Parisian materialists.

The contrast between France and Spain is most highly developed in the disparity between the national "sports" of the two countries. The emphasis that Hemingway places on bullfighting is easily recognized through Jake Barnes' interest in it and his feeling for it. We see something of the traditional and ritualistic aspects of the bullfight in Jake's description. We also note his admiration for the meaningfulness of the forms of the bullfight and of the passes, and the recognition that each *torero* tests his integrity each time he encounters the bull. Furthermore, the *torero* faces death, not as the man who is killed during the unloading and running of the bulls, but in an art form where each act has not only beauty but meaning. The whole ceremony, then, is the antithesis of the meaningless world Jake Barnes and his friends live in. This is the "sport" of Spain. Jake Barnes is one of the initiated who have *aficion*, who have the subjective feeling about what goes on in the bullring, and who understand the deeper meanings behind the bullfight. He does not react emotionally only, like those who fail to give Juan Belmonte his due, but can appreciate artistically both the worth of the young Romero and the great dignity of Belmonte in this "sport" which is played always in the face of death.

Bicycle racing, the contrasting sport of France, is another thing. Having lunch with the team manager of one of the bicycle manufacturers, Jake is told that the Tour de France is "the greatest sporting event in the world."[29] But there is no dignity in bicycle racing. It is, if it can be called such, a materialistic sport, where everything important can be taken care of, and where there is very little of the element of chance. As Jake reports, "[The bicycle riders] did not take the race seriously except among themselves. They had raced among themselves so often that it did not make much difference who won. Especially in a foreign country. The money could be arranged."[30]

There is neither the dignity nor the heavy masculinity of the bullfighter in the picture of the bicycle racers. The racers have a following of French girls with "Rue de Faubourg Montmartre chic" who seem to be almost community property, for Jake cannot make out which girl belongs to which racer. The racers whisper jokes they think the girls should not hear, and then will not repeat them. They are quite unlike Romero, who remains with his cuadrilla apart from society until the point when he quite aggressively approaches Brett. He is so direct that Jake can analyze his every move and correctly interprets his glance that indicates things are "understood." Nor are the bicycle racers exposed, as Romero is, to a horn wound or fatality. Bicycle racing does not involve the potentially tragic element of a direct confrontation with death. The leader of the bicycle racers ridiculously has an attack of boils which forces him to sit on the small of his back. He blushes when one of the girls hears him tell how he is going to ride the next day with the air touching his boils. These are sportsmen, not men. Jake makes no direct comparison of bicycle racing to the bullfight, but he does make one ironic comment that makes the point beautifully. "The Spaniards, they [the French] said, did not know how to pedal."[31] The mechanical act of pedalling is completely unimportant in contrast to the traditions and meaningful forms of the bullfight. Jake, who travels annually from one country to another as though on a religious pilgrimage, and who watches almost all of the preliminary activities as well as the bullfight itself, does not bother to watch the bicycle racers start the next morning. In fact, he indicates to the team manager that he would prefer not to be wakened for the event.

The meaninglessness and sterility of life in Paris or in France becomes evident in the implicit comparison to Spain. The meaninglessness caused by the disruption of social patterns resulting from the war is symbolized most effectively in the geographical or national contrast by two passages illustrating the present condition of the two countries. France is a far more modern and progressive country. The concept of change is evident, and Bill Gorton, though he loves the city and is glad to be back, takes a dim view of one of the changes.

> We walked along under the trees that grew out over the river on the Quai d'Orléans side of the island. Across the river were the broken walls of old houses that were being torn down.
>   "They're going to cut a street through."
>   "They would," Bill said.[32]

In contrast, when Jake returns to Spain, he finds almost everything the way he remembers it. Symbolically, the Ayuntamiento is the center of the old civilization, unchanging, the home of the history of the town.

> I went to the Ayuntamiento and found the old gentleman who subscribes for the bull-fight tickets for me every year, and he had gotten the money I sent him from Paris and renewed my subscriptions, so that was all set. He was the archivist, and all the archives of the town were in his office. That has nothing to do with the story. Anyway, his office had a green baize door and a big wooden door, and when I went out I left him sitting among the archives that covered all the walls, and I shut both the doors, and as I went out of the building into the street the porter stopped me to brush off my coat.
>
> "You must have been in a motor-car," he said.
>
> The back of the collar and the upper part of the shoulders were gray with dust.[33]

The description is obviously important. Here is the seat of a society, the society of Spain. From here Jake goes to the cathedral to pray, and becomes disappointed with himself for being such a bad Catholic. It is interesting, however, that when praying for the bullfighters, he treats them much as Montoya treats their pictures, "[praying] separately for the ones I liked, and lumping all the rest. . . ."[34] Further, he begins to think about making money, and this reminds him of Count Mippipopolous. The most important quality of the description of the Ayuntamiento, however, is that the dust that Jake had accumulated on his coat during the drive from Bayonne becomes symbolic of the Spanish earth. In the epilogue Jake arrives at San Sebastian and wistfully makes a symbolic gesture to the dust of Spain. "At the hotel I paid the driver and gave him a tip. The car was powdered with dust. I rubbed the rodcase through the dust. It seemed the last thing that connected me with Spain and the fiesta."[35]

Spain, then, is at the center of tradition and represents the old truths,

Critical Insights

the old concepts, the old ways. France is the new way, the materialistic direction, the country of twentieth-century change. The movement between the two countries is especially important in terms of a parallel development in the cast of characters. The novel begins in France, where there are no meaningful rituals and, of course, no heroes. Jake's coterie of friends intrude upon his planned vacation with Bill Gorton and enter into the land of meaning. After Jake and Bill return from their fishing trip in the mountains the stage is set for the representatives of the materialistic world to make their impact on the world of tradition. Although Jake at first chooses to remain loyal to his Paris friends, the final victory is won by Romero, the representative of Spain. He wins because this is the land of tradition, a land where the hero may still live. And the victory of the hero has a strong effect on Jake Barnes. The geographical movement in the novel parallels and enforces the gradual shift in emphasis from one character to another.

For as Jake tells the story, he gradually shifts his focus. He begins his narration with a description of Cohn; the first book is primarily devoted to Cohn and Brett and himself. In the second book emphasis is transferred from Cohn and Brett to Mike and Brett and finally to Romero and Brett. Romero completely replaces the other suitors by the end of Book II. In Book III, which serves as an epilogue, Jake is left alone, but returns to Spain to rescue Brett.

Both Earl Rovit[36] and Mark Spilka[37] make the interesting point that Cohn functions essentially as Jake's "double." What they neglect, however, is that Cohn represents only Jake's passive and romantic side when there is still another important side to be considered. Jake is a more complex character than he seems to be. He is the only character in the novel, with the possible exception of Bill Gorton, who is at home in both of the environments. He lives a comfortable, fairly controlled life in France until Brett Ashley interferes, and he is equally comfortable and at home in Spain until once again Lady Brett and all of his friends intrude. It should be remembered that Jake has made the trip to Spain a number of times. He is familiar with bullfighting, has been recognized as having *aficion*, and has never broken the rules of loyalty—until, of course, he arranges the meeting between Romero and Brett.

Perhaps the reason for his disloyalty can be seen in a comparison of the two aspects of his personality represented by Cohn and Romero. If we use the sociological terminology of David Riesman's *The Lonely Crowd*, these differences can perhaps be clarified. Robert Cohn might be classified as a man who might well use his tradition-directed background, but who has no basic "inner-direction" for coping with the value-less "other-directed" post-war society in which he finds himself. Cohn is Jewish, but he has broken from the traditional Jewish way of life. He is, in fact, ashamed of his Jewish background. He learned to box to counteract a feeling of inferiority when he was treated as a Jew. And he received a "strange sort of satisfaction" at having his nose flattened. But with the Jewish tradition to fall back on, Cohn takes a different course. He becomes an editor and then a novelist. Like an insect who points his feelers out into the world and then responds to what it feels, he is constantly putting out his own antennae. He has never had set in motion the "internal gyroscope" of an inner-directed man. He is completely unable to make up his mind about anything until he falls in love. Having broken from his tradition, and with no strong sense of himself, he is as empty as a man can be. He is completely dominated by Frances, or would be except for what Jake would later call his hard, stubborn, Jewish streak, which is the only strength he has. Later, he is dominated by Lady Brett, but this time because he is completely overpowered by his infatuation for her. As Jake points out, Cohn gets his romantic ideas from very impractical books. He is extremely conscious of his failure to live, and even speaks to Jake about it.

When Jake asks him if he has had any fun the night before, Cohn gives a well-qualified answer. "No, I don't think so."[38] This is the same type of reaction evidenced in the one Spanish peasant on the bus ride who had been to America and whose traditions had been confused. When asked if he likes the bullfight, he says, "Yes. I guess I like them."[39]

Cohn is much closer than Jake to the Anderson type of "wounded" hero that Hemingway had satirized in *The Torrents of Spring*. He is self-interested, with a tendency toward emotionalism, and with a strong belief that a romantic interest with the right woman in the right environment is what he needs in order to "live." He believes that a change of environment will solve his problems when he is, like an Anderson hero, trying to escape from one woman to another. Just as he believes that he can find "life" in romantic South America, he also believes that his sexual interlude with Brett is a great love, and thus allows himself to be destroyed by her. In this respect, as Spilka has pointed out, he is much like Jake Barnes in the early part of the novel, who believes that if he were not physically wounded he would be able to provide Brett with all of the qualities necessary for her happiness.

The major difference between the two men is in the nature of the wound. Cohn is psychologically wounded, while Jake is physically wounded. Jake has been unmanned by the war, although left with all of his masculine drives. He is not self-centered, as Cohn is, and his passivity is largely a device that he has used in order, as he says, to keep from making trouble. Though he loves Brett and is dominated by her for a large part of the novel, he is finally able to recognize her emotional limitations. As he says, "I suppose she only wanted what she couldn't have."[40] As a wounded man, we do not expect heroic activity from Jake, especially on a physical level. But we do expect him to act with integrity. In the one important decision he has to make in the novel, he fails.

The most significant "action" in the novel involves Jake's choice of whether or not to introduce Brett to Romero. Strangely enough, Jake as narrator tells us very little about the reasons for this decision, which is the crucial moral action in the novel. Thus, what he has chosen to tell us about Spain and his recapitulation of the differences between France and Spain become exceptionally important to an understanding of Jake Barnes and of the novel itself.

When Jake is not under pressure, he makes the "right" decision in terms of his loyalty to Montoya, bullfighting, and the subjective, traditional way of life. Montoya asks his advice after Romero has been invited to the American ambassador's suite at the Grand Hotel. Jake tells Montoya not to deliver the message to Romero, and they talk about the dangers to the career of the young torero. The major danger seems to be older women who collect bullfighters. In his advice to Montoya, Jake is loyal to the bullfight and to all that it represents in the novel.

But when Lady Brett asks for Jake's help in meeting Romero, Jake lacks the integrity to deny her wishes. He becomes, as Cohn later calls him, a "pimp," and is disloyal to those things that he has respected. It is at this point in the novel that Jake has the opportunity to act with integrity, and it is at this point in the novel that he fails. He refuses the role of the hero.

His failure, however, is only a partial failure, because his reasons for sending Brett away with Romero are complex. For one thing, he is getting even with Cohn for running away with Brett, and it is rather easy to trace the change from pity toward Cohn at the beginning of the novel to hostility after his discovery that Cohn and Brett have been away together. As he confesses to Brett, "I'm not sorry for him. I hate him, myself."[41] But in his act of disloyalty he is, at the same time, destroying that part of himself that, as Rovit and Spilka suggest, Cohn represents. Even more important, he is replacing Cohn with another figure and another part of himself, the masculine and heroic side that has been powerless and inactive since his wound. Finally, he may even be trying to punish and destroy the bitch goddess, the tempting sorceress, by mating her with a surrogate lover, Romero.

Jake Barnes is not totally passive; rather, he has elements of strength and areas of belief that he is unable to maintain in the face of human conflicts and a changing world. Between the idea of how he should act and the reality of how he does falls the shadow of his wound. He is, like his namesake, the man with the hollow "thigh." But he is just as much Romero on one side of his character as he is Cohn on the other. Romero becomes the symbol for what he could have been had he not been wounded and had there been no twentieth-century moral revolution in the material world. Both Jake and Romero have *aficion*, and Jake understands Romero's motives in the bullring as though he *were* Romero. They both have the same attitudes toward honor. When Mike tells Jake the story about Romero's defeat of Cohn through Romero's refusal to be defeated (Romero kept trying to hit Cohn and refused to shake his hand), we recognize that this is the way Jake would have acted had he been able. After Jake has sent Brett off with Romero, for example, he has far more courage than he has had previously. Instead of backing away from trouble, as he had when Cohn once threatened to hit him for his remarks about Brett, Jake now actually starts a fight.

> I swung at him and he ducked. I saw his face duck sideways in the light. He hit me and I sat down on the pavement. As I started to get on my feet he hit me twice. I went down backward under a table. I tried to get up and felt I did not have any legs. I felt I must get on my feet and try and hit him.[42]

But Jake is unable to get up. His attitude, however, is the same as Romero's, and is very unlike Mike's who says. "He didn't knock me out. I just lay there." Even more important, perhaps, is the feeling Jake has about not accepting Cohn's apology. Again he wishes to act as Romero has acted. Jake returns to the hotel, and Bill tells him to go see Cohn. Jake says, "The hell with him," but Bill insists that he go. Jake climbs another flight of stairs, knocks on Cohn's door, and identifies himself as "Barnes," not "Jake." He at first refuses to allow Cohn to call him by his first name. Then he is reminded once more that this was how he had felt when he had come home from a football game after being hit in the head. His immediate reaction to the concept of "home" is that he suddenly wants a "deep, hot bath, to lie back in." He refuses to forgive Cohn, reminds him that he had called him a pimp and then thinks, "I did not care. I wanted a hot bath. I wanted a hot bath in deep water."[43]

As he finds out later he wishes to react very much like Romero acted after his physical defeat by Cohn; but he is incapable. He is unable to face the complexity of the world, is unable to live by the code that Romero uses to preserve his integrity. Instead, he decides that he does not really care and symbolically wishes to retire from the world into an obviously symbolic womb.

The contrast between the actions of Jake and Romero emphasizes the unheroic nature of Jake as protagonist. Romero is the hero, the bullfighter who lives his life "all the way up." He lives according to his traditions, even refusing to speak English any more than absolutely necessary because bullfighters should not know English. He preserves his integrity despite the physical punishment he receives from Cohn. Then he erases the whole incident, as Jake realizes, by his performance in the traditional ritual of the bullfight. Like the true hero, Romero faces every trial successfully. He even temporarily conquers the temptress, a feat that none of the other males has been able to accomplish. He can conquer because he is what might be called the "tradition-directed" hero.

Life is far more simple for Romero than for the expatriates. Living the restricted life of a bullfighter with his cuadrilla, he has fewer choices to make. He must work his own individuality into the definitely traditionalized ritual of the bullfight. He is presented at each corrida with a certain number of bulls to kill ritualistically—bulls which he has not been allowed to choose, although his manager might help in the selection. Most important, his profession is his way of life, and he lives within it. It includes a code of honor that he may respect and live by. It is not the audience that is to be pleased at each corrida. As Jake understands, Romero does it for himself. He does not, like the "other-directed" individual, do things to please others and to justify himself in their terms. Nor does his older counterpart, Belmonte.

Carlos Baker overlooks the one point that Jake's description of Juan Belmonte serves in the novel. Belmonte, too, is a bullfighter who lives his life "all the way up." He is an old Romero whose popularity has diminished, but who maintains at least some degree of his old integrity. As Jake explains, Belmonte is careful about the selection of bulls and has lost his belief in the "great moments" of bullfighting. But unlike the inactive Count Mippipopolous, Belmonte continues to test himself despite his illness and thus he preserves some of his dignity and integrity. He is a sick man, in constant pain, but he does not allow the reaction of the crowd to destroy his composure. Worst of all, he is the mythological hero who cannot at his age—or could not, even in his best years, Jake tells us—do the things the crowd now expects of him. Jake's description of Belmonte in the ring shows more contempt for the crowd than for Belmonte. At the end of the passage, Belmonte, untouched by the crowd, goes back to take his part in the ritual.

Also Belmonte imposed conditions and insisted that his bulls should not be too large, nor too dangerously armed with horns, and so the element that was necessary to give the sensation of tragedy was not there, and the public, who wanted three times as much from Belmonte, who was sick with a fistula, as Belmonte had ever been able to give, felt defrauded and cheated, and Belmonte's jaw came further out in contempt, and his face turned yellower, and he moved with greater difficulty as his pain increased, and finally the crowd were actively against him, and he was utterly contemptuous and indifferent. He had meant to have a great afternoon, and instead it was an afternoon of sneers, shouted insults, and finally a volley of cushions and pieces of bread and vegetables, thrown down at him in the plaza where he had his greatest triumphs. His jaw only went further out. Sometimes he turned to smile that toothed, long-jawed, lipless smile when he was called something particularly insulting, and always the pain that any movement produced grew stronger and stronger, until finally his yellow face was parchment color, and after his second bull was dead and the throwing of bread and cushions was over, after he had saluted the President with the same wolf-jawed smile and contemptuous eyes, and handed his sword over the barrera to be wiped, and put back in its case, he passed through into the callejon and leaned on the barrera below us, his head on his arms, not seeing, not hearing anything, only going through his pain. When he looked up, finally, he asked for a drink of water. He swallowed a little, rinsed his mouth, spat the water, took his cape, and went back into the ring.[44]

Belmonte, as seen here, is one of the undefeated. In a sense his dignity is unsurpassed even by Romero.

There is the same essential difference, then, between Belmonte and Cohn that there is between Romero and Cohn. Both Romero and Belmonte refuse to accept defeat, but Cohn collapses completely after Brett has left and he has taken out his spite on Jake. He lies with his face to the wall, cries, and begs for both forgiveness and sympathy. Finally, he leaves the scene of the fiesta before the last act, sneaking out almost unobserved.

It is apparently the bullfighter, then, who serves as the best example of how one can face life. Here in the Romero-Belmonte figure is the only character, or combination of characters, who successfully resists all of the forces imposed on him from the outside world. In Romero's refusal to be defeated by physical punishment at the hands of Cohn and, more important, to be dominated by Lady Brett Ashley is found the important lesson of the concepts of honor and integrity that are based in a traditional way of life and are given solidity by it.

Thus, when Jake deliberates whether to introduce Brett to Romero and later to deliver her to him, he is not only choosing between his loyalties to materialism represented by his friends from France and those traditional values represented by Spain and Montoya, he is also choosing between two aspects of his own personality. Unconsciously, he is delivering Brett to his own better self and destroying the Cohn relationship and that part of himself that is passive. Even more, he may be unconsciously trying to punish Lady Brett by introducing her to the dominant male figure—the hero he cannot be.[45]

Lady Brett Ashley has dominated all of the males. She is very much like the street vendor's girl attendant who is described at the beginning of Chapter V, immediately after the chapter devoted to Brett and Jake's relationship. "I passed the man with the jumping frogs and the man with the boxer toys. I stepped aside to avoid walking into the thread with which his girl assistant manipulated the boxers. She was standing looking away, the thread in her folded hands."[46] Although Brett becomes a goddess of the fiesta, she is a false goddess. She is a temptress who destroys, and then hates those, like Cohn, who suffer from her destruction.

Jake, too, comes to hate Cohn. "I'm not sorry for him. I hate him, myself," he says, before Brett tells him about her love for Romero. After Jake warns her that she should not become involved with Romero, he becomes suddenly angry. They find Romero in the bar and converse while they wait for him to join them.

> "I've always done just what I wanted."
> "I know."
> "I do feel such a bitch."
> "Well," I said.
> "My God!" said Brett, "the things a woman goes through."
> "Yes?"[47]

Jake then joins his other friends and fights with Cohn. After the fight he seems to change in his attitude toward Brett. Instead of showing his anger and jealousy, he is quite sympathetic and helpful to her. He seems to enjoy Romero's conquest of the bull as much as Brett does, and his narration concentrates all the attention upon Romero and the older bullfighter Belmonte. After the bullfight he gets drunk on absinthe that tastes "pleasantly bitter." On this last night of the fiesta, he is drunker than he has ever remembered being.

This is a fitting conclusion to the action of the novel. The hero has departed with what he thinks to be the goddess. If this were a romantic novel, it would end here, or Jake would go on to tell an adapted version of the heroic myth, which traditionally ends in the marriage of the hero and the goddess.[48] Lady Brett, however, will not play the role of goddess. She is, as Robert Lewis has recognized, the woman in Ecclesiastes whose "heart is snares and nets."[49] She is the temptress, and though Romero is the traditional hero, he is not the protagonist of the novel. Thus, the epilogue is concerned with the result of the union of the hero and the temptress and the effects of the union on the narrator. Of major significance in the epilogue is the fact that the heroic figure has replaced the passive figure and that this replacement affects Jake Barnes' attitude toward Lady Brett.[50] In the beginning of the epilogue Jake makes a reluctant and ironic acceptance of France, but only because he is a wounded man. He rationalizes that France is an easy country to live in. It is a country where loyalties do not conflict and where one's integrity is thus not always being tested. There is, however, something shameful about his choice.

As his attitude toward her changes in this last book nothing seems shameful any longer in his relation to Brett. At the beginning of the novel Jake is so emotionally disturbed by Brett that he cannot sleep. When they meet at the dance, he wants to take her away immediately. They are both disturbed at his inability to consummate their love, and Jake is in almost a constant state of torment. On one occasion Brett seems able to provide him with some makeshift physical release, but there is usually none at all. While they are in Spain at the fiesta, Jake is still under her control, and he is very upset when Brett forces him to introduce her to Romero. He witnesses Romero's triumph and then leaves for San Sebastian where he has time to think and to swim. It is immediately after his immersion that he receives the "S.O.S." telegram from Brett and answers it. His initial reaction is one of self-contempt. "That seemed to handle it. That was it. Send a girl off with one man. Introduce her to another to go off with him. Now go and bring her back. And sign the wire with love. That was it all right. I went to lunch."[51]

It has not been as simple as this, of course. Jake reports the action without commenting on his own emotional involvement. He has punished both Cohn and Brett for their escapade, and he has exposed Brett to the traditional masculine hero who has wiped out her experience with Cohn. Jake has also had time for some reflection, and his attitude toward Brett is quite different when he returns to Spain. By the time he finds her in Madrid, he is in almost complete control of himself. His attitude toward Brett is fatherly, if not actually condescending. He kisses her, but notices that her mind is on something else. He comforts her rather than allowing her to comfort him. His control is not easy to maintain. The effort is obviously difficult, and can be seen in his response to her questions, with clipped answers that steer away from any involvement. She seems to sense this and is slightly helpful when she tells him he does not have to get drunk. Later in the cab he puts his arm around her, but there is no longer the frantic need that he had previously felt. The two cab scenes, one at the beginning of the novel and one at the end, make some rather nice distinctions. In the first,

> Brett was leaning back in the corner, her eyes closed. I got in and sat beside her. The cab started with a jerk.
>
> "Oh, darling, I've been so miserable," Brett said.
>
> The taxi went up the hill. . . . The street was dark again and I kissed her. Our lips were tight together and then she turned away and pressed against the corner of the seat, as far away as she could get. Her head was down.
>
> "Don't touch me," she said. "Please don't touch me."[52]

But at the end, when Jake gets in beside Brett,

> . . . I settled back. Brett moved close to me. We sat close against each other. I put my arm around her and she rested against me comfortably. . . .
>
> "Oh, Jake," Brett said, "we could have had such a damned good time together."
>
> Ahead was a mounted policeman in khaki directing traffic. He raised his baton. The car slowed suddenly pressing Brett against me.
>
> "Yes," I said. "Isn't it pretty to think so?"[53]

The imagery in the first cab scene is dark. It is night. The second scene takes place in the brightness of the sun. Such symbolism is slightly ambiguous, however. It might be interpreted as a continuation of the day-night difference of two different worlds, more prevalent in *A Farewell* to *Arms*, but certainly a part of *The Sun Also Rises*; and it could also indicate the clarity with which Jake is finally able to view the situation, in keeping with other passages in the novel where light and truth seem to be synonymous, as at the bullfight. But the most important distinctions to be made are less ambiguous.

In the first passage, the cab starts; in the second, it stops. In the first, the two are tense with emotion and Brett breaks away from him after the kiss; in the second she moves closer to him and then sits "comfortably" with his arm around her. The policeman's raised baton reminds him at once of both his own incapacity and, equally important, Brett's selfishness and lack of understanding. What has become clear to Jake from the slight victory he has gained through Romero is the recognition that Brett could never become a woman even if he were not wounded. She would not let her hair grow for Romero because of her vanity; she could not destroy Romero, and neither could she change for him. Psychologically, she can no more be a woman than Jake can be a man. His ironic reply, "Isn't it pretty to think so" to Brett's "we could have had such a damned good time together" brings the novel full circle, for Jake had earlier known but could not accept the fact that the only reason she wanted him was because she could not have him. There is no more hope now than at the beginning of the novel, but Jake is apparently far more resigned to his condition. He is dedicated, after watching Romero's conquest, to preserving himself against the forces of the temptress. Jake learns to accept the inevitable, as preached in Ecclesiastes, that "All is vanity and vexation of spirit."

The Sun Also Rises, then, is essentially a satire on mankind, much as Ecclesiastes can be looked at as a satire on the vanity of human attempts to find meaning in life. The novel falls into the category of those works on the "Vanity of Human Wishes" theme. Jake looks at all experience and finds it lacking. There are no simple answers for the individual— especially the wounded man—and no code is going to eliminate the problems and perplexities of human relationships in a traditionless world, although it would be pretty to think so. The materialistic world of France is bereft of meaning, and the world of Spain, with its obscure value system and its rigid traditional code is too demanding for the wounded man. Jake finds some solace in nature, however, and he has learned something about integrity from the heroic Romero-Belmonte figure in contrast to the "lost" expatriates. Jake is no hero, but he has learned something from the hero figure—a contempt for the crowd and a certain indifference to his own fate. There are to be no more illusions. And with this knowledge comes a certain compassion for Lady Brett and a recognition of the need for restraint in his association with her. Thoreau had said that he did not want to practice resignation "unless it was quite necessary." Jake Barnes, the wounded man in the rapidly changing traditionless and heroless twentieth century, seems to find it necessary.

Notes

1. A. E. Hotchner, *Papa Hemingway*, p. 51.

2. Part of the reason for this, of course, was Hemingway's use of the Gertrude Stein quotation "You are all a lost generation." The assumption was, and sometimes still is, that Jake Barnes is part of the "all." Henry Seidel Canby (*American Memoir* [Boston, 1947]) says that *The Sun Also Rises* "reflected the life of psychological derelicts floating in alcohol and tormented by oversensitive nerves. Yet these derelicts, expatriated in Paris, were evidently symbolic of a change in values, more easily seen in these neurotics than in better-balanced youngsters of the new generation at home" (p. 339).

3. Ernest Hemingway, *The Sun Also Rises* (New York, 1926), p. 36. All page references are to The Scribner Library Edition, SL 5.

4. Andrew Turnbull, ed., *The Letters of F. Scott Fitzgerald*, p. 205.

5. Actually he is from the Midwest, but is representative of a more conservative environment.

6. Note that in "The Killers," for example, Nick Adams does not want to think about what has happened in the café. He cannot help thinking about it in the sense of remembering it, but he does not want to think about the implications.

7. *The Sun Also Rises*, p. 148.

8. Henry David Thoreau, *Walden*, ed., Sherman Paul (Boston, 1957), p. 62.

9. *The Sun Also Rises*, p. 148.

10. See William James, *Essays in Pragmatism*, ed., Alburey Castell (New York, 1961).

11. *The Sun Also Rises*, p. 149.

12. Ernest Hemingway, *Death in the Afternoon* (New York, 1932), p. 4.

13. This discussion of Jake's moral position is limited to Jake's statements and actions within the novel. For an excellent discussion of Hemingway's concept of morality and immorality, see Max Westbrook, "The Stewardship of Ernest Hemingway," *The Texas Quarterly* (Winter, 1966), pp. 89-101.

14. *The Sun Also Rises*, p. 149.

15. *Ibid.*, p. 130.

16. *Ibid.*

17. *Ibid.*, p. 233.

18. *Ibid.*, p. 61.

19. *Ibid.*, p. 65.

20. *Ibid.*, p. 72.

21. *Ibid.*, p. 53.

22. *Ibid.*, p. 52.

23. *Ibid.*, p. 106.

24. *Ibid.*, p. 76.

25. *Ibid.*, p. 156.

26. *Ibid.*, pp. 109-110.

27. *Ibid.*, p. 132.

28. *Ibid.*

29. *Ibid.*, p. 236.

30. *Ibid.*

31. *Ibid.*

32. *Ibid.*, p. 77.

33. *Ibid.*, p. 86.

34. *Ibid.*, p. 97.

35. *Ibid.*, p. 232.

36. See Earl Rovit, *Ernest Hemingway*, pp. 152 ff.

37. Mark Spilka, "The Death of Love in *The Sun Also Rises*," in Carlos Baker, ed., *Ernest Hemingway: Critiques of Four Major Novels* (New York, 1962), pp. 18-25.

38. *The Sun Also Rises*, p. 37. Note Macomber's selection of a drink and the reason for it. "I suppose it's the thing to do," . . . "Tell him to make three gimlets." (*The Short Stories of Ernest Hemingway* [1953], p. 3.)

39. *Ibid.*, p. 107.

40. *Ibid.*, p. 31.

41. *Ibid.*, p. 182.

42. *Ibid.*, p. 191.

43. *Ibid.*, p. 194.

44. *Ibid.*, pp. 214-215.

45. In this sense, Jake would be making an attempt to destroy Brett's illusion that she is capable of love. Brett is obviously the "new" woman. She wears a man's hat and

is accepted easily by the homosexuals at the beginning of the novel. Jake must feel that she will be forced into a traditional female role by the extremely masculine Romero. The confusion of sexual roles in France is quite evident in the novel.

46. *The Sun Also Rises*, p. 35.

47. *Ibid.*, p. 184.

48. See Lord Raglan, *The Hero* (New York, 1956), p. 150, for a description of the characteristics of the typical ritual pattern.

49. Robert W. Lewis, *Hemingway on Love*, p. 34.

50. An interesting approach for an analysis of the relationship of Jake to Lady Brett would be the use of Berne's *Games People Play* (New York, 1964). Jake Barnes plays "Wooden Leg," and Brett plays "Let's You and Him Fight" through much of the novel.

51. *The Sun Also Rises*, p. 239.

52. *Ibid.*, pp. 24-25.

53. *Ibid.*, p. 247.

Works Cited

Baker, Carlos. *Ernest Hemingway: A Life Story*. New York: Charles Scribner's Sons, 1969.

_____. *Hemingway: The Writer as Artist*. Princeton: Princeton University Press, 1956, ad ed.

_____ (ed.). *Ernest Hemingway: Critiques of Four Major Novels*. New York: Charles Scribner's Sons, 1962.

Berne, Eric, M.D., *Games People Play: The Psychology of Human Relationships*. New York: Grove Press, Inc., 1964.

Canby, Henry Seidel. *American Memoir*. Boston: Houghton Mifflin Company, 1947.

Fitzgerald, F. Scott. *The Letters of F. Scott Fitzgerald*. Edited with an Introduction by Andrew Turnbull. New York: Charles Scribner's Sons, 1963.

Hemingway, Ernest. *Death in the Afternoon*. New York: Charles Scribner's Sons, 1932.

_____. *A Farewell to Arms*. New York: Charles Scribner's Sons, 1929.

_____. *The Short Stories of Ernest Hemingway*. New York: Charles Scribner's Sons, 1953.

_____. *The Sun Also Rises*. New York: Charles Scribner's Sons, 1926.

_____. *The Torrents of Spring*. New York: Charles Scribner's Sons, 1926.

Hotchner, A. E. *Papa Hemingway*. New York: Random House, Inc., 1966.

James, William. *Essays in Pragmatism*. Edited with an Introduction by Alburey Castell. New York: Hafner Publishing Company, 1961.

Lewis, Robert W., Jr. *Hemingway on Love*. Austin: University of Texas Press, 1965.

Riesman, David, et al. *The Lonely Crowd: A Study of the Changing American Character*. New York: Doubleday & Company, Inc., 1955.

Rovit, Earl. *Ernest Hemingway*. New York: Twayne Publishers, Inc., 1963.

Spilka, Mark. "The Death of Love in *The Sun Also Rises*." *Ernest Hemingway: Critiques of Four Major Novels*. Carlos Baker (ed.). New York: Charles Scribner's Sons, 1962.

Thoreau, Henry David. *Walden*. Edited with an Introduction and Notes by Sherman Paul. Boston: Houghton Mifflin Company, 1957.

Westbrook, Max. "The Stewardship of Ernest Hemingway." *The Texas Quarterly* (Winter 1966), 89-101.

The Sun Also Rises:
A Reconsideration

Donald T. Torchiana

Despite forty-odd years of shining existence, *The Sun Also Rises* is still read by the best of our Hemingway men as though it were an off-shoot of T. S. Eliot's *Waste Land*. Sadly enough, no amount of angry denial by Hemingway himself has had much effect in removing the identification. In his latest edition of *Hemingway: The Writer as Artist*, Carlos Baker persists in entitling his chapter on the book "The Waste-landers." Though any number of statements from this chapter could be used to suggest the dogged insistence of its title, I shall pick out but one as provocative and central: "Brett . . . is . . . the reigning queen of a paganized wasteland with a wounded fisher king as her half cynical squire."[1] Perhaps even more arresting is Philip Young's stubborn as-sertion, coming after Hemingway's publication of *A Moveable Feast*, that "despite quite a lot of fun *The Sun Also Rises* is still Hemingway's *Waste Land*, and Jake is Hemingway's Fisher King . . . . once again here is the protagonist gone impotent, and his land gone sterile."[2] Both these critics are equally explicit in deeming the drift of the book a jour-ney to nowhere, a study in futility, and a picture of the Lost Generation. Once again, Young is the more colorful in his attempts to talk around Hemingway's rather furious rejection of that reading:

> Some support for this [Hemingway's] position can be found in the novel it-self. Not quite all the people in it are "lost"—surely Romero is not—and the beauty of the eternal earth is now and then richly evoked. But most of the characters do seem a great deal of the time if not lost then terribly un-sure of their bearings, and few readers have felt the force of Hemingway's intention. The strongest feeling in the book is that for the people in it (and one gets the distinct impression that other people do not matter very much) life is futile, and their motions like the motions of the sun of the title (as it appears to our eyes): endless, circular, and unavailing. Further, for all who

remember what the Preacher said in this well-known Biblical passage, the echo of "Vanity of vanities; all is vanity" is rather loud. Thus what Hemingway proposed to do and what he did again seem two things, but it is doubtful that this hurts the book.[3]

If Young's is a worship of the intentional fallacy carried to the point of martyrdom, a reader may turn to Sheridan Baker's recent chapter on the book to discover a variation on that dedication that denies Hemingway's intention this time on the fact of testicles, not vanity. However Baker's previous devotions to chivalric romance may have aided him in this discovery, his outright refusal of Hemingway's blunt statement that Jake was not emasculated must be read to be believed:

> Testicles and the lack of testicles—an idea Hemingway consistently associates with bullfighting, using the Spanish slang *cojones*—are clearly symbols of power and failure in *The Sun Also Rises.* . . . But whatever Hemingway's private picture of Jake's disfigurement and however that picture may have changed over the years, the similarity of Jake's deprivation to that of a steer is too insistent to be set aside.[4]

On this score—a refining on the *Waste Land* image of the novel by reducing it to a testiculate sunset—a recent critic had seemed to come to my rescue by arguing that, after all, the novel could hardly be called a study in disillusion and despair. In his essay "*Cabestro* and *Vaquilla*: The Symbolic Structure of *The Sun Also Rises*," Dewey Ganzel held that the bullfight rather than Eliot's poem was the proper analogy for the book. Although generally agreeing with him, I must hastily part critical company with Mr. Ganzel when he identifies Jake as a "working steer," calls Cohn, of all people, a fighting bull, and slips Brett into the role of a female fighting bull, the *vaquilla*, all of which seems to me as severely arbitrary an inversion of Hemingway's intentions as any done him by the resolute Wastelanders above.[5]

They are not without my sympathy. For, as F. Scott Fitzgerald so shrewdly observed in the year of the book's appearance, "In the mutilated man I thought Ernest bit off more than can yet be chewn between the covers of a book, then lost his nerve a little and edited the more vitalizing details out. He has since told me that something like this happened."[6] I suspect that Fitzgerald alludes to painfully sexual scenes, originally in the manuscript, revealing Jake's virility and its frustration. Accordingly, beyond removing the *Waste Land* sticker and the badge of futility from the book, I shall also turn to the bullfight, as Mr. Ganzel has done, as the analogy for the novel's structure. But I shall discover Jake, not Cohn, at the center of the book from first to last where, after the manner of a bullfighter, not a *cabestro*, he may be said to dominate the action. Thus, in trying to persuade a new generation that *The Sun Also Rises* still deserves attention on these new grounds, however shrill the objections from Fiedler, Edel, and those Hemingway used to dismiss as his New York critics, I shall open by stressing Hemingway's dislike of Eliot and his *Waste Land* point of view; then offer the alternative that the novel does indeed celebrate this enduring earth of ours, as Hemingway said it did; and finally, stretching matters a bit, take another look at the bullfight as the key to the novel's structure. So then, to the lists.

i

Hemingway's contempt for T. S. Eliot, especially during the years immediately following publication of *The Waste Land*, is immediately apparent in the aspersions implied in the story "Mr. and Mrs. Elliot" which appeared in the *Little Review*'s autumn-winter number for 1924-25. If that slander were not enough, Hemingway had also chosen to make his feelings explicit in 1924 in the October issue of the *Transatlantic Review*. The occasion was a tribute to the recently dead Joseph Conrad. One short passage is instructive:

It is agreed by most of the people I know that Conrad is a bad writer, just as it is agreed that T. S. Eliot is a good writer. If I knew that by grinding Mr. Eliot into a fine powder and sprinkling that powder over Mr. Conrad's grave Mr. Conrad would shortly appear, looking very annoyed at the forced return, and commence writing I would leave for London early tomorrow morning with a sausage grinder.

One should not be funny over the death of a great man, but you cannot couple T. S. Eliot and Joseph Conrad in a sentence seriously. . . .[7]

In later years Hemingway was still able to wisecrack at Eliot's expense, although his contempt seems milder and even good-natured.[8] But with the strong hint of Mr. Elliot's impotence in the notorious story and then the even stronger hint of Mrs. Elliot's resolute Lesbianism, a reader might well expect an equal aversion in the novel. That aversion appears in fact almost at the beginning. Now it is conventional to fix upon Georgette, the little prostitute, and her remark that everyone is sick, as proof that we are indeed being ushered into another instance of the modern *Waste Land*. Yet in truth the little prostitute blithely scorns the homosexuals and affected writers that surround Braddocks—Cohn's, not Jake's, literary companion. In other words, the novel opens by introducing Robert Cohn and then moves on to record Jake's encounter with a literary set that includes Cohn and exhibits many of the traits that Hemingway had so nastily discovered in the Elliots.

Jake's pleading nausea as an excuse to rid himself of queer company is but the beginning of his, and Hemingway's, pointed revulsion against an American literary culture and life that could produce a Mencken, become absorbed in Hudson's *The Purple Land*, and, I would submit, breed a T. S. Eliot. Very little has been said of the fact that the novel from beginning to end is virtually an unrelieved attack on America. The waste land of the novel is a time and place we never see but have dinned into us with unrelieved disdain: the America of Wilson, Bryan, Ford, and Coolidge. More than once we learn that Paris is ruined by American tourists of the Woman's Club variety. Prohibition and its hypocrisy are constantly ragged. We rightly sneer at the pilgrims from Dayton, Ohio, on their way to Lourdes. The American ambassador to Spain is signalled to be the least comprehending of the entire throng watching Romero on the last day. Consequently, at the book's beginning, when locked in the midst of American writers and artists and patrons like the Braddocks, Cohn, and Frances Clyne, with attendant homosexuals in tow, we are not surprised to be introduced to Robert Prentiss, especially when told that "he was from New York by way of Chicago, and was a rising new novelist. He had some sort of an English accent." Thereafter we get the full flavor of his arch, fruity, affected conversation. Any waste land inflicted upon us is American, not Parisian.

Jake too is a writer of sorts, and Bill is a very successful one. Both have a great capacity for love of place and readily admit to being from Chicago and Kansas City. But neither cares to return to America, especially Jake. In fact, the alienated or expatriated American is held up as the true one, while we gather that the so-called good Americans at home are somehow morally at fault. As Bill quips to Jake: "You're an expatriate. You've lost touch with the soil. You get precious." The opposite is the truth. One major theme of the book emerges altogether early then, namely, Jake's love of the earth, in this case the legendary Paris of sunshine, Seine, flowering chestnut trees, and memorials to military courage. This is hardly the Anglo-American world where April is the cruellest month. Later in *The Green Hills of Africa* Hemingway was to make himself explicit on the subject:

> Our people went to America because that was the place to go then. It had been a good country and we had made a bloody mess of it and I would go, now, somewhere else as we had always had the right to go somewhere else and as we had always gone. You could always come back. Let the others come to America who did not know that they had come too late. Our people had seen it at its best and fought for it when it was well worth fighting for. Now I would go somewhere else.[9]

With this heavy criticism of America, its childishness and naiveté personified in Cohn, the arrested adolescent, and his literary crowd, we are ushered into the real antidote to Eliot's *Waste Land*—the Paris of the Twenties—and its actuality, the grim fastness of distant America.

Finally, if we scrutinize Jake in his newly discovered America of the European continent, we must recognize how very unlike any Fisher King he is. In the first place, he is virile, not sterile, nor even a psychological victim, as Hemingway has been at great anatomical pains to explain. Setting off to work in Paris at the beginning of Chapter V, Jake cannot record enough of the many morning sights, smells, and sensations that delight him in his fair city, unlike Eliot's City man gloomily crossing London Bridge, coming or going to his despised bank. As the opposite of the Fisher King, Tiresias, or the generally solemn, weary, slightly deracinated and highly literary voice of *The Waste Land*, Jake, as every critic comments, has courage and friendliness a plenty with common sense to match them. But I would go further by noting his generally good spirits and ability to laugh that rise so easily to the generally hilarious Bill and Mike. But he also harbors another quality singularly missing in Eliot's Fisher King—Jake is a fighter. As Brett explains, "You've a hell of a biblical name, Jake." He does indeed. He wrestles with life. There is nothing passive or foredoomed about him. Moreover, unlike Eliot and the Tiresias of his poem, Jake is an extremely humble man, a trait summed up in his admission to Brett that "Nobody ever knows anything." He is also a just man, forged in the disaster of the Great War, the great injustice that lies behind the book. As Hemingway once wrote, "Writers are forged in injustice as a sword is forged."[10] Like Bill, Jake is extremely sensitive to the injustice done to a Negro boxer in Vienna; he is acutely aware, as a newsman, of the difficulties of getting a true story; he won't compromise events or the telling of them, even the story of how Lady Brett came to her desperate condition. Best of all, the War has taught him impartiality—even during his jealous hatred of Cohn he admits to the man's finer qualities.

Hemingway held that the great crime of war—"Never think that war, no matter how necessary, nor how justified, is not a crime"[11]—might nevertheless teach us that virtue of impartiality. As he wrote at the conclusion of World War II:

> We have come out of the time when obedience, the acceptance of discipline, intelligent courage and resolution were most important into that more difficult time when it is a man's duty to understand his world rather than simply fight for it.
>
> To understand we must study. We must study not simply what we wish to believe. That will always be skillfully presented for us. We must try to examine our world with the impartiality of a physician. This will be hard work and will involve reading much that is unpleasant to accept. But it is one of man's first duties now.[12]

Jake comes very close, in his striving to understand the new world, to that impartiality of a physician rather than to the bias of a literary doctor. His exuberant fishing, his physical maiming and psychological health, his religionless Catholicism, his love of the sun's rising rather than any implied setting, all make him very nearly a direct answer to Eliot's essentially Protestant, urban, hectoring Anglo-American Brahman.

ii

On the score of Gertrude Stein's remark, "You are all a lost generation," one may only ceaselessly repeat that Hemingway has sworn again and again that his novel was written to counter the idea of his generation's being more lost than any other. One of Hotchner's cranked-up Hemingway conversations shows his objection to be actually a commonplace, lifted as it is from several unacknowledged sources:

That passage from Ecclesiastes, that sound lost? . . . Look, Gertrude was a complainer. So she labeled that generation with her complaint. . . . Nobody I knew at that time thought of himself as wearing the silks of the Lost Generation, or had even heard the label. We were a pretty solid mob. The characters in *Sun Also Rises* were tragic, but the real hero was the earth and you get the sense of its triumph in abiding forever.[13]

In *A Moveable Feast*, Hemingway devoted a whole chapter to mulling over Miss Stein's phrase. While admitting, with Ney's statue in mind (it also appears in the novel), that "all generations were lost by something and always had been and always would be," Hemingway's predominant sentiment in the chapter is caught in his reflection, "I thought of Miss Stein and Sherwood Anderson and egotism and mental laziness versus discipline and I thought who is calling who a lost generation?" However vicious or warmhearted Hemingway could be about Gertrude Stein, the point I wish to make here has been thoroughly overlooked. No matter how much anger Harold Loeb experienced on being the actual model for Cohn—and the vulgarity of *The Way it Was* seems to have underscored the likeness—an even closer literary resemblance would seem to be that of the fictional Cohn and Hemingway's perverse portrait of the sham Miss Stein.

Cohn, as all agree, is a pretty hopeless case. He is really a boy, at best a man formed by women who weeps easily and has nonsensical ideas about titled ladies, sportsmanship, and the worth of W. H. Hudson. He doesn't drink to speak of, doesn't like Paris or fishing or bullfights, lacks breeding, is full of literary pretensions. Worst of all, he is pronouncedly a restless man, a creature who even took an inner pleasure in getting his nose flattened at Princeton, in fact, for all his bravado, a man who while sensitive to insult almost seeks it out so that he may suffer in public. In a word, he is selfish. Hemingway at the end of his life summed up his disgust with this combination of self-seeking and the hedonism that it feeds upon in these words:

The untiring search for personal pleasure is selfishness in action. Self-exaggeration, egotism, pride, self-righteousness, self-justification and mock modesty are but branches of the tree of selfishness, whose roots run in all directions, crossing, recrossing and intertwining one another in the clay soil of personal self. Jealousy is the most insane phase of human selfishness. It is born of a selfish fear of loss or of being personally displaced by something or somebody.[14]

This appears to me to be a close résumé, abstractly speaking, of Robert Cohn, even in the matter of his frenzy over Brett's attentions to Romero, when Cohn himself admits that he must have been insane. On this concept of what might be called philosophical selfishness I would pin Cohn's resemblance to Gertrude Stein.

For it is Cohn himself who believes that his generation is liable to pass, lost to glory, and that the earth itself won't abide unless one personally seizes it. At the book's beginning Hemingway carefully distinguishes Jake and Cohn on this subject of self-concern. Jake reacts with ironic amaze at such of Cohn's plaints as "I can't stand to think my life is going so fast and I'm not really living it" or "Listen, Jake. . . . don't you ever get the feeling that all your life is going by and you're not taking advantage of it? Do you realize that you've lived nearly half the time you have to live already?" or, expectedly, "Do you know that in about thirty-five years more we'll be dead?" All these wails exemplify fear, egotism, and hedonism—but mostly fear.

Both Stein and Cohn had many fine qualities, as Hemingway repeatedly tells us. That in a sense—their being "so awful and so nice"—is why both seem such great wastes as Hemingway presents them. Both fall into an affectation of deserving merit. Neither seems to have recovered in Hemingway's eyes. At one juncture in *The Green Hills of Africa*, Gertrude Stein is condemned for having gone to pot,[15] precisely the process that Hemingway fixes on Cohn. Notoriously, the three chapters devoted to Miss Stein in *A Moveable Feast* expose her homosexuality and laziness, her hard ambition and jealousy of other writers, her lost or wasted womanhood transformed from peasant beauty to sybarite Roman emperor. The dimensions of Cohn's special perversity are far more subtle, but we sense their presence early when he rejects a bullfighter's life as an abnormal one and thus excludes himself like Gertrude Stein from life's feast. So does their itch to theorize about life and literature, an itch that clearly aligns Cohn with the male steers and makes Stein seem doubtfully feminine. Hemingway wrote in 1924: "As I have always regarded critics as the eunuchs of literature . . . But there is no use in finishing that sentence. . . . Did you, however, ever see a bull which has withstood the bad sticking of the matador, led off to the corrals by three thin steers?"[16] The answer, of course, is yes, but the point is that brave bulls and genuine writers ought to carry through, despite the critics. But Cohn and Stein did not. They lacked courage. If his fragile masculinity is redolent of the Princeton gym and the barber shop, Cohn's behavior like hers seems to be pleadingly masochistic. So much so that after levelling all about him, including for the moment Romero, Cohn is reduced to tears and bewails to Jake, of all people, his great love and the hell he has been put through. He then jumps to the rather unusual conclusion—generally settled on Jake and Hemingway—that nothing in this dreary world is of any use.

Hemingway had labeled one chapter in *A Moveable Feast* "Miss Stein Instructs." He might have just as maliciously labeled this scene "Mr. Cohn Instructs." In one fantastic parody of his break with Miss Stein, Hemingway spoofed the whole affair by blaming it on an act of near-violence done him by her maid, who had her orders from Miss Stein.[17] Here of course Jake's break with Cohn repeats that exaggeration as the real thing. In both cases jealousy was the motive. In any event, part of Miss Stein's going to pot Hemingway caught in the ease with which she passed out labels like "You are all a lost generation," or, in his fantasy account, "All you young men are alike." In Cohn Hemingway has made an excruciating study of just the reverse of these slogans, of a man who is a lost one and, unlike other men of his generation, ironic proof of Miss Stein's claim, even, I'm afraid, a way of directing the slur back to her and those who made her, if not her whole generation.

iii

But the tragedy of the novel is not wasted on the lost ones like Cohn and, I would imply, Stein. No, the tragedy belongs to those who truly love the earth and share in its death, though they endure in our minds for their love of it and turn the tragedy into a joyful, affectionate thing. For everywhere in *The Sun Also Rises* the earth is celebrated in her living and dying. In Paris we dote over the quintessence of its products—fine foods, vintage wines, Negro jazz, the movement of barges over the Seine, the glory of a Paris morning, the breeze that cools Jake's torments, even the courtesy of a count who has survived its savage wars. In Spain the earth's presence is even more dramatic. The fiesta itself arises traditionally and explosively from the rural ways and lives of those who flock in devotion and gaiety to it, the apex, explanation or apology for their lives. The mile after mile of dusty road, the icy trout streams, windswept plains, sudden rains and torrid suns underwrite the grapes, bulls, music and men, and assure their life in their continued destruction. This is the scene Cohn sleeps through. Neither grape nor bull nor trout stream nor dance means much to him, a nearsighted man in more than one way.

Hence, in taking this tragedy of the earth as Hemingway's acknowledged subject, as opposed to any idea of being especially lost, we may expect to be instructed in this love of an enduring though periodically dying earth. Hemingway's term is the Spanish word *afición*, which he defined in *Death in the Afternoon* as " . . . love of bullfights. It also means the entire bullring public, but is usually used in the generic sense to denote the most intelligent part of the public." In the novel he simply calls it passion. To be an *aficionado*, as he goes on to explain, is to know bullfighting and for that reason to be devoted to it.

Hemingway had long held to this creed of the intelligent heart. Towards the end of his life he was explicit in saying, "The heart is the noblest part of human nature. And the affections are the noblest ingredient in human nature."[18] This saintly creed may well recall St. Firminus I, a native of Pamplona, who achieved his martyrdom in the third century and had his feast celebrated, in the manner Hemingway depicts, from the 12th century on.[19] Though the saint was noted as a missionary and preacher of the gospel in the remoter areas of heathen France, the devotions of Hemingway's celebrants are pagan. Thus, despite a good deal of speculation on the different faces offered by Jake and Brett at the church door, Hemingway's own account of the festival in 1924 certainly reinforces the religionless Catholicism or pious paganism of the event:

> There are six bull fights during the Feria and Fiesta of San Firmin. San Firmin is the local deity in the system of local idolatry which the Spaniards substitute for catholicism. San Firmin, looking very much like Buddha, is carried through the streets at odd moments during the Feria.[20]

I submit then that the passions of the heart and man's affection for other men initiated into the mysteries of the earth's diurnal round comprise the religious center of a book where *aficion* is finally attested to by the laying on of hands among the adept—one of whom is the American Jake Barnes. With the onset of seven nights and days of celebration, it is right that Jake should experience a sudden unreality, imagine himself elevated into a realm void of consequences. The cry of the natives—"Hurray for wine! hurray for the Foreigners!"—articulates his exhilaration. For he is summoned to a conviviality that aims at a brotherhood where the grape dissolves any exigencies of time and space.

For that matter, Brett's being denied entrance to the church need not underline her supposed Circe nature—that highfalutin moniker fixed on her by the literary Mr. Cohn—since no sharp division is made between the reverential darkness of the church interior and the jubilant street where Brett is garlanded and set up as an image for singing and dancing men awaiting the return of a religious procession that transports San Firmin ecstatically from church to church. In spite of her later plaint, "I'm damned bad for a religious atmosphere . . . I've got the wrong kind of face," Brett in her happiness reaffirms a faith that can include rather than exclude the supposedly narrow, doctrinal Catholicism she is said to eschew. What's more, Jake, the religious center of the book—and the center of every other theme—astounds or should astound those who smell in Brett a whiff of sacrilege. For Jake prays, as an *aficionado* should, for his friends, for the bullfighters, for himself, for money, for successful fishing and a good fiesta, and so forth. Jake finally concludes that he is not being very religious. But he truly is, for by the covenant insinuated in the book, like Brett's his passion is for the heightened life of earth worshipped with awe in both bull ring and church.

An accidental death is our reminder. If the earth has taken Jake's capacity for sexual consummation from him, so also has it taken life heedlessly from Vicente Girones. This set piece, justly celebrated for its impersonal joining of all the elements of the fiesta—from Romero's brilliant killing to Brett's impulsive affair with him—offers without comment a sacrificial victim to the earth in a rite more pagan than Christian. He had been a married farmer with two children. He had returned to the fiesta year after year until his sudden death running with the bulls. Despite the widow and children on the train bringing the coffin home, Hemingway allows us to imagine the permanence that such apparently gratuitous misery underlines: "The train started with a jerk, and then ran smoothly, going downgrade around the edge of the plateau and out into the fields of grain that blew in the wind on the plain on the way to Tafalla." So too, as I shall maintain, the tragic eventualities in the pattern of the bullfight—the supreme running with the bulls— enhance the inevitable loss that the earth demands in abiding forever. That the ear of a bull, killer of Girones, victim of Romero, should end in Jake's handkerchief jammed in a drawer with cigarette stubs is a no less symbolic affirmation of the fact that love must also end but never finish.

We must turn, then, to the bullfight to grasp the essential affirmation that I have been holding up as a non-Christian counter to the idea that the book offers only the trivial misery of a lost generation or the religious condemnation of a waste land presided over by a faithless and impotent fisher king.

iv

Hemingway makes the point both in this novel and in *Death in the Afternoon* that there is no Spanish word for bullfight. The term used—*corrida de toros*—means running with the bulls, and to run well with the bulls requires a kind of courage that finds its opposite in the antics of Robert Cohn. Hemingway himself once wrote, "Courage is only another name for faith."[21] When the best bulls and men confront each other in the bull ring, the faith or confidence displayed makes the encounter a tragedy—the bull must die—yet also a rebellion against any threat of death, a sentiment Romero utters decisively in Brett's presence before his major performance: "I'm never going to die." In almost the same utterance, he boasts, "The bulls are my best friends." I take these claims to illustrate Hemingway's more explicit belief spelled out later in *Death in the Afternoon*:

> . . . rarely will a great artist with the cape and muleta be a killer. A great killer must love to kill; unless he feels it is the best thing he can do, unless he is conscious of its dignity and feels that it is its own reward, he will be incapable of the abnegation that is necessary in real killing. The truly great killer must have a sense of honor and a sense of glory far beyond that of the ordinary bullfighter. . . . he must have a spiritual enjoyment of the moment of killing. . . . One of its greatest pleasures . . . is the feeling of rebellion against death which comes from its administering. Once you accept the rule of death thou shalt not kill is an easily and a naturally obeyed com-

mandment. But when a man is still in rebellion against death he has pleasure in taking to himself one of the Godlike attributes; that of giving it. This is one of the most profound feelings in those men who enjoy killing. These things are done in pride, and pride, of course, is a Christian sin, and a pagan virtue. But it is pride which makes the bullfight and true enjoyment of killing which makes the great matador.[22]

This rebellion against death, along with a pagan pride in killing that makes the bull's tragedy dependent on the matador's honor and the crowd's passion, demands an air of aloofness, imprinted on all of Hemingway's great bullfighters, combined with an intense local identification signaled by Montoya's disgust with Romero's gadding about with international drunks, a titled English lady, and possibly the American ambassador. Spirited human intelligence and skill pitted against pure animal courage make running with the bulls at best an ancient, traditional, indigenous, epic endeavor binding the Spanish earth into a unified landscape of animal passion, human purpose, and organic rhythm which no amount of temporary human misery can violate. This near-epic unity is glanced at openly when charged landscape after charged landscape is unfurled before us, combining, after the manner of Cézanne, an insistent geometry of land, beasts, and men in the bracing air of rural coincidence:

Looking back we could see the country spread out below. Far back the fields were squares of green and brown on the hillsides. Making the horizon were the brown mountains. They were strangely shaped. . . . Then the road came over the crest, flattened out, and went into a forest. It was a forest of cork oaks, and the sun came through the trees in patches, and there were cattle grazing back in the trees. . . . As we came to the edge of the rise we saw the red roofs and white houses of Burguete ahead strung out on the plain, and away off on the shoulder of the first dark mountain was the gray metal-sheathed roof of the monastery of Roncesvalles.

"There's Roncevaux," I said.

"Where?"

"Way off there where the mountain starts."

"It's cold up here," Bill said.

"It's high," I said. "It must be twelve hundred metres."

"It's awful cold," Bill said.

Here I submit is the epitome of Spanish landscape—high, cold and near the epic site Roncevaux—a fitting memorial to the courageous faith behind a mask of aloof coldness that recalls a Roland, matures a Romero, and, as I shall try to argue, sits lightly beneath the friendly exterior of Jake Barnes. This enduring earth, then, this continuous running of brave bulls and men through centuries of Spanish soil, has about it for Hemingway the hint of holy ground, so that the peasant-centered fiesta can be the very antidote to Eliot's prescriptive verses condemning an unreal City, London's financial district, the capital of world usury. Nor can St. Mary Woolnoth's, the banker's church, offer the refuge of the Spanish countryside or the certainties and sparkle of Hemingway's springtime in Paris. The earth becomes the hero, as Hemingway claimed. Eliot's City languishes for just such holiness, unaided even by memories of Essex, Magnus Martyr, and Conrad's Marlow.

His own love of countryside and people has long been an open secret in Hemingway lore. We are not surprised to find him writing explicitly, "I have loved country all my life; the country was always better than the people. I could only care about a very few at a time."[23] Like the heady delicacy of Paris, the Spanish earth—more tragic, less self-conscious—joins in Hemingway's nostalgic celebration of an all but vanished America. Bill and Jake can still marvel at the fiesta as it dramatizes totally the life and death of significant country. Packed with peasants in black, the "solid and unbroken fiesta" absorbs all who approach it. Even on the last day, distraught Americans, gaping English, Mike's creditors, government officials, the wanderers of all nations are caught up in its saturnalia with the vaunted tragedy of the bull ring and the martyrdom of St. Firminus at its center. This is the stuff for the

American writer who has chosen not to return home, the density of felt life that those critics who carp about expatriate removal from reality— "you're not in touch with the soil"—have missed in *The Sun Also Rises*. Writing of Elio Vittorini's experience of Italy, Hemingway in 1949 contrasted such a writer's evocation of Sicily through its rainfall with those New York critics' abstract grasp of America or Italy, and, in angrily forcing the contrasts, clarifies his American love of the myriad Spanish earth:

> . . . Vittorini from the time he was old enough to leave home without per-mission at seventeen learned his native Italy in the same way American boys who ran away from home learned their own country.
>
> The Italy that he learned and the America that the American boys learned has little to do with the Academic Italy or America that periodi-cally attacks all writing like a dust storm and is always, until everything shall be completely dry, dispersed by rain.
>
> Rain to an academician is probably, after the first fall has cleared the air, H_2O with, of course, traces of other things. To a good writer, needing something to bring the dry country alive so that it will not be a desert where only such cactus as New York literary reviews grow dry and sad, inexistent without the watering of their benefactors, feeding on the dried manure of schism and the dusty taste of disputed dialectics, their only flowering a desiccated criticism as alive as stuffed birds, and their steady mulch the de-hydrated cuds of fellow critics; such a writer finds rain to be made of knowledge, experience, wine, bread, salt, vinegar, bed, early mornings, nights, days, the sea, men, women, dogs, beloved motor cars, bicycles, hills and valleys, the appearance and disappearance of trains on straight and curved tracks, love, honor and disobey, music, chamber music and chamber pots, negative and positive Wassermanns, the arrival and non-arrival of expected munitions and/or reinforcements, replacements or your brother. All these are part of rain to a good writer. . . .
>
> In this book the rain you get is Sicily.[24]

The Spanish earth, like the rain in Sicily, was to become during the Spanish Civil War proof positive that the American dead of the Lincoln Battalion would be immortal. Hemingway's later pronouncement on their continued life echoes the passage above on the mystical substance of rain. It also highlights his devotions to Spanish countryside and its yearly fiesta, his announced master theme of the novel: human tragedy on an earth that endures forever:

> The dead sleep cold in Spain tonight and they will sleep cold all this winter as the earth sleeps with them. But in the spring the rain will come to make the earth kind again. The wind will blow soft over the hills from the south. The black trees will come to life with small green leaves, and there will be blossoms on the apple trees along the Jarama River. This spring the dead will feel the earth beginning to live again.
>
> For our dead are a part of the earth of Spain now and the earth of Spain can never die. Each winter it will seem to die and each spring it will come alive again. Our dead will live with it forever.
>
> Just as the earth can never die, neither will those who have ever been free return to slavery. The peasants who work the earth where our dead lie know what these dead died for. There was time during the war for them to learn these things, and there is forever for them to remember them in.
>
> Our dead live in the hearts and minds of the Spanish peasants, of the Spanish workers, of all the good, simple, honest people who believed in and fought for the Spanish republic. And as long as all our dead live in the Spanish earth, and they will live as long as the earth lives, no system of tyranny ever will prevail in Spain.
>
> The fascists may spread over the land, blasting their way with weight of metal brought from other countries. They may advance aided by traitors and by cowards. They may destroy cities and villages and try to hold the people in slavery. But you cannot hold any people in slavery.
>
> The Spanish people will rise again as they have always risen before against tyranny.
>
> The dead do not need to rise. They are a part of the earth now and the

earth can never be conquered. For the earth endureth forever. It will outlive all systems of tyranny.

Those who have entered it honorably, and no men ever entered earth more honorably than those who died in Spain, already have achieved immortality.[25]

As a matter of fact, Hemingway came to see those American dead in Spain as joined with those others who fought in our own Civil War.[26]

Thus the tragedy of the bull ring, stemming from the strength and virtues of the Spanish landscape, concentrates the tragedy of Jake and his friends, a tragedy comprehensible to the initiated, whether from Italy, America, Africa or wherever—wherever being those specific locales ranged over the world that Hemingway loved and, metaphorically, claimed as his lost America. Jake Barnes takes his place in a pantheon of American heroes, that includes Robert Jordan, a precisionist from even farther west than Kansas City, who act out Hemingway's rediscovery of his native land. Like those later veterans of Spain, Jake does his duty like the airman he once was. The same may be said on a more mystical level of Romero, if one keeps in mind the demands of the traditional bullfight audience. In neither case does death in the ring or in bed prevail. For in *The Sun Also Rises*, America and Spain, Jake and Romero, join hands on the Spanish earth to outlast that threat. Hemingway seldom made the point more clearly—tragedy's exultation over death, the daily drama of Jake and Romero—than when he wrote:

It was a saying of Milton that, "Who best can suffer, best can do." The work of many of the greatest men, inspired by duty, has been done amidst suffering and trial and difficulty. They have struggled against the tide and reached the shore exhausted, only to grasp the sand and expire. They have done their duty and been content to die. But death has no power over such men; their hallowed memories still survive to soothe us.[27]

V

What is the structure of this tragedy—or perhaps I should say this life of earth or bull ring with its tragedy always imbedded and awaiting us? If it cannot be the circular, futile thing, that critics lead us to believe, and if the tragedy itself is a much more joyous, pagan thing than any Christian lament over the lacrimae rerum might allow, then the bull ring must be the test of any new theory of structure. Since it lies at the center of the book, I shall argue that its drama is the drama of the novel.

According to Hemingway, bullfighting demonstrates man's dominance over animals, the bull being one of the most formidable. Hemingway goes so far as to picture the final third of the contest, the faena, in terms of religious and tragic ecstasy:

> . . . the faena that takes a man out of himself and makes him feel immortal while it is proceeding, that gives him an ecstasy that is, while momentary, as profound as any religious ecstasy; moving all the people in the ring together and increasing in emotional intensity as it proceeds, carrying the bullfighter with it, he playing on the crowd through the bull and being moved as it responds in a growing ecstasy of ordered, formal, passionate, increasing disregard for death that leaves you, when it is over, and the death administered to the animal that has made it possible, as empty, as changed and as sad as any major emotion will leave you.[28]

Such emotion, I hope to show, lies close to the feeling Hemingway rouses at the end of *The Sun Also Rises*. It is not a feeling of futility, for all its sadness. Alive, Jake is increasingly superior in the last portion of the novel to the death of his own sexual power. Overwhelmed increasingly by the animalism all around him, he nevertheless prevails and dominates as a man. Let us contemplate his persistent domination of the book.

Jake is no bullfighter. He kills no one. Nor had Hemingway written *Death in the Afternoon*, the source of my recent quotations, until some years after this novel. Nevertheless, in October 1923, he published news stories in the *Toronto Star* on both bullfighting and Pamplona, obvious sources for his fiction as was so much of his journalism during those years. Dwelling upon the ancient, pagan, and tragic origins of the spectacle in both articles, he offers to explain in the first the structure of the fight. He insists that it is not to be confused with sport. Instead, "It is a tragedy. A very great tragedy. The tragedy is the death of the bull. It is played in three definite acts." Hemingway goes on to explain each of the acts, all together a tragedy that "symbolizes the struggle between man and beasts" where vulgarity is the worst sin a bullfighter can commit. In the first the bull arrives promptly met by picadors defending their mounts with lances. The horses are gone in the second act; the matador places the banderillas which, if correctly planted, further confuse the bull and slow him down. The third act promises the death of the bull, the chore of the matador, who has actually been in command since the opening of hostilities in the first act. His killing must be perfect. With the time and place of the sword thrust rigidly prescribed, the matador must constantly dominate the bull by close work with the muleta right down to the killing. Summing up matters in this first article, Hemingway wrote of the matador: "He must be proficient in all three acts of the fight. In the first he uses the cape and does veronicas and protects the picadors by taking the bull out and away from them when they are spilled to the ground. In the second act he plants the banderillos. In the third act he masters the bull with the muleta and kills him."[29] As Hemingway was to elaborate in *Death in the Afternoon*, all the bull's likely victories occur in the first act, considered the trial. Thereafter he faces sentencing in the second act and execution in the third. The drift is both preordained and non-Anglo-Saxon. The great requirements are bright sunshine and a windless day, hardly the concomitants, say, of *Lear*, *Hamlet*, or for that matter *The Waste Land*.

I shall not claim, as has Dewey Ganzel, that Cohn must be considered the bull if this scheme is to fit the novel—although he is stupidly dangerous when, like the bulls in Pamplona, we find him isolated from his companions. Nor, if you choose to cast Cohn in the role of the fighting bull, could he be said to make much of a fight of the book. Unlike the ideal, vicious, fearless, fighting bull, Cohn has little breeding, less bravery, and no proximity to the wolf, Hemingway's analogue for such a bull. Nevertheless, Jake has a formidable enough opponent, which he dominates like a good matador at the risk of his manhood and without inflicting needless pain.

I speak of the totally bad form, to one degree or another the poor faith, in the long run the collective animality—attractive, vicious, magnificent, and irrational—exhibited by Jake's friends. The bull is, so to speak, the undeterred compulsions of those friends. Their tragedy is imaginatively like that of the bull—an irrational, determined, even deliberate charge into dissolution maddened by the impetus of the War. By contrast, Hemingway insists in Jake that the ultimate dissolution of bull, man or earth must be met with style, cheerfulness, control, and even artistically bestowed indifference. Playing this role as close to his companions as love will allow, Jake's countering them gives their tragedy significance.

How then does this tripartite structure of the bullfight match up imaginatively with the three sections of the novel? Though the likeness isn't perfectly exact, the parallels exist in a rough but startling way. Just as the bullfight is a series of downhill actions for the bull, with the matador hopefully looking better and better—Hemingway saw the bull moving through three stages, lofty, slowed, and leaden—so during the three sections of the book Jake's friends are brought to a virtual standstill. Cohn, Brett, Mike, even to some extent Bill, isolated in their baffled desires become more and more dangerous because at the same time more and more ashamed, abandoned, busted or exhausted until they are brought around, humanized or politely dismissed by the quietly resolute Jake. Thus in the first book, and perhaps beyond to include the arrival of Bill and Mike before the departure for Spain, animalism seems to triumph on all sides. Even Robert Cohn finds himself a success at cards, a published novelist of a bad book, and very much the possessive and deserving swain of a titled lady, who at the end has agreed to go off with him to San Sebastian. Brett, though in love with Jake and miserable for keeping this tryst from him—the refrain of the last song they dance to is "Don't Two Time Me"—quite successfully inflicts her unintentional cruelties on him. She stands Jake up, bedazzles the Count, runs off with Cohn, and returns with Mike in tow. Nor is Mike as gentle or thoughtful as we might have expected, harping drunkenly before Jake on Brett's sexual attractiveness. Even Bill, befuddled as he is when we first meet him at the beginning of Book II, holds forth on the subject with more than enough insistence. Minor figures, too, like Frances Clyne, Harvey Stone, the Braddockses, and the American tourists give Jake sore moments. However, although a few horses are nicked, like Jake's concierge the first time she meets Brett, and the patronne's daughter after her run-in with Georgette, Jake manages to keep his entourage off each other and himself by a combination of skillful dodges, compassionate understanding, as with Brett and Harvey Stone, and iron determination to get on with his own work. In fact, for all their confused verve and mad comings and goings, Jake quietly dominates them by seeming not to. He has even made out the itinerary for Spain, when all in good humor leap off for the fiesta, knowing they will be in touch with each other, thanks to Jake's painstaking.

The explosion of the fiesta at Pamplona corresponds to the increased confusion of all but Jake, although he is harried enough. As the matador brings out the best in a bull by placing the banderillas right, so Jake attempts to bring out the best in his friends—what more conducive to deep-felt friendship than a fiesta?—yet each act of friendship also goads the jealousy, the disgust, the false heroics, the sluttishness in, respectively, Mike, Bill, Cohn, and Brett. Jake *intends* nothing of the sort. But in keeping with my analogy, a reader senses that Jake quickly faces the inevitable, the compulsive nature of their behavior and so in humoring them along unaffectedly draws them out, even tires them and himself in fighting his delaying action—Roncevaux again—

where only he and perhaps Bill hold on. In one famous passage, Bill inadvertently hints that Jake's role is that of the unfortunate friend-making steers. In another Mike accuses Cohn of being a steer—hanging around when he's not wanted. But Jake is no steer, and Cohn's unmanly dependence is but the worst part of a collective animality that knocks Jake off his feet. Old Jake, the human punching bag, as Bill dubs him, nevertheless gets on his feet again and is left standing with Cohn run off to Paris in shame, Brett in bed with Romero, and Mike in general disgrace. Jake himself has been called a pimp, is out of favor with Montoya, and has been knocked silly. Such are the rewards for enlivening the existence of his friends—the bulls. We are ready for the last act, the faena.

In the third book, out of Pamplona, Jake does more than hold on. Although Mike is left to live on credit and Bill drifts off, the challenge of animality however weakened remains dangerous and unpredictable in Brett's call for help. Quelling now the beast in himself, Jake gallantly returns to Spain. Like the matador at one with the bull at the moment of the kill, he seeks Brett out and brings her away. At the close of the novel he may well retort to her thought at what might have been, "Isn't it pretty to think so," but at this expected halt in traffic we not only realize that their life can be no different, we are also persuaded that the traffic will move on, that Jake will come to Brett's rescue again, and that their meeting then, as at the book's beginning, will be repeated. So the earth turns, the earth Jake loves, the earth that breeds such people and such bulls—vicious, simple, hostile, grand—but Jake has braved them and will brave and love again. He brings out the best in his friends, if we consider the entire course of his running with them, while Cohn the boxer brought out the worst.

vi

These considerations lead me to a no less audacious conclusion. Namely that *The Sun Also Rises* is a novel of sculptured masses, the phrase and configuration which delighted Hemingway in the bull ring, here seen in a series of mounting dangers which Jake faces without flinching, gifted, as he is, as an American who believes that death is a friend, since it is the only thing a man may be certain of.[30] Like the bullfighters he praises at the book's beginning, he too lives his life up to the hilt. The French and the English, who do not always show up well in the novel, contrast with Jake. They, the life-lovers, the animal-lovers, the gold-sniffers, the real fantastics at Pamplona, lack Jake's keen thought, yes, intellectual respectability, grounded as his actions are on the certainty of death. To write of Hemingway that " . . . nowhere in Hemingway's work does there glimmer even the faintest suggestion that one's life can be ordered by thought, or that it is at all desirable to attempt such an offering. . . . the Hemingway hero lacks the intellectual resources to achieve a distance from his suffering, to contemplate it, and to learn something from it fundamental about himself"[31]—to write thus, or to parrot Yeats and claim that "Jake lacks much conviction,"[32] is tacitly to conceive of the novel as at best an understated, ironic, pur-gatorial rendition of *The Waste Land*. Little more than bumptious hu-mor, a stiff upper lip, the code hero of the Twenties, or an anatomy of society patently lifted from *Huckleberry Finn* can be the stale rewards for such a reading. On the other hand, to remember Hemingway's re-mark that Descartes was unduly sanguine "when he wrote in the seven-teenth century, 'Good sense is, of all things among men, the most equally distributed'"[33] or that "the world of a man's life is, for the most part, the world of his thoughts"[34] may help fix the dimensions of Jake Barnes that I have been urging: a man of common sense indeed but also a man whose devotion to the bull ring has taught him the value of cou-rageous rationality, a trait he exhibits with increasing intensity as he moves through his turbulent heavens—fishing, reading, writing, cheer-ful and friendly concern for his fellows—in a preordained dying world. His thoughts, doubts, judgments and intellection triumph over the equally precious animalism that has been his tormentor, main spring and personal tragedy. As with Romero in the ring, Jake's manner and thought are one since the earth does endure forever.

Notes

1. *Hemingway: The Artist as Writer* (Princeton: Princeton University Press, 1963), 3rd ed., p. 90.

2. *Ernest Hemingway: A Reconsideration* (University Park: Pennsylvania State University Press, 1966), pp. 87-88.

3. *Ibid.*, p. 87n.

4. *Ernest Hemingway: An Introduction and Interpretation* (New York: Holt, Rinehart & Winston, 1967), pp. 50-51. For Hemingway's statement that Jake's "testicles were intact and not damaged," see George Plimpton's interview in *Writers at Work, Second Series* (New York: Viking, 1965), p. 230.

5. "*Cabestro* and *Vaquilla*: The Symbolic Structure of *The Sun Also Rises*," *Sewanee Review*, LXXVI (Winter 1968), 26-48.

6. *The Letters of F. Scott Fitzgerald*, ed. Andrew Turnbull (New York: Scribners, 1963), p. 205.

7. "Conrad, Optimist and Moralist," *By-Line: Ernest Hemingway*, ed. William White (New York: Scribners, 1967), pp. 132-33.

8. See for instance *Death in the Afternoon*, pp. 139-40, and *A Moveable Feast*, pp. 110-13.

9. *The Green Hills of Africa*, p. 285.

10. *Ibid.*, p. 71.

11. "Foreword," *Treasury for the Free World*, ed. Ben Raeburn (New York: Arco, 1946), p. xv.

12. *Ibid.*, p. xiii.

13. *Papa Hemingway* (New York: Random House, 1966), pp. 49-50.

14. "Advice to a Young Man," *Playboy*, XI (January 1964), 227.

15. *The Green Hills of Africa*, pp. 65-66.

16. "New York," *Transatlantic Review*, I (May 1924), 355.

17. "My Own Life," *The New Yorker Scrapbook* (Garden City, N.Y.: Doubleday, Doran, 1931), pp. 156-57.

18. *Playboy*, 225.

19. Rev. Alban Butler, *The Lives of the Saints*, rev. by Herbert Thurston and Donald Attwater, IX (London, 1934), p. 310.

20. "Pamplona Letter," *Transatlantic Review*, II (September 1924), 301.

21. *Playboy*, 225.

22. *Death in the Afternoon*, pp. 232-33.

23. *The Green Hills of Africa*, p. 66.

24. "Introduction" to Elio Vittorini, *In Sicily* (New York: New Directions, 1949), n.p.

25. "On the American Dead in Spain," *Somebody Had to Do Something: A Memorial to James Phillips Lardner* (Los Angeles, 1939), pp. 4-5.

26. "The Last Commander and Unpublished Letters," *American Dialog*, I (October-November 1964), 10.

27. *Playboy*, 227.

28. *Death in the Afternoon*, pp. 206-07.

29. "Bull Fighting a Tragedy," *By-Line: Ernest Hemingway*, pp. 97-98.

30. *Death in the Afternoon*, p. 66.

31. Robert Evans, "Hemingway and the Pale Cast of Thought," *American Literature*, XXXVIII (1966), 168.

32. David Fuchs, "Ernest Hemingway, Literary Critic," *American Literature*, XXXVI (1965), 447.

33. Mary Hemingway, "Life with Papa," *Flair*, II (January 1951), 116.

34. *Playboy*, 226.

Hemingway's Morality of Compensation_____

Scott Donaldson

Books should be about the people you know, that you love and hate, not about the people you study up about. If you write them truly they will have all the economic implications a book can hold.[1]

—Ernest Hemingway

I

While voyaging back to the United States in 1833, Ralph Waldo Emerson puzzled over a definition of morals. His thoughts, he admitted in his journal, were "dim and vague," but one might obtain "some idea of them . . . who develops the doctrine in his own experience that nothing can be given or taken without an equivalent."[2] In Emerson's sublime optimism, he weighted the scales of equivalence in favor of the taker. Only the half-blind, as he observes in his essay on "The Tragic," had never beheld the House of Pain, which like the salt sea encroached on man in his felicity. But felicity was man's customary state, for he lived on the land, not at sea. If pain disturbed him, he could rest in the conviction that nature would proportion "her defence to the assault" and "that the intellect in its purity, and the moral sense in its purity, are not distinguished from each other, and both ravish us into a region whereinto these passionate clouds of sorrow cannot rise."[3]

On this issue, Emerson's Concord voice sounds in off-key opposition to that of Emily Dickinson in western Massachusetts, who wrote of the primacy of pain in the equation of compensation:

> For each extatic instant
> We must an anguish pay
> In keen and quivering ratio
> To the extasy

For each beloved hour

Sharp pittances of years—

Bitter contested farthings—

And Coffers heaped with Tears!⁴

For her, the transactions of life have been costly; cosmic usurers demand payments of anguish, at unconscionable interest, for each momentary joy. But it is a debt that *"must"* be paid, however unfair the terms.

Ernest Hemingway, throughout his fiction but especially in *The Sun Also Rises*, sides with Dickinson in this hypothetical quarrel. The cost of joy, ecstasy, or happiness comes high, yet it must be met. Like the poet from Amherst, he expressed his view of compensation in the metaphor of finance—a metaphor which runs through the fabric of his first novel like a fine, essential thread, a thread so fine, indeed, that it has not before been perceived. The classical statement against Hemingway's lack of moral sensitivity in this book was made by James T. Farrell, who described the characters as "people who have not fully grown up" and the moral outlook as amounting "to the attitude that an action is good if it makes one feel good."⁵ Among others, even the perceptive Philip Young seems at first (later, he changed his mind) to have read *The Sun Also Rises* in this way: "Jake's disability excepted, always, the book now seems really the long *Fiesta* it was called in the English edition, and one's net impression today is of all the fun there is to be had in getting good and lost."⁶ That was not the impression, clearly, that Hemingway meant to convey. Lunching with a group of professors from the University of Hawaii in 1941, he advised against their students reading *A Farewell to Arms*. "That's an immoral book. Let them read *The Sun Also Rises*. It's very moral."⁷

It is Jake Barnes who explicitly states the code of Hemingway's "very moral" novel. Lying awake at Pamplona, Jake reflects that in having Brett for a friend, he "had been getting something for nothing" and that sooner or later he would have to pay the bill, which always came:

I thought I had paid for everything. Not like the woman pays and pays. No idea of retributions or punishment. Just exchange of values. You gave up something and got something else. Or you worked for something. You paid some way for everything that was any good. I paid my way into enough things that I liked, so that I had a good time. Either you paid by learning about them, or by experience, or by taking chances, or by money. Enjoying living was learning to get your money's worth and knowing when you had it. You could get your money's worth. The world was a good place to buy in.[8]

It is understandable that Jake, sexually crippled in the war, should think that he has already paid for everything; and it is an index of his maturity, as a man "fully grown up," that he comes to realize that he may still have debts outstanding, to be paid, most often and most insistently, in francs and pesetas and pounds and dollars.

For Jake's philosophical musing is illustrated time and again in the profuse monetary transactions of *The Sun Also Rises*. On the second page of the novel, one discovers that Robert Cohn has squandered most of the $50,000 that his father, from "one of the richest Jewish families in New York," has left him; on the last page of the book, that Jake has tipped the waiter (the amount is unspecified) who has called a taxi for him and Brett in Madrid (pp. 4, 247). Between the beginning and the end, Hemingway specifically mentions sums of money, and what they have been able to purchase, a total of thirty times. The money dispensed runs up from a franc to a waiter to the fifty francs that Jake leaves for his *poule*, Georgette, at the dancings, to the two hundred francs which Count Mippipopolous gives to Jake's concierge, to the $10,000 the count offers Brett for a weekend in her company. Mostly, though, the monetary amounts are small, and pay for the food, drink, travel, and entertainment that represent the good things in life available to Jake.

Hemingway reveals much more about his characters' financial condition and spending habits than about their appearance: the book would be far more useful to the loan officer of a bank than, say, to the missing person's bureau, which would have little more physical information to go on, with respect to height, weight, hair and eye color, than that Brett had short hair and "was built with curves like the hull of a racing yacht" (p. 22) and that Robert Cohn, with his broken nose, looked as if "perhaps a horse had stepped on his face" (pp. 3-4). When Hemingway cut 40,000 words out of the first draft of *The Sun Also Rises* but retained these ubiquitous references to the cost of things, he must have kept them for some perceptible and important artistic purpose.

II

In fact, he had several good reasons to note with scrupulous detail the exact nature of financial transactions. Such a practice contributed to the verisimilitude of the novel, denoting the way it was; it fitted nicely with Jake's—and his creator's—obsession with the proper way of doing things; and mainly, it illustrated in action the moral conviction that you must pay for what you get, that you must earn in order to be able to buy, and that only then will it be possible, if you are careful, to buy your money's worth in the world.

In the early 1920's exchange rates in postwar Europe fluctuated wildly. Only the dollar remained stable, to the benefit of the expatriated artists, writers, dilettantes, and party-goers who found they could live for next to nothing in Paris. Malcolm Cowley and his wife lived there the year of 1921 in modest comfort on a grant of $1,000, twelve thousand francs by that year's rate.[9] By the summer of 1924, when Barnes and his companions left for the fiesta at Pamplona, the rate was still more favorable, almost 19 francs to the dollar.[10] And you could get breakfast coffee and a brioche for a franc or less at the cafés where Hemingway, expatriated with the rest, wrote when the weather turned cold.[11] There were even better bargains elsewhere, and the Hemingways, somewhat strapped once Ernest decided to abandon journalism for serious fiction, found one of the best of them in the winter of 1924-

1925, at Schruns in the Austrian Voralberg, where food, lodging, snow and skiing for the young writer, his wife, and son came to but $28.50 a week.[12] Europe was overflowing with (mostly temporary) American expatriates, living on the cheap. Any novel faithful to that time and that place was going to have to take cognizance of what it cost to live and eat and drink.

Hemingway regarded most of his fellow Americans on the left bank as poseurs pretending to be artists, but "nearly all loafers expending the energy that an artist puts into his creative work in talking about what they are going to do and condemning the work of all artists who have gained any degree of recognition." The tone of moral indignation in this dispatch, one of the first that Hemingway sent the *Toronto Star Weekly* from Paris in 1922, is emphasized by the anecdote he includes about "a big, light-haired woman sitting at a table with three young men." She pays the bill, and the young men laugh whenever she does: "Three years ago she came to Paris with her husband from a little town in Connecticut, where they had lived and he had painted with increasing success for ten years. Last year he went back to America alone."[13]

To the writer, single-minded in his dedication to his craft, the time-wasting of café habitués represented the greatest sin of all. It was the work that counted, and talking about art was hardly a satisfactory substitute. As Jake remarks, setting forth an axiom of Hemingway's creed, "You'll lose it if you talk about it" (p. 245).[14] In the posthumously published *A Moveable Feast*, Hemingway laments having accompanied the hypochondriacal Scott Fitzgerald on an unnecessarily drawn out trip to Lyon. Nursing his traveling companion, he "missed not working and . . . felt the death loneliness that comes at the end of every day that is wasted in your life."[15] Observing the playboys and playgirls of Paris waste their lives on one long hazy binge, Hemingway as foreign correspondent felt much the same disgust that visits Jake after the revels at Pamplona, when he plunges deep into the waters off San Sebastian in an attempt to cleanse himself.

What distinguishes Jake Barnes from Mike and Brett, who at least make no pretenses toward artistic (or any other kind of) endeavor, and from Robert Cohn, a writer who is blocked throughout the novel, is that he works steadily at his regular job as a newspaperman. He is, presumably, unsupported by money from home, and he spends his money, as he eats and drinks, with conspicuous control. Above all, he is thoughtful and conscientious in his spending. Sharing a taxi with two fellow American reporters who also work regularly and well at their jobs but at least one of whom is burdened, as he is not, by "a wife and kids," Jake insists on paying the two-franc fare (p. 37). He does the right thing, too, by Georgette, the streetwalker he picks up at the Napolitain. Not only does he buy her dinner as a preliminary to the sexual encounter she has bargained for, but upon deserting her for Brett, he leaves fifty francs with the patronne—compensation for her wasted evening—to be delivered to Georgette if she goes home alone. The patronne is supposed to hold the money for Jake if Georgette secures another male customer, but this being France, he will, Brett assures him, lose his fifty francs. "Oh, yes," Jake responds, but he has at least behaved properly (p. 23), and Jake, like his creator, was "always intensely interested in how to do a thing," from tying flies to fighting bulls to compensating a prostitute.[16] Besides, he shares a double kinship with Georgette: she too is sick, a sexual cripple, and she pursues her trade openly and honestly.

The case is different with Lady Ashley, who acquires and casts off her lovers nearly as casually as Georgette, but does so without thought of the consequences to others. There is a certain irony in Brett's telling Jake that it was wrong of him to bring Georgette to the dance, "in restraint of trade" (p. 22). Surely this is a case of the pot and kettle, for she has arrived in the company of a covey of homosexuals. More to the point, it is women like Brett—and even, to a lesser degree, Cohn's companion Frances Clyne—who provide unfair competition to the streetwalkers of Paris.

After an unsatisfactory time with Brett, Jake Barnes returns to his room, where he immediately goes over his bank statement: "It showed a balance of $2,432.60. I got out my checkbook and deducted four checks drawn since the first of the month, and discovered I had a balance of $1,832.60. I wrote this on the back of the statement" (p. 30). This is make-work, an attempt to delay thinking about the love for Brett that he cannot consummate. But it is also characteristic of Jake's meticulousness about money. The surprising thing, in fact, is that Jake should have spent as much as $600 in any given month, for he is a man who tries very hard always to get his money's worth. He knows whom to write to secure good bullfight tickets, and he reserves the best rooms in the best hotels at the best price. In Bayonne, he helps Bill buy "a pretty good rod cheap, and two landing-nets," and checks with the tourist-office "to find what we ought to pay for a motor-car to Pamplona": 400 francs (pp. 90-91). At Burguete, he bargains to have the wine included in the twelve-pesetas-a-day hotel room he and Bill share, and they make certain at dinner that they do "not lose money on the wine" (pp. 109-111). He is annoyed when Cohn sends a wire of only three words for the price of ten ("I come Thursday"), and takes revenge by answering with an even shorter telegram ("Arriving tonight") (p. 128). After the fiesta, when a driver tries to overcharge Jake for a ride from Bayonne to San Sebastian, he first works the price down from fifty to thirty-five pesetas and then rejects that price too, as "not worth it" (pp. 231-232). Jake is careful to fulfill his obligations, but he will not be taken advantage of. Once, in church, regretting that he is such a rotten Catholic, he even prays that he will "make a lot of money" (p. 97), but here the verb is important, for he next begins thinking about how he might make the money. He does not pray or even hope to *have* a lot of money, or for it to descend upon him from the trees or the deaths of relatives. Robert Cohn and Mike Campbell remind him, often and painfully, of what inherited money, or the promise of it, can do to undermine a man.

III

Though physically impotent and mentally tortured, Jake Barnes remains morally sound, while Mike Campbell, Robert Cohn, and Brett Ashley, who are physically whole, have become morally decadent. As Baker observes, *The Sun Also Rises* has "a sturdy moral backbone," deriving much of its power from the contrast between Barnes-Gorton-Romero, who constitute the "moral norm" of the book, and the morally aberrant trio of Ashley-Campbell-Cohn.[17] What has not been observed is that money and its uses form the metaphor by which the moral responsibility of Jake, Bill, and Pedro is measured against the carelessness of Brett, Mike, and Robert. Financial soundness mirrors moral strength.

Bill Gorton is the most likable of the crew at the fiesta. Modeled upon the humorist Donald Ogden Stewart, Bill regales Jake with topical gags about Mencken, the Scopes trial, literary fashions, and middle-class mores. An enthusiast, he finds every place he visits equally "wonderful" (pp. 69-70). The adjective is a private joke between Barnes and Gorton, for Bill knows as well as Jake that when things are really wonderful, it is neither necessary nor desirable to say so. Thus, hiking through the magnificent woods at Burguete, Bill remarks simply, "This is country" (p. 117). The five days they share at Burguete stand in idyllic contrast to the sickness and drunkenness which characterize both Paris and Pamplona. It is not that Bill and Jake do not drink together on the fishing trip; they drink prodigious quantities of wine. But it is drinking for the pleasure they have earned, both through hard work (in contrast to Cohn, Gorton is a producing writer) and through the rigors of the outdoor life they choose to pursue on vacation. Furthermore, Bill knows when not to drink. After dinner at Madame Lecomte's and a long walk through Paris, Jake proposes a drink. "No," says Bill. "I don't need it" (pp. 77-78).

The first thing Jake says about Bill Gorton is that he is "very happy. He had made a lot of money on his last book, and was going to make a lot more" (p. 70). He has paid for his fiesta, and like all who have earned "the good things," he is careful of the rights of others. In Vienna, he tells Jake, he had gone to an "enormous . . . prize-fight" in which a "wonderful nigger" knocked a local boy cold and aroused the anger of the crowd. People threw chairs into the ring, and not only was the victorious fighter deprived of payment (he had agreed not to knock out the local fighter), but his watch was stolen. "Not so good, Jake. Injustice everywhere," as Gorton remarks. Conscientious about money matters, he is disturbed by a world where fights are fixed and debts go unpaid. So, though tight and on holiday, Bill lends the cheated fighter clothes and money and tries to help him collect what's owed to him (pp. 71-72).

Bill's comic determination to purchase stuffed animals foreshadows Jake's serious reflections on compensation. Passing a Paris taxidermist's, Bill appeals to Jake to buy

"Just one stuffed dog. I can take 'em or leave 'em alone. But listen, Jake. Just one stuffed dog."

"Come on."

"Mean everything in the world to you after you bought it. Simple exchange of values. You give them money. They give you a stuffed dog." (p. 72)

His affinity for spending money on the ridiculous emerges again at Pamplona, when he buys Mike eleven shoeshines in a row. "Bill's a yell of laughter," Mike says, but Jake, who unlike them has not had much to drink, "felt a little uncomfortable about all this shoeshining" (pp. 172-173). Still, Bill's expenditures buy amusement for himself and others (including, of course, the reader), and these otherwise merely amusing incidents serve to illustrate the principle of exchange of values: to obtain stuffed dogs, shoeshines, or drinks, you must deliver payment.

IV

Robert Cohn, for whom Gorton conceives an immediate dislike, does not belong with the party at Pamplona. A romantic, he is understandably unable at first to conceive that his weekend with Brett at San Sebastian has meant nothing to her, but he forfeits any claim to sympathy by his subsequent stubborn and violent unwillingness to accept that obvious fact. Terribly insecure, he takes insult after insult from Frances and Mike without retaliation, though he is ready enough, anachronistically, to fight with his "best friend" Jake over what he construes as insults to Brett. A Jew in the company of Gentiles, he is a bore who takes himself—and his illusions—far too seriously. Unlike Jake, he has not "learned about" things. He does not know how to eat or drink or love. It is no wonder that Harold Loeb, unmistakably recognizing himself in Hemingway's portrait of Cohn, "felt as if he had developed an ulcer" and, decades later, attempted to vindicate himself in his autobiography.[18]

Still, it would be possible to pity Cohn for his dominant malady (is not romantic egotism a less unlovely illness than nymphomania or dipsomania?) were it not for his callous and opportunistic use of the money he has not earned. His allowance ($300 a month, from his mother) comfortably stakes him to his period of expatriation. He has written a novel which has been "accepted by a fairly good publisher," but it is not, clearly, a very good novel, and now the well has run dry. In his idleness, he hangs around Jake's office, disturbing his work, and even proposes to pay Jake's way as his companion on a trip to South America, a continent he invests with an aura of romance (pp. 9-20). How Hemingway felt about such proposals was later made clear in *A Moveable Feast*, when he reflected, in connection with the trip to Lyon with Fitzgerald, that he "had been a damned fool to accept an invitation for a trip that was to be paid for by someone else."[19] But biographical evidence is hardly necessary to make the point that Cohn, whose money comes to him through no effort of his own but fortuitously because of the accident of his birth, does not understand the proper way of spending it: the point is made implicitly by a number of incidents in *The Sun Also Rises*.

Having inherited a great deal of money, he has wasted nearly all of it on a little magazine—and in maintaining the prestige that came to him as its editor. He is consistently lucky in gambling, but that does him more harm than good. What comes too easily has a pernicious effect on him as a person. While he was in New York to see his publisher, for example, several women had been nice to him as a budding novelist.

> This changed him so that he was not so pleasant to have around. Also, playing for higher stakes than he could afford in some rather steep bridge games with his New York connections he has held cards and won several hundred dollars. It made him rather vain of his bridge game, and he talked several times of how a man could always make a living at bridge if he were ever forced to. (pp. 8-9)

Cohn wins a 100-peseta bet with Gorton that Mike and Brett will not arrive as scheduled at Pamplona, but the bet costs him any possibility of friendship with Bill. Gorton wagers, in fact, only because Cohn's arrogance in parading inside knowledge of Brett's and Mike's habits makes him angry. Furthermore, when the wager has been agreed on, Cohn first does Bill the indignity of asking Jake to remember it, and then, to make amends after he has won, pretends that it really does not matter (pp. 95, 98-99).

What most damns Cohn, however, is his habit of buying his way out of obligations to women. Frances Clyne, one of the bitchiest women in Hemingway's fiction, reveals this practice of Cohn's in a devastating scene. Flat broke and not so young or attractive as she once was, Frances is being packed off to England so that her paramour may see more of the world—and, he surely hopes, of Lady Ashley:

"Robert's sending me. He's going to give me two hundred pounds [about a thousand dollars] and then I'm going to visit friends. Won't it be lovely? The friends don't know about it, yet."

She turned to Cohn and smiled at him. He was not smiling now.

"You were only going to give me a hundred pounds, weren't you, Robert? But I made him give me two hundred. You're really very generous. Aren't you, Robert?"

"I do not know," Jake reflects, "how people could say such terrible things to Robert Cohn." But Frances can say them, and get away with it, because they are absolutely true. Cohn, in fact, has disposed of another girl, his "little secretary on the magazine," in just the same way, except cheaper (pp. 48-50). It is in his attempt to buy his way out of entanglements, without expending anything of himself, that Robert Cohn most viciously breaks the moral code of compensation.

Furthermore, there are suggestions in the book that Cohn is tight-fisted with his money. He has, apparently, tried to bargain with Frances. He directs Jake to buy him a double-tapered fishing line, but says he will pay later instead of now (p. 81). After unleashing a stream of insults against Cohn ("Don't you know you're not wanted?"), Mike Campbell tells Bill Gorton, who is about to remove Cohn from the slaughter, to stay. "Don't go," Mike says. "Robert Cohn's about to buy a drink." The clear implication is that Robert Cohn rarely buys drinks (p. 142).

Mike, on the other hand, is more than willing to buy drinks, whenever—which means rarely—he has any money. As is true of all the other major characters in the book, Hemingway reveals a good deal about Mike's financial condition and habits. Brett, Jake tells Robert, is going to marry Mike Campbell. "He's going to be rich as hell some day" (p. 38). Cohn refuses to believe that Brett will marry Mike—and indeed, the matter remains in doubt at the end of the novel—but there is no question about Mike's potential wealth. He is trying, Brett says, to get his mother to pay for her divorce so they can be married. "Michael's people have loads of money" (p. 63). But for the moment, he makes do on a rather skimpy allowance, and is not even allowed to write checks. When he needs funds, he must "send a wire to the keeper" (p. 82).

Mike Campbell is held under strict financial control for the best of reasons: he is totally irresponsible about money. With his anticipated future wealth serving as a promissory note, he sponges off everyone in sight and simply does not pay his debts. After suffering a business collapse, he has had to resort to bankruptcy, an ungentlemanly if legal way of evading creditors. It is, as Brett realizes when she introduces him, one of the two most important and typical things about the man she intends to marry. The other is that he drinks far too much: "This is Bill Gorton. This drunkard is Mike Campbell. Mr. Campbell is an undischarged bankrupt" (p. 79).

Mike is no more conscientious about settling his debts to friends than to his former business "connections." Yet he possesses a certain self-deprecatory wit, and Bill Gorton, especially, is drawn to him. Bill likes Mike so much, in fact, that is very difficult for him to admit that Mike does not meet his obligations. One night in Pamplona, Mike, Bill, and Bill's girl Edna are thrown out of a bar by the police. "I don't know what happened," Bill says, "but some one had the police called to keep Mike out of the back room. There were some people that had known Mike at Cannes. What's the matter with Mike?" "Probably he owes them money," Jake says. "That's what people usually get bitter about." The next morning, Bill remembers the incident more clearly: "There was a fellow there that had helped pay Brett and Mike out of Cannes, once. He was damned nasty." The night before, Bill had emphatically defended his friend: "They can't say things like that about Mike." But in the light of dawn, he modifies the statement: "Nobody ought to have a right to say things about Mike. . . . They oughtn't to have any right. I wish to hell they didn't have any right" (pp. 189, 204). Bill's own loyalty to Mike finally crumbles when, after the fiesta, another incident makes it clear *why* they have the right.

Jake, Bill, and Mike have hired a car together, and stop at "a very Ritz place" in Biarritz where they roll dice to see who will pay for the drinks. Mike loses three times in a row, but cannot pay for the third round:

> "I'm so sorry," Mike said. "I can't get it."
> "What's the matter?"
> "I've no money," Mike said. "I'm stony. I've just twenty francs. Here, take twenty francs."
> Bill's face sort of changed. (p. 229)

He had had just enough money for his hotel bill in Pamplona, Mike explains, though it turns out that Brett has given him all of her cash to pay his bill. Neither can Mike help pay for their car, and his promise to send Jake what he owes is hardly reassuring.

Mike continually banters about his bankruptcy, as if making light of the obligations might somehow cause them to disappear. "I'm a tremendous bankrupt," he remarks. "I owe money to everybody." He will not go down into the ring after the running of the bulls because "it wouldn't be fair to my creditors." As Mike observes, "One never gets anywhere by discussing finances," but he is unable to resist touching the wound by discussing his own (pp. 192, 200, 230). There is the story, for example, of the medals and Mike's tailor. Invited to "a wopping big dinner" in England where medals are to be worn, Mike prevails upon his tailor to supply him with some medals which had been left by another customer for cleaning. When the dinner fizzles out, he goes to a night club and passes the medals around. "Gave one to each girl. Form of souvenir. They thought I was hell's own shakes of a soldier. Gave away medals in a night club. Dashing fellow." The story delights his audience, but it had not seemed so funny to his tailor. If it was foolish to set too great store by military medals, as did the chap who had left them with the tailor, it was quite wrong to propose to wear medals that one had not earned. Mike has fought in the war, and "must have some medals," but he does not know which ones and has never sent in for them. He is careless about them, quite as willing to don other people's ribbons as he is to spend other people's money (pp. 135-136).

Brett shares with Mike a carelessness of personal behavior which stems from a lifetime of having had things done for her. Her room in Madrid, for example, "was in that disorder produced only by those who have always had servants" (p. 241). She makes appointments and does not keep them. She accepts the generosity of others as if it were her due. The Paris homosexuals, one feels certain, were paying her way. Count Mippipopolous finances her champagne binge. "Come on," she says at Pamplona. "Are these poisonous things paid for?" (p. 144). In the bar of the Palace Hotel in Madrid, she asks Jake, "*Would* you buy a lady a drink?" (p. 244). She has been given, she admits, "hell's own amount of credit" on her title (p. 57). And, of course, she and Mike had jointly run up the bills they could not settle at Cannes. Moreover, she satisfies her demanding sexual appetites at the expense of others, effectively turning Robert into a steer, Mike into a swine, and Jake into a pimp. She is clearly not what Madame Duzinell, Jake's concierge, calls her after the bribe of 200 francs from the count, "très, très gentille" (p. 52).

Oddly, though, Brett observes a strict code in connection with her sexual activity. She will not accept money for her favors. Thus she rejects the count's offer of "ten thousand dollars to go to Biarritz [or Cannes, or Monte Carlo] with him" (p. 33). She pays Mike's way, not vice versa, out of the Hotel Montoya. Though Romero pays the hotel bill in Madrid, she will take nothing else from him. "He tried to give me a lot of money, you know. I told him I had scads of it. He knew that was a lie. I couldn't take his money, you know" (p. 242). In sending Romero away, against the urgings of the flesh, she has done the right thing at the cost of real personal anguish. She will be neither a whore nor "one of those bitches that ruins children" (p. 243).

Furthermore, Brett's apparent nymphomania can be at least partly excused by the unhappy circumstances of her past life. She has lost one man she loved in the war, and married another ("Ashley, chap she got the title from") who has returned quite mad from serving as a sailor. "When he came home," Mike explains, "he wouldn't sleep in a bed. Always made Brett sleep on the floor. Finally, when he got really bad, he used to tell her he'd kill her. Always slept with a loaded service revolver. Brett used to take the shells out when he'd gone to sleep. She hasn't had an absolutely happy life" (p. 203). Like Jake, she still suffers from war wounds. Like him, too, she articulates her awareness of the law of compensation. If she has put chaps through hell, she's paying for it all now. "Don't we pay for all the things we do, though?" (p. 26).

Brett's case is far more ambiguous than that of Robert Cohn or Mike Campbell. If she recklessly imposes nearly insupportable burdens on others, she carries an even heavier burden herself. Morally, she is neither angel nor devil, but somewhere, rather fascinatingly, in between. It is almost as if Hemingway himself were alternately attracted to and repelled by Brett. In Carlos Baker's biography there is a strong implication that Hemingway either had or wanted to have an affair with Duff Twysden, the prototype for Brett. In the fall of 1925, Duff sent Hemingway a note asking for a loan: "Ernest my dear, forgive me for this effort but can you possibly lend me some money? I am in a stinking fix but for once only temporary and can pay you back for *sure*. I want 3,000 francs—but for Gods sake lend me as much as you can."[20] In the novel, as if to protect Duff, Hemingway transfers her behavior to Mike Campbell: it is he and not Brett who asks, repeatedly, for loans.

V

Hemingway's insistence on the need to earn, and to pay for, what you get is in no way a statement in support of materialism, for it is accompanied by disgust with the crooked and corrupting values of the commercial world. Eager to line their pockets, the merchants of Pamplona double prices during the fiesta (p. 159). Away go the café's marble-topped tables and comfortable white wicker chairs, to be replaced by cast-iron tables and severe folding chairs: "The café was like a battleship stripped for action." The warship's objective, of course, is to relieve peasants and tourists alike of their cash. At the start of the fiesta, the peasants confine their drinking to the outlying shops, where wine sells for 30 centimes a liter. "They had come in so recently from the plains and the hills that it was necessary that they make their shifting in values gradually. . . . Money still had a definite value in hours worked and bushels of grain sold. Late in the fiesta it would not matter what they paid, nor where they bought." When the peasants reach the stage of heedlessness (epitomized by the futile death of one of them during the running of the bulls), they will have lost any sense of the dignity of labor, of hours worked and bushels sold (pp. 152-153).

The cancer of commercialism also threatens to infect bullfighting. Romero is forced to face a dangerously bad bull, who cannot see well the lure of the cape, because the promoters have paid for the bull and "don't want to lose their money" (p. 217). The crowd sends a volley of cushions, bread, and vegetables into the ring where Belmonte, ill and more cautious than he once had been, is performing his art. "Belmonte was very good. But because he got thirty thousand pesetas and people had stayed in line all night to buy tickets to see him, the crowd demanded that he should be more than very good." His greatness had been "discounted and sold in advance," and nothing he could do would satisfy those who watched him do it (pp. 213-214, 216).

Montoya, an *aficionado* who represents bullfighting's conscience, puts up all the good toreros at his hotel, and keeps in his room framed photographs of the bullfighters he "really believed in." The pictures of the commercial bullfighters, though, are consigned first to a desk drawer and then to the waste basket (p. 132). Montoya welcomes Jake, a fellow *aficionado*, and is grateful for his advice not to deliver to Romero his invitation from the American ambassador. "People take a boy like that," the hotel-keeper explains. "They don't know what he's worth. . . . They start this Grand Hotel business, and in one year they're through" (pp. 171-172). Montoya is even inclined to forgive Jake his friends, but that tolerance dissolves when he sees "Pedro Romero with a big glass of cognac in his hand, sitting laughing between me [Jake] and a woman with bare shoulders, at a table full of drunks. He did not even nod" (p. 177). When Jake and his companions check out, Montoya does "not come near" them (p. 228).

Romero, however, remains immune to the disease of commercialism—and the caution unto cowardice it is likely to breed. He wants and expects to make money as a bullfighter: when Brett reads in his hand that there are thousands of bulls in his future, "Good," he replies, and in an aside to Jake in Spanish, "At a thousand duros apiece." But he has not yet begun to compromise his bullfighting, as Belmonte has, by insisting on manageable bulls with smallish horns (pp. 185, 214). And Hemingway invokes the metaphor of profit and loss in comparing Pedro's afternoon of triumph to the jeers that had greeted Belmonte: "Pedro Romero had the greatness. He loved bull-fighting, and I think he loved the bulls, and I think he loved Brett. Everything of which he could control the locality he did in front of her all that afternoon. . . . But he did not do it for her at any loss to himself. He gained by it all through the afternoon" (p. 216). His willingness to take chances, one of the ways, as Jake has reflected, in which you could pay "for everything that was any good," gives the bullfight, his relationship with Brett, and the fiesta itself a kind of dignity.

It hardly matters that "the Biarritz crowd" does not appreciate what he has accomplished, with either his bad bull or his good one (pp. 217-218). Hemingway obviously regards the rich English and American tourists from Biarritz, come for one day of the quaint fiesta at Pamplona, with undisguised scorn. Those who buy false wares, like the secretly manipulated boxer toys hawked on the streets of Paris, deserve no more than they get (p. 35).

The depth of this contempt can be measured against the sympathetic portrayal of Wilson-Harris, the Englishman who fishes and plays three-handed bridge with Jake and Bill at Burguete. When his companions must leave, Harris, (as the Americans call him) insists on buying them a bottle of wine apiece. The atmosphere is one of warm camaraderie, punctuated by Harris's regret that Bill and Jake must leave. As they board the bus for Pamplona, Harris presses still another gift upon each of them: a dozen flies that he has tied himself. "They're not first-rate flies at all," he insists. "I only thought if you fished them some time it might remind you of what a good time we had." It has been a good time indeed, so that Jake first wishes Harris were coming along to Pamplona but then reflects that "You couldn't tell how English would mix with each other, anyway" (pp. 129-130). But you can tell: a man who spends his holiday trout fishing in the Pyrenees and who behaves so generously would not have mixed at all well with the perpetually carousing crew at the fiesta.

Hemingway's major characters in the novel are all, with the exception of Romero, English and American, and each is easily distinguishable from the others. The foreigners, though, he tends to stereotype. Most of the Europeans in the book are, of course, French or Spanish, and these two nationalities are characterized almost solely on the basis of their attitude toward money. French standards of value are epitomized by Jake's concierge, who will not admit shabbily dressed friends of Jake to his quarters and who conveniently changes her mind about Brett—from "a species of woman" to "a lady . . . of very good family"—on the strength of a bribe (pp. 32, 52). In *The Sun Also Rises*, Frenchmen always have their hands out, like the dining-car conductor who pockets ten francs but does nothing to earn them (p. 85). In an interior monologue, Jake dissects the French national character. He has just overtipped a waiter in Bayonne: "Everything is on such a clear financial basis in France. It is the simplest country to live in. No one makes things complicated by becoming your friend for any obscure reason. If you want people to like you you have only to spend a little money. I spent a little money and the waiter liked me. He appreciated my valuable qualities" (p. 233). Repetition and the pun on "valuable qualities" underscore the heavy irony of this passage. For Jake obviously prefers Spain to France, just as he prefers bullfighting, a sport which cannot be fixed, to Viennese prizefights and French and Belgian bicycle-racing where the contestants "had raced among themselves so often that it did not make much difference who won. . . . The money could be arranged" (p. 236).

Spaniards, unlike Frenchmen, were likely to be friendly for no good financial reason at all. The Basques, for example, share a crowded bus with Bill and Jake, and all share their wine, the Americans from bottles they have just bought, the Spanish from their wine-skins. When the bus stops at a *posada* in a small town, Bill and Jake each have an *aguardiente*, at twenty centimes apiece. "I gave the woman fifty centimes to make a tip, and she gave me back the copper piece, thinking I had misunderstood the price." Two of the Basques join them, and the cost of the drinks is split equally between them (pp. 103-106). On the opening day of the fiesta at Pamplona, Spanish peasants in a wine-shop will not let Jake and his friends pay for wine and food. They will accept in return only "a rinse of the mouth from the new wine-bag" Jake has bought, at the "lowest price," because the shopkeeper discovers he intends to drink out of it, not resell it in Bayonne (pp. 155-157). Spanish peasants, with their ethic of sharing, display a dignity and readiness for fellowship not to be thought of among the French.

The minor character who best exemplifies the morality of compensation is the Greek Count Mippipopolous. It is possible to regard him solely as the sort of aging voluptuary that he appears, on the surface, to be. But to do so is to miss the point. It "means any amount to him" to buy fine champagne directly from Baron Mumms (p. 56). All he wants out of wines, he says, is to enjoy them (p. 59). When Brett objects to his ordering a bottle of 1811 brandy, he reprimands her in his customary tough English:

"Listen, my dear. I get more value for my money in old brandy than in any other antiquities."
"Got many antiquities?"
"I got a houseful." (p. 62)

It is the same with food, and with women: the count can enjoy them properly because he has a sense of values acquired through long and painful experience.[21] Count Mippipopolous has been involved in seven wars and four revolutions. In Abyssinia when he was twenty-one, two arrows went clean through his body: he shows Brett and Jake the scars. He is "one of us," as she remarks after this demonstration, because like them he has paid in suffering for the pleasures he now pursues (p. 60). The temptation to judge the count by puritanical standards (Jake last sees him at Zelli's, surrounded by three girls he has just picked up) is tempered by an awareness that he has earned his pleasure, and that generosity and loyalty, as well as hedonism, form facets of his code.

VI

After delivering himself of his thoughts on the need to pay for the good things, Jake Barnes concludes rather cynically, "It seemed like a fine philosophy. In five years . . . it will seem just as silly as all the other fine philosophies I've had" (p. 148). Hemingway, however, did not abandon the code of compensation Jake had enunciated, but continued to regard the rich—and the lure of easy money—as threats to artists in general and himself in particular. Money, he wrote John Dos Passos in 1929, "had been the ruination of too many of their friends. Don Stewart had taken up with Jock Whitney, to say nothing of selling his soul to Hollywood for a $25,000 contract. John Bishop's career had been spoiled by his wife's munificent income. The search of eternal youth had clearly sunk the Fitzgeralds."[22] In *Green Hills of Africa*, he cited money as the first way in which American writers are destroyed. When they have made some money, they "increase their standard of living and they are caught. They have to write to keep up their establishments, their wives, and so on, and they write slop."[23]

For his own part, as becomes clear in *A Moveable Feast*, he quite specifically blamed the demise of his idyllic first marriage on the predatory rich who had followed Hadley, Bumby, and himself to the Voralberg:

When you have two people who love each other, are happy and gay and really good work is being done by one or both of them, people are drawn to them. . . . Those who attract people . . . do not always learn about the good, the attractive, the charming, the soon-beloved, the generous, the understanding rich who have no bad qualities and who give each day the quality of a festival and who, when they have passed and taken the nourishment they needed, leave everything deader than the roots of any grass Attila's horses' hoofs have ever scoured.[24]

Especially in the long story "The Snows of Kilimanjaro," Hemingway excoriated himself, in the guise of the writer-narrator Harry, for drinking and playing with the rich and letting his talent erode through idleness. "It was strange, too, wasn't it," Harry thinks, "that when he fell in love with another woman, that woman should always have more money than the last one."[25] That was exactly the case with Pauline, Hemingway's second wife, and as Philip Young has divined, the story is partly "a special and private . . . analysis of his past failures as a writer of prose fiction, as of 1936." He had not published a first-rate book since *A Farewell to Arms*, seven years before, and like Harry, contemplated with despair all the stories he had not written.[26] Though it was not really his wife's fault, though he had destroyed his talent himself, still it was her money that gave him the chance to spend what he had not earned and was not paying for. Perhaps it was not coincidental that in his other major fiction of the 1930's, Hemingway depicted his most coolly vicious female characters of all in Margot Macomber and Helene Bradley, the rich, writer-collecting adventuress of *To Have and Have Not*.

But the morality of compensation found expression not only in the fiction of the thirties, but throughout Hemingway's works. Both in *A Farewell to Arms* (1929) and *Across the River and into the Trees* (1950), his protagonists are virtually obsessed with their obligations. After making his "separate peace" with the war, a totally justifiable escape, Frederic Henry nonetheless feels "damned lonely" and tortures himself with recurring thoughts that he has deserted in a conventional way. Colonel Cantwell, facing his certain death, carefully discharges his outstanding debts: he sends ducks to the waiter at the Gritti Palace Hotel, returns his girl's emeralds and her portrait, and makes her a gift of the shotguns that have served him so well.[27] All of Hemingway's major protagonists share this sense of obligation—to political belief (Robert Jordan), to craft (Santiago as well as Romero), to wife and family (Harry Morgan). Though Hemingway himself was divorced three times, his heroes never cast off commitments. They pay their bills in full, sometimes at the cost of their lives.

A teacher in Oak Park, Illinois, an upper-middle-class suburb noted for nothing so much as its respectability, once wondered "how a boy brought up in Christian and Puritan nurture should know and write so well of the devil and the underworld."[28] But Ernest Hemingway carried with him always an inheritance from the community where he grew up, a faith in the efficacy and staying power of certain moral values. Strongest among these was the axiom that you had to earn your happiness, though the price might come exceedingly high, with its corollary that easy money could ruin a man. In his first novel, Hemingway imposed this standard on the expatriate world of the early 1920's. At the end of the last book he wrote, looking back on those years as an idyll when he had worked hard and loved well and taken nothing without making full payment, his nostalgia found expression in the same metaphor which runs through *The Sun Also Rises*: "Paris was always worth it and you received return for whatever you brought to it. But this is how it was in the early days when we were very poor and very happy."[29]

From *American Literature* 43, no. 3 (1971): 399-420. Copyright © 1971 by Duke University Press. All rights reserved. Used by permission of the publisher.

Notes

1. Quoted in Carlos Baker, *Hemingway: The Writer as Artist* (Princeton, N.J., 1963), p. 197.

2. *Selections from Ralph Waldo Emerson*, ed. Stephen E. Whicher (Boston, 1957), pp. 14-15.

3. Ralph Waldo Emerson, "The Tragic," *Dial*, IV (April, 1844), 515-521.

4. Poem 125, I, pp. 89-90, *The Poems of Emily Dickinson*, 3 vols., ed. Thomas H. Johnson (Cambridge, Mass., 1958). In the 1891 edition, this poem was titled "Compensation."

5. James T. Farrell, "*The Sun Also Rises*," *New York Times* (August 1, 1943). Reprinted in *Studies in The Sun Also Rises*, ed. William White (Columbus, Ohio, 1969), pp. 53-57.

6. So Young wrote in his 1952 *Ernest Hemingway*. By 1966, when he published a revised and expanded edition of the book, the sentence quoted and the paragraph that contained it had been excised and telescoped into but six words: "Despite quite a lot of fun *The Sun Also Rises* is still Hemingway's *Waste Land*. . . ." Compare Philip Young, *Ernest Hemingway* (New York, 1952), pp. 54-60, with Philip Young, *Ernest Hemingway: A Reconsideration* (New York, 1966), pp. 82-88.

7. Quoted in Carlos Baker, *Ernest Hemingway: A Life Story* (New York, 1969), p. 429.

8. Ernest Hemingway, *The Sun Also Rises* (New York, 1926), p. 148. Further citations to this text will be indicated in parentheses.

9. Malcolm Cowley, *Exile's Return* (New York, 1951), pp. 79-81.

10. For information on the rate of exchange as of June 30, 1924, I am indebted to Murray Weiss, editor of the *International Herald Tribune*.

11. Baker, *Writer*, p. 18.

12. Baker, *Life*, p. 174.

13. Baker, *Writer*, p. 6. Charles A. Fenton, *The Apprenticeship of Ernest Hemingway* (New York, 1958), pp. 124-125.

14. Hemingway said much the same thing to Mary Lowry, a fellow reporter on the *Toronto Star*, in the fall of 1923. See Fenton, p. 253.

15. For the full account of the trip to Lyon, see Ernest Hemingway, *A Moveable Feast* (New York, 1964), pp. 125-160.

16. Fenton, pp. 150-151.

17. Baker, *Writer*, pp. 82-83, 92.

18. Baker, *Life*, p. 223. Loeb's autobiography was entitled *The Way It Was* (New York, 1959).

19. Hemingway, *Feast*, p. 138.

20. Baker, *Life*, p. 196.

21. Earl Rovit explores the theme of the hierarchy of values in the novel, taking Count Mippipopolous as his point of departure. See Rovit, *Ernest Hemingway* (New York, 1963), pp. 149-155.

22. Baker, *Life*, p. 250.

23. Ernest Hemingway, *Green Hills of Africa* (New York, 1935), p. 23.

24. Hemingway, *Feast*, pp. 188-192.

25. "The Snows of Kilimanjaro," *The Short Stories of Ernest Hemingway* (New York, 1955), p. 60.

26. Young, *Reconsideration*, pp. 75-76.

27. See for example Ernest Hemingway, *A Farewell to Arms* (New York, 1929), pp. 232, 243, 245, 251; and Ernest Hemingway, *Across the River and into the Trees* (New York, 1950) pp. 303-308.

28. Fenton, p. 2.

29. Hemingway, *Feast*, p. 192.

Love and Friendship/Man and Woman in *The Sun Also Rises*_____

Sibbie O'Sullivan

It would be naive to say that *The Sun Also Rises* is a joyous book, or even a hopeful one; it is, of course, neither. Most often interpreted as a picture of post-war aimlessness and anomie, Hemingway's 1926 novel is usually said to be the bible of the Lost Generation, a modern-day courtesy book on how to behave in the waste land Europe had become after the Great War. However valid this interpretation may be, it is limiting and unduly pessimistic. It necessitates a particularly negative reading of the characters in the book and undervalues Hemingway's intuitive awareness of cultural and historical forces and the impact they have on personal relationships. Most damaging of all, the consensual interpretation fosters the harmful propagation of sexist stereotypes and ignores Hemingway's knowledge of and respect for the New Woman. Instead of reading *The Sun Also Rises* as the death of love,[1] we can read it as a story about the cautious belief in the survival of the two most basic components of any human relationship: love and friendship. Examined this way, the novel is a rather extraordinary document that unites the two separate sexual spheres of the nineteenth century and in so doing breaks away from the moral imperatives of the Victorian age while demonstrating the possibility of love's survival in the more realistic but nihilist twentieth century.

The coaxial themes of love and friendship inform this book in such subtle ways that they are easily overlooked even though they are the forces which motivate the characters' behavior. In the case of Jake Barnes and Lady Brett Ashley they form the basis of their relationship. Too often this relationship is laid waste by stereotypical thinking. The cliché runs like this: Jake, unmanned in the war, is not only physically but spiritually impotent and allows himself to be debased by Brett, that "non-woman," that "purely destructive force." Such critical abuse is understandable when we realize that Brett is considered part of that long American tradition of the dark-haired, bad woman. She must be termed "promiscuous" and a "nymphomaniac" if her sexual behavior is to be explained at all. The mainspring of such a tradition is that "nice girls don't do it." But we've already seen in the short stories that Hemingway refuses to bind his female characters to such strictures. His women do "do it," and with relish.

Hemingway seems to take for granted that Brett is a sexually active woman. And though he did not consciously set out to create the New Woman, Hemingway's Brett is a fine example of one. Before examining Brett's character in terms of the love/friendship theme of the novel let us briefly examine the milieu from which she emerged.

* * *

The modern woman did not suddenly rise up from the rubble of 1918. On both sides of the Atlantic Brett's predecessors had for some time rebelled against personal circumstances and societal restrictions. Though it is agreed that the so-called New Woman emerged as a type during the "naughty nineties," as William Wasserstrom points out, "After 1860 Americans of even the straightest gentility preferred girls with spunk."[2] It was well known in Europe how independent and free-wheeling American girls were; Henry James founded his literary career on such types. By European standards American ladies had great freedom of movement. Frances Kemble remarked on unescorted teenage girls "lounging about in the streets" of New York.[3] Before 1860 chaperonage of unmarried women was neither enforced nor required, and though this practice was reintroduced in 1880, it was popular only with the upwardly mobile.[4]

In both America and England the rise of industry and business brought men and women into close proximity. Though American women entered the clerical occupations before their British sisters, by the end of the nineteenth century the business office had been sexually integrated in both countries. The combination of more women leaving the home and women working closely with men moved to create a different mode of female behavior—women were perceived as beginning to "act like men." As K. G. Wells remarked in 1880, "Instead of grace, there has come in many women an affectation of mannishness as is shown in hats, jackets, long strides, and a healthful swinging of the arms in walking."[5] More radical behavior included smoking, drinking, living alone ("latch-key girls"), and sexual activity. The dissemination and use of birth control increased. Though such "liberated" activity was often frowned upon, it was alluring for many people, at least on an unconscious level. *Trilby*, George Du Maurier's 1894 novel, was wildly popular and took America by storm. Leading a bohemian existence, earning a living as an artist's model, dressing like a man when she felt like it, the title character defied the stupidity and insidiousness of Victorian propriety. Five years later in London, the 1889 premiere of Ibsen's *A Doll's House* ushered in the decade of the New Woman with a more somber but nonetheless resounding bang. The New Woman had entered the imagination of Western society.

Non-fictional modes of female behavior which had a liberating effect swept over America in the form of the British Blondes, a burlesque troupe which began its American tour in the 1870s. These British imports struck a new standard of feminine beauty. Even so proprietary a critic as William Dean Howells admired the "new buxom image of beauty they represented."[6] By the 1890s, this buxomness, a lower class trait, softened, elongated, and moved up to a more respectable rung of the social ladder and became the Gibson Girl. By 1913 the "hipless, waistless, boneless" (and, we must not forget, breastless) flapper appeared.[7] It seems, indeed, that women were becoming "mannish," as the de-emphasis of breasts implies.

But more important than how female these women looked was how they behaved. All three types of women, the British Blondes, the Gibson Girl, and the flapper, had the ability to be "pals" with men, to sustain friendships as opposed to courtships. This ability helped to break down long existing gender boundaries. Actresses and dancers, because they travelled with male actors and musicians, were not bound to conventional, sexually segregated behavior; their necessarily intimate living conditions worked against the Victorian fetish for modesty. Though such Broadway behavior earned actresses the reputation of being loose, it also promoted a free and easy exchange between male and female, a healthy demystification of "the opposite sex." In the case of the Gibson Girl, her behavior was more circumspect but still high-spirited and modern. She was more elegant than voluptuous, very athletic and healthy, progressive and college-educated. Though not overtly sexual, she was not without sensuality. The Gibson Girl was the representative woman for the novelists of the Progressive Era.[8] She was not dependent on men, yet valued their friendship; she would not hesitate to marry the "right one."

The flapper, by 1913 "the preeminent model of female appearance,"[9] not only looked but behaved like a man. She smoked, drank, drove, slept around, and earned a living. Her arrival coincided with "Sex o'clock in America."[10] Her behavior was "assertive, and independent, she experimented with intimate dancing, permissive favors, and casual courtships or affairs. She joined men as comrades, and the differences in behavior of the sexes were narrowed."[11] Her live-for-today attitude was announced in Owen Johnson's 1914 novel *The Salamander* and later immortalized by F. Scott Fitzgerald. She was destined to become part of Hemingway's lost generation.[12]

As expected, the push for female freedom, whether advanced by fashion, birth control or the vote, met with strong opposition. As women became more militant in their demands for equality, what were once only implications of female inferiority became flat pronouncements. While the British Blondes were showing their legs, male obstetricians virtually took over the birth process in America.[13] By pronouncing "the truth" about women's bodies men attempted to effect control over those bodies. In 1873, Anthony Comstock successfully lobbied Congress to prohibit the dissemination of birth control information. A year earlier Comstock founded the New York Society for the

Suppression of Vice, an organization successful in shutting down Broadway productions and banning selected novels from the mails. The extent of Comstock's influence is best gauged by remembering that in 1915 then President Wilson appointed him as delegate to an International Purity Conference. It is a measure of how virulent and persistent the original Moral Majority was when we recognize that Comstock's campaign against vice spanned those same years in which women made the greatest strides in sexual and political freedom.

Of course, any loosening of the social strictures for women represented an assault on male omnipotence. The nineteenth-century demarcation of gender roles was fiercely guarded. The myth of the self-made man conspired with the Cinderella myth to make women hostages of the home and men absentee husbands and fathers pursuing the higher calling of business. A book such as *The Awakening* is a good index of how ignorant many men probably were of the inner lives of women.

This emotional segregation of women and men had obvious consequences. It accounts for the intense relationships between female friends as well as the sad and deplorable conditions of many Victorian marriages.[14] It burdened women with the preservation of all morals and manners, while it forced men to do homage to the unbending demands of progress. It safeguarded the male ego by denying that "nice" women had erotic drives, thereby insuring male sexual adequacy. It interpreted any change in female behavior as a threat to male dominance; the new mannish behavior was particularly threatening because it called into question heretofore supposedly self-evident gender distinctions. Fear of women was, as Peter Gay points out, an international preoccupation of the nineteenth century.[15]

But however fearful and discouraged at first, this mannish behavior of women had positive results. It helped to bring the two worlds of men and women closer together. And such bringing together had to be undertaken by women and actualized through a transformation of their behavior because it is less frightening for a woman to be masculinized than it is for a man to be feminized. Theron Ware discovered that the emergence of a man's sensual nature leaves him open to emotional and physical collapse, but Brett Ashley's deviant temperament gives her strength, determination, and resilience. The genius of Brett Ashley lies not in Hemingway's ability to create the Great American Bitch but in his ability to create woman as Friend.

* * *

The Sun Also Rises reflects the changing sex role patterns prevalent in Western society during the thirty years before its publication. In many ways this first novel is Hemingway's goodbye kiss to the Victorian ethos under which he was raised. As an expatriate, as a World War I veteran, as a young husband and father, and as an artist, Hemingway, since the age of eighteen, had lived an unconventional life. Living as he did in Europe he saw firsthand the shifting social structures that transformed the old order into the new. His sensibilities were equally attuned to both pre- and post-World War I mores. He was not so ignorant as to believe that 1918 had changed everything; it certainly had not changed Robert Cohn, the traditional, romantic, chivalric, and backward-looking character we meet when the book opens.

Cohn, of course, is a bridge figure. He lives in the waste land but does not adhere to its values. He represents the dual concepts of manly adventure and romantic love so important in the nineteenth century.[16] When we meet him he is engaged to Frances Clyne, a woman with "the absolute determination that he [Cohn] should marry her."[17] Though he wants to venture to South America and asks Jake Barnes, the book's narrator, to go with him, he physically silences Jake when Jake suggests in front of Frances that he and Cohn take a weekend trip to nearby Strasbourg. Frances, it seems, is the jealous type.

By focusing the first two chapters on Cohn and the dual concerns of romantic love and adventure, Hemingway establishes a backdrop against which the rest of the book is played. That backdrop becomes, as Cohn's daydream of South America fades, the conventional theme of courtship and marriage—in other words, the typical theme of the Victorian novel. Of course, conventional marriage does little to erode the rigid boundaries between men and women, and Robert and Frances act out scenes which accentuate, in a progressively negative manner, the worst attributes of both sexes. She becomes a nasty woman tremendously afraid of not being married, and he becomes a chump willing to take her verbal abuse lest he break into tears, as he habitually does whenever they "have a scene." The demise of this relationship is nothing less than a wicked parody of the engagement/marriage ritual itself. Fifty pages into the novel we see already that the old way offers nothing but anger and humiliation.

In Chapter II another Victorian ritual is enacted, but with a twist: Jake gets a prostitute but does not sexually use her. As he explains, "I had picked her up because of a vague sentimental idea that it would be nice to eat with some one" (16). Jake's motive is not sexual fulfillment or an escape from a dull marriage bed, but companionship. Prostitute or not, Georgette is recognized by Jake as a fellow human being, not as a mere commodity to buy and discard. But however kindly Jake treats Georgette his actions still reflect the rigid gender roles of the nineteenth century. The underbelly of the conventional Victorian marriage was, after all, prostitution; the erotic restrictions placed on wives encouraged husbands to use whores for sexual release, experimentation, and erotic delight. Coming as it does after the parody of Victorian marriage that Robert Cohn and Frances Clyne represent, this chapter enacts the inevitable decline of such a relationship were it to go on. When Jake introduces Georgette to some acquaintances as his "fiancée" the connection between marriage and prostitution becomes unmistakable.

So far the male-female relationships fall within the scope of the typical Victorian ethos of courtship/marriage, and customer/prostitute. With the entrance of Lady Brett Ashley the focus shifts. Brett's arrival in Chapter III trumpets a new set of relationships. Since Brett is neither a wife nor a prostitute, it is fitting that she emerge from an environment alien to these two opposites; hence she arrives with a group of homosexual men. Her mannishness is thus established through this group, but since she quickly leaves that group and bonds with Jake we learn that her inclinations are orthodox and acceptable. We know that she is not a lesbian, and that her association with male homosexuals, instead of being a detriment, enhances her attractiveness.

As soon as Brett and Jake begin talking we realize theirs is no conventional relationship. Their dialogue bristles with familiarity. Jake asks, "Why aren't you tight?" and Brett answers by ordering a drink. The jabs continue:

> "It's a fine crowd you're with Brett," I said.
> "Aren't they lovely? And you, my dear. Where did you get it?" (22)

The "it," of course, refers to Georgette. As this exchange indicates, Brett and Jake share a public language (remember that Cohn is with them) that includes mild insult and sarcasm. It is a language in which the indefinite pronouns need not be identified. The verbal volley continues on the dance floor and in the taxi, where, alone at last, Brett confesses to Jake, "Oh, darling, I've been so miserable."

What we know so far about Brett's and Jake's relationship is this. First, as the dialogue reveals, Jake and Brett are friends. No matter what else their relationship may be it has a solid base in friendship; such benign verbal ribbing only takes place between friends. Secondly, they share a history. Reference to Brett's drinking habits and how out of character it is for Jake to pick up a whore indicate a more than superficial knowledge of each other's habits. Thirdly, Brett has control. She neatly declines two dances with Cohn and instigates her and Jake's departure. And fourthly, there seem to be two languages operating for them: public and private. It is by the latter that the truth is revealed.

And the truth isn't pretty. They are in love with each other but because of Jake's wound that love cannot be sexually fulfilled. They have tried making love but failed: "I don't want to go through that hell again" (26). Love is "hell on earth" but they continue to see each other.

There is a sense of things being out of control; at the end of the taxi ride Brett is shaky, and later when Jake returns alone to his apartment he cries himself to sleep. When Jake leaves Brett it is at another bar and in the company of another man.

This pattern of public/private behavior shapes Brett's and Jake's relationship in an important way. Jake accepts Brett's need for public display, her need to breeze around Paris with as many men as possible. He also accepts her need to tell him about it privately. After she interrupts his sleep to recap her night's adventure with the Count, Jake comments to himself, "This was Brett, that I had felt like crying about" (34). Though there is probably disgust in his voice at this point, there is also resignation, resignation that the woman he loves acts in such peculiar and unstable ways.

The ability to listen, the capacity to care, are not faculties belonging to Jake alone. Brett is also tender and solicitous in private moments. During her second visit to Jake with Count Mippipopolous, when she sees that Jake is a bit shaky, she sends the Count off to get champagne. As Jake lies face down on the bed Brett gently strokes his head. "Poor old darling. . . . Do you feel better, darling? . . . Lie quiet" (55). Though her actions are kind and genuine, Brett does not allow this moment to blunt the truth. When Jake, perhaps succumbing to her touch, to her motherly devotion, asks, "Couldn't we live together, Brett? Couldn't we just live together?" she answers the only way she knows how:

> "I don't think so. I'd just *tromper* you with everybody. You couldn't stand it."
> "I stand it now."
> "That would be different. It's my fault, Jake. It's the way I'm made." (55)

When the count returns with the champagne all three go out and Jake and Brett talk once more in their public manner until out on the dance floor. Brett, in the privacy of Jake's arms, recites again what is fast becoming her litany, thus closing Book I: "Oh, darling, . . . I'm so miserable" (64).

These two small scenes are interesting for what they tell us about how easily Brett and Jake merge the traditional sex roles. The two qualities of granting freedom and lending an ear that Jake exhibits in the first scene clash with the stereotypical image of the muscle-bound, closed-mouth husband/boyfriend who "doesn't want to hear about it." If Jake's attentiveness and meekness in the face of Brett's gallivanting seem in some ways feminine (Jake as the suffering wife?), then in the second scene Brett reenacts a particularly masculine ritual, character-ized by the "line": "I love you babe, but I can't stay tied to one woman. I'm just that kind of man." Brett's version of this "line" is not delivered with any hint of bravado or cruelty as it has been delivered by men to countless women in books and movies, but as an assessment of, almost as an apology for her personality. What is striking about these role re-versals is how easily and naturally they appear and reappear through-out the couple's interactions. Brett's behavior, especially, flows back and forth between being soft and caring, and hard and straightforward. Jake has the ability to snap back after a painful relapse. Such flexibility is unthinkable in traditional relationships where sex roles are rigid. Robert Cohn and Frances Clyne do not have this kind of flexibility. One reason Brett leaves Romero at the end of the novel is that he de-mands that she conform to the rigid traditional female role.

If I over-emphasize that Jake's and Brett's departure from stereotyp-ical male-female behavior is a positive dimension of their relationship, I do so because so many critics judge the couple's behavior in a nega-tive way when measured against those stereotypes. Mark Spilka is one critic who is most ungenerous. In his essay "The Death of Love in *The Sun Also Rises*," Spilka sees Jake as emotionally impotent, as an emo-tional adolescent, and as a man of little integrity; according to Spilka, Jake has defaulted on his maleness. Brett fares no better. She is "the freewheeling equal of any man" who engages in the "male preroga-tives of drink and promiscuity." She is a woman who allows her "natu-ral warmth" to be replaced with "masculine freedom and mobility." Under such conditions, "there can be no serious love."[18] Obviously

Spilka identifies "serious love" with traditional male-female gender roles. Though he acknowledges the general damage to love wrought by World War I, he points specifically to the damage done when woman "steps off the romantic pedestal [and] moves freely through the bars of Paris, and stands confidently there beside her newfound equals."[19] Such narrow-minded thinking not only oversimplifies a very complicated novel but blinds the reader to what demonstration of "serious love" there is in the book.[20]

Hemingway has a much broader definition of love than Spilka does, and he examines it in many types of relationships and under many different conditions. Such early stories as "The End of Something," "My Old Man," and "The Battler," indicate that Hemingway was less concerned with the outward form of a relationship and whether it conformed to the standard perception of a love relationship—heterosexual love that ends in marriage —than with the inner workings of such relationships. "The Battler" especially supports the suspicion that for some years before he wrote *The Sun Also Rises* Hemingway was interested in couples who deviated from the standard sex roles. Generally perceived as a story about homosexuality, as of course it is, "The Battler" is also a story about marriage roles, therefore a story about male-female behavior.

There is no reason why Brett's and Jake's behavior should be gauged by traditional gender roles since those roles have been modified to suit the couple's needs. Brett is, after all, the New Woman, and her claim to sexual freedom, though irksome to the critics, is both attractive and perplexing to her fellow characters. Jake cannot be the traditional man because he is impotent. Freed from the pressure to prove his worth through sexual intercourse, Jake must develop other means of asserting his personality.

Both Brett and Jake expect little of each other and have a relationship in which they agree to accept each other as they are. Early in the book Jake describes Brett's two worst habits to Robert Cohn: "She's a drunk" (38), and "She's done it twice" (39), referring to Brett's marrying men "she didn't love." Brett gives a clear self-assessment when she speaks of her intention to return to Mike: "He's so damned nice and he's so awful. He's my sort of thing" (243). Because Jake accepts Brett as she is he has been able to maintain their relationship for as long as he has. We should remember that Cohn and Pedro Romero do not accept Brett as she is and therefore lose her. Brett, too, accepts Jake as he is. They can never be completely, physically united, and for a woman as sexually alive as Brett this loss is deep and sad.

At the end of Book I the boundaries have been drawn. Brett and Jake, the New Woman and the shattered veteran, conduct a relationship based on the honest assessment of each other's failings. In any other arms Brett's lament of "darling I'm so miserable" could pass for a comment on the progress of a particular night's activities, but in Jake's arms it is properly received for what it is: a statement about Brett's soul. This kind of emotional shorthand conveyed in private moments through a private language is the backbone of Jake's and Brett's relationship and a testament to its strength. Though imperfect, their friendship is imbued with the survival mechanisms of honesty, shared histories, and serious love.

Book II begins by depicting male-male friendships, first in Paris and then in Spain. In many aspects Jake's friendship with Bill Gorton is similar to his with Brett. Though they are frequently separated, the two men can quickly restore intimacy. Bill's retelling of his experiences in Vienna is not only some of the best dialogue Hemingway ever wrote, but a wonderful example of that familiar speech we first heard between Jake and Brett. For instance, there is the shared knowledge of each other's drinking habits:

"How about Vienna?"
"Not so good, Jake. Not so good. It seemed better than it was."
"How do you mean?" I was getting glasses and a siphon.
"Tight Jake, I was tight."
"That's strange. Better have a drink." (70)

Then there's the flippant talk about values: "'Simple exchange of values. You give them money. They give you a stuffed dog.' 'We'll get one on the way back'" (72); and the personal litany, in this case Bill's "Never be daunted. Secret of my success. Never been daunted. Never been daunted in public" (73).

Once Bill and Jake leave Paris they become more intimate; the pastoral Spanish setting invokes an even more private speech which allows them to discuss religion, literature, and personal problems such as Jake's impotency. (Though Jake's problems are not discussed at any length, and though his answers are frequently evasive or non-committal, the subject is mentioned often enough in a number of dialogues to warrant being designated a topic of conversation.) Physical closeness is established by the freedom of movement between each other's rooms and by Jake watching Bill shave and dress. At one point, Bill even declares his love for Jake:

> "Listen. You're a hell of a good guy, and I'm fonder of you than anybody on earth. I couldn't tell you that in New York. It'd mean I was a faggot." (116)

Other examples of intense male interaction are the scenes with Wilson-Harris, the English angler Bill and Jake meet in Burguete, and with the aficionados in Pamplona. Wilson-Harris is very candid about how much he likes Bill and Jake. The sheer joy of buying his friends drinks almost overcomes him. At one point he says, "I say Barnes. You don't know what this all means to me" (129). When Jake and Bill leave to return to Pamplona, Wilson-Harris gives them each a present, a valentine of hand-tied fishing flies.

Not all male-male relationships are as successful as this. Once the characters are in Spain, Robert Cohn's presence grates on both Jake and Bill. Jake, of course, has reason to dislike Cohn because he recently vacationed with Brett. Jake is very forthright about his resentment:

I was blind, unforgivingly jealous of what had happened to him. The fact that I took it as a matter of course did not alter that any. I certainly did hate him. (99)

Bill's dislike seems rooted in prejudice: "Well, let him not get superior and Jewish" (96). But even Jake and Bill cannot hold on to their hatred of Cohn for too long. Bill says to Jake:

"The funny thing is he's nice, too. I like him. But he's just so awful."
"He can be damn nice."
"I know it. That's the terrible part." (101)

This assessment of Robert Cohn is so similar to Brett's assessment of Mike ("He's so damned nice and he's so awful") that the parallel should not be overlooked. Appearing when they do, these assessments frame the events at Pamplona. They remind us that friendship holds both the promise of betrayal as well as of forgiveness.

Carlos Baker[21] and others often divide the novel's characters into two groups: those who are solid, and those who are neurotic. Baker puts Jake, Bill, and Romero in the former category, and Cohn, Brett, and Mike in the latter. As fair as this division may seem on the surface, it belies the truth of human interaction and negates the web of friendship in which all the characters, at one time or another, are enmeshed. And what a complicated web it is. Throughout the fiesta the characters form new pairs or groups as they partake of the festivities. Everyone at one time or another shares the other's company. Of all the characters Brett seems most in control of choosing her companions. She maneuvers it so that, with one exception, she is never alone with Cohn. In contrast, she frequently asks Jake to go off with her alone, by now a rather predictable action.

Though Brett may behave consistently with Jake, she demonstrates new facets of her personality while interacting with others in the group. When we first see her in Pamplona she seems to have lost all patience with Cohn. "What rot . . . What rot . . . What rot" (134) she keeps repeating in response to his self-aggrandizement. She is sufficiently irked to put aside the charm that was so evident in Book I. A few pages later, however, she's protecting Cohn from Mike's drunken barbs. "Come off it, Michael. You're drunk. . . . Shut up, Michael. Try and show a little breeding" (141). The next day at dinner Brett once again runs interference between Cohn and Mike; this time her refrain is, "Pipe down, Mike. . . . Oh, pipe down, Mike, for Christ's sake!" (177). But even Brett has her limits as, a few pages later, she purposely scorns Cohn in order to make him go away: "For God's sake, go off somewhere. Can't you see Jake and I want to talk? . . . If you're tight, go to bed. Go on to bed" (181). Knowing that such an outburst is out of character, Brett checks with Jake to see if she's done the impolite, but necessary thing: "Was I rude enough to him? . . . My God! I'm so sick of him!" (181).

Jake says at one point to Brett, "Everybody behaves badly. . . . Give them the proper chance" (181). Not only does this foreshadow Jake's own bad behavior when he arranges for Brett to meet Romero, but it explains everyone else's bad behavior as well. However, it does not excuse that behavior. When a critic such as Baker defines the moral norm of the novel as "the healthy and almost boyish innocence of spirit . . . carried by Jake Barnes, Bill Gorton, and Pedro Romero,"[22] he conveniently releases these three, already identified as the "solids," from responsibility for their actions. But if we look at the histories and current behavior of Jake, Bill, and Romero, we see that it is anything but boyish and innocent. There is nothing boyish about being in war and being wounded; nothing innocent about picking up whores, being blind drunk in Vienna, and defiling the code of the bullfighters by running off with an engaged woman. It is, however, boyish to think that one can get away with such things. But even boys discover there are consequences to such actions. Jake, for instance, suffers for pimping for Brett. Bill, who is good at bailing out strange boxers, is nowhere in sight when Cohn knocks out Mike and Jake. And it is doubtful that

Pedro Romero can ever completely earn back Montoya's respect. Keeping these facts in mind, one reasonably concludes that the so-called "neurotics" behave in a better manner because they do not uphold false values and then act against them. Instead, they are consistent: Mike is consistently a drunk, so awful, so nice; Brett consistently exercises her right to sleep with whomever she wants and remains open and honest about it; and Cohn consistently acts like a "wounded steer," a sobriquet he earned early in the novel.

The separation of the group into two factions creates barriers if not as visible, surely, at least, as damaging as those erected between the sexes. Such barriers highlight how friends betray but not how they forgive one another. And in Brett's case, because she is grouped with the neurotics, she suffers under a double onus: she becomes the neurotic female, the "bitch," the "nymphomaniac." Clearly, it is the double standard and nothing else that permits the critics, both male and female, to criticize Brett for sleeping with Cohn and Romero while not criticizing Cohn and Romero for the same act. But Hemingway is not interested in erecting barriers but in destroying them. He does not see behavior as either male or female. Nor does he see passion as something solely inter-sexual. In *The Sun Also Rises*, bonding and passion occur in mysterious ways. There is no difference in the intensity of what Wilson-Harris feels for Jake and Bill and what Brett feels for Romero. Brett, however, is allowed the sexual expression of her intensity whereas Wilson-Harris would not be, even if his feelings were sexual. The bond that Jake establishes with Montoya is special because it is validated both by intensity and physical touch. Though this touch is not overtly sexual it certainly suggests sexuality because it is the symbol of a shared passion, just as the touching of sexual partners represents mutual passion.[23]

The above relationships, considering their brevity, their passion, and the intensity of mutual attraction between their participants, would be like one-night stands or casual affairs, were they to exist in the sexual dimension. I am not suggesting that we belittle the effects of sexual

Critical Insights

union, or that Brett's escapade with Romero is as inconsequential as Wilson-Harris's fishing trip. What I am suggesting is that there are parallels between male bonding and heterosexual bonding which should not be overlooked, and that both forms of bonding are as easily established as they are destroyed. By removing the sexual barriers which unduly place the burden of bad behavior on sexually active women (as Jake points out the woman pays and pays and pays), we see that Brett's transgression is no worse than Jake's; in fact, Brett's may have fewer repercussions. We can assume with good reason that Mike will take Brett back after her fling with Romero, but we are not as certain about a reconciliation between Jake and Montoya. True to form, Hemingway remains aloof in making clear any moral certainties. But one thing for certain is that Hemingway wants us to look at all the characters' behavior and not just Brett's. The structural parallels in the novel are too clear to ignore.

What seems to be more important than who does what to whom and why is the acceptance of the mysteries of behavior, and of bonding in particular. Those characters who survive the best are the ones who have cultivated a certain sense of negative capability. The ability to accept simultaneously two opposing ideas or modes of behavior becomes a means of survival. Those characters who do not have this capability end up exiled from the web of relationships established at Pamplona. Hence it is Cohn and Romero, those representatives of the traditional male role, who are ultimately excluded from any relationship with Brett, the object of their desires. Rigidity of values and, since these two men were Brett's lovers, a corresponding rigidity of erectile tissue are not what keeps Brett. Jake, it seems, wins again.

Book III opens with Jake's observation that "it was all over" (227). Ostensibly referring to the fiesta, Jake's statement is also an assessment of the condition of the web of relationships woven in the previous two hundred pages. It is in shreds. Brett has taken off with Romero. Cohn has left in disgrace, Jake is blind drunk for the first time in the novel, and Mike, as we presently discover, is penniless. Book III is, initially, a book of departures, but by the close of the book Jake and Brett have reunited, thus reconstructing the web. Jake and Brett have no parting scene; her departure with Romero, like Cohn's departure, takes place under cloak of night. We do see, however, the partings of Mike and Bill. Each has a different destination: Mike for Saint Jean de Luz, Bill for Paris and points west, and Jake for San Sebastian. We have no clue as to when these gentlemen will meet again, if at all.

Both Bill and Jake are visibly irritated at Mike for deceiving them into thinking he had money. When he learns that Mike is broke, "Bill's face sort of changed" (229). And after learning from Mike that Brett paid his hotel bill, Jake questions him repeatedly about Brett's financial well-being: "She hasn't any money with her? . . . Hasn't she any at all with her?" (230). Clearly, Mike has become persona non grata. We're less sure on what terms Bill and Jake part. Their relationship has always been catch-as-catch-can, each going his separate way then re-uniting in a burst of intimacy. Their parting words still exude that good-old-boy camaraderie first heard during their reunion at the beginning of Book II, but something is curiously missing from this final good-bye. As they part in private, neither of them knowing when they will meet again, neither man mentions past events. Bill, who very con-sciously encourages Jake to get drunk at the end of Book II in order to "Get over your damn depression" (223), now has nothing to say. No words of encouragement, compassion, or advice, though he knows full well the extent of Jake's involvement with Brett and therefore the pain he must be suffering. Clearly, Bill makes no attempt at intimacy as a departing gesture. Unfortunately, Hemingway is predictably silent about how Bill's behavior impresses Jake. We are not told, either overtly or by facial expression, how Jake feels when Bill tells him "I have to sail on the 17th" and will not be in Paris when Jake returns. We are not told if Jake or Bill waves as the train pulls out, only that "Bill was at one of the windows" (231). We can not know if this scene repre-sents the ordinary way two male friends say good-bye, or if it repre-sents a deeper rent in their friendship. What we do know, however, is that once Jake is alone his thoughts turn to friendship. He likes France because money will buy friends; in France "No one makes things complicated by becoming your friend for any obscure reason" (233).

But we also know by now that such thoughts are only partial truths. Jake, perhaps more than any other character, knows how obscure and unfathomable friendship can be. He knows that few situations and even fewer relationships offer up a fixed set of truths; as he states halfway through the book: "I did not care what it was all about. All I wanted to know was how to live in it" (148).

In San Sebastian Jake takes long, solitary swims, and hides behind irony and sarcasm in an attempt to recover from the events at Pamplona. We realize how damaged Jake has been by these events through his attitude towards others. Not only does he put friendship on a monetary basis by deciding which waiters he wants for "friends," but he discourages any form of bonding with men of his own station. He purposely snubs the bicycle team manager. This uncharacteristic but telling action is a good measure of Jake's suffering when we recall how easily and eagerly he bonded with Wilson-Harris and Montoya. Now, not even the purely masculine comradeship between fellow sportsmen appeals to Jake.

But the habit of loving is a most difficult one to break. Though Jake responds to Brett's telegram with his by now characteristic sarcasm, he nonetheless reserves a seat on the Sud Express and whisks off to Madrid. Their reunion exhibits all the tenderness and caring one wishes Bill had exhibited at his departure. Jake not only physically comforts Brett by holding and kissing her, but he solicits her words: "Tell me about it," he says. And when Brett rambles on with her story despite her refrain of "let's not talk about it," Jake is still attentive and caring. Though his answers are one word responses this does not necessarily indicate a lack of concern on Jake's part, but rather an instinct that less is more. When one friend is hurting, sometimes the best thing another friend can do is listen. Jake does exactly this. But not without a price.

Involvement, of course, means pain. Jake could have just as easily wired Brett some money; he knew already she was broke. But their friendship cannot be measured in monetary terms. Later at the bar and the restaurant, Jake begins to show the effects of his rescue mission. When Brett once more brings up the matter of Romero, he responds, "I thought you weren't going to ever talk about it" (245). The amount of food and alcohol he consumes seems to keep his mouth full so he won't have to talk, to speak what's on his mind. When Brett admonishes him that he doesn't have to get drunk, Jake replies, "How do you know" (246). She backs off, he finishes one more glass and they go for a taxi ride.

In effect they are back at the beginning when they took their first taxi ride together. But however similar the two scenes seem, something has changed. The web has begun to mend. Friendship is renewed. Jake, by rescuing Brett, reaffirms his love for her, and Brett, by recognizing her own faults and deciding not to be a bitch, recognizes the danger of passion for passion's sake. This realization, taking place as it does outside the narrator's scope of vision, can only be measured by its after effects. Brett's tears, her trembling, her sudden smallness, her hesitation in feeling proud for deciding not to be "one of these bitches that ruins children" (243), are completely believable, as is her heretofore uncharacteristic refusal of alcohol at dinner. Her concern at dinner that Jake not get drunk is genuine, almost motherly, what any good friend would do.

* * *

Hemingway has said that the more applicable epigraph for his novel is the one from Ecclesiastes and not the one attributed to Gertrude Stein. We must take the author's word on some things; the very title bears this out. If this novel exhibits traits of Stein's lost generation, it also exhibits the cyclical nature of friendship, its rhythm of disintegration and renewal. Brett's and Jake's relationship may have been dealt a cruel blow by fate or the First World War, but it is anything but lost, sadistic, and sick. It, and the bullfights, are the only lasting things in the book. Contrary to what many readers believe, Brett Ashley is a positive force, a determined yet vulnerable woman who makes an attempt to live honestly. Her struggle in choosing to marry one man while loving another strangely coincides with Hemingway's own dilemma. For a year before the novel's publication he wrestled with whether or not to divorce Hadley Richardson, his first wife, and marry Pauline Pfeiffer.

Hemingway broke with convention by creating a brilliant example of the New Woman and dismantled nineteenth century gender lines by uniting love with friendship. His masculine ego did not suffer one iota in the process. He, unlike many of his critics, believes as Jake Barnes does: "In the first place, you had to be in love with a woman to have a basis of friendship" (148).

From *Arizona Quarterly* 44, no. 2 (Summer 1988): 76-97. Copyright © 1988 by University of Arizona. Reprinted with permission of University of Arizona.

Notes

1. Mark Spilka, "The Death of Love in *The Sun Also Rises*," in *Ernest Hemingway: Critiques of Four Major Novels*, ed. Carlos Baker (New York: Charles Scribner's Sons, 1962), pp. 18-25.

2. William Wasserstrom, *Heiress of All the Ages: Sex and Sentiment in the Genteel Tradition* (Minneapolis: University of Minnesota Press, 1959), p. 27.

3. Lois W. Banner, *American Beauty* (New York: Alfred A. Knopf, 1983), p. 79.

4. Banner, p. 132.

5. K. G. Wells, "Transitional American Woman," *Atlantic Monthly*, 278 (1880), 820-821.

6. Banner, p. 123.

7. Banner, p. 166.

8. Banner, p. 171.

9. Banner, p. 176.

10. James R. McGovern, "The American Woman's Pre-World War I Freedom in Manners and Morals," in *Women's Experience in America, An Historical Anthology*, eds. Esther Katz and Anita Rapone (New Brunswick: Transaction Books, 1980), p. 358n.

11. McGovern, p. 350.

12. In Ernest Earnest's *The American Eve Fact and Fiction, 1775-1914* (Urbana: University of Illinois Press, 1974), the author makes a nice argument that the novelists

of the nineteenth century did not truthfully depict the American woman and therefore these novels have misrepresented what real women were like before World War I. "They were vastly more lively, able, full blooded, and interesting human beings than we have been led to suppose" (270). If this is the case, it is easy to understand how shocked the reading public must have been at the flapper's lifestyle, though in reality she was nothing unusual.

13. G. J. Barker-Benfield, *The Horrors of the Half-Known Life: Male Attitudes Toward Women and Sexuality in Nineteenth-Century America* (New York: Harper & Row, 1976). This is a well-documented history of nineteenth century gynophobia.

14. Carroll Rosenberg-Smith, "The Female World of Love and Ritual: Relations Between Women in Nineteenth-Century America," *Signs*, 1 (1975), 1-29.

15. Peter Gay, *Education of the Senses*, Vol. 1 of *The Bourgeois Experience: Victoria to Freud* (Oxford: Oxford University Press, 1984), p. 197.

16. Martin Green, *The Great American Adventure* (Boston: Beacon Press, 1984). According to Green the two main types of novels in the nineteenth century were the domestic novel, which focused on romantic love, and the adventure novel which justified imperialism and national expansion.

17. Ernest Hemingway, *The Sun Also Rises* (New York: Charles Scribner's Sons, 1970), p. 5. All quotations are from this edition and will be cited in the text.

18. Spilka, p. 20.

19. Spilka, p. 20.

20. Spilka, fortunately, has been challenged. Some of the critics who have given *The Sun Also Rises* a more positive reading include the following: Richard B. Hovey, "*The Sun Also Rises*: Hemingway's Inner Debate," *Forum* [Houston], 4 (1966), 4-10; Robert W. Lewis, Jr., *Hemingway on Love* (Austin: University of Texas Press, 1965); Linda Wagner, "*The Sun Also Rises*: One Debt to Imagism," *Journal of Narrative Technique*, 2 (1972), 88-98; Roger Whitlow, *Cassandra's Daughters: The Women in Hemingway* (Westport: Greenwood Press, 1984); and Delbert E. Wylder, "The Two Faces of Brett: The Role of the New Woman," *Kentucky Philological Association Bulletin* (1980), 27-33.

21. Carlos Baker, *Hemingway: The Writer as Artist* (Princeton: Princeton UP, 1973).

22. Baker, p. 82.

23. "Men would come in from distant towns and before they left Pamplona stop and talk for a few minutes with Montoya about bulls. These men were aficionados. . . . When they saw that I had aficion, and there was no password, no set questions that could bring it out, rather it was a sort of oral spiritual examination with the questions always a little on the defensive and never apparent, there was this same embarrassed putting the hand on the shoulder, or a 'Buen hombre.' But nearly always there was the actual touching. It seemed as though they wanted to touch you to make it certain" (*The Sun Also Rises*, 132).

Performance Art:
Jake Barnes and "Masculine" Signification in *The Sun Also Rises*

Ira Elliott

Lesbians and gay men figure in no fewer than eight Hemingway short stories published between 1925 and 1933. The tone of these stories and their attitudes toward homosexuality fluctuate between outright scorn ("The Mother of a Queen") and apparent acceptance ("A Simple Enquiry").[1] Homosexuals also appear, albeit in lesser roles, in many of Hemingway's major novels, from his first full-length fiction, *The Sun Also Rises*, to his posthumously published *Islands in the Stream*. Homosexuality is also touched upon in *A Farewell to Arms*, *Death in the Afternoon*, *To Have and Have Not*, and *A Moveable Feast*.

Gender categories and gender reversals are, moreover, central thematic concerns in works as diverse as *The Sun Also Rises*, *A Farewell to Arms*, *Islands in the Stream*, and *The Garden of Eden*, in which the question of gender constitutes the basis of the story.[2] As Jeffrey Meyers points out, in *A Farewell to Arms*, *For Whom the Bell Tolls*, *Islands in the Stream*, and *The Garden of Eden*, "the lovers experiment in dyeing their hair the same color and cutting it the same length in order to exchange sexual roles and merge their identities."[3] Hair, in fact, functions throughout Hemingway's work as the principal image by which gender is made known. In *The Sun Also Rises*, for instance, Brett Ashley, epitome of the Modern Woman, "wore a slipover jersey sweater and a tweed skirt, and her hair was brushed back like a boy's. She started all that." Whatever is meant by "all that," Brett, a "damned fine-looking" woman,[4] evokes androgyny and gender ambiguity in both physical appearance (her hair) and attire (her jersey).[5]

In both his life and his work, Hemingway remained ambivalent about sex and gender.[6] While his later work in particular demonstrates, in Sylvia O'Sullivan's words, how his "public and private selves circulate with his hypermasculine and submerged feminine selves,"[7] a great deal of his fiction retreats from the possibility of multiple sexual identities and fluid gender roles even while acknowledging the inherent instability of gender.

Certainly the unexpected reemergence of the theme of androgyny in *The Garden of Eden*, striking with such force and urgency, supports Mark Spilka's assertion that questions of gender play a major and often-overlooked role in Hemingway's fiction. It is not difficult to see why the early novels (*The Sun Also Rises* and *A Farewell to Arms*) may rightly be regarded as the place "where the loss of androgynous happiness initially occurs."[8] As American culture undertakes a reevaluation of gender/sexual politics, Hemingway is, as Jerry Varsava suggests, proving to be a "more influential writer than we ever thought he was . . . more influential than he ever *intended* to be" (Varsava's emphasis).[9]

* * *

My project is to consider the ways in which Jake Barnes's male identity is called into question by the genital wound he suffered during the First World War, and the ways in which his fractured sense of self functions in relation to homosexuality and the homosexual men he observes at a *bal musette* in the company of Brett Ashley. Jake's attitude toward the homosexuals—the way he degrades them and casts them as his rivals—will, I believe, reveal the extent to which sexual categories and gender roles are cultural constructions. Close readings of several key passages in the novel will at the same time uncover the reasons behind Jake's own inability to openly accept, if not fully endorse, the potentialities of gender/sexual mutability.

I take as my starting point the recent work of theorist Judith Butler, whose influential book *Gender Trouble* maintains that "the heterosexualization of desire requires and institutes the production of discrete and asymmetrical oppositions between 'feminine' and 'masculine,' where these are understood as expressive of 'male' and 'female.'"[10] This process suggests that "the gendered body is performative," and, in fact, "has no ontological status apart from the various acts which constitute reality." Insofar as "the inner truth of gender is a fabrication," "genders can be neither true nor false, but are only produced as the truth effects of a discourse of primary and stable identity." The notion of a "primary and interior gendered self" is, therefore, a cultural construction which creates the "illusion" of such a disguised self. That gender is itself a kind of *"performance of drag . . . reveals the imitative structure of gender itself—as well as its contingency"* (Butler's emphasis).[11]

With respect to the "crowd of young men, some in jerseys and some in their shirt-sleeves" (20) that Jake encounters at the *bal musette*, external signs—that is, behavioral or performative acts—lead Jake to "read" the men as homosexual. The various signs by which their homosexuality is made known are these: their "jerseys" and "shirt-sleeves," their "newly washed, wavy hair," their "white hands" and "white faces," their "grimacing, gesturing, talking" (20). While it may be argued that the idea of performativity ("grimacing, gesturing, talking") is here conflated with the notion of the homosexual as a morphological "type" ("newly washed, wavy hair"; "white hands" and "white faces") created by a congenital condition,[12] I maintain that what may at first seem to be morphological is in fact performative: these men are "types" not owing to natural physical features, but rather because they have created themselves as a "type" in order to enact (perform) the role of homosexual.

Their casual dress and careful grooming suggest a "feminine" preoccupation with physical appearance. Their hair appears to be styled ("wavy"), like a woman's, while their "white hands" suggest delicacy, their "white faces," makeup or powder. Just as the feminized Jew of the novel, Robert Cohn, is mocked for his excessive barbering (99), the homosexuals are scorned for their obvious concern with appearance. Rather than exhibiting the reticence and rigidity associated with masculinity, they are overly and overtly expressive, uninhibited in the use of their bodies and voices. Jake's "diagnosis" is confirmed, his own masculinity momentarily consolidated, by the policeman near the door of the bar, who, in a gesture that bonds the two "real" men and marginalizes the homosexuals as "other," looks at Jake and smiles (20).

But what is it, really, that Jake "reads"? It is not the sexual orientation of the men but rather a set of signs, a visual (and aural) field—the body—upon which is inscribed, and through which is enacted, their otherwise concealed sexuality. The young men have their homosexuality "written" on their faces and on their bodies. They "perform" their sexuality through facial expressions and physical gestures. Just as Jake's wound remains unnamed, so, too, homosexuality is never mentioned; both are instead disclosed through, in the words of Arnold and Cathy Davidson, "sexual and textual absences." The reader, like Jake, "must read the ostensible sexual preference of the young men from the various signs provided and thereby decode covert private sexuality from overt public sociability."[13] Homosexuality is therefore not simply a matter of erotic object choice and same-gender sex. It is also a way of being, for the performativity of the young men indicates—is, in fact, predictive of—their bedroom behavior.

What Jake "reads" is not, therefore, sexuality, but gender. In Butlerian terms, Brett's companions are "imitating" the "wrong" gender. Sexual identity can be determined through careful observation of behavior, and sex and gender collapse into a single "truth" manifest in appearance. The "feminine," regarded as the exclusive province of the female, is seen as inscribed within/on the female body. Its appropriation by the male constitutes a gender transgression which in and of itself becomes the visible sign of homosexuality. The homosexual reveals himself through a performative "error," and, by this logic, the feminine, effeminate, or feminized man is always homosexual.

According to Jonathan Dollimore, the notion that sex and (performative) "truth" are connected leads to the supposition that sexual deviation is a "deviation from the truth . . . [which is] embodied in, and really only accessible to, normality."[14] This in turn implies that "there is something like an 'error' involved in what they [homosexuals] do . . . a manner of acting that is not adequate to reality."[15] This perverse "error" is not only enacted in sex but also in "performance" or self-presentation. Boys will be boys only if boys act like boys; when boys act like girls— that is, do not conform to gender/ed expectations—they are acting, in public or in private, in ways "not adequate to reality."

Jake objects not so much to homosexual behavior (which is unseen) but to "femininity" expressed through the "wrong" body. Gender-crossing is what troubles Jake; the rupture between a culturally-deter-mined signifier (the male body) and signified (the female gender) disrupts the male/female binary. But what if the young men had not crossed the gender line, if their behavior were "in accord" with their sex, if they, in short, acted the way Jake expects men to act? He would then have no "signs" of their homosexuality.

The perception that the young men are enacting the "wrong" gender leads to the conclusion that they are inauthentic, that the projection of a "feminine" persona is a parody, a send-up of the female's "proper" role. Just as their presumed sexual deviation is a "deviation from the truth," a behavioral "error," so the way they act in public is a deliberate "deviation" from the "truth" of their gender. Although one could argue that the men are "camping" in order to destabilize the notion of fixed (naturalized) gender characteristics—that theirs is a conscious deployment of gender for strategic political ends—Jake cannot allow for the possibility that they might truly *be* the way they *act*. He cannot believe that these men are *really* like that ("feminine") because they are male.

When Jake sees one of the men dancing with Georgette, the prostitute he picked up earlier in the evening, he describes her "tall blonde" partner as dancing "big-hippily, carrying his head on one side, his eyes lifted as he danced" (20). In other words, he danced like a woman, for "big-hippily" evokes the maternal body—or perhaps the "bump-and-grind" of a "loose" woman who wishes to call attention to her genital area. That his head is carried "on one side" implies that a pose has been struck, that he is unbalanced, somehow "off." His gaze, moreover, is not where it should be—on the female object—but somewhere else, an indication that he is not firmly grounded or well-focused but given to wandering (sexual promiscuity?). "Eyes lifted," he stares dreamily into space, like a screen beauty in a seductive Hollywood photograph. Indeed, Hollywood erotica, magazine "glamor shots," and even Christian iconography depict the female as exposed, inviting, and passive through the position of her head, which is often thrown back in ecstasy/ agony. This same receptivity and vulnerability is recalled in the homosexual's dancing, his head tilted to "one side." And when the music stops, "another one of them" asks Georgette to dance, and Jake knows that "they would all dance with her," for "they are like that" (20).

Just what he means by "like that" remains ambiguous; he neither explains nor reflects upon what precisely they are "like" or why they might be that way.[16] I take Jake to mean, however, that homosexuals enjoy flirting with what they perceive as the exotic or marginalized, for the prostitute represents yet another form of "deviant" desire or "perverted" sexuality. She is, moreover, like all women, alien to the homosexual's erotic life, just as the homosexuals are foreign to the conception of manhood expressed in the novel.

Homosexuals, then, enjoy sporting with, or teasing, the "fallen" woman. Her own "corrupted" sexuality provides them with a non-threatening plaything which they are able to trade among themselves (as they presumably trade sexual partners, hopping from one bed to another). While Georgette is unaffiliated with the homosexual men in terms of their sexuality, she is aligned with them because of her professional promiscuity. What's more, her very name, a feminized version of George (where the masculine is taken for the universal), suggests that she is a feminized man—another "performance of drag" that underscores *male* promiscuity.

Brett uses the homosexuals in a similar manner—"when one's with the crowd I'm with, one can drink in such safety" (20)—and her confidence (perhaps the only wholly unambiguous response to these men, as well as the clearest evidence that they are in fact gay) does not seem to greatly disturb Jake. What offends him is the deployment of the female body as an item of exchange. Georgette is present owing entirely to his transaction with her, but in his case she would be used "properly"—that is, for heterosexual exchange—if only he could do so. Yet the fact that he cannot appropriate her body for the "manly" purpose for which she is intended affiliates Jake with the homosexuals. Although his desire is "normal," his body prevents him from actualizing his "manhood." Jake's inability to perform sexually corresponds to the homosexual's inability to perform his "correct" gender. Jake's sexual inadequacy and the homosexual's gender transgression are therefore conjoined: neither can properly signify "masculinity."

When the men first enter the bar, Jake overhears a part of their conversation which relates to Georgette: "One of them saw Georgette and said: 'I do declare. There is an actual harlot. I'm going to dance with her, Lett. You watch me.' The tall dark one, called Lett, said: 'Don't be rash.' The blonde one answered: 'Don't worry, dear'" (20). Their theatricality and the staginess of the scene itself is underscored by the dramatic presentation of their dialogue, for the colon is a formal device borrowed from the drama (and is employed in the novel only in this instance). Their mannered speech also sounds theatrical and declamatory. The insertion of "do" in "I declare" strikes one as an archaism out of the drawing rooms of the nineteenth century. Reminiscent of the speech of the upper-class, whose diction represents a kind of cultural power, the archaic form of address also recalls the stereotypical southern belle, whose inflection feeds into the construction of the southern woman as artificial and insincere. Like the belle of the Old South, the homosexual affects an aristocratic pose which is arch and pretentious, and both exhibit a "superior, simpering composure" (20). That the blonde "declares" that he sees an "actual" harlot intensifies the split between the "real" and the "feigned," the "true" and the "untrue." Georgette's reality is, in Jake's mind anyway, a titillation for the men, a contrived danger (like Brett's relationship to the homosexuals) that poses no threat. That which is termed "rash" is "rash" only insofar as it unites the authentic (a "real" female) with the inauthentic (a "false" female—

the homosexual). But even this is not a real danger, for both the prostitute and the homosexual are presented as poor copies of an original (authentic) female.

The very existence of the gay man—"feminine" desire expressed through the male body, "feminine" behavior enacted by a man—calls into question not only naturalized sex/gender roles, but also such oppositions as seen/unseen, disclosed/undisclosed, real/illusory.[17] That the homosexual appears to hold together "qualities that are elsewhere felt as antithetical: theatricality and authenticity . . . intensity and irony, a fierce assertion of extreme feeling with a deprecating sense of its absurdity,"[18] leads one to entertain the possibility that the contemporary gay man possesses—and this, I believe, is specific to time, place, race, and class—"a heightened awareness and appreciation for disguise, impersonation, the projection and the distinction between instinctive and theatrical behavior."[19] As gay-identified novelist John Rechy put it at the 1991 Out/Write Conference in San Francisco, the so-called gay sensibility "may be marked by its risking of extremes, a duality often revealed within seeming contradictions."[20]

It is also notable that "it is not Brett who elicits Jake's obvious and immediate attraction"[21] when she enters the bar, but rather her homosexual companions: "I was very angry. Somehow they always made me angry. I know they are supposed to be amusing, and you should be tolerant, but I wanted to swing on one, any one, anything to shatter that superior, simpering composure" (20). The urge to physically assault the homosexual man—what we now call "gay bashing," which many theorists argue constitutes an attack on the "feminine" rooted in misogyny—quite clearly derives from Jake's anger; but what, precisely, is he so angry about? The source of his rage is in part his frustration at being unable to categorize the homosexual within the male/female binary. That these men represent and enact gender nonconformity violates the cultural boundaries established to demarcate appropriate social and sexual behavior. Any attempted remapping of these culturally agreed upon borders exposes the arbitrariness of their frontiers, which in turn calls for a rethinking of the ontological groundwork of sex/gender itself. At the same time, his anger is self-hatred displaced onto the homosexual, for Jake has lost (physically and psychologically) his signifying phallus. What's more, the tolerance he knows he should have for the homosexuals may also be the same tolerance he hopes Brett will have for him and his sexual failing.

In a cultural system that authorizes a single mode of self-presentation for each gender, transgressing the binary law of male/female constitutes a crime. Just as homosexuality is often constructed as "a crime against nature," so, too, this crime, or sin, against naturalized gender performance must be punished: Jake wishes "to shatter that superior, simpering composure" which he sees as a homosexual or "feminine" trait. Robert Cohn's manner is also described as "superior." To whom or what the homosexual is "superior" is not expressed, but Jake apparently believes that they are, or think that they are, "superior" to him. He is also disturbed by their "simpering composure," though one may wonder whether it is their composure itself which troubles Jake, or its simpering nature. In either case, the ostensibly heterosexual man here feels threatened by the homosexual's acceptance and assertion of his presumably "incorrect" gender behavior. If he is superior to Jake, then it is axiomatic that Jake is inferior to him, for Jake himself hopes that he signifies what he is not, namely, the potent and powerful heterosexual male.

What Jake is unable or unwilling to acknowledge (disclose) is that his relationship to women resembles that of the homosexual. Though for different reasons, both Jake and the homosexual man do not relate to women in accordance with the demands of a heterosexual/heterosexist culture. What Jake desires but cannot do is to perform sexually with women, the same performance rejected by the homosexual. While the homosexual rejects heterosexual performance, he does so in favor of an alternative. Jake, on the other hand, is bound by a "masculine" signification and desire which is "untrue"—he cannot *do* what his appearance suggests he can. The homosexual signifies differently, Jake not at all, and so the homosexual is seen as "superior."

Jake's body stands, as it were, between himself and his desires; the homosexual's "perverse" desire, however, circumvents the "natural" physical act. It is therefore not the homosexual's denial or disinterest in women which offends Jake but the renunciation of naturalized male desire. When he looks at the homosexual man, what Jake sees is the body of a male that does not perform as a "man"; when he regards himself what he sees is the body of a male that lacks the sign of "manliness." This tends to support Jonathan Dollimore's observation that "the most extreme threat to the true form of something comes not so much from its absolute opposite or its direct negation, but in the form of its perversion . . . [which is] very often perceived as at once utterly alien to what it threatens, and yet, mysteriously inherent within it."[22]

For Hemingway, himself something of a "sexual puritan,"[23] "sexual perversion is inseparable from intellectual and moral corruption."[24] This is just one instance of how the nineteenth-century "medical model" of homosexuality, which regarded same-gender sex as a "congenital abnormality," absorbed the centuries-old construction of homosexual behavior as "a sinful and evil practice . . . [so that] the older conception remained active within the new."[25]

What Judith Sensibar says about John Campton in *A Son at the Front* applies equally well to Jake Barnes (and Hemingway). She declares that Wharton's Campton is "a victim of his culture's rigid gender classifications and patriarchal exchange systems," and that "his refusal to examine his own sexuality is caused partly by his rigid belief in masculinist gender classifications."[26] This is similar to Butler's belief that "institutional heterosexuality both requires and produces the univocity of each of the gendered terms that constitute the limit of gendered possibilities within an oppositional, binary system."[27] Jake can account for the homosexual man only by associating him with aristocratic pretensions or with "femininity," which Jake perceives in the gay man's "superior," southern-belle-like manner—behavior Hemingway elsewhere associates with the "mincing gentry."[28]

In the following chapter (4), Jake's affiliation with the homosexual and with gender reversal is even more pronounced. While undressing for bed, he sees himself in the mirror: "Undressing, I looked at myself in the mirror of the big armoire beside the bed. That was a typically French way to furnish a room. Practical, too, I suppose. Of all the ways to be wounded. I suppose it was funny. I put my pajamas on and got into bed" (30). While the digression concerning the armoire might at first appear to be an attempt to avoid seeing himself or talking about what he sees, it is actually a symbolic corollary of Jake's wound. Just as the armoire represents "a typically French way to furnish a room," so the penis is "typical" of the male body. Whereas the armoire is "practical," however, Jake's member is not (at least in relation to his sex life); rather, it is all "furnishing." In relation to the female, the homosexual's sex is similarly "furnishing." That Jake regards his wound as "funny" recalls his earlier observation that homosexual men "are supposed to be amusing," though clearly neither are a source of much humor. Both are instead ironic objects of derision. What Jake sees in the mirror has come to be mere ornamentation.[29] That which is present signifies absence—not of desire but of ability. The mirror reflects appearance; it does not reveal essence. At the same time, the "external signs" which it presents can, if "read" correctly, provide the clues necessary to apprehend "inner truth." In Jake's case, that "truth" is his fractured sense of masculine identity. In holding the mirror up to himself, what Jake discovers is his close affiliation with the homosexual men.

Inasmuch as Jake considers himself to be heterosexual, the novel posits the site of sexuality in gendered desire rather than sexual behavior. What distinguishes Jake from the homosexual men is gender performance and erotic object choice. By this logic, it follows that sexuality is determined by gender identification rather than sexual activity. Jake's sex can no longer penetrate a woman (and so all sexual relations are apparently ruled out), but he remains heterosexual by virtue of his desire. If the men from the bar discontinued same-gender sex, they would presumably remain homosexual. Sexual identity issues not from the sex act but from covert desire or overt social behavior.

When Jake finally gets into bed, his "head start[s] to work," and he again thinks how his was a "rotten" way to be wounded—and "on a joke front like the Italian" at that—another unfunny joke (31). His wound is an accident which cannot be named, just as homosexuality is the love that dare not speak its name. His "reduced" stature as a man is further signified by his name, a monosyllabic diminutive which suggests that his identity, like his body, has been cut off, foreshortened, reduced. Jake has "given more" (31) than his life, for his manhood has been sacrificed, or at least compromised, and with it the potential for offspring, his link to the future.[30]

The scene continues: "I lay awake thinking and my mind jumping around. Then I couldn't keep away from it, and I started to think about Brett and all the rest of it went away. I was thinking about Brett and my mind stopped jumping around and started to go in sort of smooth waves. Then all of a sudden I started to cry. Then after a while it was better and I lay in bed and listened to the heavy trams go by and way down the street, and then I went to sleep" (31). This is a highly problematic passage not only because of the vagueness of the language (what precisely is "it"?) but also because of the uncertain signification assigned Jake. If we regard these lines as a masturbatory fantasy either for Jake or for a projected male reader, the "it" that he "couldn't keep away from" may be taken to refer to the body itself, the part with which Jake is most preoccupied. Once he has focused his attention on "it"— and nothing suggests that his thoughts alone are what he "couldn't keep away from"—he "started to think about Brett and all the rest of it went away." Now the "it" may be the wound and his reflections on his injury, but he may also be talking about his wounded sex itself, where "sex" is understood to be the male member. That is to say, what "went away" might be the maimed part of himself, leaving Jake free to fantasize that his wound has been healed, his body restored to wholeness, health, and a "correct" masculine morphology. If, on the other hand, what "went away" is the male member itself, then Jake imagines himself in the female subject position. In this case, his body has not been restored (even psychologically) but reinscribed.

The trams, a variation on the familiar phallic image of the penis as a powerful forward-moving train, are, like Jake's own maleness, removed from himself, detached and no longer a function of his body, but outside him and "way down the street." Kenneth Lynn goes so far as to suggest that Jake is a man "whose dilemma is that, like a lesbian, he cannot penetrate his loved one's body with his own."[31] While this comparison betrays Lynn's lack of understanding of lesbian sexuality, it is nevertheless an acute observation as it pertains to Jake's ruptured sense of male identity. It remains unclear, however, whether Jake's masculinity is in question because of the lost body part (morphology) or because of his inability to express what is regarded as masculine—that is, heterosexual performativity. This loss is later seen in relation to homosexuality itself, when Jake's wound is directly linked to homosexual identity.

This linkage occurs about midway through the novel, during the fishing trip Jake takes with his friend Bill Gorton before the fiesta. The fishing episode is one of what Wendy Martin calls Hemingway's "pastoral interludes, in which his male characters seek relief from social tensions," part of a tradition in American fiction "that begins with Cooper and Brackenridge and extends through Hawthorne, Melville, and Twain."[32] This "pastoral interlude" is also a "set piece" profoundly colored by the homoerotic element. Like the Arcadian adventures described in more specifically "gay texts"—the fishing trip in Forster's *Maurice*, for example—Jake and Bill's "relief from social tensions" represents "relief" or escape from the bonds of mainstream morality. *Maurice*'s "greenwood" of erotic possibilities has its antithesis in another kind of "set piece" found in Anglo-American literature, the man-to-man combat featuring two males as signifiers of the "masculine," the most famous example being perhaps the "Gladiatorial" chapter in Lawrence's *Women in Love*. In *The Sun Also Rises* the physical battle between male rivals is most overtly expressed in the bullfight, where two such signifiers are the man and the bull. And just as Jake is a spectator at the bullfight rather than a participant, so, too, he can only look on as other men (Robert Cohn, Mike Campbell, Pedro Romero) compete for the affections of Brett Ashley. The arena where "real" men compete—whether the bullring or the bedroom—is for Jake a foreclosed area of emotional and psychic involvement.

Whether "greenwood," bullring, or battlefield, these episodes are intense moments of male bonding, which for Mario Mieli (and I concur) is always an expression of a "paralysed and unspoken homosexuality, which can be grasped, in the negative, in the denial of women."[33] While alone and apart from the world, Bill teases Jake by asking him if he knows what his real "trouble" is: "You're an expatriate [Bill explains]. One of the worst type. . . . You've lost touch with the soil. You get precious. Fake European standards have ruined you. You drink yourself to death. You become obsessed by sex. You spend all your time talking, not working. You are an expatriate, see? You hang around cafés" (115). Jake's association with the old world places him within the shadow of European decadence, which is seen as a performance, a role unbecoming to him. That he has "lost touch with the soil" suggests that Jake is estranged from enduring values, for "the earth abideth forever."[34] Jake has become "precious," "ruined" by "fake European standards," so that his very identity has been compromised, if not corrupted, by foreign influences. Similarly, Jake's body has been corrupted by a foreign object, perhaps a mortar shell. This has in turn transformed his corporeal existence into something foreign or other—not quite a "whole" man but certainly not a woman. Jake has come to inhabit the demi-monde, the world of the outcast, the lost, the homosexual—the decadent other *par excellence*. What's more, like Lawrence's, Hemingway's "anxieties about homosexuality were conjoined with class antagonism"[35]—his antipathy for the rich, the "mincing gentry."

Jake, like the homosexual, is a habitué of cafés, where one "does" very little except talk, and the homosexual, the female, and the Jew are constructed as overly discursive. (Another of Hemingway's fears was that writing—talking—was unmanly, for it is not "doing.") The gay man, however, is like a woman in that he "hangs around" and doesn't work much. His only "work" is nightwork related to sex, just as the "proper" work for a woman is to serve her man. Even Brett, the independent Modern Woman, exists only in relation to men—Jake, Mike, Robert, Pedro, Count Mippipopolous, the homosexuals.

Bill goes on to say that Jake doesn't work, after all, and that while some claim he is supported by women, others insist that he's impotent. A man who is supported by women is of course not a "real" man, but what Bill means by "impotent" is ambiguous. He may believe that Jake is sexually impotent or that as a decadent American who has adopted "fake" European standards he is psychically impotent. In either case, the link between non-normative sexuality and decadence is clear. Jake responds to Bill by saying, "I just had an accident." But Bill tells Jake, "Never mention that. . . . That's the sort of thing that can't be spoken of. That's what you ought to work up into a mystery. Like Henry's bicycle" (115). Once again, just as homosexuality is the love that dare not speak its name, so Jake's "accident" should not be discussed. "Henry's bicycle" is a reference to Henry James and the "obscure hurt" he suffered while a teenager—either a physical wound which rendered him incapable of sexual performance or a psychic "hurt," the realization of his homosexuality.[36] The failure to perform in the culturally prescribed way (heterosexually) is therefore figured as "de-masculinizing."

Jake and Bill then banter about whether Henry's wound was suffered while riding a bicycle or a horse, with attendant puns on "joystick" and "pedal" (116). When Jake "stands up" for the tricycle, Bill replies, "I think he's a good writer, too." He adds that Jake is "a hell of a good guy":

Listen you're a hell of a good guy, and I'm fonder of you than anybody on earth. I couldn't tell you that in New York. It'd mean I was a faggot. That was what the Civil War was about. Abraham Lincoln was a faggot. He was in love with General Grant. So was Jefferson Davis. Lincoln just freed the slaves on a bet. The Dred Scott case was framed by the Anti-Saloon League. Sex explains it all. The Colonel's Lady and Judy O'Grady are Lesbians under the skin. (116)

That Jake opts for the tricycle over the horse as the instrument of Henry's "unmanning" implies that the modern world of the machine has had a negative, disruptive effect on traditional male/female roles. When Bill acknowledges that Henry, in spite of his wound, was "a good writer" (could still perform as an artist), he is also reassuring Jake that he can still perform as a good friend and "proper" man—fishing, eating, drinking. Jake will not be banished from the homosocial realm where all "good guys" go to escape from the debilitating influence of women.

* * *

While Jake may now occupy an uncertain place between the genders, Bill continues to be "fonder" of him than anybody. Defending himself from any potential "charge" of homosexuality, Bill quickly adds that had they been in New York, he wouldn't be able to voice his affection for Jake without being a "faggot"; European decadence makes it possible to speak the unspeakable. Without belaboring Bill's mock history of the Civil War, we should remark that "sex explains it all." The "truth" of the self is revealed, after all, in sex; and homosexuality (in this instance, lesbianism) is inscribed in the body, concealed "under the skin." If we recall that male homosexuality may be "read" in external signs, it appears here that lesbian sexuality is not similarly marked by gender nonconformity, that concealed lesbian identity cannot be discerned through observing performance but only by unmasking what is hidden in the body, under the skin. This seems to suggest that lesbianism is congenital, while male homosexuality is performative.

The novel concludes with the justly famous scene of Jake and Brett together in a cab: "'Oh, Jake,' Brett said, 'we could have had such a damned good time together.' Ahead was a mounted policeman in khaki directing traffic. He raised his baton. The car slowed suddenly pressing Brett against me. 'Yes,' I said. 'Isn't it pretty to think so?'" (247). Earlier in the novel, Georgette pressed against Jake while in a cab (15), and now Brett is thrown against the body of a man who desires more than he can do; he wants not just "pressing" but penetration. Once again the symbolic policeman is present, but this time he isn't smiling; he and Jake are no longer members of the same "club." This time his raised baton is a rebuke. The policeman, a "manly" authority figure, is not only "mounted" (and perhaps "well-mounted") on a horse (suggesting a "stud" or "stallion" while recalling Henry's "accident") but also a uniformed presence whose "raised" baton is suggestive not only of an erect phallus but also of the baton of a conductor or military officer, two whose role is to orchestrate the performance of others, though Jake can no longer perform.

The sun, almost always figured as "male" (and in most Indo-European languages grammatically of the "male gender"), "ariseth" and "goeth down," as does a male. The earth, a female/maternal signifier, "abideth forever," and "the soil," it will be recalled, is what Jake has "lost touch" with. As Arnold and Cathy Davidson note, "Jake's last words readily devolve into an endless series of counter-statements that continue the same discourse: 'Isn't it pretty to think so?' / 'Isn't it pretty to think isn't it pretty to think so?'" This "negation," as the Davidsons call it, closes the novel and returns us to its title, for "only the earth—not heroes, not their successes or their failures—abideth forever."[37] The use of so "feminine" a word as "pretty" further underscores Jake's mixed gender identification as well as the "feminine" qualities of life which abide forever.

If there is hope for Jake—that is, for those confined by their culture's "rigid gender classifications"—it may be found, paradoxically enough, in the image of the homosexual man and the "feminized" male, in the "possibility of a consciousness integrating both the masculine and feminine," in the recognition that "patriarchy as a cultural phenomenon . . . can destroy a man's ability to develop his fullest potential."[38] Similarly, that Jake and Brett share the public space of the bar may signal "the possibility of new kinds of relationships for women and men in the twentieth century."[39]

Notes

1. Although I here use the designations "lesbians" and "gay men" for the sake of convenience (and at the risk of historical inaccuracy), I elsewhere employ the terms "homosexual" and "gay man" interchangeably. Except where otherwise noted, "homosexual" and "homosexuality" should be understood to refer exclusively to males. The eight stories I have in mind are "Mr. and Mrs. Elliot," "Che Ti Dice La Patria?" "A Simple Enquiry," "A Pursuit Race," "The Sea Change," "The Mother of a Queen," "The Light of the World," and "The Last Good Country."

2. For an account of the editing process which led to the published version of *The Garden of Eden*, and for a discussion of the plot lines omitted, see Robert E. Fleming's article, "The Endings of Hemingway's *Garden of Eden*," *American Literature* 61 (May 1989): 261-70.

3. Jeffrey Meyers, *Hemingway: A Biography* (New York: Harper and Row, 1986), 434.

4. Ernest Hemingway, *The Sun Also Rises* (1926; reprint, New York: Scribner's, 1954), 22. Subsequent references to this novel will be noted parenthetically within the text.

5. The relationship between hair and (sexual) power is of course a common one. In *Wars I Have Seen*, for example, Gertrude Stein notes that girls who "kept company with Germans" during World War II had their heads shaved (London: Batesford, 1945), 160. Hair and barbering are also mentioned in four other places in *The Sun* (83, 97, 101, 150), and Hemingway once wrote an unpublished short story entitled, "A Story of a Man Who Always Wanted to Have Long Hair." See Wendy Martin, "Brett Ashley as New Woman in *The Sun Also Rises*," in *New Essays on "The Sun Also Rises,"* ed. Linda Wagner-Martin (New York: Cambridge Univ. Press, 1987), 76.

6. Probably the best critical biographies for background on Hemingway's childhood and troubled family life—his relationship to his parents and his androgynous "twinship" (Lynn) with sister Marcelline—are James R. Mellow's *Hemingway: A Life Without Consequences* (New York: Houghton Mifflin, 1992), Kenneth Lynn's *Hem-*

ingway (New York: Fawcett Columbine, 1987), and Meyers's *Hemingway: A Biography.*

7. Sylvia O'Sullivan, *Hemingway vs. Hemingway: Femininity and Masculinity in the Major Works* (Ph.D. diss., Univ. of Maryland, 1986), abstract in *Dissertation Abstracts International* 48 (1987): 127A.

8. Mark Spilka, *Hemingway's Quarrel with Androgyny* (Lincoln: Univ. of Nebraska Press, 1990), 4.

9. Jerry A. Varsava, "En-Gendered Problems: Characteral Conflict in Hemingway's *Garden*," *LIT: Literature Interpretation Theory* 3 (1991): 131.

10. Judith Butler, *Gender Trouble: Feminism and the Subversion of Identity* (New York: Routledge, 1990), 17.

11. Butler, 136-37.

12. The pallor of the young men evokes the familiar vampiric construction of the gay man and lesbian, figures of the night who prey on innocents and by sucking their blood "convert" them to a "perverted" way of life. The fear of homosexual "contamination" (especially "contamination"/"conversion" of the young) is a typical homophobic strategy which relies on the homosexual's ability to "pass" as heterosexual in mainstream society. The idea of the homosexual as carrier of moral and physical disease was fully deployed during the McCarthy period and during Anita Bryant's antigay "Save Our Children" campaign of the 1970s. Today's so-called Religious Right follows in the footsteps of such ignoble movements. See Barry D. Adams, *The Rise of a Gay and Lesbian Movement* (Boston: Twayne, 1987); John D'Emilio and Estelle B. Freedman, *Intimate Matters: A History of Sexuality in America* (New York: Harper and Row, 1988); and James Levin, *The Gay Novel in America* (New York: Garland, 1991). For a discussion of the "polluted body," see Mary Douglas, *Purity and Danger: An Analysis of Concepts of Pollution and Taboo* (New York: Praeger, 1966); and, for an examination of how these stereotypes work in relation to the AIDS pandemic, see Cindy Patton, *Inventing AIDS* (New York: Routledge, 1990) and Simon Watney, *Policing Desire: Pornography, AIDS and the Media* (Minneapolis: Univ. of Minnesota Press, 1989). For a recent discussion of the reemergence of the vampire legend in popular culture, see Pat H. Broeske's article in *The New York Times*, "Hollywood Goes Batty for Vampires" (26 April 1992), and, of course, Anne Rice's vampire novels.

13. Arnold E. and Cathy N. Davidson, "Decoding the Hemingway Hero in *The Sun Also Rises*," in *New Essays on "The Sun Also Rises,"* ed. Linda Wagner-Martin (New York: Cambridge Univ. Press, 1987), 89. For a reading of *The Sun* similar to the Davidsons' and my own, though with a different slant from our respective pieces, see Debra A. Moddelmog's excellent article, "Reconstructing Hemingway's Identity: Sexual Politics, the Author, and the Multicultural Classroom," *Narrative* 1 (October 1993): 187-206.

14. Jonathan Dollimore, *Sexual Dissidence: Augustine to Wilde, Freud to Foucault* (Oxford: Oxford Univ. Press, 1991), 69.

15. Michel Foucault, Introduction to *Herculine Barbine: Being the Recently Discovered Memoirs of a French Hermaphrodite*, trans. Richard McDougall (New York: Pantheon, 1980), x-xi.

16. According to Peter Griffin, Hemingway's naturalized conception of homosexu-

als was based on their "tendency to overreact or, better, to misreact, because their emotions were somehow short-circuited. Usually afraid to let their genuine feelings show, they would either amplify or suppress their response—keeping up a static of excitement or affecting ennui—in order to hide themselves. In speech and writing, everything for them had to be more, or less, than it was" (*Less Than a Treason: Hemingway in Paris* [New York: Oxford Univ. Press, 1990], 50).

17. Such binarisms were suggested to me by Eve Kosofsky Sedgwick's proposition that "many of the major nodes of thought and knowledge in twentieth-century Western culture as a whole are structured—indeed, fractured—by a chronic, now endemic crisis of homo/heterosexual definition" (*Epistemology of the Closet* [Berkeley: Univ. of California Press, 1990], 3).

18. Richard Dyer, *Heavenly Bodies: Film Stars and Society* (London: Macmillan, 1987), 154.

19. Jack Babuscio, "Camp and the Gay Sensibility," in *Gays and Film*, ed. Richard Dyer (London: British Film Institute, 1977), 45.

20. Quoted by Joan Fry in "An Interview with John Rechy," *Poets & Writers* 20 (May/June 1992): 25-34.

21. Davidson and Davidson, 89.

22. Dollimore, 121.

23. Scott Donaldson, *By Force of Will: The Life and Art of Ernest Hemingway* (New York: Viking, 1977), 180.

24. Dollimore, 67.

25. Dollimore, 46.

26. Judith Sensibar, "'Behind the Lines' in Edith Wharton's *A Son at the Front*: Rewriting a Masculinist Tradition," *Journal of American Studies* 24 (1990): 192.

27. Butler, 22.

28. Ernest Hemingway, *Death in the Afternoon* (1932; reprint, New York: Lyceum-Scribner Library, 1960), 205. Also, see Robert Scholes and Nancy R. Comley, "Hemingway's Gay Blades," *differences: A Journal of Feminist Cultural Studies* 5 (1993): 116-39. Two of the best places to begin further reading on the aristocracy and homosexuality are Susan Sontag's seminal 1964 essay, "Notes on 'Camp,'" in *Against Interpretation* (New York: Delta-Dell, 1966), 275-92; and Eve Kosofsky Sedgwick's equally important *Between Men: English Literature and Homosexual Desire* (New York: Columbia Univ. Press, 1985).

29. Hemingway writes in *A Moveable Feast* (1964; reprint, New York: Bantam, 1979): "If I started to write elaborately, or like someone introducing or presenting something, I found that I could cut that scrollwork or ornamentation out and throw it away and start with the first true simple declarative sentence I had written" (12). The "true simple declarative sentence," stripped of "scrollwork" and "ornamentation," because both are seen to be dishonest and excessive, was the aesthetic ideal which would serve equally well in life and literature.

30. Hemingway took great pains in selecting both the titles of his books and the names of his characters. The androgynous names Brett and Frances are no accident. Robert Jordan of *For Whom the Bell Tolls*, whose father, like Hemingway's, committed suicide, has two first names (Jordan can also be a woman's name—for example, the

---

professional golfer Jordan Baker in *The Great Gatsby*). Frederic Henry in *A Farewell to Arms* has two first names as well, which, because there is no patronymic, indicates that the link to the father has been severed. Kenneth Lynn traces the source of both Frederic and Catherine Barkley's names to Barklie Henry, "the husband of a Whitney heiress" whose wife, like Catherine, had "a tough time giving birth to their first child" (239, 297-98). Like the dissatisfied wife in "Cat in the Rain" (1925), Catherine is referred to in *A Farewell* as "Cat"; she is "reborn" in the person of Catherine Bourne in *The Garden of Eden*. As for Jake Barnes, his name may derive from lesbian salon hostess Natalie Barney, writer Djuna Barnes, or the rue Jacob/Hotel Jacob, where many Americans stayed upon first arriving in Paris in the 1920s. Such androgynous names and sources for names recall the various personas Hemingway assumed throughout his life—Papa, Hemingstein, Dr. Hemingstein, Ernie, and so forth.

31. Lynn, *Hemingway*, 323.

32. Martin, "Brett Ashley as New Woman in *The Sun Also Rises*," 77-78.

33. Mario Mieli, *Homosexuality and Liberation: Elements of a Gay Critique*, trans. David Fernback (London: Gay Men's Press, 1980), 34.

34. The fact that the sun rises but Jake does not suggests not only his "lost manhood" but also the loss of all "masculine" values. He is a member of the "lost generation" in two respects: he is lost in the chaos of a changing world, and lost in terms of nineteenth-century values that no longer abide.

35. Dollimore, 268.

36. See R. W. B. Lewis, *The Jameses: A Family Narrative* (New York: Farrar, Straus and Giroux, 1991), 117.

37. Davidson and Davidson, 103-04.

38. Nancy McCampbell Grace, *The Feminized Male Character in Twentieth-Century Fiction: Studies in Joyce, Hemingway, Kerouac and Bellow* (Ph.D. diss., Ohio State University, 1986), abstract in *Dissertation Abstracts International* 48 (1988): 2334 A.

39. Martin, 81.

Reading Around Jake's Narration:
Brett Ashley and *The Sun Also Rises*_____

Lorie Watkins Fulton

Contradiction lies at the heart of *The Sun Also Rises*. This is apparent before the narrative action even begins; Hemingway pairs Gertrude Stein's famed phrase about the "lost" post-war generation with the very different verse from Ecclesiastes emphasizing regeneration. The novel begins with a two-part epigraph at odds with itself. Hemingway's plot also turns on contradictory notions. In this story that he considered a tragedy, everyone celebrates but no one finds true happiness.[1] Through the seemingly pointless pursuit of pleasure, each character searches for meaning in a post-war world that denies the possibility of any sort of meaning at all. Most paradoxically, the novel's protagonist, Jake Barnes, tries to define himself as a man even as a war-related genital wound denies him the most basic assertion of manhood, sexual gratification. Given this depth of contradiction, it seems odd that critics have taken Brett Ashley, the novel's other major character, at face value for so long. Brett is one of Hemingway's richest female characters; her personality gradually emerges as an intriguing mix of femininity and masculinity, strength and vulnerability, morality and dissolution. Yet after Edmund Wilson first tagged her as "an exclusively destructive force" (238), his perception, for the most part, remained unchallenged for decades.

Following Wilson's lead, critics quickly labeled Brett as a "bitch." Members of what Roger Whitlow terms the "Brett-the-bitch" (51) school of criticism include Leslie Fiedler, who describes Brett as a "demi-bitch" (319), John Aldridge, who calls her a "compulsive bitch" (24), and, more recently, Mimi Gladstein, who labels her as part "bitch-goddess" (61). Even those who shy away from the actual term "bitch" tend to delineate Brett in other destructive ways. For example, in demonstrating differences between Brett and her real-life counterpart in this *roman à clef*, Duff Twysden, Bertram D. Sarason glibly brands

Brett as a woman "who made castration her hobby" (10). A few of the more sympathetic, yet still fundamentally conflicted readings of Brett try to excuse her behavior as a result of her putative pursuit of self-destruction.[2] Whitlow maintains that Brett "is a self-induced 'sufferer,' but [. . .] she is *not* a bitch" because nymphomania motivates her self-destructive actions (58). In "Women and the Loss of Eden in Hemingway's Mythology," Carol H. Smith does not use the term "nymphomania," but states that Brett "hopes to find in the drug of sex a way to forget the future and the past" (133).

Truly affirmative readings of Brett have begun to emerge; however, they still form the critical minority.[3] Many charges against Brett remain unchallenged or insufficiently challenged, and the majority of critics continue to view her as a flawed character. Linda Patterson Miller notes that Brett remains one of the "Hemingway women most often maligned and misread" ("In Love" 10). Kathy G. Willingham writes that even critics "who do take a somewhat positive view toward her [Brett] do so in an apologetic and equivocal manner, intimating a lack of conviction and signifying that perhaps there is indeed something wrong with her" (35).

Such misinterpretations stem from the fact that we as readers see Brett as Jake sees her, and his ideas about Brett seem conflicted at best. Scott Donaldson asserts that "Jake Barnes tells the story of *The Sun Also Rises* so unobtrusively and convincingly that it never occurs to us to challenge his view of events" (26). But maybe we should question Jake's narration as it pertains to Brett. He seems, perhaps unconsciously, to associate women with manipulation. For example, as he walks "down the Boulevard to the Rue Soufflot" early one morning he notices "flower-women [. . .] arranging their daily stock" and a puppeteer's "girl assistant" as she "manipulate[s]" the vendor's toys (*SAR* 43). After all, Jake emphatically says more than once, "To hell with Brett. To hell with you, Lady Ashley" (38). His dismissal sounds like an attempt to convince himself of her worthlessness, and this attitude could color his narration, which certainly seems questionable in other respects. In the excised original opening of the novel, Jake even admits that his narration will not "be splendid and cool and detached" because he "made the unfortunate mistake, for a writer, of first having been Mr. Jake Barnes" ("Beginning" 133-34).[4] Jake more subtly points to his own unreliability concerning Brett later when he reflects, "Somehow I feel I have not shown Robert Cohn clearly. The reason is that until he fell in love with Brett, I never heard him make one remark that would, in any way, detach him from other people" (*SAR* 52). Jake tellingly connects his misrepresentation of Cohn to Cohn's falling in love with Brett. If this affair so skewed Jake's perception of Cohn, what must it have done to his feelings about her?

Jake all but admits that he blames his desire for Brett on Brett herself: "Probably I never would have had any trouble if I hadn't run into Brett when they shipped me to England. I suppose she only wanted what she couldn't have" (*SAR* 39). Besides showing that Jake holds Brett responsible for his unhappiness, his statement points ironically to a seldom-acknowledged equality of purpose between these two characters. In desiring Brett, he too longs for that which he cannot have. A damning example of Jake's biased narration appears in chapter seventeen, detailing events surrounding the fiesta. Just after Brett begins her affair with bullfighter Pedro Romero, Jake sees her "coming though the crowd in the square, walking, her head up, as though the fiesta were being staged in her honor, and she found it pleasant and amusing" (210). However, we discover on the next page that he has totally misrepresented her desire for attention; Brett only wants to talk to Jake, and when he suggests a walk through the crowded upper end of the park, the area filled with "fashionably dressed people," she does not want to go because she does not "want staring at just now" (211). In this scene, Jake clearly ascribes motives and emotions to Brett that the text does not support, and he makes other, similar assumptions about her throughout the novel.

While Jake obviously narrates through his own prejudices, he remains our primary source of information about Brett. Unfortunately, what she actually says provides little insight into her character because she communicates largely with pat British expressions, and her words frequently contradict her actions. For example, she meets Jake in the *bal musette* and says that she plans never "to get tight any more" and then orders a brandy and soda with her next breath (*SAR* 29). Jake obviously knows more about Brett than he directly reveals. When Cohn asserts that Brett would never "marry anybody she didn't love," Jake replies "She's done it twice" (46-47), giving us a piece of information about her life outside the text. Readers familiar with the excised first chapter know that before she married Lord Ashley, Brett divorced a husband whom she had married "to get away from home" ("Beginning" 131), but neither this first husband nor the implication that Brett experienced a problematic childhood appear in the published novel. The extremely daunting problem for readers longing for a glimpse of the "real" Brett Ashley, then, lies in knowing how to extricate valuable information from Jake's narrative prejudices.

As early as 1947, George Snell suggested that *The Sun Also Rises* "is an interesting novel by reason of its investigation of submerged meanings, and for what is symbolic in the relationships of its strangely assorted personnel" (162). Undeniably, a great deal of this novel's action occurs beneath the surface, and readers must interpret Jake's narrative carefully to discern much of what goes on. Brett voices what could serve as Hemingway's credo for the novel near the conclusion when she tells Jake that she will not talk about her affair with Romero; instead, she will "just talk around it" (*SAR* 249). In much the same fashion, Jake's narration frequently seems to "talk around" Brett. By searching for the submerged facets of her character, the unseen portion of that fabled Hemingway iceberg, readers can penetrate Jake's sketchy, prejudiced narration and begin to value Brett as a fully developed character engaged, like Jake, in learning how to live in a world where the rules have irrevocably changed.

2

By resisting different critical charges against Brett and re-examining the basis for those charges within the text we can begin to uncover concealed aspects of her character. The most damning critical charges against Brett, the ones that delineate her as a "bitch" with devastating powers, seem rooted in two portions of the text: Jake's aforementioned assertion that he would probably have had no problems after his injury had he not met Brett, and Cohn's description of Brett as Circe, the goddess who turns men into swine. These constructions of Brett, however, go against the logic of the text. Obviously, she did not cause Jake's real problem, his wound, and Cohn, who according to Jake "had been thinking for months about leaving his wife and had not done it because it would be too cruel to deprive her of himself," almost certainly became a pig long before he met Brett (*SAR* 12).

Moreover, Brett's actions prove that she attempts to nurture others, not destroy them. Gladstein acknowledges Brett's "mothering qualities" and feels that these traits keep Brett from becoming a "pure bitch-goddess" (61).[5] While some feel that Brett mothers those around her in an attempt to provide some sort of sexual healing, her actions certainly satisfy something within herself as well.[6] She frequently chastises Mike and patronizes him almost as she would a small child. When she attempts to placate him after he first confronts Cohn she says, "Don't spoil the fiesta" in much the same way she might say "play nicely" to a toddler (*SAR* 148). As she leaves the group to nurse Romero after his fight with Cohn, she charges Jake with the task of watching out for Mike, but she still "look[s] in" on Mike herself on at least one other occasion (215). Furthermore, readers know that Brett nursed Jake through his recovery in a military hospital, and Mike says that his relationship with Brett also began because she "was looking after me" (206).

In the excised portion of the original first chapter, Hemingway gives a clue about why Brett feels compelled to mother those around her; she had a son with her second husband, Lord Ashley, and because of that,

Ashley refused to grant her a divorce ("Beginning" 131). We also learn that Brett prided herself on "the speed with which they [she and Mike] got passports and raised funds" when she left Ashley (132). Her emphasis on speed suggests that she escaped rather than simply left, especially given that we later learn from Mike in the text proper that Ashley repeatedly threatened to kill her (*SAR* 207). Brett emphasizes what she takes pride in, the speed with which she escaped, to deflect attention from what she cannot regard with pride, leaving her child with an abusive husband. Therefore, her need to mother those around her probably stems from the pain and guilt born of leaving her child in order to save herself.

Another critical misconception about Brett assumes that she is vain about her personal appearance. Jake presents her as a primarily self-interested individual who uses her beauty as a weapon and to "add [. . .] up" her conquests (*SAR* 30). As a result, critics like Fiedler see Brett as a "terrible goddess, the avatar of an ancient archetype" (319), and Gladstein likewise interprets her as an Aphrodite figure worshipped by the novel's men, and for whom they "prostitute themselves" (60). Jake emphasizes the powerful effect of Brett's beauty upon everyone who sees her. When Cohn first meets Brett, he gazes upon her with "eager, deserving expectation" as if he "saw the promised land" (*SAR* 29). He later tells Jake that he finds her "remarkably attractive," and that she possesses a "certain fineness" (46). Count Mippipopolous alludes to a quality similar to that "certain fineness" when he remarks, "You got class all over you" (46, 64). Bill Gorton first says upon seeing Brett, "Beautiful lady" (80), and even the women who work in the wine shop in Pamplona, apparently awed by Brett's appearance, come to the window and stare at her when she first walks down the street (142). It seems little wonder, then, that Miller describes Brett as a woman "who is aware of and trapped by her beauty" ("In Love" 10-11).

While the text makes much of Brett's attractiveness, she seems somewhat less sure of her appearance. Beauty may, as Miller believes, trap Brett, but Brett seems less aware of her appeal than Miller assumes. Brett agrees with Jake's assertion that she likes to "add [. . .] up" her conquests (*SAR* 30), but possibly because they afford her a much-needed source of reassurance. In the excised text, the omniscient narrator (whom Hemingway only later identifies as Jake) reveals the nontraditional nature of Brett's beauty: "She was not supposed to be beautiful, but in a room with women who were supposed to be beautiful she killed their looks entirely. Men thought she was lovely looking, and women called her striking looking" ("Beginning" 133). Perhaps because her attractiveness does not conform to traditional standards of beauty, Brett considers that "her looks were not much" and feels flattered when various artists ask her to sit for them (133). This deleted information casts a very different light upon how Brett views herself. For example, when Mike asks Jake, "Don't you think she's beautiful?" Brett's response, "Beautiful. With this nose?" (*SAR* 85), no longer seems a ploy to generate further compliments. In fact, her self-deprecating question may conceal a genuine insecurity about her appearance. Another sign of this uncertainty appears in Brett's reluctance to allow the *riau-riau* dancers to encircle her. She seems uncomfortable when they choose her as "an image to dance around," and instead wants to join the dance herself (159). Like Romero in the similar scene occurring after he kills the bull that killed Vicente Girones, if Brett functions as a goddess here, she seems a most unwilling deity.

Some critics connect Brett to the decidedly less powerful figure of the prostitute, rather than the goddess. Even revisionist critics seeking to redeem Brett as a character place her in conjunction with Georgette Hobin, the prostitute Jake entertains before Brett comes onto the scene.[7] The two characters do seem to exchange places as Brett goes off with Jake and Georgette remains with Brett's homosexual friends, but there is a distinct difference between the two women—Georgette can be purchased by the highest bidder, but Brett is not for sale. While Brett frequently allows various men to foot her bills, she does not, as Patrick D. Morrow suggests, function as "the group's prostitute in that most all her relationships sooner or later become based on money"

(56). Morrow proposes that Jake becomes Brett's "primary client" because he gives her "all he possibly can" (55), but Morrow's theory overlooks the fact that Jake does not attempt to buy Brett. Although several other men try to purchase her favors, she only accepts things from those who do not want to buy her, or, like Jake, know that they cannot. For example, Brett turns down the count's offer of ten thousand dollars in exchange for accompanying him on a trip to Biarritz, and only accepts things from him after making it clear that he cannot purchase her favors (*SAR* 41). Readers can also see this resistance in her financial interactions with Romero. Even though she refuses to take money from him as he leaves, telling him that she has "scads of it," she remarks that it "doesn't matter now" when she learns that he has already paid her hotel bill in advance (246-247). Romero's payment truly does not matter to Brett now that he has left and does not expect anything in return for his investment (247). Despite attempts by other characters to depict Brett as a prostitute, including Mike's numerous references to her as a "piece" and the concierge's characterization of Brett as "a species of woman" engaged in "a dirty business" (84-85, 39-40), Brett's actions resist such definitions.

Nor does Brett merely pay psychologically, as Jake implies with his realization that as a woman, she "pays and pays and pays" (*SAR* 152). Brett does pay in that fashion, but she also shows a pecuniary reserve at odds with Jake's exclusion of her from a financial definition of payment. We first see this reserve about financial matters when Brett dryly responds to Mike's suggestion that she purchase a new hat with "Oh, we've so much money now" (85). It surfaces again when, upon arriving in Pamplona, Brett sees a shop advertising wine for "30 Centimes A Liter" and decides, "That's where we'll go when funds get low" (142). Readers see the ultimate evidence that Brett pays her way both financially and psychologically when she funds Mike's stay in Pamplona; he freely admits that she "put up most of what I gave to old Montoya" (233).

A final catchall criticism of Brett linked to Jake's sketchy description of her holds that like many women characters in Hemingway's novels, she is a fundamentally weak, narrowly drawn character.[8] In "Hemingway's Women," Miller refutes such assertions by pointing to Hemingway's iceberg theory and positing that "some readers do not read between the lines to feel more than they understand. Some readers miss the underlying emotional complexity which inheres in Hemingway's art and in his heroines" (5-6). Miller further maintains that within the male-oriented frameworks of Hemingway's novels, "the female characters easily seem too narrowly drawn" (3).

However, with the exception of Jake, all of Hemingway's characters in *The Sun Also Rises*, male and female alike, seem somewhat narrowly drawn. Jake provides a lot more information about Brett than about male characters such as Bill or Montoya. In fact, Jake gives Brett a depth of character rivaling any other in the novel. She easily seems the most racially tolerant member of the group when she accepts the African-American percussionist at Zelli's as "a great friend of mine" and appreciates him as a "Damn good drummer." Her attitude of acceptance contrasts markedly with Jake's rather racist observation that the drummer "was all teeth and lips" (*SAR* 69). In light of the anti-Semitic humor that Hemingway directs at Cohn, attributing such open-mindedness to Brett might seem a bit of a stretch, but she nevertheless displays an appealing generosity of spirit.[9] Additionally, she exhibits a subtle wit as she delicately pokes fun at the count's speech patterns when she asks, "Got many antiquities?" (68). Her word choice recalls the count's earlier observation that Brett has "got class all over" her (64), as does his reply—"I got a houseful" (69). Hemingway highlights another of Brett's virtues, the ability to keep a secret, through a conversation she has with Mike. While Mike claims that "she tells all the stories that reflect discredit on me" (139), the text proves the groundlessness of his accusation. It's Mike, not Brett, who tells the story about his giving away someone else's war medals in a bar. She mentions at least two other "stories"—one concerning his recent court experience and another about his counsel (141)—however, because Mike refuses to tell those tales, readers remain in the dark about them. In contrast, Mike seems more than willing to relate information that Brett would rather keep quiet, most notably when he recounts Cohn's comment likening Brett to Circe:

> "Look, Brett. Tell Jake what Robert calls you. That *is* perfect, you know."
> "Oh, no. I can't."
> "Go on. We're all friends. Aren't we all friends, Jake?"
> "I can't tell him. It's too ridiculous."
> "I'll tell him."
> "You won't, Michael. Don't be an ass."
> "He calls her Circe," Mike said. "He claims she turns men into swine. Damn good. I wish I were one of these literary chaps." (148)

Brett clearly wishes that Mike had kept this information to himself, but he seems compelled to tell this story that reflects discredit on Brett. He reflects even greater discredit upon himself by committing the very offense of which he earlier accused her.

3

By acknowledging the shortsightedness of these and other judgments of Brett, we can begin to recognize that she functions as much more than a player in Jake's quest for self-definition: "I did not care what it [the world] was all about. All I wanted to know was how to live in it. Maybe if you found out how to live in it you learned from that what it was all about" (*SAR* 152). Brett also engages in a quest of her own, a similar pursuit that, in many ways, parallels Jake's. His emphasis on Brett's self-destructive behaviors, though, masks this search by making her appear mentally unbalanced. Jake's portrayal of her even leads Whitlow to suggest that "Brett's mind is, then, seriously disordered and filled with guilt" (57). But no character in this novel seems completely stable emotionally or mentally, and Brett hardly appears more psychologically affected than Jake. Jake's foul mood after Brett leaves with Romero, what Bill suggestively calls his "damn depression" (*SAR* 227), even causes Morrow to speculate that Jake actually spends his subsequent stay in San Sebastian at some type of mental hospital.[10] Jake's latest philosophy of living concerns the notion of paying for what you get. He thinks, "Enjoying living was learning how to get your money's worth and knowing when you had it. You could get your money's worth. The world was a good place to buy in." He then goes on to reveal that this philosophy simply marks the latest of several attempts to create meaning when he elaborates, "It seemed like a fine philosophy. In five years, I thought, it will seem just as silly as all the other fine philosophies I've had" (152). Jake, like Count Mippipopolous, has apparently learned how to "buy in" the world, but not how to live in it.

Rather than pursuing some sort of neurotic self-destruction, Brett, like Jake, simply searches for a way to make meaning of the changed world the war has thrust upon her. Like Jake, Brett searches unproductively for meaning through organized religion. When Jake describes himself as "pretty religious," Brett challenges that claim by declaring, "Oh, rot. [. . .] Don't start proselyting to-day" (*SAR* 213). Her doubt appears justified; Jake earlier comments to Bill that he "technically" professes Catholicism as his religion, but does not even know what he means by that qualification (129). Initially, other people block Brett from reaching out to religion. As she tries to enter the church in Pamplona, she is "stopped just inside the door because she had no hat" (159). When later she does gain access, she stays in the chapel for only a moment and then whispers to Jake, "Let's get out of here. Makes me damned nervous" (212). Brett recognizes that religion does not present any viable options for her and remarks, "I'm damned bad for a religious atmosphere" (212). Jake's observation that Brett's "praying had not been much of a success" echoes his own earlier failed attempt at prayer in the cathedral, a similar effort that ends in self-blame when he thinks, "I only wished I felt religious and maybe I would the next time" (212, 103).

While neither protagonist finds comfort in religion, Jake finds a measure of comfort in the natural world. The fishing episode at Burguete depicts Jake mostly at peace. Brett, however, does not even explore nature as a source of spiritual comfort. She apparently already knows that nature holds little potential for her, telling Jake "I couldn't live quietly in the country" (*SAR* 62). E. Roger Stephenson asserts that Hemingway removes Brett from the fishing episode because she is "out of place in the world of tranquility and peace that Jake and Bill experience" (37). It is more likely that Brett senses the natural world does not offer a woman the same opportunities it does Jake. Wendy Martin proposes that Brett avoids the country because she "knows that it is the urban centers that provide mobility and choices for the new woman, not the country with its traditionally limited vision of woman as reproductive being" (79). Or Brett could simply dislike the outdoors; she hardly seems much of a nature-lover. We rarely see Brett in a natural setting, and when we do, she usually occupies the decidedly limited natural environment of the park. And she does not even seem comfortable there. For example, when she walks to the park with Jake on the night that she seduces Romero, she can only sit there, surrounded by "the long lines of trees [that] were dark in the moonlight" for a moment before shivering and asking to leave (*SAR* 186-187). Whatever the reason, nature offers Brett little opportunity. She cuts herself off from exploring its possibilities when she asserts, "I won't fish" (88), and then somehow manages to avoid making the trip to Burguete altogether.

While Jake finds a comfort in nature unavailable to Brett, Brett searches through her sexual activities for a comfort that Jake cannot access. Critics have seen Brett's affairs as everything from a fairly innocuous search for reassurance to evidence of nymphomania.[11] While Brett certainly does enter into these affairs for some type of reassurance, the types of men she chooses as lovers suggest that she also uses her sexuality to search vicariously for meaning. Outside of her relationships with Jake and Mike—the long-standing connections that she maintains as part of her fundamental support system—she chooses to carry out her affairs with men who profess to believe in some sort of moral code. Cohn, the first of Brett's temporary lovers, seems a romantic type basically untouched by war. Mark Spilka aptly describes him as "the last chivalric hero, the last defender of an outworn faith" (109). Brett turns to Count Mippipopolous as her next candidate for a partner. However, she quickly cuts short the possibility of a relationship when he says that love "has got a place in my values." Brett challenges him when she replies, "You haven't any values. You're dead, that's all" (*SAR* 67). Because she vests such hope in the power of love, she cannot conceive of love as only one among many values.

Next, Brett enters into a romance with Romero that seems to have the most promise of any affair in the novel. In addition to his tight green trousers, Romero's belief in the code of the bullfight fires Brett's immediate attraction. When the affair first begins, Brett tells Jake, "I feel altogether changed," and Jake notes that she certainly does look "radiant" and "happy" (*SAR* 211). She seems to have found what she has searched for throughout the novel: great sex with a man who might possibly understand her and, more importantly, help her to understand herself. Predictably, though, she ends this affair as well when Romero tries to remake her into the more womanly sort of partner he desires by urging her to grow her hair longer. Brett remains true to herself, the self that Romero wants to change, and tries to cover her pain when she explains the situation to Jake, joking "Me, with long hair. I'd look so like hell." Given her insecurities about her appearance, when she tells Jake "It was rather a knock his being ashamed of me" (246), she almost certainly understates her reaction. Even though Brett says that Romero would have "gotten used" to the way she looked (247), she does not totally believe it. Hemingway evidences Brett's uncertainty by way of another of her defensive jokes; when she tells Jake that Romero wanted to marry her, she dryly adds, "After I'd gotten more womanly, of course" (246).

Brett tells Jake that she might have prolonged her liaison with Romero if she "hadn't seen it was bad for him." By deciding not to lead Romero on, she takes an important step in defining a system of belief for herself. When she resolves not "to be one of these bitches that ruins children" (*SAR* 247), she moves toward her own definition of morality, a more promising approach than searching for validation through the beliefs of her various lovers. By equating her ability to choose "not to be a bitch" with "sort of what we have instead of God" (249), she sets about defining her own moral code. Gerry Brenner speculates that Brett's decision represents a moral watershed and that with it, she "threatens to be his [Jake's] moral equal if not his superior" (50). Whether Brett becomes morally superior to Jake or not, her decision to define her own morality indicates that like him, she definitely searches for a way to make sense of the changed world around her.

In direct contrast to Brett, Jake seems much less willing to ponder the flexibility of moral categories. During one sleepless night he thinks that morality consisted of "things that made you disgusted afterward" and then decides, "No, that must be immorality," before dismissing the topic entirely as "a lot of bilge" (*SAR* 152). The way Jake quickly pushes the issue aside suggests that his search for a fulfilling life will be less successful than Brett's. With her analytical nature, she faces difficulty more readily than Jake does. The odds favor Brett because she can think through and talk out her problems; in contrast, Jake simply avoids thinking of such things. Until Jake can analyze both his needs and the choices that he makes, he will probably continue to search unsuccessfully for a mode of living that satisfies him.

4

Besides engaging in a quest for self-definition that equals Jake's in significance, Brett also plays a substantial, active role in their relationship. However, because Hemingway depicts the relationship exclusively from Jake's perspective, Brett's role does not become immediately apparent. Jake reveals the depth of his feeling for Brett when his stoic narrative breaks down and he admits that he "was blind, unforgivingly jealous of what had happened to" Cohn (*SAR* 105). But what, exactly, does Jake envy? Jake does not begrudge Cohn the sex alone, or he would hate Mike equally; Jake must resent Cohn because he can both love Brett *and* have sex with her, something Jake knows he can never do. Because readers know how Jake feels about Brett, and that his love for her results in many a sleepless night, he easily garners our sympathy. As a result, Brett sometimes comes off as a tease, leading Jake on and using him for entertainment when she does not have a lover.

Approaching the relationship from a more objective perspective, however, broadens the possibilities. If readers can get past the emotional bias of Jake's narration, the bond between him and Brett seems much more symbiotic than his description indicates. Hemingway suggests that a value exists in the relationship which Jake cannot see because of his own impossible desire. Readers know that Brett values Jake highly. While her lovers come and go, her relationship with Jake remains constant. When she tries to stay away from him, she cannot, and Brett even says that she does not see Jake because she *wants* to, but because she *has* to (*SAR* 35). Hemingway demonstrates her dependence on Jake when, in a fruitless attempt to separate from him, she leaves for San Sebastian with Cohn. The night before she leaves, she tells Jake that she must go because their parting will create a more positive situation, "Better for you. Better for me" (62). When she returns, she acknowledges the futility of her attempt by looking directly at Jake and saying, "I was a fool to go away" (81). Brett pushes Jake away and pulls him back to her throughout the novel in what Whitlow calls a "tease-withdraw-suffer syndrome" (58). Perhaps Jake highlights the depth of Brett's need for the relationship, a need so strong that Whitlow terms it a "syndrome," to conceal his own need for her. Jake's stance of ironic detachment is his most effective tool for masking his own dependence. Readers can observe this attitude clearly in thoughts like the one he has after receiving Brett's telegram near the novel's end: "That was it. Send a girl off with one man. Introduce her to another to go off with him. Now go and bring her back. And sign the wire with love. That was it all right" (*SAR* 243).

While Jake's stoic attitude successfully distances him, readers can still discern the depths of his desire when he occasionally drops his detached pose. Hemingway depicts one such instance after Brett leaves with Romero and Jake observes, "The three of us [Jake, Bill, and Mike] sat at the table, and it seemed as though about six people were missing" (*SAR* 228). Jake's actions after the fiesta further betray his need for Brett. He implies that he lingers in nearby San Sebastian because he suspects that Brett will need him when her affair with Romero reaches its inevitable end; as Jake notes, "I had expected something of the sort" (243).

Jake also makes their relationship appear one-sided by obscuring how he benefits from it. Despite his frequent protests to the contrary, he does profit from his association with Brett. Sukrita Paul Kumar proposes that Brett's "illusion of confident cheer and security" draws "the men of an after-war sick world to her" (103). Jake's sexual fixation on Brett almost eclipses how they enjoy each other's company in the other ways that Kumar's observation suggests. They have many of the same interests and friends, and Hemingway makes Brett the only woman, indeed the only other character besides Bill, who can verbally hold her own with Jake.

Ironically, however, most of the benefits that Jake derives from their association involve sex. Most obviously, Brett provides Jake with a convenient way to maintain a pretense of social normalcy concerning his sexuality. While Jake's friends know about his injury, Brett provides a useful cover for him with various acquaintances, like the count, that do not. For instance, when the count asks why Jake and Brett do not marry, she deflects his question with the rather inane excuse, "We have our careers" (*SAR* 68).

Chaman Nahal convincingly argues that in addition to providing this sexual cover, Brett possibly even gives Jake some sort of "perverted sexual satisfaction" in the scene where the count leaves them alone in Jake's apartment while he goes to purchase champagne (44).[12] Whether Jake receives, or even can receive, any sort of direct sexual pleasure from Brett, it seems clear that, as Kumar suggests, he derives "vicarious pleasure out of her sexual adventures" (107). Jake even says, "I have a rotten habit of picturing the bed-room scenes of my friends" (*SAR* 21). Later, he seems to derive a definite surrogate pleasure from Brett's interaction with Romero. Hemingway makes this especially evident when the three meet in the bar just as the affair begins and Jake reflects:

> I noticed his skin. It was clear and smooth and very brown. There was a triangular scar on his cheek-bone. I saw he was watching Brett. He felt there was something between them. He must have felt it when Brett gave him her hand. He was being very careful. I think he was sure, but he did not want to make any mistake. (189)

Jake watches the interaction between the two prospective lovers much as he would a bullfight, and his emphasis on Romero's careful avoidance of error recalls his earlier descriptions of Romero's confrontations in the ring. Moreover, the novel's language suggests a similarity between Brett's affairs and bullfights in passages that conflate the two. In one such passage describing a bullfight Jake notes, "There were no tricks and no mystifications. There was no brusqueness. And each pass as it reached the summit gave you a sudden ache inside. The crowd did not want it ever to be finished" (223). Such language links sexuality to sport and suggests that both give Jake a thrill by association.

The main advantage Jake derives from his connection to Brett, however, seems as much psychological as sexual; she gives him a legitimate focus for mourning what has happened to him. Hemingway demonstrates this early in the novel as Jake lies in bed thinking of his injury:

I lay awake thinking and my mind jumping around. Then I couldn't keep away from it, and I started to think about Brett and all the rest of it went away. I was thinking about Brett and my mind stopped jumping around and started to go in sort of smooth waves. Then all of a sudden I started to cry. (*SAR* 39)

Contemplating Brett allows the stoic Jake to feel the pain of all that he has lost in a way he can accept. He repeatedly dismisses any reference to his injury with a joke, but thinking of Brett allows him to refocus the pain caused by his "shameful" wound. Wanting the woman he cannot have appears infinitely more acceptable to him than grieving the sexuality he has lost. More importantly, with Brett, Jake can commiserate with someone who truly loves him and mourns his loss almost as much as he does.[13]

5

Brett must possess truly extraordinary qualities to occupy such a prominent position in Jake's life; however, she also represents all that he can never have, and she sometimes appears as a "bitch" or "narrowly drawn" character because his conflicted mind projects that image of her. If we read beyond Jake's narrative bias, we can see that Hemingway creates Brett as a character worthy of Jake's devotion, a real woman with complexities equaling his own. Martin believes that the final scenes between Brett and Jake show them moving toward a "genuine friendship," and that Hemingway represents this progress with the "coldly beaded" glasses of wine that mirror the "moisture beaded" wine bottles that Bill and Jake share in another scene of mutual friendship on the Irati River (Martin 80). However, the basic components of Brett and Jake's friendship already exist; the two characters only need to acknowledge the relationship as such. Yet by focusing on the sexual relationship they cannot have, Brett and Jake overlook the value of the friendship they already possess. While Jake may become, as Martin states, the only man who does not try to possess Brett because his wound "has made it impossible for him to make a physical claim" on her (70), he has an even more powerful psychological claim. When Brett tells Count Mippipopolous, "I haven't a friend in the world. Except Jake here" (*SAR* 65), her joking manner conceals a deeper truth. The ensuing exchange between her and the count, which begins when the count criticizes her characteristic verbal reserve, makes clear the main reason that she considers Jake her friend:

> "Why don't you just talk?"
>
> "I've talked too ruddy much. I've talked myself all out to Jake."
>
> "I should like to hear you really talk, my dear. When you talk to me you never finish your sentences at all."
>
> "Leave 'em for you to finish. Let any one finish them as they like."
>
> "It is a very interesting system," the count reached down and gave the bottles a twirl. "Still, I would like to hear you talk some time." (65)

Jake cannot make love to Brett, but in spite of that, or perhaps because of it, he becomes the only man she actually talks to. When Brett tells Jake, just before she begins her affair with Romero, "You're the only person I've got, and I feel rather awful to-night" (185), she acknowledges that only Jake understands her, or even tries to.

Clearly, Hemingway has already put the fundamentals of a friendship into place; Brett and Jake have shared the tragic experience of war, and, as a result, they listen to and support one another in their own ways. Friendship ultimately presents the only option for them; when Jake proposes a more serious commitment, that they "just live together," Brett refuses, remarking, "I don't think so. I'd just *tromper* you with everybody. You couldn't stand it" (*SAR* 62). She values her connection with Jake too much to jeopardize it with such an experiment, and even Jake acknowledges the proximity of friendship to love when he thinks, "you had to be in love with a woman to have a basis of friendship" (152). In fact, he might even unconsciously rank friendship as superior to love; his equation sets love as the basis of friendship, and thus establishes friendship as the more advanced, developed relationship.

Read through the lens of this friendship, the novel's concluding scene seems more optimistic than readers commonly think. Kumar echoes a fairly standard interpretation of the novel's conclusion when she states that the tragedy of *The Sun Also Rises* resides "in the disability of the otherwise strong man who suffers from acute loneliness in his inability to achieve the wholeness of a relationship with the other sex, despite his having found the right woman" (106). However, Hemingway implies that the real tragedy is the likelihood that if Jake possessed full sexual capabilities, his deep connection to Brett could not exist. Brett seems unaware of this probability when she laments that she and Jake "could have had such a damned good time together." Conversely, Jake's oft-quoted response, "Isn't it pretty to think so?" (*SAR* 251), suggests his belief that the romantic relationship could never have flourished long-term. While it might seem pleasant to think that this narrative could have ended happily if only Jake had escaped the war unscathed, he has already eliminated this possibility. Brett earlier says that Jake "wouldn't behave badly" if she rejected him; in response, Jake replies without hesitation, "I'd be as big an ass as Cohn" (185). In the end, Hemingway intimates that if Jake could have a sexual relationship with Brett, then he would become just another of her lovers, a passing distraction doomed to an eventual rejection. Given this likelihood, if readers view the couple's relationship as an unrealized friendship, it becomes something to celebrate rather than lament. By transcending the physical, their connection represents the possibility for a true, lasting camaraderie, a stable connection offering each of them something much more substantial than the sexual union that they think they desire. Freed from the limits of Jake's perspective, we as readers can see that Hemingway has bound these two characters together for life. Their friendship will help them to survive, and indeed has already contributed to their healing. This mutually beneficial connection becomes more significant and lasting than any romantic relationship in the novel. As such, it might form part of Brett's alternative, post-war morality, part of "what we have instead of God" (249).

Notes

1. Shortly after the publication of *The Sun Also Rises*, Hemingway ended a 16 November 1926 letter to Maxwell Perkins with the statement: "It's funny to write a book that seems as tragic as that and have them take it for a jazz superficial story. If you went any deeper inside they couldn't read it because they would be crying all the time" (Bruccoli 50).

2. When Roger Whitlow first tried to rescue Brett from the misnomer of "bitch" in *Cassandra's Daughters: The Women in Hemingway*, he theorized that some readers might superficially construe Brett's behavior as "bitchlike" (51).

3. Perhaps Brett's most loyal supporter, Linda Wagner[-Martin] asserted as early as 1980 in "'Proud and Friendly and Gently': Women in Hemingway's Fiction" that reading Brett "as a Hemingway hero is not implausible" (243). In *Concealments in Hemingway's Works*, Gerry Brenner implies just such a heroic status when he speculates that, at the end of *The Sun Also Rises*, "Brett might achieve the ethical ideal he [Jake] professed to be seeking" (50). Most recently, Kathy G. Willingham argued in "The Sun Hasn't Yet Set" that Brett "provides a model no less significant, important, or romantic than any of the male code heroes" (34). Other notable affirmative readings of Brett include Wendy Martin's "Brett Ashley as New Woman in *The Sun Also Rises*" and Delbert E. Wylder's "The Two Faces of Brett," studies of Brett as a "New Woman" of the 1920s, a reaction against Victorianism (68; 90-91).

4. I feel justified in referring to the excised text here and in other instances because this material, cut from the galleys at the last minute, informed Hemingway's composition of the novel. His deletions, as Wagner[-Martin] notes in "'Proud and Friendly and Gently,'" actually encouraged misinterpretation, leaving "readers too little direction" (242). While not a part of Hemingway's published text, the discarded material nevertheless sheds valuable light upon many aspects of the novel.

5. Wylder similarly notes that while the novel does celebrate Brett as "bitch-goddess," she also plays the role of mother to a group of men who behave like adolescents (92).

6. For example, Martin states that Brett "still plays the redemptive role of trying to save men through her sexuality" (71). Wylder notes Brett has an affair with Cohn in part because she believes it might be "'good for him'" (92).

7. In *Hemingway's Genders*, Nancy Comley and Robert Scholes propose that the

scenes with Georgette create a frame prefiguring Brett's entrance into the text (43). In "Hemingway's Women," E. Roger Stephenson asserts that Brett "recognizes her kinship" with Georgette as a virtual prostitute, a role "recognized by others in the novel, too" (36). Martin also suggests that while "Brett mirrors the traditional wife and the prostitute," she "will be neither" (72).

8. In "Hemingway's Women: A Reassessment," Linda Patterson Miller writes that a "belief that Hemingway's heroines are weak *in* character and weak *as* characters has persisted over time" (3). In one example, Edwin Muir states that Brett "never becomes real" (qtd. in Whitlow 49). Allen Tate similarly writes that Brett "is more caricature than character" (qtd. in Whitlow 49). In *The Hemingway Women*, Bernice Kert also implies such weakness, arguing that Hemingway's heroines embody his fantasies while his more destructive women mirror his prejudices (347; 134). More recently, Stephenson has theorized that Hemingway's women "are very difficult to discuss by themselves" because "Hemingway *uses* them to characterize his men" (35). Similarly, Jamie Barlowe's summary of female-authored criticism about *The Sun Also Rises* lists many negative interpretations of Brett as an object against which Jake defines himself (26-27).

9. Although undeniably anti-Semitic, Hemingway's treatment of Cohn falls short of mean-spiritedness. In "Humor and *The Sun Also Rises*" Scott Donaldson notes, "Jewish jokes, especially, were part of Hemingway's heritage. At school he was called Hemingstein, apparently because he was careful in money matters, and rather enjoyed the nickname" (20).

10. Morrow's argument that Jake "acts like a sanitarium patient" seems quite valid. Morrow notes, among other things, that Jake never mentions the name of the "hotel" at which he stays, finds comfort in watching the visiting nurses, and engages in what seems like a "therapeutic" daily routine. Morrow also points out that, as in an institutional setting, "meals constitute the high points" of Jake's days, and he often acts "drugged and tense, at the edge of breakdown" (60).

11. In her introduction to *New Essays on The Sun Also Rises*, Linda Wagner-Martin asserts, "Brett is a product of war-ravaged Europe. She must have physical affection, in quantity, for reassurance" (5). See endnote #2 for nymphomania references.

12. Specifically, Chaman Nahal argues that "In the stillness of the moment, both Jake and Brett see the uncommon and the unthinkable as their present demand—a demand which comes with an insistence and compels obedience. The simple adverb 'then,' repeated a little later as 'then later,' shows the fulfillment of that urge, while the forward action of the novel is at a standstill." Nahal speculates that Hemingway conceals this sexual moment within his text because "he may not have been sure in advance of the limit to which Jake's privation would take him" (44).

13. Brett occupies a similar position in that she apparently remains married to Ashley throughout the course of the novel. Although Jake tells Bill that Mike and Brett are going to marry (*SAR* 81), the count has earlier observed, "when you're divorced, Lady Ashley, then you won't have a title" (64). Brett obviously retains her title, and given her husband's refusal to agree to the divorce, will probably continue to do so. In a way, she is just as unmarriagable as Jake, and that gives her all the more reason to value his place in her life.

Works Cited

Aldridge, John W. *After the Lost Generation*. New York: McGraw-Hill, 1951.

Barlowe, Jamie. "Re-Reading Women II: The Example of Brett, Hadley, Duff, and Women's Scholarship." In Broer. 23-32.

Brenner, Gerry. *Concealments in Hemingway's Works*. Columbus: Ohio State UP, 1983.

Broer, Lawrence R. and Gloria Holland. Eds. *Hemingway and Women: Female Critics and the Female Voice*. Tuscaloosa: U of Alabama P, 2002.

Bruccoli, Matthew J. Ed. *The Only Thing That Counts: The Ernest Hemingway/ Maxwell Perkins Correspondence 1925-1947*. New York: Scribner's, 1996. 48-50.

Comley, Nancy R. and Robert Scholes. *Hemingway's Genders: Rereading the Hemingway Text*. New Haven: Yale UP, 1994.

Donaldson, Scott. "Humor in *The Sun Also Rises*." In Wagner-Martin. 19-42.

Fiedler, Leslie A. *Love and Death in the American Novel*. 1966. Third edn. New York: Scarborough House, 1982.

Gladstein, Mimi Reisel. *The Indestructible Woman in Faulkner, Hemingway, and Steinbeck*. Ann Arbor: UMI Research Press, 1986.

Hemingway, Ernest. *The Sun Also Rises*. 1926. New York: Simon and Schuster, 1954.

_____. "*The Sun Also Rises*: The Beginning Cut From the Galleys." In Svoboda, Frederic Joseph. *Hemingway and The Sun Also Rises: The Crafting of a Style*. Lawrence: UP of Kansas, 1983. 131-137.

Kert, Bernice. *The Hemingway Women*. New York: W.W. Norton, 1983.

Kumar, Sukrita Paul. "Woman as Hero in Hemingway's *The Sun Also Rises*." *Literary Endeavor* 6.1-4 (1985): 102-108.

Lewis, Robert W. Ed. *Hemingway in Italy and Other Essays*. New York: Praeger, 1990.

Martin, Wendy. "Brett Ashley as New Woman in *The Sun Also Rises*." In Wagner-Martin. 65-82.

Miller, Linda Patterson. "Hemingway's Women: A Reassessment." In Lewis. 3-9.

_____. "In Love with Papa." In Broer. 3-23.

Morrow, Patrick D. "The Bought Generation: Another Look at Money in *The Sun Also Rises*." In *Money Talks: Language and Lucre in American Fiction*. Ed. Roy R. Male. Norman: U of Oklahoma P, 1981. 51-69.

Nahal, Chaman. *The Narrative Pattern in Ernest Hemingway's Fiction*. Cranbury, NJ: Associated UP, 1971.

Sarason, Bertram D. "Lady Brett Ashley and Lady Duff Twysden." *Connecticut Review* 2.2 (1969): 5-13.

Smith, Carol H. "Women and the Loss of Eden in Hemingway's Mythology." In *Ernest Hemingway: The Writer in Context*. Ed. James Nagel. Madison: U of Wisconsin P, 1984. 129-144.

Snell, George. *The Shapers of American Fiction*. 1947. 2nd edn. New York: Cooper Square, 1961.

Spilka, Mark. "The Death of Love in *The Sun Also Rises*." In *Modern Critical Views: Ernest Hemingway*. Ed. Harold Bloom. New York: Chelsea House, 1985. 107-118.

Stephenson, E. Roger. "Hemingway's Women: Cats Don't Live in the Mountains." In Lewis. 35-48.

Wagner[-Martin], Linda W. "'Proud and Friendly and Gently': Women in Hemingway's Early Fiction." *College Literature* 7 (1980): 239-247.

_____. Ed. and introd. *New Essays on The Sun Also Rises*. Cambridge: Cambridge UP, 1987. 1-18.

Whitlow, Roger. *Cassandra's Daughters: The Women in Hemingway*. Westport, CT: Greenwood, 1984.

Willingham, Kathy G. "The Sun Hasn't Set Yet: Brett Ashley and the Code Hero Debate." In Broer. 33-53.

Wilson, Edmund. *The Wound and the Bow: Seven Studies in Literature*. New York: Oxford UP, 1947.

Wylder, Delbert E. "The Two Faces of Brett: The Role of the New Woman in *The Sun Also Rises*." In *Critical Essays on Ernest Hemingway's The Sun Also Rises*. Ed. James Nagel. New York: G. K. Hall, 1995. 89-94.

The "Whine" of Jewish Manhood:
Rereading Hemingway's Anti-Semitism, Reimagining Robert Cohn_____

Jeremy Kaye

Introduction

Even though Hemingway wrote several Jewish characters in his career, debates surrounding his anti-Semitism predominantly hinge on his portrait of Robert Cohn.[1] The scholarly archive on Hemingway's negative, if conflicted, characterization of Cohn is virtually unified in its belief that *The Sun Also Rises*'s infamous Jewish boxer conforms to anti-Semitic stereotype. After all, critics reason, he is the novel's "primary whipping boy" (Traber 238), and he is also Jewish; these two things cannot be coincidental.

Allen Tate inaugurated this critical castigation of Cohn with a devastating 1926 review of Hemingway's novel in *The Nation*. Tate calls Cohn a "most offensive cad," a "puppet," and a "Jewish bounder" (43). Without significant exception, Cohn's marginalized status has gone unchallenged ever since. Nearly four decades later, in 1964, Leslie Fiedler was still echoing Tate's negative sentiments, describing Cohn as "the despised Robert Cohen [*sic*], Jewish butt of *The Sun Also Rises*" (64). Jonathan Freedman, in a 2003 essay investigating modernism and anti-Semitism, describes the novel in these terms:

> Jake Barnes, the castrated, war-wounded narrator, is shadowed by Robert Cohn, the alcoholic, former boxing champion at Princeton, now besotted with Lady Brett Ashley, with whom he has a brief affair about which he *whines* for most of the novel and whose new boyfriend, a matador, he savagely beats at the end of the novel. ("Lessons" 423, emphasis added)

Freedman contends that this negative portrait of Cohn typifies a "remarkably consistent pattern of response with respect to the figure of the Jew" within American modernism (423). This remarkable consistency, in Freedman's estimation, has caused many critics to place Cohn with other anti-Semitic representations of Jews in the modernist canon: Meyer Wolfsheim, criminal Jewish financier and fixer of the World Series in F. Scott Fitzgerald's *The Great Gatsby*; Simon Rosedale, the wealthy Jew who cannot seem to assimilate fully into the social elite in Edith Wharton's *The House of Mirth*; and even "those damned jews" or "yitts" in Ezra Pound's *Cantos*. Yet, unlike Freedman and other critics, I am not so sure that the characterization of Robert Cohn is an open-and-shut case of anti-Semitism.

In titling this essay "the whine of Jewish manhood," I have used the word "whine" to suggest two important aspects of my approach toward Cohn. The word first pays homage to several generations of Hemingway's readers and critics who have condemned Cohn as a "whiner"— unable to "take it like a man" the way that Jake Barnes can, unable to live up to a model of Hemingwayesque masculinity that prides itself on suffering or "emotional restraint."[2] Secondly, I use the word whine to draw attention to its long association with Jewish men. When critics such as Freedman refer to Cohn as a "whiner,"[3] they are tapping into an anti-Semitic tradition relegating Jewish men to a feminized, less-than-male status. As Daniel Boyarin has recently shown, "In the antisemitic [*sic*] imaginary of Europe (and perhaps Africa and Asia as well) Jews have been represented traditionally as female" (69). Such discourse seeks to pathologize the Jewish man as feminine within a tradition that privileges an idealized masculinity based on Western ideals of manhood such as strength, stoicism, adequacy, heterosexuality, and, most importantly, figurative possession of the phallus (see Silverman 15-51).

Largely represented in the Western cultural imagination through such anti-Semitic tropes as the wimp, sissy, bookworm, or whiner, the Jew, in obvious contrast to an idealized masculinity, is symbolically castrated, lacks the phallus. We see this conventional scripting of race and gender drawn upon repeatedly in critical readings of *The Sun Also Rises*: Jake Barnes as the figure of "white" or phallic masculinity, and

Cohn, the Jew, as the figure of a deviant, less-than-white masculinity.[4] Yet the majority of criticism concerning Cohn fails to consider the transgressive possibilities deployed by his Jewishness. As the work of Daniel Boyarin and others in the "new Jewish cultural studies" so clearly demonstrates, theories about the construction and deployment of white masculinity rely on the abjected status of Jewish masculinity (see, e.g., Boyarin and Boyarin). While previous critics treated the feminized Jewish male character as "anti-Semitic [*sic*] fantasy," Boyarin instead calls for scholarship reclaiming the subversive possibilities of a figure belonging to a "culture of men . . . resisting, renouncing, and disowning the phallus" (69, 68).

My reading of Cohn explores a critical engagement between such work on Jewish masculinity and work exploring what Thomas Strychacz has called "Hemingway's theaters of masculinity." Recent pathbreaking criticism has explored the construction and deployment of masculinity in Hemingway's work through issues of performativity, masochism, and fetishism.[5] Taking my cue from such scholarship, I ask several questions: How can we use the Jewish male's disruption of hegemonic masculinity to rethink one of modernism's most infamous and most vilified Jewish characters? How can we talk about Cohn's Jewishness without treating it as a stereotype of Jewish inferiority? Moreover, how can we talk about the "whiteness" of Hemingway and Jake Barnes without viewing it as the source of racist/subjugating/anti-Semitic practices? How can we reimagine Cohn, not as an *object* of anti-Semitism as critics have cast him, but rather as an *agent* of Jewish manhood, disrupting the novel's privileged pairing of hegemonic and Hemingwayesque masculinity?

Whereas many critics have relegated Cohn's Jewishness to the margins of the novel (either as pure anti-Semitic stereotype, or as unimportant to a reading),[6] I would argue instead for its centrality. The fact that critics abide so willingly by the conventional racial scripting of Robert Cohn is ironic, not least because Cohn literally has the penis Jake lacks. Cohn is the novel's figure of hyper-masculinity. He, not Jake, has an affair with Lady Brett and boxes his way through both Jake and Pedro Romero. Jake's narration may be obsessed with Cohn in part because Cohn possesses the penis that Jake desperately wants and needs. This obsession manifests itself in the novel's first ten pages, filled not with Jake Barnes's exploits, but with Robert Cohn's. At times an object of Jake's affection ("I rather liked him" [*SAR* 7][7]), at other times an object for Jake's rage and anxieties ("I certainly did hate him" [99]), Cohn is easily the most talked-about character in *The Sun Also Rises*, inspiring feelings of love, desire, envy, or revulsion in almost every character in the novel. We might even say that Cohn exerts a certain control over the narrative, that his energy makes the novel more interesting and alive when he is present.

Critics are not wrong in characterizing Hemingway's representation of Cohn as anti-Semitic, yet why is Jake's animosity toward Cohn so often reconstituted in critical readings? Many of Hemingway's critics and biographers are quick to apologize for the author, deeming his use of anti-Semitic slurs "regrettable," but equally quick to add, as Carlos Baker does, that "like Frost, Pound, and Eliot, to name a few— [Hemingway] was born into a time when such epithets were regrettably commonplace on most levels of American society" (xvii).[8] Biographer Jeffrey Meyers lists twenty-two Jewish friends and acquaintances of Hemingway, implying that even if the author's portrait of Cohn was anti-Semitic, Hemingway himself could not have been because he kept Jewish company (72, 586). "Jewish jokes were part of Hemingway's heritage," rationalizes Scott Donaldson, before drawing our attention to the strange biographical fact that schoolmates had nicknamed Hemingway "Hemingstein" (20). Hemingway himself, in a 1926 letter to his publisher Maxwell Perkins, felt compelled to defend his portrait of Cohn against charges of anti-Semitism, defiantly asking, "Why not make a Jew a bounder in literature as well as in life? Do jews always have to be so splendid in writing?" (*SL* 240). In 1949, Bantam Press got into the act when, in a post-Holocaust edition of *The Sun Also Rises*, their editors expurgated the novel's one use of the slur "kike," all six uses of the adjective "Jewish," and six out of eleven appearances of "Jew" and "Jews" (Gross 149).

Much of this critical predicament is built into Hemingway studies as a discipline which, for better or worse, often privileges biography as a tool for interpreting the fiction. Debra A. Moddelmog, in her book *Reading Desire*, articulates how scholarship ostensibly about Hemingway's writing has worked instead to construct and reconstruct his persona. She notes that "the attention he has received is so clearly overdetermined and thus makes visible what is often hard to see: that critics' desires play an integral role in the construction of authors and the interpretation of their works" (2). Following Moddelmog, we can begin to see that the desire of scholars for the "real" or "true" Hemingway not to be anti-Semitic actually informs how they have read and interpreted the novel's anti-Semitism.[9]

This interrogation of anti-Semitism from the site of production—was Hemingway anti-Semitic or wasn't he?[10]—is necessarily limited. Once Hemingway has been either *outed* as anti-Semitic or *defended* from charges of anti-Semitism, the only thing left for the critic to do is articulate exactly how the portrait of Cohn is or is not anti-Semitic, how it does or does not deploy Jewish stereotypes. But the novel's central racial hierarchy remains intact: Hemingway/Jake's white masculinity on top, and Cohn's feminized, less-than-white Jewishness below. In attempting to rectify anti-Semitism, such critics explain anti-Semitism, but they never explain Cohn's Jewishness as a possible source of identification and agency. Because critics have most often explored Cohn from the site of Hemingway's *production*, they overlook the site of *reception*. Here the question "Was he or wasn't he anti-Semitic?" can be reformulated as "Can a new reading of Cohn's Jewishness emerge that neither Hemingway nor his critics account for?"

Historicism, Anti-Semitism, and the Difference of the Jew's Body

In *How Jews Became White Folks and What That Says About Race in America*, anthropologist Karen Brodkin locates the 1920s and 1930s as the "peak of anti-Semitism in America" (26). Anti-Semitism flourished, for example, in the realm of higher education because "Jews were the first of the Euro-immigrant groups to enter colleges in significant numbers" (Brodkin 30). Fearing that Jews would use a university education as a way to become assimilated into "white" American culture, Columbia University placed a cap on Jewish admissions in 1919, and soon was followed by other Ivy League schools viewing Jews as "unwashed, uncouth, unrefined, loud, and pushy" (Brodkin 30). It is no surprise, then, that Robert Cohn first becomes "race-conscious" (*SAR* 4), as Hemingway terms it, at Princeton: "No one had ever made him feel he was a Jew, and hence any different from anybody else, until he went to Princeton" (4).

Historical context is crucial for understanding the function of Jewishness in *The Sun Also Rises*, although not only as a way, as most critics would have us believe, to excuse Hemingway's anti-Semitism as symptomatic of the rampant racism-cum-nativism permeating the modernist period. Whereas apologetic commentators depict Hemingway and other modernist writers as merely *reflecting* the era's dominant racial ideologies, it is crucial to see that such writers also took part in *creating* such ideologies. Walter Benn Michaels's important rereading of modernism, *Our America*, argues that "the great American modernist texts of the '20s must be understood as deeply committed to the nativist project of racializing the American" (13). For Michaels, "Americanness" must always be understood as "whiteness," not as a biological-scientific category, but as a socially constructed and historically changing marker of racial and cultural identity. *The Sun Also Rises*, as an exemplary model of what Michaels calls "nativist modernism," fosters a hegemonic version of "white" Americanness in a context where immigrant groups such as Jews, Italians, and Irish, among others, are racialized as non-white.[11]

Defining Jews as non-white aliens proved no easy task, however, not least because of their ability to "pass" as "white" via intermarriage and other methods of assimilation such as dress, education, occupation, and language. To combat the racial anxiety caused by the Jew's facility for "slip[ping] back and forth into white Americanness" (Itzkovitz 178), late nineteenth and early twentieth century nativist writers made the Jewish body a focal point for the construction and articulation of the Jew's racial difference. Strategies for distinguishing "the Jew" from "the white American" at the site of the body were deployed across juridical, medical, and literary discourses. Sander Gilman, in *The Jew's Body*, analyzes historical representations of the Jewish male body—the Jewish voice, feet, uneven gait, circumcised penis, the "stink" of the Jewish flesh, and the ubiquitous hook nose—to reveal how such discourses described the Jew's body and his physiognomy in order to "set him apart as diseased" and render him "black," "mongrel," and "racially inferior" to the "white" national ideal (43, 172-74). Gilman's work suggests how period discourses deliberately conflated notions of the Jew's physical difference with notions of psychical difference, so that the Jew's exterior body (hook nose, e.g.) could be made to signify his interior nature (Jew as corrupt and/or amoral).

The Great Gatsby's Meyer Wolfsheim offers us an opportunity to apply Gilman's observations to the representation of the Jew in modernist literature. Published one year before *The Sun Also Rises*, Fitzgerald's portrait of the infamous Jewish gambler and bootlegger has become one of the best-known and most often critiqued descriptions of the Jew in American literature:

> A small, flat-*nosed* Jew raised his large head and regarded me with two fine growths of hair which luxuriated in either *nostril*. After a moment I discovered his tiny eyes in the half-darkness. . . . [H]e dropped my hand and covered Gatsby with his expressive *nose*. . . . Mr. Wolfsheim's *nose* flashed me indignantly. . . . His *nostrils* turned to me in an interested way. . . . As he shook hands and turned away his tragic *nose* was trembling. (64-7, emphasis added)

Critical Insights

Notably, it is Wolfsheim's body (his expressive, tragic nose) that makes his Jewishness visible, and excludes him from the WASPish whiteness of Nick Carraway. The anxiety with which Carraway draws attention to Wolfsheim's nose (six references in three pages) suggests that Wolfsheim embodies the stereotype of Jewish physical difference so perfectly, so grotesquely, that it is almost impossible for Carraway or readers to distinguish Wolfsheim as a particular Jew. Even though Fitzgerald's narrator "outs" Wolfsheim as a Jew by calling him one, Wolfsheim could never be mistaken for "white." He is "the Jew"—a different species altogether.[12]

Hidden Threat: Muscle Jews, White Male Fetishism, and the Construction of Cohn

The trouble with Robert Cohn in Hemingway's novel, and the reason why Jake's narration is obsessed with containing him, is that if Jake Barnes did not repeatedly *call* Cohn a "Jew," we would never know that Cohn was Jewish. Certainly, Hemingway's narrator is guilty of pointing out the "Jewishness" of Cohn's body,[13] but more often Jake performs rather envious appraisals of Cohn's body. For every reference to Cohn's "flattened" nose or "sallow" skin, we have many more references to his having a tennis player's body, a boxer's body, a body that turns Jake into a "human punching-bag" and "massacre[s]" Pedro Romero (*SAR* 199, 201). Cohn's body seems quite healthy compared to Jake's war-wounded, impotent body. In fact, readers are never given a very good sense of Jake's body. When Jake does look at his "wound," he quickly turns away, too ashamed to look for longer than a moment: "Undressing, I looked at myself in the mirror. . . . Of all the ways to be wounded. I suppose it was funny. I put on my pajamas and got into bed" (30). In comparison, Jake's narration often appears obsessed with gazing upon Cohn's body: "He was nice to watch on the tennis-court, he had a good body, and he kept it in shape" (45).

Cohn is not the weak and sickly caricature of anti-Semitic fantasy.

Rather, he embodies Max Nordau's idea of the "Muscle Jew." Nineteenth-century Zionist Nordau called for a "new Jewish body" produced through "sport" and "exercise" in order to combat the "inherent neurological weaknesses of the Jew" (Gilman 53-4). This discourse allowed the Jewish subject to shed physical stereotypes of Jewishness (such as a sick and feeble body) and identify instead with the dominant category of "white" masculinity (a muscular body). Cohn, for instance, becomes a boxer to "counteract the feeling of inferiority and shyness he had felt on being treated as a Jew at Princeton" (*SAR* 3). Through boxing, the "painful self-consciousness" he feels at being made "race-conscious" (4) turns into a "certain inner comfort" that comes with "knowing he could knock down anybody who was snooty to him" (3). Boxing allows Cohn a sort of psychical assimilation, a sense that he is no more different than anyone else. Boxing also affords him physical assimilation, as his transformation into a Muscle Jew rids him of the stereotypes of Jewish embodiment exemplified by his hook nose, "permanently flattened" in a boxing accident which Jake describes as "certainly improv[ing] [his nose]" (3). Rather than the hyper-visibility attendant on having a non-white racial body, Cohn's rebuilt, muscular body gives him invisibility. As a boxer, Cohn is absorbed into the hegemonic body of 1920s American whiteness. He becomes simply another member of the crowd, unmemorable and invisible: "I never met any one of his class who remembered him," writes Jake (3-4). "If he were in a crowd nothing he said stood out" (45).

Some critics have tried to account for the fact that Cohn's Jewish body is not very different from Jake's white body. For instance, Walter Benn Michaels suggests that "Hemingway's obsessive commitment to distinguishing between Cohn and Jake only makes sense in the light of their being in some sense indistinguishable" (27). Although he takes us part of the way in deconstructing the binary that separates the white Jake from the Jewish Cohn, Michaels is clear to distinguish their indistinguishability, noting, "[I]t is the similarity of the 'imitation' to the real thing" (73). As a Jew, Cohn can only "imitate" masculinity, while Jake embodies the "real thing." I would suggest, however, that Cohn's function in the novel is far more radical than merely to imitate Jake's white masculinity. Cohn performs white masculinity so well, in fact, that he exposes its very nature as a construct rather than an essential identity.

While we would never confuse Meyer Wolfsheim with the white masculine ideal, Cohn often embodies this ideal better than Hemingway's surrogate, Jake Barnes. For instance, Cohn has been educated at Princeton, an Ivy League bastion of genteel white male culture, while we never know where or if Jake went to college. Cohn is a member of one of the richest and oldest families in New York, whereas Jake, the rootless expatriate, must work and does not have a family, or at least never mentions one. Furthermore, Cohn performs hyper-masculinity in the novel with his tendencies toward sexuality, aggression, and violence. Because Cohn is so close to the white masculine ideal, his Jewishness becomes even more threatening to Jake. The Jewish Cohn as a "threat" to whiteness registers with Daniel Itzkovitz's notion of "Jewish difference [being] all the more threatening because it [is] lurking somewhere behind an apparent bodily sameness" (181). It is precisely because the racial boundary between the two men is so thin that Jake must continually reiterate with verbal insults Cohn's status as a Jew, labeling him a "Jew" and a "kike" at various points in the novel. Jake's own failure to live up to the white masculine ideal means that he must compensate for his lack with repeated denigrations of Cohn's Jewishness.

Cohn's Jewishness, then, is an almost wholly imaginary creation on the part of Hemingway/Jake, situated equally within his/their masculine pose and narrative desire. For Jake, Cohn's Jewishness operates along the lines of the psychoanalytic notion of the fetish, the unsuitable substitute object of desire with its commonly invoked formula: "I know very well, but still . . . ."[14] If we follow this formula, we can recast this statement for Jake as, "I know very well that I must reject Cohn because he is Jewish, but still I need him all the same." Paradoxically, Cohn is not only the hated object of racial "difference" in the novel, the Jewish scapegoat onto whom Jake projects his worst fears and anxieties, but also the object Jake *needs* for his (and Hemingway's) versions of white identity to remain stable. Jake cannot be white—where whiteness is defined by the possession of the phallus—without the Jewish Cohn. Cohn is the fetish object holding in place the "dominant fiction" (Silverman 15-51) that structures masculinity in the novel.

The usefulness of Cohn's Jewishness as a fetish giving integrity to Jake's masculinity corresponds with the notion of "Hemingway's fetishism" theorized by Carl P. Eby in his recent book bearing the same title. Eby successfully demonstrates how Hemingway's "fetishization of race" works so that he can define himself "as 'white' and 'male' in relation to an insistent and ever-present racial and sexual otherness" (157). This structure of fetishistic disavowal and masculine consolidation with regard to racial bodies becomes particularly problematic, and even takes on a homoerotic character, when we remember what Jake is lacking, what he needs from Cohn in order to maintain a white masculine subject position. As Jake is missing the necessary object for the coherence of phallic masculinity—the penis itself—we can extrapolate that he sees Cohn as a symbol for his lost penis. Thus Cohn makes Jake "whole" again. It is as if Jake says, "I know very well that Cohn cannot have my lost penis, but still . . . ." Cohn's presence—indeed, his penis—allows Jake to deny his own castration (symbolic and literal) and project that lack onto Cohn's Jewishness. In order for this denial to function, however, Jake must first identify with Cohn, because Cohn has the penis he needs, before he can reject him as a Jew, thereby disavowing Cohn's importance in the making of his manhood.

This dialectical relationship of identification and disavowal structures the novel's tropes of whiteness and masculinity. It also proves that Jake cannot be the sole point of identification in the novel, as he would have to be in order for us successfully to "read" Cohn as a purely anti-Semitic stereotype. Because Jake must identify with Cohn (and his Jewish penis) in order to cover up his own lack, Jake's narration creates a chain of identification leading readers to identify with Cohn as well, even though the novel seems programmatic in its efforts to prevent such identification. In order to disavow this "perverse," unwanted identification with Cohn, Hemingway's readers must become complicit in his subjugation. Acknowledging Cohn's performative function in *The Sun Also Rises* would open up a field of racial disavowal and desire that would challenge the novel's myth of masculine wholeness. Instead, most readers accept Hemingway's scapegoating of Cohn in order that the novel's powerful figuration of Hemingwayesque masculinity can endure unscathed.

Cohn's importance to the novel's racial structure is perhaps best understood after he leaves the narrative in Pamplona. Unlike most critics who reason that Cohn's exit from the novel "marks the dismissal of the Jewish question" (Meyerson 104), I would argue that his Jewishness becomes most important to the novel at exactly this juncture. After Cohn's departure, everything falls apart for Jake: the sacred art of bullfighting is profaned; the fiesta ends with Jake feeling "[l]ow as hell" (*SAR* 222); and his and Brett's idealized love for one another is lost. Cohn's absence from this last quarter of the text exacerbates Jake's masculine dissolution because he no longer has the fetish object that has consolidated his identity. Yet Cohn's psychological presence persists even after he is physically gone, becoming a sort of structuring absence that drives (if not disrupts) the narrative. A great deal of dialogue in the last chapters of the novel concerns Cohn: "'Is Cohn gone?'" (206); "But her Jew has gone away" (210); "I feel sorry about Cohn" (222); "Oh, to hell with Cohn" (222); "What do you suppose he'll do?" (222); "that damned Cohn" (243). Cohn's stubborn refusal to be forgotten constitutes his subversive potential.

Parody, Polo Shirts, and the Performance of Whiteness

Hemingway's recent critics have been reluctant to explore Cohn's subversive potential. Contemporary critical work has continued in the vein of Tate, Fiedler, Michaels, and others, blaming Cohn for his failure to become white, and thereby re-inscribing his marginalization. In a recent essay exploring the construction of whiteness in *The Sun Also Rises*, Daniel S. Traber argues that because Cohn wants to be assimilated into the dominant whiteness, he "accept[s] legitimized hierarchical notions of racial superiority and discard[s] the subversive potential of his own otherness" (243). According to Traber, Cohn "fails to be a transgressive source at the level of social marginality" (243). Traber's analysis, even with its attention to the constructedness of whiteness in the novel, still relies too heavily on the language of agency in its discussion of Cohn. Words like "accepts," "discards," and "fails" suggest that Cohn has some level of control over his status as a Jew. On the contrary, Cohn's enforced marginalization as a Jew cannot be anything but transgressive, as it draws out the instability of whiteness itself.

This is not to suggest that Cohn has no agency in the novel. Rather, Cohn's agency lies in the fact (not the choice) of his Jewishness. Cohn exceeds and disrupts the grand narrative of white masculinity as set up by Hemingway/Jake, best seen if we return to the novel's last few scenes before Cohn leaves the narrative. Having just knocked Jake unconscious for insulting Brett, Cohn retreats to his hotel room where he "was crying. There he was, face down on the bed, crying" (*SAR* 193). This image of Cohn crying face down on the bed secures his ultimate humiliation, apparently offering readers and critics definitive proof of his status as a "whining Jew." At least implicitly, this is the scene that critics refer to when arguing for Cohn as a Jewish stereotype. Hemingway depicts Cohn here as breaking all sorts of masculine codes. Cohn's violent verbalizing of his love for Brett ("I just couldn't stand it about Brett . . . I loved Brett so" [194]), his pain at the realization that he is simply another of her many discarded lovers, seems to play in stark contrast to Jake's stoic refusal to verbalize his own feelings for Brett. Yet because we have already seen Jake himself crying alone in bed over his unfulfilled love for Brett ("I was thinking about Brett and . . . all of a sudden I started to cry" [31]), Cohn's humiliation, which should give Jake satisfaction, instead only increases Jake's anxiety.

Such anxiety is most evident if we focus on an unusual aspect of this scene: Jake's repeated mention of Cohn's white polo shirt. Directly after he describes Cohn as crying face down on the bed, Jake notices Cohn's polo shirt: "He had on a white polo shirt, the kind he'd worn at Princeton" (*SAR* 194). Jake mentions this shirt three times in less than one page: "white polo shirt," "white shirt," and "his polo shirt" (194). The polo shirt is a fetish object par excellence, signifying for Jake both Cohn's undergraduate aura and his Jewishness. Presumably Cohn started wearing polo shirts as an undergraduate at Princeton to conceal his racial otherness and avoid "being treated as a Jew." Jake's obsession with the shirt reveals his envy of Cohn's upper class status and Princeton education.[15] If Cohn's polo shirt suggests his failed attempt at assimilation into the genteel whiteness of Princeton, Jake's fixation on it exposes both whiteness and masculinity as performances. For both Jake and Cohn, racial identity has more to do with behavior or performance (including costume) than with racial essence or being.

Not only does Cohn embody the white masculine ideal better than Jake, but we could even say that Cohn performs whiteness so well that he parodies it. After crying to Jake about his unrequited love for Lady Brett, Cohn's next act in the novel—perhaps in overcompensation for his outburst of weakness—is an attempt to embody a hyper-masculine hero: "He nearly killed [Pedro Romero] the poor, bloody bull-fighter. Then Cohn wanted to take Brett away. Wanted to make an honest woman of her, I imagine. Damned touching scene" (*SAR* 201). Cohn's efforts to perform heroic masculinity are complicated by his uncertainty about the masculine ideal itself. Should he act the part of the romantic hero, the knight in shining armor who wants to rescue Brett from a life of unmarried sin? Or should he emulate Jake Barnes's long-suffering masculinity of "emotional restraint," remaining stoic and silent, never articulating his feelings for Brett? Cohn consistently undercuts every gesture of masculinity he attempts. He valiantly "do[es] battle for his lady love" (178), but then cries and begs Romero's forgiveness, wanting to shake hands with him and Lady Brett.

Ron Berman has recently drawn attention to Cohn's apparent uncertainty about which model of masculinity to follow: "Some of Robert Cohn's problems are native, but possibly the most serious ones arise from his assimilation of and to the wrong models [of masculine behavior]" (44). Berman sees Cohn as the exemplar of an outmoded "false chivalry," as a type of "fake gentleman" (44). And yet, Cohn's status as a "fake gentleman" has everything to do with his status as a Jew: "Even where an effort is made, the Jew cannot escape his identity, cannot make the transition to civility and urbanity" (40). While Berman is correct in arguing that Cohn adheres to "wrong models" of masculinity, such an argument implicitly reinscribes the notion that the novel contains a "right model" of masculinity. In fact, Cohn's inability to choose a "right" masculinity exposes the fact that all masculinities in the novel are "wrong," that a true or authentic model of Hemingwayesque masculinity does not exist.

Kaja Silverman reminds us of the impossibility of ever truly inhabiting a "right" model of masculinity when she refers to ideal masculinity as "the dominant fiction." In *Male Subjectivity at the Margins*, she argues that this "right" model, based on the myth of the "adequacy of the male subject" (16), is dependent on the alignment of the phallus and the penis. For Silverman, drawing on Lacan, the phallus is not the same as the male sex organ. No male subject can actually "have" the phallus. Rather, the phallus represents the universal desire of all subjects to deny the fundamental castration or "lack" upon which male subjectivity is founded. Crucial to Silverman's formulation is the idea that the phallus needs the penis for ideal masculinity to work, and that their "disjuncture" threatens "a collective loss of belief in the whole of the dominant fiction" (2).

Richard Fantina, in an excellent recent essay, uses Silverman's distinction between the phallus and the penis to explore Jake Barnes's status as a "male masochist." Fantina argues that because Jake "lacks a full complement of male genitalia" (86), his maimed body enacts this "disjuncture" of the penis from the phallus that, as Silverman urges, contains transgressive possibilities. Yet even though Jake obviously does not have a penis, he is able to maintain the phallus by fetishizing such objects as Cohn's Jewishness and his polo shirt. Jake has the phallus without the penis, while Cohn has the penis without the phallus. As long as Jake and Cohn are together, the dominant fiction remains intact. However, when Cohn leaves the novel in Pamplona, he takes his penis with him, and this threatens, in Silverman's words, the "whole of our 'world'" (1). This shattering of the dominant fiction can only come when Cohn's abjected Jewishness is not present in the narrative. Only then can Jake articulate his failure to live up to the white masculine ideal.

The idea that Jake and Brett might end up together has been alive in the novel ever since the early scene in Paris where Jake tells Brett that he loves her, and begs her not to go off with Count Mippipopolous: "Oh, Brett, I love you so much. . . . Couldn't we live together, Brett? Couldn't we just live together?" (*SAR* 54-5). That Jake cannot help verbalizing his love for Brett at this point in the narrative shows how difficult it is for him to enact the stoic silence of idealized white masculinity. Jake's position in this scene relative to Brett—"I lay face down on the bed" (55)—clearly foreshadows Cohn's humiliating position later in the novel. Yet while many readers tend to define Cohn by his lying down and whining about Brett, readers tend when defining Jake to privilege the novel's last scene, in which he reasserts his stoicism.

At the end of the novel, Brett and Jake make one final effort to embody the dominant fiction; the unrealizable, romantic ideal of white heterosexual coupling that seems to contain the text's (if not the Lost Generation's) hope for regeneration. Lady Brett has just left the bullfighter Pedro Romero, refusing to marry him, and has gone to Madrid to find her soul mate Jake. Jake and Brett sit close together as they travel by taxi down Madrid's Gran Via: "Brett moved close to me. We sat close against each other. I put my arm around her and she rested against me comfortably. . . . 'Oh, Jake,' Brett said, 'we could have had such a damned good time together.' . . . 'Yes,' I said. 'Isn't it pretty to think so?'" (*SAR* 247). Despite their physical closeness, the gap between the two is now unbridgeable, and they both acknowledge defeat.

If Jake's "isn't it pretty to think so" reveals his refusal to live the lie of the dominant fiction, we must not underestimate the importance of Cohn's absence to this refusal. Because Cohn's Jewish penis is not there, Jake's identity cannot be sutured whole, and he finally is made to confront what he always was—a phallus without a penis. Readers, on the other hand, are left to wonder whether Jake would have ever come to this recognition if the Jewish Cohn was still present in the novel. If that was the case, the novel's famous last phrase could easily have been another slur against the Jewish Cohn rather than one of the most enduring lines in American literature.

From *The Hemingway Review* 25, no. 2 (Spring 2006): 44-60. Copyright © 2006 by the Hemingway Society. All rights reserved. Reprinted with permission of the Hemingway Society.

Notes

Many thanks to Steve Axelrod, Richard Hishmeh, Amy Vondrak, and (especially) Michael LeBlanc for their help with this essay.

1. Hemingway's other Jewish characters are minor in comparison to Cohn. Two well-known examples are Al from "The Killers," whom Robert E. Meyerson calls "[t]he most sinister Jew Hemingway ever portrayed" (99), and the more sympathetic Doc Fischer from "God Rest You Merry, Gentlemen."

2. For more on suffering as foundational to Hemingway's vision of manhood, or on his aesthetic of "emotional restraint," see Fantina 89-92 and Strychacz 14-52, respectively.

3. Sanford Pinsker in *The Schlemiel as Metaphor* regards Cohn as a "whiner par excellence" (40).

4. Here and throughout I deploy the term "white" to oppose Jew—rather than the more commonly invoked "WASP" or "Gentile"—in the interest of an accurate histori-

cal rendering of race in the modernist era. In the decades prior to World War II, Jewishness was not only characterized by religious and cultural difference, but, significantly, took on a racial character as well. While Jews would almost certainly be considered "white" in today's America, in the 1920s Jews bore the mark of the racialized subject, considered "off-white" or "not-quite-white" (Brodkin). Anthropologist Karen Brodkin narrates this historical transformation in *How Jews Became White Folks*, explaining the processes and discursive contexts that "made Jews a race and that assigned them first to the not-white side of the American racial binary, and then to its white side" (22). It was not until the post-WWII (and post-Holocaust) era, explains Brodkin, that American Jews would be considered "just as white as the next white person" (35). For a similar account of how Jews have "been both white and Other" (176) within a larger argument about the historical constructedness of whiteness as a racial formation, see Jacobson 171-99.

5. Gender studies have long been a staple of Hemingway scholarship (see Comley and Scholes), with important books by Strychacz, Fantina, and Eby exemplifying the best recent work on masculinity.

6. As Robert E. Meyerson puts it, "[I]f Cohn's function in Hemingway's tale is clear, what is not so clear is the purpose of rendering Cohn a Jew. . . . For the most part, references to Cohn's Jewishness or to Jews in general are just the mindless pot shots of trigger-happy loose tongues. The impetus behind them is not specific" (97, 100). Michael Reynolds posits that the novel's anti-Semitism is "irrelevant to the reading of the novel" (54). Carlos Baker adds, "Hemingway's anti-Semitism was no more than skin deep; it was mainly a verbal habit rather than a persistent theme like that of Pound" (xvii).

7. All quotations from *The Sun Also Rises* are from the Scribner's edition and are cited parenthetically in the text.

8. See also Reynolds ("Hemingway is a historical result, no better or worse than the America in which he was raised" [54]); Gross; and Rudat.

9. Ironically, Moddelmog's point is best exemplified in what is to my knowledge the only article that defends (rather than demonizes) Cohn. In his little-cited 1957 essay, "In Defense of Robert Cohn," Arthur L. Scott argues that Cohn is "worth saving" (309); however, his defense of Cohn is really a defense of Hemingway, agreeing with the latter's statement that, "'If you think the book is anti-Semitic you must be out of your mind'" (310). See also Kenneth S. Lynn, who after juxtaposing Hemingway's real-life "insensate desire to 'get' Harold Loeb" with Jake Barnes's "ambivalently sympathetic" (296) portrait of Robert Cohn, interprets this disparity in terms of Hemingway's persona: "A complicated man, Ernest Hemingway" (295).

10. I am indebted to Jonathan Freedman for this formulation. See "Lessons" 421.

11. Although both Irish and Jews would be considered white later in the century, it is crucial to understand both groups as non-white in the period under investigation (see Brodkin on Jews; see Ignatiev for a similar argument regarding the Irish in America).

12. Josephine Z. Knopf reads Wolfsheim as a "villainous Jew" alongside Cohn as a "schlemiel," noting that "as Jewish figures both are inauthentic and unrealistic failures" (61).

13. One of Jake's first descriptions of Cohn is that he "read too much and took to

wearing spectacles" (*SAR* 3), evoking images of the Jewish bookworm. Moreover, at several points in the text, Jake describes Cohn's skin as "sallow," possibly alluding to a stereotypic yellowness or sickliness of the Jew's skin (see Gilman 194-209). Examples include: "Cohn's face was sallow" (142); "[Cohn's] face had the sallow, yellow look it got when he was insulted . . ." (178); "[Cohn's] face was sallow under the light" (190).

14. For this construction of fetishistic disavowal, see Žižek 18-9.

15. As Harold Loeb puts it, "Hem had mixed feelings for the Ivy League and the Rich. My guess is that it was his combination of envy, suspicion and admiration for these categories that complicated his relations with Scott Fitzgerald and perhaps myself" ("Hemingway's Bitterness" 19).

Works Cited

Baker, Carlos. "Introduction." *Ernest Hemingway: Selected Letters, 1917-1961*. Ed. Carlos Baker. New York: Scribner's, 1981. ix-xxi.

Berman, Ron. "Protestant, Catholic, Jew: *The Sun Also Rises*." *The Hemingway Review* 18.1 (Fall 1998): 33-48.

Boyarin, Daniel. "Homotopia: The Feminized Jewish Man and the Lives of Women in Late Antiquity." *Differences* 7.2 (Summer 1995): 41-81.

Boyarin, Jonathan and Daniel Boyarin, eds. *Jews and Other Differences: The New Jewish Cultural Studies*. Minneapolis, MN: U of Minnesota P, 1997.

Brodkin, Karen. *How Jews Became White Folks and What That Says About Race in America*. New Brunswick, NJ: Rutgers UP, 1998.

Comley, Nancy and Robert Scholes. *Hemingway's Genders: Rereading the Hemingway Text*. New Haven, CT: Yale UP, 1994.

Donaldson, Scott. "Humor in *The Sun Also Rises*." In *New Essays on The Sun Also Rises*. Ed. Linda Wagner-Martin. Cambridge: Cambridge UP, 1987. 19-42.

Eby, Carl P. *Hemingway's Fetishism: Psychoanalysis and the Mirror of Manhood*. Albany, NY: SUNY Press, 1999.

Fantina, Richard. "Hemingway's Masochism, Sodomy, and the Dominant Woman." *The Hemingway Review* 23.1 (Fall 2003): 84-105.

Fiedler, Leslie. *Waiting for the End*. New York: Stein and Day, 1964.

Fitzgerald, F. Scott. *The Great Gatsby*. New York: Scribner's, 1953.

Freedman, Jonathan. "Lessons Out of School: T. S. Eliot's Jewish Problem and the Making of Modernism." *Modernism/Modernity* 10.3 (September 2003): 419-29.

Gilman, Sander. *The Jew's Body*. New York: Routledge, 1991.

Gross, Barry. "Dealing with Robert Cohn." In *Hemingway in Italy and Other Essays*. Ed. Robert W. Lewis. New York: Praeger, 1990. 123-30.

Hemingway, Ernest. "God Rest You Merry, Gentlemen." *Winner Take Nothing*. New York: Scribner's, 1933. 41-50.

_____. "The Killers." *Men Without Women*. New York: Scribner's, 1927. 78-96.

_____. Letter to Maxwell Perkins. 21 December 1926. *Ernest Hemingway: Selected Letters, 1917-1961*. Ed. Carlos Baker. New York: Scribner's, 1981. 239-40.

_____. *The Sun Also Rises*. New York: Scribner's, 1926.

_____. *The Sun Also Rises*. New York: Bantam, 1949.

Ignatiev, Noel. *How the Irish Became White*. New York: Routledge, 1995.

Itzkovitz, Daniel. "Secret Temples." In *Jews and Other Differences: The New Jewish Cultural Studies*. Eds. Jonathan Boyarin and Daniel Boyarin. Minneapolis, MN: U of Minnesota P, 1997. 176-202.

Jacobson, Matthew Frye. *Whiteness of a Different Color: European Immigrants and the Alchemy of Race*. Cambridge, MA: Harvard UP, 1998.

Knopf, Josephine Z. "Meyer Wolfsheim and Robert Cohn: A Study of a Jewish Type and Stereotype." In *Ernest Hemingway's The Sun Also Rises*. Ed. Harold Bloom. New York: Chelsea House, 1987. 61-70.

Loeb, Harold. "Hemingway's Bitterness." *Connecticut Review* 1.1 (October 1967): 7-24.

Lynn, Kenneth S. *Hemingway*. New York: Simon and Schuster, 1987.

Meyers, Jeffrey. *Hemingway: A Biography*. New York: Harper and Row, 1985.

Meyerson, Robert E. "Why Robert Cohn? An Analysis of Hemingway's *The Sun Also Rises*." In *Critical Essays on Ernest's Hemingway's The Sun Also Rises*. Ed. James Nagel. New York: G. K. Hall, 1995. 95-105.

Michaels, Walter Benn. *Our America: Nativism, Modernism, and Pluralism*. Durham, NC: Duke UP, 1995.

Moddelmog, Debra A. *Reading Desire: In Pursuit of Ernest Hemingway*. Ithaca, NY: Cornell UP, 1999.

Pinsker, Sanford. *The Schlemiel as Metaphor: Studies in Yiddish and American Jewish Fiction*. Carbondale, IL: Southern Illinois UP, 1991.

Reynolds, Michael S. *The Sun Also Rises: A Novel of the Twenties*. Boston: Twayne, 1988.

Rudat, Wolfgang E. H. "Anti-Semitism in *The Sun Also Rises*: Traumas, Jealousies, and the Genesis of Cohn." In *Hemingway: Up in Michigan Perspectives*. Ed. Frederic J. Svoboda and Joseph J. Waldmeir. East Lansing, MI: Michigan State UP, 1995. 137-47.

Scott, Arthur L. "In Defense of Robert Cohn." *College English* 18.6 (March 1957): 309-14.

Silverman, Kaja. *Male Subjectivity at the Margins*. New York: Routledge, 1992.

Strychacz, Thomas. *Hemingway's Theaters of Masculinity*. Baton Rouge: Louisiana State UP, 2003.

Tate, Allen. "Hard Boiled." In *Critical Essays on Ernest Hemingway's The Sun Also Rises*. Ed. James Nagel. New York: G. K. Hall, 1995. 42-3.

Traber, Daniel S. "Whiteness and the Rejected Other in *The Sun Also Rises*." *Studies in American Fiction* 28.2 (Fall 2000): 235-53.

Žižek, Slavoj. *The Sublime Object of Ideology*. London: Verso, 1989.

The Pedagogy of *The Sun Also Rises*_____

Donald A. Daiker

> Pain is the teaching emotion.
>
> —Edward Albee, *The Zoo Story*

> When you teach, you learn so much.
>
> —Paavo Jaarvi, Music Director, Cincinnati Symphony Orchestra

"He who teaches others, teaches himself," wrote the great Moravian educator and reformer John Amos Comenius almost four centuries ago. Comenius believed that teachers learn in the very act of teaching because "the process of teaching in itself gives a deeper insight into the subject taught" (47).

Educators past and present agree with Comenius that teachers learn by teaching. The sixteenth century encyclopaedist Joachim Fortius believed that "if a student wished to make progress, he should arrange to give lessons daily in the subjects which he was studying, *even if he had to hire pupils*" (Gartner 15, ital. mine). The 19th century English educator Andrew Bell writes, "That the teacher profits far more by teaching than the scholar does by learning, is a maxim of antiquity, which all experience confirms—'*Docemur docento*'—'He who teaches learns'" (75). The American psychologist Jerome Bruner tells this story of teaching quantum theory to college students:

> I went through it once and looked up only to find the class full of blank faces—they had obviously not understood. I went through it a second time and they still did not understand it. And so I went through it a third time, and that time I understood it. (88)

Sandra Cisneros agrees that turning students into teachers is one of the best ways of enhancing their learning. When asked to identify an appropriate writing assignment for students reading her award-winning novel *The House on Mango Street*, Cisneros replied, "My assignment as a teacher would be to have the students write the Cliffs Notes. When you teach is when you have to look at the text deeply" (7).

Ernest Hemingway's brilliant novel *The Sun Also Rises* (1926) demonstrates that teaching can be a powerful source of learning for the teacher. Jake Barnes, the novel's narrator and protagonist, tries to teach Lady Brett Ashley, the woman he loves but cannot have, the importance and significance of bullfighting. Brett fails to understand the lesson, but in teaching Brett Jake himself becomes the learner. In the novel's closing pages, most clearly in the final Madrid sequence, Jake puts into practice the knowledge he has internalized from teaching Brett, becomes the metaphorical bullfighter, and thereby ends forever his mutually destructive relationship with Lady Brett.

That *The Sun Also Rises* is a novel about teaching and learning[1]—what Terrence Doody calls "a novel of education" (217)—is established in its opening paragraph when Jake Barnes tells us that Robert Cohn disliked boxing but "learned it painfully and thoroughly to counteract the feeling of inferiority and shyness he had felt on being treated as a Jew at Princeton." Jake adds that Cohn had been a "star pupil" of boxing coach Spider Kelly, who "taught all his young gentlemen to box like featherweights" (*SAR* 11).[2]

But the importance of teaching and learning in *The Sun Also Rises* extends well beyond the boxing ring. Learning is the key to the philosophy of life that Jake articulates, and Hemingway endorses, in the novel's central chapter XIV:

> You paid some way for everything that was any good. I paid my way into enough things that I liked, so that I had a good time. Either you paid by learning about them, or by experience, or by taking chances, or by money. Enjoying living was learning to get your money's worth and knowing when you had it. You could get your money's worth. The world was a good place to buy in. (*SAR* 152)

Jake asserts in this passage that "learning" is one of the major sources of enjoyment in life. By learning about food and drink, books and travel, languages like French and Spanish, and sports like boxing and fishing, Jake gets his money's worth of life's pleasures. Jake's goal in life, he explains, is "learning to get your money's worth and knowing when you had it."

Aside from friendship, Jake derives most pleasure from bullfighting, which he has learned about thoroughly if not yet painfully. Jake carefully reads bull-fight newspapers like *Le Toril* (38), he travels to Pamplona and other venues to watch bull-fights "every year" (*SAR* 102), and he "often" (137) talks about bulls and bull-fighters with Montoya, the hotel proprietor, and other *aficionados*, those who are "passionate about the bull-fights" (136). Jake has learned bull-fighting so well that Montoya places "his hand on [Jake's] shoulder" in recognition of a fellow *aficionado* (136).

Jake has learned to get his money's worth of enjoyment from bullfighting, and through the central portions of the novel he teaches his friends about it. Even before the bullfights begin, he teaches Bill Gorton about the unloading of the bulls and the role of the steers in quieting them down (*SAR* 138). He later helps Bill, Mike Campbell, Robert Cohn, and Brett Ashley see that bulls use their horns like boxers, with a left and a right (144). He explains that bulls are "only dangerous when they're alone, or only two or three of them together" (145).

But Jake's teaching focuses on Lady Brett Ashley. During the second day of bull fights, Jake completely ignores Mike Campbell beside him in order to become Brett's teacher: "I sat beside Brett and explained to Brett what it was all about" (*SAR* 171). Significantly, Jake and Brett are seated in barreras, according to *Death in the Afternoon* the location most conducive to teaching and learning: "If you are going [to a bullfight] with some one who really knows bullfighting and want to learn to understand it and have no qualms about details a barrera is the best seat . . ." (33). "I had her watch Romero," Jake says (171), and in so doing he helps Brett try to understand how close the young bullfighter always works to the bull and how his bullfighting gives real emotion. Brett had earlier called the bullfight a "spectacle" (169), but with Jake's instruction it becomes "more something that was going on with a definite end, and less of a spectacle with unexplained horrors" (171). Above all, Jake tries to teach Brett to understand Romero's importance and his greatness: "Romero had the old thing, the holding of his purity of line through the maximum of exposure, while he dominated the bull . . ." (172). Jake at first believes that his teaching of Brett is successful—he uses the key phrase "she saw" no fewer than four times in a single paragraph to indicate his conviction that Brett is learning from his instruction and Romero's example. "I do not think Brett saw any other bullfighter," Jake says (171).

But Jake's teaching fails. Although Brett sees the purity of Romero's cape work, she misses his larger importance—symbolically represented by the bull's ear that, along with "a number of Muratti cigarette-stubs," Brett shoves "far back" into her hotel drawer in Pamplona (*SAR* 203). Brett's leaving behind the ear presented by popular acclamation to Romero, and then by Romero to her, shows that she is like the American tourists who "don't know what he's worth . . . , don't know what he means" (176). Interested primarily in Romero's "looks" (172), Brett manipulates Jake into introducing her to the bullfighter so that she can go to bed with him. Their affair causes bloody fights between Cohn and Jake and then between Cohn and Romero, as well as pain and anguish for Cohn, Mike, Jake, Romero, and finally Brett herself.

But Jake eventually learns the lessons that Brett misses. During the final bullfight of the fiesta, Jake makes no attempt to teach Brett. He speaks to her only to answer procedural questions, not to instruct. Instead, Jake concentrates on the personal relevance of Romero's work in the bullring, especially Romero's capacity for erasing the hurt of Cohn's beating: "He was wiping all that out now. Each thing he did with this bull wiped that out a little cleaner" (*SAR* 223). What Jake learns from Romero's "course in bull-fighting" (223) is that it is possible to clean up the messes in our lives. To this new knowledge he can now apply the earlier lesson he sought to teach Brett: it is through maximum exposure that you dominate the bull or any other force that, like Brett,[3] threatens to destroy you. Jake is beginning to internalize his own teaching, to apply to his own life what he has tried but failed to teach Lady Brett.[4]

When at the end of the novel he travels to Madrid to answer Brett's calls for help—Romero has left her, not the other way around—Jake has so well internalized the lessons he had earlier tried to teach Brett that he lives them. That is, in ending once and for all a relationship that drives Brett into other men's arms and prompts Jake himself to commit acts he acknowledges to be immoral, Jake puts into practice the wisdom that he has learned from Romero's bullfighting and that Brett has failed to learn. Jake the teacher has become Jake the learner.

First, Jake follows Romero's example of maximum exposure in two major ways: by leaving the safety of France, "the simplest country to live in" because "everything is on such a clear financial basis," for the complexities of Spain, where people become your friend for "obscure" reasons and where "you could not tell about anything" (*SAR* 237); and then by responding to Lady Brett's cry for help—"COULD YOU COME HOTEL MONTANA MADRID AM RATHER IN TROUBLE" (242, 243)—with an immediate and unequivocal *YES*. Jake is always most exposed when he is alone with Brett—like the bulls she becomes most dangerous when detached from the herd (145)—especially when they are alone together in a bedroom. During the early bedroom scene in Paris Jake becomes so "low" and so obviously dispirited by Brett's refusal to live with him that Brett says, "Don't look like that, darling" (63). In agreeing to meet Brett at her Madrid hotel room, in moving from "the terrain of the bull-fighter" to "the terrain of the bull" (217), Jake is knowingly—and courageously—exposing himself to another potentially debilitating bedroom scene.[5]

Even within the terrain of the bull, Romero controls virtually every element of the bullfight. During the final day of bullfighting, after Romero has begun his affair with Brett, "Everything of which he could control the locality he did in front of her all that afternoon" (*SAR* 220). All of Romero's movements were "so slow and so controlled" (221). Jake exerts the same control over Brett when the two meet in Madrid, although his control is evinced in more subtle ways than Romero's. For instance, it is Jake—and not Brett—who chooses Botin's restaurant for lunch and later decides on a taxi ride through town. Jake's control, even dominance, is further manifest in his understated sense of humor, a trait notably absent from the Paris bedroom scene. When Brett claims that Romero wanted to marry her, Jake responds with skeptical humor: "Maybe he thought that would make him Lord Ashley" (246). When Brett later invites Jake to think about Romero's comparative youth, Jake again replies with humor: "Anything you want me to think about it?" (248).

Jake's full control of the situation and himself as well as his dominance of Brett is shown in several other ways during the Madrid sequence. When they embrace for the first time, Jake is not swept away by passion but fully in control of his thoughts and sensations: "I could feel she was thinking of something else. She was trembling in my arms. She felt very small" (*SAR* 245). Later, as Brett and Jake are about to leave the Hotel Montana, Jake is still fully in control of the situation and of Brett: "I could feel her crying," Jake says at one point and, moments later, "I could feel her shaking" (247). Jake's dominance is also reflected in Brett's echoing his words. Moments after Jake tells Brett that she "ought to feel set up," Brett says, "I feel rather set up" (247, 248).[6] Still later, at the Palace Hotel bar, Jake separates himself from Brett theologically as he had earlier distanced himself emotionally. Thus when Brett asserts that "deciding not to be a bitch" is "sort of what we have instead of God," Jake challenges her use of the inclusive plural pronoun: "'Some people have God,' I said. 'Quite a lot'" (249).

Jake remains in control of Brett during the novel's penultimate scene in Botin's restaurant. There Jake eats "a very big meal" accompanied by four bottles of *rioja alta* (249), prompting many readers of *The Sun Also Rises* to conclude that Jake, still in thrall to Brett, is getting drunk to drown his sorrows.[7] Nothing could be further from the truth. Although Brett is convinced that Jake is getting drunk, her perspective is no more to be trusted here than her earlier thinking that going off with Cohn would be "good for him" (89). When Brett tells Jake not to get drunk because "You don't have to," she has no idea what she is talking about; preoccupied with herself as ever, she has not bothered to learn anything about Jake since he set her up with Romero. Brett has not the slightest knowledge, for instance, of Jake's swimming, diving, and self-restoration in San Sebastian, which is indeed one reason why he doesn't have to get drunk.[8]

Mistaken though she may be, Brett's belief that Jake is trying to get drunk is understandable. After all, she has seen him drink three martinis at the Palace bar in addition to three bottles of wine plus two glasses of wine from a fourth bottle at Botin's. That's probably enough alcohol to make even an inveterate drinker like Jake legally "drunk": it's likely that his blood-alcohol content exceeds legal limits and that he could not pass a breathalyzer test. But Jake's words and actions make clear that both at Botin's and afterwards he has achieved an emotional sobriety that enables him to control his relationship with Brett.

If Jake had been actually trying to get drunk instead of merely drinking a good deal, he would not have eaten "a very big meal" of roast young suckling pig—"My God! What a meal you've eaten," Brett exclaims (*SAR* 248)—because food slows the absorption of alcohol into the blood stream.[9] And he would not be drinking *rioja alta*, one of the lightest and most delicate (and finest) of the world's wines.[10] Instead, as at the end of Book II, when Jake acknowledges that he has gotten "drunker than I ever remembered having been" (227), he would be drinking a potent brew like absinthe.

If Jake had become not only legally drunk but functionally intoxicated by drinking *rioja alta* with Brett, his vision would have been affected, as it was earlier in Pamplona when he had drunk not only wine but "much too much brandy" and his hotel room had started to "go round and round" (*SAR* 151, 153). Similarly, when Jake purposely got drunk on absinthe, he saw his bed go "sailing off" before that "wheel-ing" sensation subsided and his world seemed only "to blur at the edges" (228). But in Madrid, Jake's emotional sobriety is underscored by his clarity of vision: "the houses looked sharply white" (251).

Whereas Brett's word is often not to be trusted, especially in the Ma-drid sequence, Jake tells the truth here as he does throughout the novel.[11] Thus when Jake denies that he is getting drunk, we should take him at his word—especially since he has freely acknowledged earlier instances when he had been in various stages of inebriation. For exam-ple, Jake admits to being "a little drunk" (*SAR* 29) in Paris, and "quite drunk," "very drunk" (151), and then "drunker than I ever remembered having been" (227) in Pamplona. The common Latin expression "*in vino veritas*" applies to Jake in two ways: he utters truth when he is drinking wine, and he tells the truth about the effects of the wine or al-cohol he is drinking.

Jake's denial that he is getting drunk takes on even greater force and persuasiveness because of its syntactic form—one of Hemingway's *trios*, three crisp consecutive assertions that essentially repeat each other. A trio is Hemingway's most powerful means of syntactic empha-sis, to be taken at face value without irony or qualification. Thus when Hemingway's "Hills Like White Elephants" concludes with the trio, "'I feel fine,' she said. 'There's nothing wrong with me. I feel fine'" (*CSS* 214), we can be certain that, even when confronted by her lover's lies and evasions, even in the midst of pain and rejection, Jig will main-tain her values, independence, and self-control. By the same token, the response of Count Mippipopolous to Brett's calling him dead—"No, my dear. You're not right. I'm not dead at all" (*SAR* 68)—makes clear that Brett is badly mistaken. Significantly, the scene at Botin's restau-rant closes with a trio of Jake's: "'I'm not getting drunk,' I said. 'I'm just drinking a little wine. I like to drink wine'" (250). Jake's trio tells us to believe him when he rejects Brett's accusation that he is getting drunk. It is another sign of Jake's control of the situation and his domi-nation of Brett.

But the novel's most significant trio occurs earlier as Jake's train from San Sebastian arrives in Madrid: "The Norte station in Madrid is the end of the line. All trains finish there. They don't go on anywhere" (*SAR* 244). This trio takes on special importance because Jake echoes it in his next-to-last spoken utterance. "I'll finish this" (250), Jake declares, the moment before leaving Botin's for a taxi ride through Madrid with Brett. Jake's determination to "finish this"—remember that Count Mippipopolous tells Brett, "you never finish your sentences at all" (65), and Brett admits, "I can't stop things" (187)—is a clear assertion of his control and dominance, and carries three-fold significance. First, Jake's statement suggests his resolve to get his money's worth from the wine he has paid for (Brett, like Mike Campbell, is penniless, a metaphor for her/their emotional bankruptcy); he has now learned how to get his money's worth of life's pleasures. Second, by finishing "this," Jake will not be leaving a mess behind for others to clean up, as he had earlier in Pamplona when, after he had made it possible for Brett and Romero to go off together, "A waiter came with a cloth and picked up the glasses and mopped up the table" (191). Finally, and most significantly, Jake's "I'll finish this" announces his determination to end, once and for all, his romance with Lady Brett Ashley.

The novel's final four paragraphs—Hemingway at his richest and best—show that Jake has internalized the lessons of life implicit in Romero's bullfighting, the lessons Jake has learned from his attempts to teach them to Brett. Like Romero in the bullring, Jake fully controls everything that transpires in the "very hot and bright" Madrid sunshine. It is Jake, not Brett, who tells the taxi driver "where to drive," in contrast to the earlier cab ride in Paris where he had asked Brett, "Where should I tell him" to drive? (*SAR* 32). But the key word in this paragraph is "comfortably." For the first time in the novel, Jake feels comfortable when alone with Brett. In Paris Brett had made Jake cry and beg, in Pamplona she had made him act immorally, but in Madrid Brett no longer exerts control over Jake. Even when they are seated "close against each other" and when his arm is around her, Jake tells us that Brett "rested against me *comfortably*" (251, my emphasis). Unlike the Paris cab ride, where Jake stares at Brett ("I saw her face in the lights from the open shops . . . then I saw her face clearly. . . . Brett's face was white" [33]) and kisses her on the lips, during the Madrid cab ride Jake is not even looking at Brett. He most certainly is not after a kiss, but is focused instead on their surroundings (the white houses), the weather (hot), and their route (the Gran Via).

However comfortable Jake now feels with Brett beside him, Brett herself is tense and miserable. For probably the first time in her life she has been rejected by a lover. Although she wants to believe—and wants Jake to believe—that it is she who has made Romero go, her words and acts gradually reveal to both Jake and the reader that Romero has left Brett, not the other way around.[12] Although Brett tells Jake that Romero "really" wanted to marry her after she had "gotten more womanly" (*SAR* 246), her behavior—throughout the hotel scene she cries, shakes, trembles, cries some more, and constantly looks away[13]—shows how depressed Romero's desertion has left her. So do her words. Perhaps the most telling index of Brett's emotional state is her decision to go back to Mike Campbell: "He's so damned nice and he's so awful. He's my sort of thing" (247).

Brett's equating herself to a "thing" shows just how badly she feels about herself, how far her self-esteem has fallen because of Romero's rejection. The depth of self-loathing reflected in Brett's seeing herself as a "thing" echoes Belmonte's disparagement of the bullfighter Marcial as "the sort of thing he knew all about" (*SAR* 219). Because Brett already feels so low, she no longer cares that Romero's having paid the bill at the Hotel Montana makes her a prostitute: "It doesn't matter now," she tells Jake[14] (247). It is a combination of Brett's depression and self-pity that leads her to reach out romantically to Jake for what proves to be the final time. In Paris, dancing with Jake, she had asked if he was "bored" before suggesting that they "get out of here" together (31); in Pamplona Brett had asked, "Do you still love me, Jake?" (187) before persuading him to introduce her to Romero; and now in Madrid

Brett once again tries to tap into Jake's love for her, this time by evoking the might-have-been: "'Oh, Jake,' Brett said, 'we could have had such a damned good time together'" (251).

What makes Brett's come-on to Jake different this time is Jake's response. Significantly, Jake does not respond immediately. At first he says nothing. He does not turn to face Brett, and he certainly does not stare at her as earlier. Rather, he is looking straight ahead to see "a mounted policeman in khaki directing traffic." That Jake takes his time in responding shows that he has taught himself the lessons of Pedro Romero, whose work in the bullring is "so slow and so controlled" (*SAR* 221) and whose passes are "all slow, templed and smooth" (223). That Jake does not look at Brett also recalls Romero's work in the bullring: "Never once did he look up" (220).

The richly complex final image of the novel—the raised baton of the khaki-clad policeman, slowing the taxi and "suddenly pressing" Brett and Jake together—underscores in multiple ways the lessons Jake has learned through teaching Brett about Romero's bullfighting. The policeman's "khaki" suggests war, as had the "very military" (*SAR* 242) appearance of the postman delivering Brett's second telegram; each is a forceful reminder of the origin of Jake's injury as well as a sign of his current vulnerability. Like Romero in the center of the ring, Jake is fully exposed because he locates himself wholly within the terrain of his bull—Lady Brett.

Brett's enticing "we could have had such a damned good time together" is the emotional equivalent for Jake of the bull's final charge. Unaware of Jake's self-teachings, Brett of course expects Jake to share her nostalgia and to embrace her self-pity. But she is badly mistaken. Earl Rovit is right in asserting that the raised baton of the policeman is "symbolic of the new command" that Jake has gained over himself and his relationship with Brett (158). But there is more here. The raising of the policeman's baton recalls Romero's drawn sword as he is about to kill. At the moment of the killing, "for just an instant" (222), Romero and the bull "were one," in the same way that Jake and Brett come together briefly when the taxi's sudden slowing momentarily presses them against each other. What happens in the bullring—"There was a little jolt as Romero came clear" (222)—exactly parallels what occurs in the taxi, what Hemingway in *Death in the Afternoon* calls "the moment of truth" (174): "'Yes,' I said. 'Isn't it pretty to think so?'" (*SAR* 251). Brett has to be taken aback—jolted, if you will—by Jake's refusal to indulge in her fantasies, but Jake has cleared himself of future romantic involvement by asserting that under no circumstances could he and Brett have lived happily ever after. As someone who "had been having Brett for a friend" (152), and as someone who knows that she "can't go anywhere alone" (107), Jake will not leave Brett stranded and penniless in Madrid; he arranges and pays for "berths on the Sud Express for the night" (247) so that he can return her to Michael,[15] her "sort of thing."

Jake's full control of his relationship with Brett, suggested by his choosing when and how they will leave Madrid, is manifest in the novel's famous final line. Spoken only after a deliberate pause following Brett's *cri de coeur*, Jake's words reveal through humor and irony the emotional distance he has achieved from Brett. Jake's initial "Yes" seems to imply his agreement with Brett, but it is an ironic affirmative immediately negated with "Isn't it pretty to think so?" Jake's control here is demonstrated not simply through what he says but how he says it. For example, his using the word "pretty" to mean not *pleasing*, *attractive*, or *good* but rather *foolish*, *silly*, or *ridiculous* deliberately echoes Brett's earlier equally ironic question, "Hasn't he [Mike] been pretty?" (*SAR* 185). Jake is subtly reminding Brett that it is her inability to remain faithful to Mike—and perhaps to any one man—that makes "a damned good time" for her unlikely.

Hemingway's late manuscript changes—two major additions and one important revision—help reinforce Jake's full control at the close of the novel[16] (Hemingway, *SAR Facsimile* II: 615-616). One key addition to the manuscript first draft is Jake's line, "I'll finish this," an unequivocal assertion that Jake is in charge and knows exactly what he must do. A second major addition is the sentence "He raised his baton" to the novel's penultimate paragraph. The raised baton also suggests Jake's power and authority. The important revision concerns the novel's final line, which apparently went through three stages:

> "Yes," I said. "It's nice as hell to think so."
> "Yes," I said. "Isn't it nice to think so"
> "Yes," I said. "Isn't it pretty to think so?"

Each revision shows Jake in firmer control. Hemingway may have eliminated the profanity in the first version above because Jake's swearing earlier in the novel almost always indicates his anger and at least a partial loss of control.[17] He may have gradually changed the form of Jake's utterance from a statement to a question—including a question mark in the final version—to achieve the sense of understatement that often characterizes Hemingway's most important utterances.[18] Finally, by substituting "pretty" for "nice," Hemingway allowed Jake to appropriate Brett's earlier term to make clear that he is the one now in charge of their relationship.[19] Significantly, the last words in the novel are Jake's.

The control that Jake evinces from the moment he arrives at Madrid's Norte Station until the moment he dismisses Brett's fantasies as "pretty" is clear evidence that in trying to teach others, especially Brett, about bullfighting he has in fact succeeded in teaching himself. By teaching others, he has taught himself that, like Romero with his final bull, it is possible to move beyond and even erase past mistakes and misdeeds:

> The fight with Cohn had not touched his spirit but his face had been smashed and his body hurt. He was wiping all that out now. Each thing that he did with this bull wiped that out a little cleaner. (*SAR* 223)

Following Romero's example, Jake wipes out his past emotional beatings in Paris and Pamplona. In the sunshine of Madrid's Gran Via, he becomes the metaphorical bullfighter who, fully exposed, "Out in the centre of the ring, all alone" (222), controls and dominates the force that threatens to destroy him by making Brett "realize he was unattainable . . ." (172). Jake the teacher has evolved fully into Jake the learner.

Notes

1. A number of commentators on *The Sun Also Rises* have recognized its educational theme although no one I've read has identified Jake as simultaneous teacher and learner. Earl Rovit, for example, calls *Sun* an "epistemological" novel and speaks of Jake's "painful lessons in learning how to live" (149). Linda Wagner refers to Jake's "initiation" and "education" (69), and Lawrence Broer to the "self-study course in emotional pragmatism" that Romero provides Jake (137). Ernest Lockridge notes that under "Barnes's tutelage," Brett receives a "bullfight-appreciation lesson" (80), while Robert Fleming focuses on the "lessons" that Jake learns first from Count Mippipopolous and then from Pedro Romero ("Importance of Count Mippipopolous" 144).

2. All quotations from *The Sun Also Rises* are from Scribner's 2003 edition and are cited parenthetically in the text.

3. Carl Eby is right in asserting that although Robert Cohn and Jake Barnes are each by turns a steer and a bull, Brett "is invariably a 'bull'" (308). For especially insightful discussions of the role of bullfighting in *The Sun Also Rises*, see Ganzel and Josephs.

4. For critical readings of *The Sun Also Rises* that focus on Jake's growth and the novel's positive ending, see Baskett, Benson, Budick, Daiker, Ganzel, Petite, and especially Vopat.

5. Jake rescues Brett, H. R. Stoneback writes, because he "places great importance on 'the values'—and one of the values is loyalty, generously assisting old friends who are 'in trouble'" (286).

6. Earlier, by contrast, it had been the other way around: it was Jake who had echoed Brett's words, who had gotten "into the habit of using English expressions in [his] thinking" (*SAR* 153).

7. See for example Balassi (115), Reynolds (62), and Svoboda (94). For an opposing view, see Vopat (103).

8. Vopat refers to San Sebastian as "Jake's Rest and Recuperation leave," convincingly arguing that its "lessons are still with him" when he arrives in Madrid (100-101).

For detailed and sensitive discussions of the San Sebastian episode, see Knodt and Steinke.

9. In *Death in the Afternoon*, Hemingway speaks of dining "on suckling pig at Botin's" as one of life's highest pleasures (104), clearly an experience that would be diminished if one were drunk.

10. In *Death in the Afternoon*, which offers many insights into *Sun*, Hemingway describes Rioja Alta and Rioja Clarete as "the lightest and pleasantest of the red wines" (461).

11. That Jake characteristically tells the truth is underscored by his admitting to the rare occasion when he doesn't: "I lied," he confesses, in telling Romero that he had seen two of his bullfights when he had in fact seen only one (*SAR* 178).

12. Hemingway readers are close to unanimous in rejecting my assertion that it is Romero who leaves Brett. See for example Gladstein, Comley and Scholes, Lewis, and Spilka. The latter refers to Brett's "charitable withdrawing of her devastating love" for Romero (179).

13. In Hemingway, a person's looking away usually signals either dishonesty or reluctance to accept an pleasant truth. In the Paris bedroom scene Jake lies "face down on the bed" (*SAR* 61) because he would rather not accept the impossibility of his relationship with Brett. Later Robert Cohn is "lying, face down, on the bed in the dark" (197), a sign of his unwillingness to acknowledge Brett's indifference. The innkeeper in Burguete, who knows she is overcharging Jake and Bill for their room, "put her hands under her apron and looked away. . . ." When Jake protests, she "just took off her glasses and wiped them on her apron" (115).

14. Earlier it was important for Brett's self-esteem that she not think of herself as a prostitute. That's why she rejected the Count's extravagant offer of "ten thousand dollars"—not because she "knew too many people" in Biarritz, Cannes, or Monte Carlo (*SAR* 41). The latter explanation is only what Brett "told him," not the real reason for her preferring to go off instead with Cohn, who offers not money but love. That Brett no longer cares that she has traded sex for money illustrates her deep despair.

15. In Hemingway's unfinished sequel to *The Sun Also Rises*, Brett has in fact returned to Michael. Probably written in 1927 and catalogued under the title "Jimmy the Bartender," this nine-page afterword to *The Sun Also Rises* shows Jake Barnes drinking at the Dingo Bar in Paris when Mike Campbell and Brett Ashley walk in together. See Fleming, "Second Thoughts."

16. Frederic Svoboda's study of the textual evolution of *The Sun Also Rises* supports my contention that Hemingway's late revisions to the novel's final chapter portray a more controlled and dominant Jake Barnes: "Jake's statements near the end of the first draft seem to project a protagonist who is more bitter and less in control of himself than the Jake Barnes of the completed novel" (40).

17. Jake usually swears only when he is angry, as when Bill Gorton asks about his relationship to Brett ("I'd a hell of a lot rather not talk about it" [*SAR* 128]) or when he receives Brett's telegram, "Well, that meant San Sebastian all shot to hell" (243).

18. After announcing his own central philosophy of life in Chapter XIV, Hemingway has Jake undercut it with "It seemed like a fine philosophy. In five years, I thought, it will seem just as silly as all the other fine philosophies I've had" (*SAR* 152).

19. For Svoboda, the novel's final sentence evolves from a "petulant and aggrieved" statement to "a wearier, yet more peaceful" one to "an even more appropriate expression of Jake's realistic, weary, yet essentially healthy accommodation to the realities of his relationship with Brett" (95).

Works Cited

Albee, Edward. *The American Dream and The Zoo Story*. 1959. New York: Penguin Books, 1997.

Balassi, William. "The Writing of the Manuscript of *The Sun Also Rises*." In Nagel. 106-125.

Baskett, Sam S. "Brett and Her Lovers." *Centennial Review* 22 (1978): 45-9.

Bell, Andrew. *Bell's Mutual Tuition and Moral Discipline*. London: C.J.G. & F. Livingston, 1832.

Benson, Jackson J. *Hemingway: The Writer's Art of Self-Defense*. Minneapolis: U of Minnesota P, 1969.

Bloom, Harold ed. *Brett Ashley*. New York: Chelsea House, 1991.

Brenner, Gerry. *Concealments in Hemingway's Works*. Columbus: Ohio State UP, 1983.

Broer, Lawrence R. "Intertextual Approach to *The Sun Also Rises*." In *Teaching Hemingway's The Sun Also Rises*. Ed. Peter L. Hays. Moscow: U of Idaho P, 2003. 127-146.

Bruner, Jerome. *The Process of Education*. New York. Vintage Books, 1963.

Budick, E. Miller. "*The Sun Also Rises*: Hemingway and the Art of Repetition." *University of Toronto Quarterly* 56 (1986-87): 319-337.

Cisneros, Sandra. "Study Guides: The Reviews Are In." Education Life. *The New York Times* 4 August 2002: 7.

Comenius, John Amos. *The Great Didactic*, Part II. Trans. M. W. Keatinge. London: A. and C. Black, Ltd., 1921.

Comley, Nancy R. and Robert Scholes. *Hemingway's Genders: Rereading the Hemingway Text*. New Haven: Yale UP, 1994.

Daiker, Donald A. "The Affirmative Conclusion of *The Sun Also Rises*." 1974. Rptd. in Nagel 74-88.

Doody, Terrence. "Hemingway's Style and Jake's Narration." 1974. Rptd. in *Ernest Hemingway: Seven Decades of Criticism*. Ed. Linda Wagner-Martin. East Lansing: Michigan State UP, 1998. 103-117.

Eby, Carl P. *Hemingway's Fetishism: Psychoanalysis and the Mirror of Manhood*. Albany: State U of New York P, 1999.

Fleming, Robert E. "The Importance of Count Mippipopolous: Creating the Code Hero." 1988. In Nagel. 141-145.

_____. "Second Thoughts: Hemingway's Postscript to *The Sun Also Rises*." In Nagel. 163-169.

Ganzel, Dewey. "*Cabestro* and *Vaquilla*: The Symbolic Structure of *The Sun Also Rises*." *Sewanee Review* 76 (1968): 26-48.

Gartner, Alan, Mary Conway Kohler, and Frank Reissman. *Children Teach Children: Learning by Teaching*. New York: Harper & Row, 1971.

Gladstein, Mimi Reisel. *The Indestructible Woman in Faulkner, Hemingway, and Steinbeck*. Ann Arbor: UMI Research P, 1986.

Hemingway, Ernest. *The Complete Short Stories of Ernest Hemingway: The Finca Vigía Edition*. New York: Scribner's, 1987.

_____. *Death in the Afternoon*. New York: Scribner's, 1932.

_____. *Ernest Hemingway: Selected Letters, 1917-1961*. Ed. Carlos Baker. New York: Scribner's, 1981.

_____. "Jimmy the Bartender." Item 530. Hemingway Collection. John F. Kennedy Library. Boston, MA.

_____. *The Sun Also Rises*. 1926. New York: Scribner's, 2003.

_____. *The Sun Also Rises: A Facsimile Edition*. Ed. Matthew J. Bruccoli. Detroit., MI: Archive of Literary Documents, 1990.

Jaarvi, Paavo. Comments during a Cincinnati Symphony Orchestra Donors' Choice Concert. 5 September 2005.

Josephs, Allen. "*Toreo*: The Moral Axis of *The Sun Also Rises*." 1986. In Nagel. 126-140.

Knodt, Ellen Andrews. "Diving Deep: Jake's Moment of Truth at San Sebastian." *The Hemingway Review* 17 (Fall 1997): 28-37.

Lewis, Robert W. "Tristan or Jacob?" 1965. Rptd. in Bloom. 63-75.

Lockridge, Ernest. "The Primitive Emotion that Drives Jake Barnes." 1990. In *Readings on The Sun Also Rises*. Ed. Kelly Wand. San Diego, CA: Greenhaven, 2002. 79-93.

Nagel, James, ed. *Critical Essays on Ernest Hemingway's The Sun Also Rises*. New York: G. K. Hall, 1995.

Petite, Joseph. "Hemingway and Existential Education." *Journal of Evolutionary Psychology* 12 (1991): 152-164.

Reynolds, Michael S. *The Sun Also Rises: A Novel of the Twenties*. Boston: Twayne, 1988.

Rovit, Earl. *Ernest Hemingway*. New Haven, CT: College and University P by special arrangement with Twayne, 1963.

Spilka, Mark. *Hemingway's Quarrel with Androgyny*. Lincoln: Nebraska UP, 1990. 175-183.

Steinke, Jim. "Brett and Jake in Spain: Hemingway's Ending for *The Sun Also Rises*." *Spectrum* 27 (1985): 131-141.

Stoneback, H. R. *Reading Hemingway's The Sun Also Rises: Glossary and Commentary*. Kent, OH: Kent State UP, 2007.

Svoboda, Frederic Joseph. *Hemingway and The Sun Also Rises: The Crafting of a Style*. Lawrence: Kansas UP, 1983.

Vopat, Carole Gottlieb. "The End of *The Sun Also Rises*: A New Beginning." 1972. Rptd. in Bloom. 96-105.

Wagner, Linda W. "*The Sun Also Rises*: One Debt to Imagism." 1972. In Nagel. 63-73.

Life Unworthy of Life?
Masculinity, Disability, and Guilt
in *The Sun Also Rises*_____

As Michael S. Reynolds and others have noted, the intense campaign of persona-building that Hemingway engaged in after being
wounded in World War I makes it difficult to assess his level of anxiety
over degeneration through disability. Even so, the cultural research of
Joanna Bourke and Betsy L. Nies suggests that this fear would have
been more than "in the air" for a wounded man returning from Europe.
Bourke, for instance, notes that an increase of pension claims sensi-
tized Britain to the literal costs of war-related disability and helped to
re-energize debates over which veterans "deserved" charity and which
did not (63-75). Nies, in turn, describes how similar financial concerns
and the popularization of eugenic theories in the United States combined to make the war-wounded body a site for particularly intense
fears about "degeneration."[1]

In addition to this body-obsessed cultural milieu, a seemingly minor
incident during Hemingway's recuperation in Italy may have helped ce-
ment connections between disability and moral/physical breakdown in
his mind. Quoting from the writer's correspondence, biographer James
Mellow reports that not long after Hemingway's arrival at the hospital
in Milan, "one of [his] newly-acquired friends proved to be a problem"
(70). The friend was the wealthy Mr. Englefield, "an Englishman in his
fifties, brother to one of the Lords of the Admiralty":

> Mr. Englefield, who had been "younger sonning it in Italy for about twenty
> years," had adopted him, visited him often, made a practice of bringing
> him gifts—everything from eau de cologne to the London papers and bot-
> tles of Marsala. Later in life, however, Hemingway would remember Mr.
> Englefield in an acid sketch in a letter to a friend. On his visits to the hospi-
> tal, Mr. Englefield, it seems, "got wet about wanting to see my wounds

---

Masculinity, Disability, and Guilt **331**

dressed. At the time I didn't know well-brought-up people were like that. I thought it was only tramps. I explained to him that I was not that way and that he couldn't come to the hospital anymore and that I couldn't take his Marsala." (Mellow 70)

This incident has been interpreted as contributing in a general way to Hemingway's awareness of sexual behaviors not acknowledged by his Midwestern home town (Vernon 39). Critics such as Eby and Elliott concur that such an incident would heighten Hemingway's interest in the idea of erotic variations and help to move him past thinking about sexual desire in binary terms. Yet while they recognize this subsequent interest in sexual variety, these readings do not stray far beyond binarism themselves, ultimately situating Hemingway's fascination within a familiar spectrum of either homosexual or heterosexual behavior signified through a socially constructed gender. (This is arguably true even in Eby's case, where Hemingway's hair fetish is tied to his fascination with "effeminate" men and "boyish" women.)

If, however, Englefield's lapse of sexual decorum was indeed triggered by arguments over seeing Hemingway's "wounds dressed," it also serves as the young writer's introduction to a wider range of beliefs specifically tied to sexuality and disability. Mr. Englefield could, for instance, have been what disability researchers call a "devotee"—a species of fetishist whose erotic desires are triggered by the sight of people with disabilities. There exists today, for instance, a large community of devotees who seek out partners with amputations; others, however, are aroused by simply associating with disabled people (Bruno 1-10). The rapidly expanding field of disability studies has done much to create a fuller understanding of this kind of fetishism, as part of its wider research on the ways cultural stereotypes intersect with the realms of myth, psychology, pseudoscience, and medicine to impact the daily lives of people with physical and mental impairments.

The Sun Also Rises articulates ideas currently debated within the field of disability studies, especially those related to the concept of the "disabled identity" (Linton 8-32). An examination of these new concepts, in turn, allows a re-evaluation of Hemingway's attitudes toward wounds and masculinity. Specifically, the experiences of emasculated war hero Jake Barnes reflect Hemingway's awareness of what researchers call a "medical model" of disability—a worldview that equates disability with pathology and that forces disabled people continually to "prove" to the world at large that they are completely "cured" and therefore "normal."[2] The novel's downbeat ending suggests that a philosophy that continually denies bodily realities can be as physically and mentally destructive as a literal wound. In the end, Jake will never achieve the psychological stability he craves because he finally accepts prevailing social and medical philosophies about his injury—and these ideas, in turn, will always leave him vulnerable to the fear that he will "degenerate" into an invalid or a "pervert." The encounter with Englefield may have alerted Hemingway to the fact that merely having a disability made one vulnerable to a new range of sexual stereotypes and cultural assumptions—and especially to the idea that disability "turns" men into homosexuals or childlike, asexual beings (Shakespeare 10, 63-65).

The specters of the eunuch and the "queer" haunt Jake Barnes and drive his search for a viable identity. In the novel, Jake's struggle to define himself as a disabled man plays out in what Thomas Strychacz calls "theatrical representations," in which he exists on a continuum of behavior "between" male characters (8, 74-80). These are men whose behavior and physical characteristics seem like exaggerated aspects of Jake's own, at least potentially. Specifically, Jake occupies a psychological middle-ground between the disabled characters Count Mippipopolous and the bullfighter Belmonte—and as he accepts or rejects these characters, we are meant to understand that he is embracing or discarding the stereotypes of able-bodiedness or disability they represent.

Generally speaking, critics have glossed over the complexity of the relationship between Jake's identity and the stereotypes linking wounds, physical power, and masculine degeneration. This oversight is due largely to the influence of Freudian thinking even within more "modern" readings of the novel that move away from the older, blatantly "heroic" and masculinist interpretations of Philip Young, Carlos Baker, and Jeffrey Meyers.[3] And so while recent interpretations have established Hemingway's awareness of gender construction and varieties of erotic desire, they consider disability primarily as a catalyst alerting Jake in a general way to the existence of a "polymorphous" sexuality. The Freudian school either aligns Jake with the stereotypical figure of the disabled man who receives a compensatory "gift" of artistic or emotional sensitivity because of his impairment, or uncritically accepts the notion that he is "turning" gay because of his injuries.

Wolfgang Rudat's essay on the Count deserves a second look at this point. Rudat identifies Mippipopolous as the only psychologically healthy disabled man in the novel, situating him within an "inspirational" discourse crafted to show how a man with injuries arguably similar to Jake's might achieve a greater sense of mental stability. Rudat explains that Brett Ashley introduces the Count as a pawn in her quasi-sadomasochistic relationship with Jake, as yet another substitute for Jake himself, and as a target for her repressed frustration:

> [When] Brett turns to Jake to assure him that the Count is one of them, that is, that the Count is also wounded, and then makes a show of telling the Count that she loves him and that he is a "darling," she is telling Jake that the Count too is sexually "wounded." . . . The Count, whom according to her own statement Brett has told that she was in love with Jake . . . knows . . . that Brett has now communicated to Jake that he, the Count, is sexually disabled. Not only does the Count take in stride the communication to another man of his own sexual status, but he actually confirms it in order to be able to explain to the other man his philosophy of life, that is, that he "can enjoy everything so well," including relations with women. (Rudat 7)

This is a persuasive analysis of the sadomasochistic elements in Brett and Jake's relationship, but because it assumes without question that the Count is literally the best-adjusted disabled man in the novel, Rudat's reading gives a distorted picture of the disability experience that Hemingway wants to articulate.

Rudat does not recognize, for instance, that the strategies for psychic healing suggested by the Count's performance—the "subduing" of sexual desire and the transference of erotic energy into "symbolic gratification" (7)—amount to little more than a passive acceptance of the asexual status that non-disabled society considers proper for the disabled. Jake knows that the Count's solution amounts to a renunciation of his sexuality. He is familiar with this kind of "cure," and he has declared it useless; alone in his hotel room, he remembers that "the Catholic Church had an awfully good way of handling [his disability.] Good advice, anyway. Not to think about it. Oh, it was swell advice. Try and take it" (*SAR* 39).

Contrary to Rudat's reading, wherein Jake realizes the larger significance of the Count's advice only gradually, Jake is instantly aware that the Count is being presented to him as a "role" model, and he resents it for reasons that would be clear to a man like Hemingway, who had had a real brush with catastrophic injury. Jake's almost complete silence during this "playful" interlude between Brett and the Count may indicate his anger over having the Count paraded in front of him as a version of what Leonard Kriegel calls "the charity cripple"—a figurehead whose injuries are assumed by the non-disabled to represent the effects of all injuries, and whose typically devil-may-care attitude is held out as worthy of emulation by other "cripples" (36-37).

Jake is silent when Brett forces the Count to undress and expose his wounds, and when she declares, "I told you [he] was one of us" (*SAR* 67), Jake recognizes her condescension toward both the Count and himself. He knows that what Brett really wants to say is, "Look, the Count is like *you*" because he has suffered severe injury and survived; by implication, the Count's boundless ebullience is something Brett hopes Jake will adopt as well, simply because she cannot stand to be around depressing or gloomy people.

The Count, in turn, is also aware of what Brett is doing, and embraces the role of "supercrip" she has offered him. He parrots the inspirational drivel she wants to hear: "You see, Mr. Barnes, it is because I have lived very much that now I can enjoy everything so well. Don't you find it is like that?" To this utopian assessment of post-disability living, Jake responds curtly, "Yes. Absolutely" (*SAR* 67). Anger and embarrassment clip his sentences, and the affect is flat and mechanical because Jake wants to limit his participation in what is essentially Brett's own private freak show.

The banter ends with a significant exchange between Brett and the Count. During a discussion of the Count's values, Brett declares, "You haven't any values. You're dead, that's all." To which the Count responds, "No, my dear. You're not right. I'm not dead at all" (*SAR* 67-68). The concept of death here is more than a metaphor for *fin de siècle* malaise and ennui among the wealthy (Gaggin 95-99): it serves to expose the liminal nature of existence for the disabled male in this society. On the one hand, the fact that Brett can so glibly declare the Count "dead" shows how close her thinking is to the eugenic/Social Darwinist stereotypes of the period. The Count's insistent and unequivocal response, in turn, gives the lie to his studied joviality and shows his own awareness of his marginalized status, revealing how desperately a disabled man must prove to others and himself that he is "worthy" to live. Hemingway's sensitivity to stereotypes of disability, rather than Jake's inability to interpret the Count's advice correctly, helps explain why the novel quickly casts such a "positive" role model into obscurity.

The next model of disability Jake encounters is the bullfighter Belmonte. This figure underscores the novel's ambivalence toward a worldview that valorizes traditional forms of masculine "performance" as "cures" for disability. The Belmonte character has been overshadowed, however, by the critical fascination with the relationship between Jake and the "damned good-looking" young matador Pedro Romero (*SAR* 170).

The tantalizing homosocial tension between Pedro and Jake diverts attention away from the dialectic that Hemingway creates though the aging matador Belmonte—a dialectic that exposes the interplay between the wounded body and public/private constructions of "honor," "masculinity," and "disability." The general view of Jake's bullfighting adventures assumes that Hemingway wants the reader to identify most with the implicitly able-bodied spectators who clamor to see the new young bullfighter. This perspective reduces Belmonte to a foil for Pedro Romero, and the graphic details of the older man's corruption and decline simply underscore the beauty and potential for greatness embodied by the younger artist.

Through Belmonte, however, readers are again forced to consider the physical and psychological costs of "supercripism" and normality-at-any-price. The matador is described as a paradox, someone who has managed to live on past his real "life": "Fifteen years ago they said if you wanted to see Belmonte you should go quickly, while he was still alive. Since then he has killed more than a thousand bulls" (*SAR* 218). Driven to perform even though he is "sick with a fistula" (218), Belmonte is kin to the jovial, wounded, and "dead" Count Mippipopolous. The tone of these passages is significant: they spare Belmonte the kind of quiet disgust reserved for other macho failures, such as Robert Cohn. By reminding the reader that Belmonte cannot reach his former heights of greatness simply because he is "no longer well enough" (219), Hemingway acknowledges the burden of social expectations on disabled men, and discards yet another faulty role model, a matador who has crafted an identity based on negation—an attempt to purge the self of any trait associated with "the invalid."

How then might Jake Barnes achieve happiness in a world shaped by the limitations of his sexually mutilated body and by cultural narratives that stigmatize deformity? The novel suggests, at least initially, that Jake might achieve a sense of wholeness if he can correctly interpret the veiled truths conveyed by Brett Ashley and Bill Gorton. These are characters who, by virtue of their unconventional worldviews, serve not so much as role models but rather as guides to show Jake how he might thrive in his otherwise oppressive and limited environment.

For her part, Brett Ashley suggests what Jake might do in the realm of the physical. She recognizes intuitively what recent work on the sexual development of disabled men and couples has confirmed, that it is possible for severely disabled people to achieve sexual satisfaction by re-training their bodies to feel erotic pleasure in different ways, through different erogenous zones (Callahan 77-78, Brown 37-38, Milam 40-43).[4]

Critics have barely considered the idea that Jake could achieve sexual satisfaction in nontraditional ways. While Debra Moddelmog's analysis of lovemaking between mutilated heroes and their "normal" lovers in *Across the River and into the Trees* and *To Have and Have Not* acknowledges that Hemingway was willing to consider the possibility of such sexual behavior (*Reading* 122-123), Chaman Nahal's indignation over moments of "perverted sexual satisfaction" (qtd. in Rudat, "Sexual Dilemmas" 2) between Jake and Brett Ashley constitutes the only critical recognition that Hemingway perhaps wanted to include the emasculated Jake in his pantheon of wounded but sexually active heroes.

However, the key moment that foreshadows the course of Jake's psychosexual development occurs not in the hotel room (as Nahal would have it), but rather in a Paris taxi when he finally gets a moment alone with Brett. Here we see how truly suitable Brett would be as a lover for Jake, because she is willing to entertain the possibility of a nontraditional erotic relationship. The meeting does not start well. "Don't touch me," she says. "Please don't touch me" (*SAR* 33). This reaction suggests a woman who knows about the nature of Jake's injury and is disgusted by thoughts of sex with man whose penis has been mutilated. But the scene does not end there. Despite her protests, Brett finally admits that she "[turns] all to jelly" at Jake's touch. Thus she affirms a capacity to experience intense physical sensation from simple stimulation—which may translate into an ability to derive satisfaction from nontraditional sex. Descriptions of her eyes also provide a kind of silent response to Jake's question about what they can "do" as lovers: Brett has been a wartime nurse (46); she has proven her ability to withstand the sight of horrific wounds—to "look on and on after everyone else's eyes in the world would have stopped looking" (34). She would not be "afraid" to have sex with a deformed man, even though "she was afraid of so many things" (34).

Through this scene, Hemingway hints at what Jake must do in order to achieve happiness and psychological stability: he must re-evaluate the effects of his wound for himself, discarding former notions about "damaged" masculinity based on cultural stereotypes. He must, in other words, rid his consciousness of the idea that sexual mutilation can only trigger mental and physical "degeneration" into homosexuality or invalidism—an idea elegantly condensed in the words of the Italian colonel who tells Jake in the hospital that he has "given more than [his] life" (*SAR* 39). But such is the power of these cultural stereotypes that there can be no epiphanic moment when Jake suddenly "sees" the truth and decides to drastically change his life. Instead, he must grope his way toward solving the riddle of his new identity, trying the best he can to interpret the random hints he is given.

Some of these hints come from Bill Gorton, who emerges as a mentor for Jake during an odd shopping trip in Paris. During this interlude, Bill's eccentric banter makes connections between dead bodies and ethics in ways designed to establish that Bill, like Brett, is someone comfortable with nonstandard bodies and perhaps able to help Jake on his journey toward psychological wholeness. When Bill and Jake are out walking in Paris, Bill stops by a taxidermist's shop and becomes strangely insistent that Jake buy something. "Want to buy anything?" he asks. "Nice stuffed dog?" (*SAR* 78).

Jake declines, but Bill will not relent. "Mean everything in the world to you after you bought it," he says. "Simple exchange of values. . . . Road to hell paved with unbought stuffed dogs" (*SAR* 78). This odd joking appeals to Jake, who remembers it later when he introduces Bill to Brett as a "taxidermist." To which Bill replies, "That was in another country. And besides all the animals were dead" (81). Bill's words have struck a chord with Jake, as well they might—by linking the notions of compromised (or "exchanged") values with "dead" bodies from "another country," Bill resurrects memories of the affable "supercrip" Count Mippipopolous and draws attention yet again to the question of how one can "overcome" or adapt to a catastrophic physical injury.

Bill's praise of out-of-place, nonstandard bodies and his certainty about their value seem to constitute a metaphorical expression of the same open-mindedness that led him to rescue a black Viennese boxer from a lynch mob earlier in the novel—a scene which Bill describes in similarly nonchalant, playful terms in order to downplay the mob's potential for violence (*SAR* 76-78). Taken together, these scenes establish Bill's importance to Jake's quest for wholeness as a disabled man. Specifically, these incidents show that Bill Gorton, like Brett Ashley, is committed to a nontraditional code of behavior allowing him to see value in bodies that the larger society would declare worthless or "dead." He seems eminently suitable as a friend for Jake: as a self-styled philosopher about what makes life worth living, Bill may be able to help Jake formulate his own principles for survival as a wounded man.

To see how Bill is only partially successful in healing Jake's psychic wounds, we must re-evaluate the quasi-erotic interlude between Bill and Jake that occurs during the Basque fishing trip in Chapter Twelve. As David Blackmore has elegantly explained, Jake's outdoor experiences foster an unexpected freedom of expression between the two men, to the extent that homoerotic desires rise "so near to the surface of Jake's personality as not to be latent" (59). Even so, I think Blackmore misses the mark when he concludes that the trip represents a victory for Hemingway's homophobia, as Jake finally falls back into "the trap of 'male homosexual panic'" (65). Like Blackmore, I believe Hemingway recognizes here that traditional concepts of masculinity—and especially *Freudian* concepts of masculinity—are too emotionally restrictive and in need of change. However, because the text links these norms and the same concepts of "normality" that stigmatize Jake's disability, I question whether the scene finally promotes the re-establishment of 19th century gender boundaries as Blackmore suggests (66).

To see the full range of ideas Hemingway presents here, it is necessary to re-evaluate the psychoanalytical play that occurs between Jake and Bill in the woods. Analyses of Gorton's highly symbolic banter by both Blackmore and Buckley confirm, in essence, that Bill copies the tactics of a skilled psychotherapist, verbally creating a "safe" space for Jake to express hidden or taboo feelings without fear of censure. Thus, Bill's graphic admission that his "fond[ness]" for Jake would make him a "faggot" in New York (*SAR* 121) is an invitation for Jake to express similar feelings as part of the "talking cure" being constructed here.

What such analyses of this psychoanalytical session fail to see, however, is that Jake's same-sex desires may not be the only cause of his problems. For instance, the war-centered double entendres that initiate Bill's well-known repartee suggest the plight of disabled veterans. Even the famous scene where Bill teases Jake with the idea of "[getting it] up for fun" (Blackmore 60) is peppered with loaded questions that echo the standard phrases of a military recruiter: "Been working for the common good?" "Work for the good of all" (*SAR* 118). Thus the text introduces a narrative thread about military service/disability that parallels the homoerotic subtext and intensifies as the joking continues between the two men.

Bill's persistent invocation of "irony and pity" further enhances this disability subtext: the phrase is a poetic crystallization of the attitudes and experiences that shaped the lives of disabled veterans during this era. Joanna Bourke, for instance, describes an "early sentimentalization" of the war-wounded that lasted until the 1920s (56). She explains that the most bathetic public responses were reserved for men with obvious deformities and amputations: in this early period, "public rhetoric judged soldiers' mutilations to be 'badges of their courage, the hall-mark of their glorious service, their proof of patriotism'" (56). According to the popular mythology of the times, a severe wound inspired more than just intense patriotism: women were supposed to be especially attracted to men with obvious injuries; these men, in turn, "were not beneath bargaining pity for love" (Bourke 56). For a time, a distinction was made between men wounded in war and those born with birth defects: the former were "broken warriors," and poems singing their praises "adopted the ironic, passive tone of the newly-styled, modern poetry" (Bourke 57).

The decline of national fascination with the war-wounded was foreshadowed by the concurrent stigmatization of veterans like Jake, whose disabilities were invisible to the public eye. Bourke reports: "The absent parts of men's bodies came to exert a special patriotic power. In the struggle for status and resources, absence could be more powerful than presence. The less visible or invisible diseases that disabled many servicemen . . . could not compete with limblessness" (59). This bias in favor of amputees translated into a pervasive resentment against men who were "merely" diseased or invisibly injured: such men were more often considered to be of inferior stock, or literally less "important" than men with obvious wounds (Bourke 59-60). During the postwar years, as the novelty of wounded men wore off and disabled veterans began to compete for resources with the civilian unemployed, this kind of resentment would even be directed against "heroic" amputees (Bourke 63-75).

Given this historical context, there is a double irony at work in the novel. According to the new rules of this modern world, Jake could "pass" as one of the most heroic of heroes. He has suffered the all-important amputation of a "part"—one which most men would probably consider the most vital "limb" of all. And yet the injury cannot be paraded in front of the public for acclaim. Because his wound must remain hidden and unknown, it must also remain "shameful."

The other resonant moment of irony and pity occurs at the point where Bill's humorous play falters. The way Bill's lighthearted tone is broken intensifies the novel's focus on disability, revealing that Freudian therapy is ill-equipped to deal with the many problems associated with a physical impairment. In the midst of "defining" Jake, Bill explains,

> You're an expatriate. You've lost touch with the soil. You get precious. Fake European standards have ruined you. You drink yourself to death. You become obsessed by sex. You spend all your time talking, not working. You're an expatriate, see? You hang around cafes.... You don't work. One group claims women support you. Another group claims you're impotent. (*SAR* 120)

On one level, this chatter reinforces the novel's well-known destabilization of sexual stereotypes by lampooning the traditionally gay or bisexual figure of the Wildean "Decadent." However, if we employ the psychoanalytical perspective established by Blackmore, Rudat, and Buckley, this babble becomes "empty speech"—the Freudian term for symbolic discourse designed to mask unpleasant truths. Seen in this light, it becomes apparent that what Bill is desperately trying—and trying *not*—to talk about is Jake's wound.

Consider first how the passage develops the character of the *expatriate*. He or she is defined, ultimately, as someone who is "impotent." This seems like an odd conclusion if one adheres to the literal definition of an *expatriate* as someone who has left his or her homeland. However, the characterization makes sense if one scratches the surface of the word to reveal the homonym beneath—"ex-patriot," a euphemism for a discharged soldier. This hidden concept exposes the wound-related anxiety here, because Jake's mutilated penis is the reason he has become an "ex-patriot" and an impotent *expatriate*. All the flaws ascribed to this decadent character—alcoholism, laziness, unemployment, sexual obsessiveness, and dependence on women—are also weaknesses stereotypically ascribed to wounded men whose injuries have supposedly destroyed all positive aspects of their former personalities (Pernick 49-52).[5]

Jake's response to Bill's prompting is simple, yet significant: countering the charge of impotence, he says, "No . . . I just had an accident" (*SAR* 120). The matter-of-fact tone here suggests that Jake may finally be able to accept his disability. He is on the verge of catharsis, of "coming out" as a disabled man (Shakespeare 50-55).

Any potential recovery is thwarted, however, by Bill's response: "Never mention that. . . . That's the sort of thing that can't be spoken of. That's what you ought to work up into a mystery. Like Henry's bicycle" (*SAR* 120). The joking is only half-hearted here: to some degree, Bill really *doesn't* want Jake to talk about his wound explicitly because his amateur therapy session (and by extension, Freudian theory in general) cannot address the range of problems associated with physical impairment. Thus Bill, the advocate of irony and pity, becomes an ironic figure—a therapist asking his patient to repress inconvenient problems.

For his part, Jake intuits the opportunity for healing presented to him here, and wants to exploit it. He notes that Bill "had been going splendidly," and wants to "start him again" on a more in-depth discussion of Jake's wound (*SAR* 120). But the task is too daunting for Bill. After a brief discussion of the nature of Henry's wound, Bill declares, "Let's lay off that" (*SAR* 121), and the conversation turns to repressed homosexuality—a more familiar (and less threatening) realm for amateur psychoanalysts.

Interpreting *The Sun Also Rises* from a disability perspective leads to a dark view of human existence, but not for the reasons most critics have discussed. Jake's struggles to find a place for himself in the postwar world help Hemingway to show that a wide and unacknowledged range of social ideas attach to physical impairment, and these cultural narratives work unobtrusively and insistently to make disability into a "master trope for human disqualification" (Mitchell and Snyder 3). A disability reading of the novel centers the work in Bill Gorton's refrain,

"Oh, Give them Irony and Give them Pity" (*SAR* 118-119). Hemingway gives us a novel where the failed romance between the hero and his lady represents the day-to-day struggle for (and with) "normality" for a generation of severely wounded survivors.[6]

The final, terrible irony of the novel is that it supports the idea that Brett and Jake *can* end their torment and be together in all senses of the word: sex is not impossible between them. However, neither Jake nor any of his well-meaning friends can rid themselves of their ingrained prejudices about disability, and these social constraints become the real obstacles to Jake's rehabilitation. The furtive sexual pleasures that Brett gives Jake are few and far between, and expressed in the classic Hemingway modes of elision, understatement, and silence indicative of guilt; for his part, Jake has internalized the stereotype of the sexually mutilated man who would be better off dead—he finally believes that "there's not a damn thing [he can] do" (*SAR* 34).

Thus, at the novel's conclusion, when Brett declares "Oh, Jake . . . we could have such a damned good time together," he can only respond, "Yes, . . . Isn't it pretty to think so?" (*SAR* 251). Although the use of "pretty" here is a "feminine" affectation, it is hardly, as Rudat has suggested (in "Hemingway on Sexual Otherness" and "Sexual Dilemmas"), the sign of Jake's life-affirming liberation from heterosexist prejudice. Rather, it is a sign that—despite occasional glimpses of his sexual potential—Jake has finally accepted the life society has mapped out for him as a disabled man. Jake will join Count Mippipopolous as a caricature of life and a toy for Brett's amusement, like one of the "pretty nice stuffed dogs" that stare at Bill Gorton from the window of a Paris taxidermy shop (*SAR* 78).

Notes

1. Discussing how racist stereotypes from the 19th century carried over into the 20th, Nies describes how the growing presence of wounded veterans in postwar America engendered a paradoxical glorification of the "fighting Nordic male" even as it fostered a widespread "collapse in the belief in the sanctity of physical borders of white soldiers" (23). According to the Lamarckian logic behind this worldview, a wounded soldier had the potential to weaken the "national health" by transmitting his "defects" into the gene pool.

2. Simi Linton defines the "medical model" as a worldview that "casts human variation as deviance from the norm, as pathological condition, as deficit, and, significantly, as an individual burden and personal tragedy." This philosophy allows non-disabled people to ignore "the social processes and policies that constrict disabled people's lives" (11).

3. Young arguably provides the most sustained examination of disabled men in Hemingway's works, as well as the most influential material for defining the nature of disability issues in *The Sun Also Rises*. Young's analysis goes beyond subsequent critics in its clarification of the disability experience, insofar as it resists the temptation to view Jake's mutilated penis as a metaphor for societal malaise. He recognizes that physical disabilities are never completely "overcome," and that they force individuals to view the world in different ways for a lifetime. Yet even Young falls back into the absolutist thinking that characterizes much Freudian thought regarding disability, suggesting that the disabled can never adapt to physical impairment that cannot be completely cured. Rather, disability becomes a totalizing flaw that causes the "primitivization" of personality (169), the core of an *idée fixe* that fuels a never-ending sense of "dis-grace" (41) and a dangerous "ambivalence" toward life.

4. In *Don't Worry, He Won't Get Far on Foot*, paraplegic author John Callahan describes achieving sexual satisfaction from a neck massage (77-78); in "Movie Stars and Sensuous Scars," Steven E. Brown relates the story of a disabled woman who trains herself to reach orgasm by rubbing her elbow (37-38); and in *The Cripple Liberation Front Marching Band Blues*, Lorenzo Milam describes a boyhood experience when he felt pleasure of sexual intensity simply by having a visitor lie next to him in a hospital bed (40-43).

5. Martin S. Pernick explains the basis for this totalizing view of disability in his analysis of eugenics and euthanasia. Specifically, he discusses the widespread belief in core genetic material known as "germ plasm" which, according to the science of the time, could be altered by environmental factors encountered after birth, such as poisons, illness, psychological shock, and wounds. Damaged germ plasm could drive a previously healthy organism into a state of physiological degeneration or "atavism" and transmit a variety of dangerous personality traits through a family bloodline (Pernick 49-52).

6. Tom Shakespeare (1996) eloquently summarizes the most common stereotypes of disabled sexuality:

> Stereotypes of disability often focus on asexuality, or lack of sexual potential or potency. Disabled people are subject to infantilization, especially disabled peo-

ple who are perceived as being 'dependent.' Just as children are assumed to have no sexuality, so disabled people are similarly denied the capacity for sexual feeling. Where disabled people are seen as sexual, this is in terms of deviant sexuality, for example, inappropriate sexual display or masturbation. (10)

Works Cited

Baker, Carlos. *Ernest Hemingway: A Life Story*. New York: Scribner's, 1969.

_____. "The Wastelanders." In *Modern Critical Interpretations: The Sun Also Rises*. Ed. Harold Bloom. New York: Chelsea House, 1987. 9-24.

Blackmore, David. "'In New York It'd Mean I Was a . . .': Masculinity Anxiety and Period Discourses of Sexuality in *The Sun Also Rises*." *The Hemingway Review* 18.1 (Fall 1998): 49-67.

Bourke, Joanna. *Dismembering the Male: Men's Bodies, Britain and the Great War*. Chicago: U of Chicago P, 1996.

Brown, Steven E. "Movie Stars and Sensuous Scars." In *Male Lust: Pleasure, Power, and Transformation*. Eds. Kay and Nagle, et al. New York: Harrington Park, 2000. 37-43.

Bruno, Richard L. "Devotees, Pretenders and Wannabes: Two Cases of Factitious Disability Disorder." *Journal of Sexuality and Disability* 15 (1997): 243-260.

Buckley, J. F. "Echoes of Closeted Desire(s): The Narrator and Character Voices of Jake Barnes." *The Hemingway Review* 19.2 (Spring 2000): 73-87.

Callahan, John. *Don't Worry, He Won't Get Far on Foot*. New York: Vintage Books, 1990.

Comley, Nancy R. and Robert Scholes. *Hemingway's Genders*. New Haven: Yale UP, 1994.

Eby, Carl P. *Hemingway's Fetishism: Psychoanalysis and the Mirror of Manhood*. New York: State U of New York P, 1999.

Elliott, Ira. "Performance Art: Jake Barnes and 'Masculine' Signification in *The Sun Also Rises*." *American Literature* 67 (March 1995): 77-94.

Gaggin, John. *Hemingway and Nineteenth-Century Aestheticism*. Ann Arbor: UMI Research, 1988.

Hemingway, Ernest. *The Sun Also Rises*. 1926. New York: Scribner's, 2003.

Kriegel, Leonard. "The Cripple in Literature." In *Images of the Disabled, Disabling Images*. Eds. Alan Gartner and Tom Joe. New York: Praeger, 1987. 31-46.

Linton, Simi. *Claiming Disability: Knowledge and Identity*. New York: New York UP, 1998.

Mellow, James R. *Hemingway: A Life Without Consequences*. New York: Houghton Mifflin, 1992.

Meyers, Jeffrey. *Hemingway: A Biography*. New York: Harper and Row, 1985.

Milam, Lorenzo. *The Cripple Liberation Front Marching Band Blues*. San Diego: MHO, 1984.

Mitchell, David T. and Sharon L. Snyder. *Narrative Prosthesis: Disability and the Dependencies of Discourse*. Ann Arbor: U of Michigan P, 2001.

Moddelmog, Debra A. *Reading Desire: In Pursuit of Ernest Hemingway*. Ithaca: Cornell UP, 1999.

Nies, Betsy L. *Eugenic Fantasies: Racial Ideology in the Literature and Popular Culture of the 1920s*. New York: Routledge, 2002.

Pernick, Martin S. *The Black Stork: Eugenics and the Death of "Defective" Babies in American Medicine and Motion Pictures Since 1915*. New York: Oxford UP, 1996.

Reynolds, Michael S. *Young Hemingway*. New York: Basil Blackwell, 1986.

Rudat, Wolfgang E. H. "Hemingway on Sexual Otherness: What's Really Funny in *The Sun Also Rises.*" *Hemingway Repossessed*. Ed. Kenneth Rosen. Westport, CT: Praeger, 1994. 169-179.

_____. "Sexual Dilemmas in *The Sun Also Rises:* Hemingway's Count and the Education of Jacob Barnes." *The Hemingway Review* 8.2 (Spring 1989): 2-13.

Shakespeare, Tom. *Untold Desires: The Sexual Politics of Disability*. London: Cassell, 1996.

Spilka, Mark. *Hemingway's Quarrel with Androgyny*. Lincoln: U of Nebraska P, 1990.

Strychacz, Thomas. *Hemingway's Theaters of Masculinity*. Baton Rouge: Louisiana State UP, 2003.

Vernon, Alex. "War, Gender, and Ernest Hemingway." *The Hemingway Review* 22.1 (Fall 2002): 34-55.

Young, Philip. *Ernest Hemingway: A Reconsideration*. University Park: Pennsylvania State UP, 1966.

RESOURCES

1899	Ernest Miller Hemingway is born to Clarence and Grace Hemingway on July 21 in Oak Park, Illinois.
1917	Hemingway works as a reporter on the *Kansas City Star.*
1918	Hemingway serves in Italy as an ambulance driver for the American Red Cross and is wounded on July 8 near Fossalta di Piave. He has an affair with nurse Agnes von Kurowsky.
1919	Hemingway is discharged from the American Red Cross and returns to the United States.
1920	Hemingway works as a reporter for the *Toronto Star.*
1921	Hemingway marries Hadley Richardson and moves to Paris.
1922	Hemingway reports on the Greco-Turkish War for the *Toronto Star.*
1923	*Three Stories and Ten Poems* is published in Paris. Hemingway's son John is born
1924	The short-fiction collection *in our time* is published in Paris.
1925	*In Our Time*, which adds fourteen stories to the earlier collection of vignettes, is published in the United States.
1926	*The Torrents of Spring* and *The Sun Also Rises* are published by Charles Scribner's Sons.
1927	*Men Without Women*, which includes "Hills Like White Elephants," is published. Hemingway divorces Hadley Richardson and marries Pauline Pfeiffer.
1928	Hemingway moves to Key West, where his son Patrick is born. Clarence Hemingway commits suicide on December 6 in Oak Park, Illinois.
1929	*A Farewell to Arms* is published.

1931	Hemingway's son Gregory is born.
1932	*Death in the Afternoon* is published.
1933	The short-story collection *Winner Take Nothing* is published.
1935	*Green Hills of Africa* is published.
1937	*To Have and Have Not* is published. Hemingway returns to Spain as a war correspondent on the Loyalist side.
1938	Hemingway writes scripts for the film *The Spanish Earth*, and *"The Fifth Column" and the First Forty-nine Stories* is published.
1940	Hemingway divorces Pauline Pfeiffer and marries Martha Gellhorn. *For Whom the Bell Tolls* is published. Hemingway buys a house, Finca Vigía, in Cuba, where he lives throughout most of the 1940s and 1950s.
1942	Hemingway's edited volume *Men at War: The Best War Stories of All Time* is published.
1944	Hemingway takes part in the Allied liberation of Paris with a partisan unit; he meets Mary Welsh.
1945	Hemingway is involved in a serious car crash; he divorces Martha Gellhorn.
1946	Hemingway marries Mary Welsh.
1947	Hemingway receives the Bronze Star.
1950	*Across the River and into the Trees* is published.
1951	Grace Hall Hemingway dies.
1952	*The Old Man and the Sea* is published.
1953	*The Old Man and the Sea* receives the Pulitzer Prize for Fiction.

1954	Hemingway is awarded the Nobel Prize in Literature.
1960	Hemingway moves to Ketchum, Idaho; he is hospitalized for various ailments, including depression.
1961	Hemingway commits suicide on July 2 in Ketchum, Idaho.
1964	*A Moveable Feast* is published.
1970	*Islands in the Stream* is published.
1972	The short-story collection *The Nick Adams Stories* is published.
1985	*The Dangerous Summer* is published.
1986	*The Garden of Eden*, an unfinished novel, is published.

Works by Ernest Hemingway_____

Long Fiction
The Sun Also Rises, 1926
The Torrents of Spring, 1926
A Farewell to Arms, 1929
To Have and Have Not, 1937
For Whom the Bell Tolls, 1940
Across the River and into the Trees, 1950
The Old Man and the Sea, 1952
Islands in the Stream, 1970
The Garden of Eden, 1986
True at First Light, 1999

Short Fiction
Three Stories and Ten Poems, 1923
in our time, 1924
In Our Time, 1925
Men Without Women, 1927
Winner Take Nothing, 1933
"The Fifth Column" and the First Forty-nine Stories, 1938
The Snows of Kilimanjaro, and Other Stories, 1961
The Short Happy Life of Francis Macomber, and Other Stories, 1963
The Nick Adams Stories, 1972
The Complete Short Stories of Ernest Hemingway, 1987

Drama and Poetry
Today Is Friday, 1926 (play)
The Fifth Column, 1938 (play)
The Spanish Earth, 1938 (documentary film script)
The Collected Poems of Ernest Hemingway, 1970
Eighty-eight Poems, 1979
Complete Poems, 1983

Nonfiction
Death in the Afternoon, 1932
Green Hills of Africa, 1935
Men at War: The Best War Stories of All Time, 1942 (editor)

Voyage to Victory: An Eye-Witness Report of the Battle for a Normandy Beachhead, 1944

Two Christmas Tales, 1959

The Wild Years, 1962

A Moveable Feast, 1964

By-Line: Ernest Hemingway, Selected Articles and Dispatches of Four Decades, 1967

Ernest Hemingway, Cub Reporter: "Kansas City Star" Stories, 1970 (Matthew J. Bruccoli, editor)

Selected Letters, 1917-1961, 1981 (Carlos Baker, editor)

Ernest Hemingway on Writing, 1984 (Larry W. Phillips, editor)

The Dangerous Summer, 1985

Dateline, Toronto: The Complete "Toronto Star" Dispatches, 1920-1924, 1985

Hemingway at Oak Park High: The High School Writings of Ernest Hemingway, 1916-1917, 1993

The Only Thing That Counts: The Ernest Hemingway/Maxwell Perkins Correspondence, 1925-1947, 1996 (Matthew J. Bruccoli, editor)

Bibliography

Baker, Carlos. *Ernest Hemingway: A Life Story*. New York: Charles Scribner's Sons, 1969.

_____. *Hemingway: The Writer as Artist*. 4th ed. Princeton, NJ: Princeton University Press, 1972.

_____, ed. *Ernest Hemingway: Critiques of Four Major Novels*. New York: Charles Scribner's Sons, 1962.

_____, ed. *Hemingway and His Critics: An International Anthology*. New York: Hill & Wang, 1961.

Balassi, William. "The Writing of the Manuscript of *The Sun Also Rises*, with a Chart of Its Session-by-Session Development." *The Hemingway Review* 6.1 (1986): 65-78.

Baldwin, Marc D. "Class Consciousness and the Ideology of Dominance in *The Sun Also Rises*." *McNeese Review* 33 (1990): 14-33.

_____. *Reading "The Sun Also Rises": Hemingway's Political Unconscious*. New York: Peter Lang, 1997.

Benson, Jackson J. *Hemingway: The Writer's Art of Self-Defense*. Minneapolis: University of Minnesota Press, 1969.

_____, ed. *New Critical Approaches to the Short Stories of Ernest Hemingway*. Durham, NC: Duke University Press, 1991.

Benstock, Shari. *Women of the Left Bank: Paris, 1900-1940*. Austin: University of Texas Press, 1986.

Berman, Ronald. *Fitzgerald, Hemingway, and the Twenties*. Tuscaloosa: University of Alabama Press, 2001.

Blackmore, David. "In New York It'd Mean I Was a . . . : Masculinity Anxiety and Period Discourses of Sexuality in *The Sun Also Rises*." *The Hemingway Review* 18.1 (1998): 49-67.

Bloom, Harold, ed. *Brett Ashley*. New York: Chelsea House, 1991.

_____, ed. *Ernest Hemingway's "The Sun Also Rises."* New York: Chelsea House, 1987.

Brenner, Gerry. *Concealments in Hemingway's Works*. Columbus: Ohio State University Press, 1983.

Brenner, Gerry, and Earl Rovit. *Ernest Hemingway*. Boston: G. K. Hall, 1986.

Brian, Denis. *The True Gen: An Intimate Portrait of Hemingway by Those Who Knew Him*. New York: Grove Press, 1987.

Bruccoli, Matthew J. *Fitzgerald and Hemingway, A Dangerous Friendship*. New York: Carroll & Graf, 1994.

Bryfonski, Dedria, ed. *Male and Female Roles in Hemingway's "The Sun Also Rises."* Detroit: Greenhaven Press, 2008.

Burgess, Anthony. *Ernest Hemingway*. London: Thames and Hudson, 1978.

Cappel, Constance. *Hemingway in Michigan*. New York: Fleet, 1966.

Comley, Nancy R., and Robert Scholes. *Hemingway's Genders: Rereading the Hemingway Text*. New Haven, CT: Yale University Press, 1994.

Curnett, Kirk. *Ernest Hemingway and the Expatriate Modernist Movement*. Detroit: Gale, 2000.

DeFazio, Albert J., III. *The Sun Also Rises*. Literary Masterpieces. Detroit: Gale, 2000.

Donaldson, Scott, ed. *The Cambridge Companion to Hemingway*. New York: Cambridge University Press, 1996.

Eby, Carl P. *Hemingway's Fetishism: Psychoanalysis and the Mirror of Manhood*. Albany: State University of New York Press, 1999.

Fantina, Richard. *Ernest Hemingway: Machismo and Masochism*. New York: Palgrave Macmillan, 2005.

Gandal, Keith. *The Gun and the Pen: Hemingway, Fitzgerald, Faulkner, and the Fiction of Mobilization*. New York: Oxford University Press, 2008.

Hays, Peter L. *Ernest Hemingway*. New York: Continuum, 1990.

_____, ed. *Teaching Hemingway's "The Sun Also Rises."* Moscow: University of Idaho Press, 2003.

Hemingway, Ernest. *Hemingway on War*. Ed. Sean Hemingway. New York: Charles Scribner's Sons, 2003.

Hinkle, James, "Some Unexpected Sources for *The Sun Also Rises*." *The Hemingway Review* 2.1 (1982): 26-42.

Kennedy, J. Gerald, and Jackson R. Bryer, eds. *French Connections. Hemingway and Fitzgerald Abroad*. New York: St. Martin's Press, 1998.

Kimmel, Michael S. *Manhood in America: A Cultural History*. New York: Free Press, 1996.

Larson, Kelli. *Ernest Hemingway: A Reference Guide, 1974-1989*. Boston: G. K. Hall, 1991.

Lee, A. Robert, ed. *Ernest Hemingway: New Critical Essays*. London: Vision Press, 1983.

Levenson, Michael, ed. *The Cambridge Companion to Modernism*. New York: Cambridge University Press, 1999.

Lewis, Robert. *Hemingway on Love*. Austin: University of Texas Press, 1965.

_____, ed. *Hemingway in Italy and Other Essays*. New York: Praeger, 1990.

Lynn, Kenneth S. *Hemingway*. New York: Simon & Schuster, 1987.

Mellow, James R. *Hemingway: A Life Without Consequences*. Boston: Houghton Mifflin, 1992.

Meredith, James H. *Understanding the Literature of World War I: A Student Casebook to Issues, Sources, and Historical Documents*. Westport, CT: Greenwood Press, 2004.

Messent, Peter. *Ernest Hemingway*. New York: St. Martin's Press, 1992.

_____. "Slippery Stuff: The Construction of Character in *The Sun Also*

Rises." *New Readings of the American Novel: Narrative Theory and Its Application.* New York: Macmillan, 1990. 86-129.

Meyers, Jeffrey. *Hemingway: A Biography.* 1985. New York: Da Capo Press, 1999.

_____, ed. *Ernest Hemingway: The Critical Heritage.* London: Routledge, 1982.

Moddelmog, Debra A. *Reading Desire: In Pursuit of Ernest Hemingway.* Ithaca, NY: Cornell University Press, 1999.

Nagel, James. "Brett and the Other Women in *The Sun Also Rises.*" *The Cambridge Companion to Hemingway.* Ed. Scott Donaldson. New York: Cambridge University Press, 1996. 87-108.

_____, ed. *Critical Essays on Ernest Hemingway's "The Sun Also Rises."* New York: G. K. Hall, 1995.

Nelson, Gerald B., and Glory Jones. *Hemingway: Life and Works.* New York: Facts On File, 1984.

Nissen, Axel. "Outing Jake Barnes: *The Sun Also Rises* and the Gay World." *American Studies in Scandinavia* 31.2 (1999): 42-57.

Pettipiece, Deirdre Ann. *Sex Theories and the Shaping of Two Moderns: Hemingway and HD.* New York: Routledge, 2002.

Reynolds, Michael S. "False Dawn: A Preliminary Analysis of *The Sun Also Rises* Manuscript." *Hemingway: A Revaluation.* Ed. Donald R. Noble. Troy, NY: Whitston, 1983. 115-34.

_____. *Hemingway: The Final Years.* New York: W. W. Norton, 2000.

_____. *Hemingway: The 1930s.* New York: W.W. Norton, 1998.

_____. *Hemingway: The Paris Years.* 1989. New York: W. W. Norton, 1999.

_____. *The Young Hemingway.* New York: Basil Blackwell, 1986.

Rovit, Earl. *Ernest Hemingway.* Boston: Twayne, 1963.

Rudat, Wolfgang E. H. *Alchemy in "The Sun Also Rises": Hidden Gold in Hemingway's Narrative.* Lewiston, NY: Edwin Mellen Press, 1992.

_____. "Hemingway, *The Sun Also Rises*—Masculinity, Feminism, and Gender-Role Reversal." *American Imago* 47.1 (1990): 43-68.

_____. *A Rotten Way to Be Wounded: The Tragicomedy of "The Sun Also Rises."* New York: Peter Lang, 1990.

Scafella, Frank, ed. *Hemingway: Essays of Reassessment.* New York: Oxford University Press, 1991.

Schwarz, Jeffrey A. "The Saloon Must Go, and I Will Take It with Me: American Prohibition, Nationalism, and Expatriation in *The Sun Also Rises.*" *Studies in the Novel* 33.2 (Summer 2001): 180-201.

Shapiro, Charles, ed., *Twelve Original Essays on Great American Novels.* Detroit: Wayne State University Press, 1958.

Sherry, Vincent, ed. *The Cambridge Companion to the Literature of the First World War.* New York: Cambridge University Press, 2005.

Spilka, Mark. *Hemingway's Quarrel with Androgyny*. Lincoln: University of Nebraska Press, 1990.

Stephens, Robert O., ed. *Ernest Hemingway: The Critical Reception*. New York: Burt Franklin, 1977.

Stoneback, H. R. *Reading Hemingway's "The Sun Also Rises": Glossary and Commentary*. Kent, OH: Kent State University Press, 2007.

Strong, Amy. *Race and Identity in Hemingway's Fiction*. New York: Palgrave Macmillan, 2008.

Strychacz, Thomas. *Hemingway's Theaters of Masculinity*. Baton Rouge: Louisiana State University Press, 2003.

Svoboda, Frederic Joseph. *Hemingway and "The Sun Also Rises": The Crafting of a Style*. Lawrence: University Press of Kansas, 1983.

Trogdon, Robert W., ed. *Ernest Hemingway: A Literary Reference*. 1999. New York: Carroll & Graf, 2002.

Tyler, Lisa. *Student Companion to Ernest Hemingway*. Westport, CT: Greenwood Press, 2001.

Wagner[-Martin], Linda. *Ernest Hemingway: A Reference Guide*. Boston: G. K. Hall, 1977.

_____. "'Proud and Friendly and Gently': Women in Hemingway's Early Fiction." *College Literature* 7 (1980): 239-47.

_____, ed. *Ernest Hemingway: Seven Decades of Criticism*. East Lansing: Michigan State University Press, 1998.

_____, ed. *Ernest Hemingway's "The Sun Also Rises": A Casebook*. New York: Oxford University Press, 2002.

_____, ed. *A Historical Guide to Ernest Hemingway*. New York: Cambridge University Press, 1987.

_____, ed. *New Essays on "The Sun Also Rises."* New York: Cambridge University Press, 1987.

Waldhorn, Arthur. *A Reader's Guide to Ernest Hemingway*. New York: Octagon Books, 1972.

_____, ed. *Ernest Hemingway: A Collection of Criticism*. New York: McGraw-Hill, 1973.

Weeks, Robert P., ed. *Hemingway: A Collection of Critical Essays*. Englewood Cliffs, NJ: Prentice-Hall, 1962.

Whitlow, Roger. *Cassandra's Daughters: The Women in Hemingway*. Westport, CT: Greenwood Press, 1984.

Wilson, Edmund. *The Wound and the Bow: Seven Studies in Literature*. Boston: Houghton Mifflin, 1941.

Young, Philip. *Ernest Hemingway*. New York: Holt, Rinehart and Winston, 1952.

_____. *Ernest Hemingway: A Reconsideration*. University Park: Pennsylvania State University Press, 1966.

CRITICAL INSIGHTS

About the Editor

Keith Newlin is Professor and Chair of the Department of English at the University of North Carolina Wilmington, where he teaches courses in American literary realism and naturalism, American modernism, and American drama. The recipient of a fellowship from the National Endowment for the Humanities, he is the author of *Hamlin Garland: A Life* (2008), coeditor of *The Collected Plays of Theodore Dreiser* (2000) and *Selected Letters of Hamlin Garland* (1998), and editor of *A Summer to Be: A Memoir by the Daughter of Hamlin Garland* (2010), *A Theodore Dreiser Encyclopedia* (2003), *American Plays of the New Woman* (2000), and Hamlin Garland's *Rose of Dutcher's Coolly* (2005) and *The Book of the American Indian* (2005). He is past president of the International Theodore Dreiser Society and the Hamlin Garland Society, and at present he is the coeditor of *Studies in American Naturalism*, distributed by the University of Nebraska Press.

About *The Paris Review*

The Paris Review is America's preeminent literary quarterly, dedicated to discovering and publishing the best new voices in fiction, nonfiction, and poetry. The magazine was founded in Paris in 1953 by the young American writers Peter Matthiessen and Doc Humes, and edited there and in New York for its first fifty years by George Plimpton. Over the decades, the *Review* has introduced readers to the earliest writings of Jack Kerouac, Philip Roth, T. C. Boyle, V. S. Naipaul, Ha Jin, Ann Patchett, Jay McInerney, Mona Simpson, and Edward P. Jones, and published numerous now classic works, including Roth's *Goodbye, Columbus*, Donald Barthelme's *Alice*, Jim Carroll's *Basketball Diaries*, and selections from Samuel Beckett's *Molloy* (his first publication in English). The first chapter of Jeffrey Eugenides's *The Virgin Suicides* appeared in the *Review*'s pages, as well as stories by Rick Moody, David Foster Wallace, Denis Johnson, Jim Crace, Lorrie Moore, and Jeanette Winterson.

    The Paris Review's renowned Writers at Work series of interviews, whose early installments include legendary conversations with E. M. Forster, William Faulkner, and Ernest Hemingway, is one of the landmarks of world literature. The interviews received a George Polk Award and were nominated for a Pulitzer Prize. Among the more than three hundred interviewees are Robert Frost, Marianne Moore, W. H. Auden, Elizabeth Bishop, Susan Sontag, and Toni Morrison. Recent issues feature conversations with Salman Rushdie, Joan Didion, Norman Mailer, Kazuo Ishiguro, Marilynne Robinson, Umberto Eco, Annie Proulx, and Gay Talese. In November 2009, Picador published the final volume of a four-volume series of anthologies of *Paris Review* interviews. *The New York Times* called the Writers at Work series "the most remarkable and extensive interviewing project we possess."

The Paris Review is edited by Philip Gourevitch, who was named to the post in 2005, following the death of George Plimpton two years earlier. A new editorial team has published fiction by André Aciman, Colum McCann, Damon Galgut, Mohsin Hamid, Uzodinma Iweala, Gish Jen, Stephen King, James Lasdun, Padgett Powell, Richard Price, and Sam Shepard. Poetry editors Charles Simic, Meghan O'Rourke, and Dan Chiasson have selected works by John Ashbery, Kay Ryan, Billy Collins, Tomaž Šalamun, Mary Jo Bang, Sharon Olds, Charles Wright, and Mary Karr. Writing published in the magazine has been anthologized in *Best American Short Stories* (2006, 2007, and 2008), *Best American Poetry*, *Best Creative Non-Fiction*, the Pushcart Prize anthology, and *O. Henry Prize Stories*.

The magazine presents two annual awards. The Hadada Award for lifelong contribution to literature has recently been given to Joan Didion, Norman Mailer, Peter Matthiessen, and, in 2009, John Ashbery. The Plimpton Prize for Fiction, awarded to a debut or emerging writer brought to national attention in the pages of *The Paris Review*, was presented in 2007 to Benjamin Percy, to Jesse Ball in 2008, and to Alistair Morgan in 2009.

The Paris Review was a finalist for the 2008 and 2009 National Magazine Awards in fiction, and it won the 2007 National Magazine Award in photojournalism. The *Los Angeles Times* recently called *The Paris Review* "an American treasure with true international reach."

Since 1999 *The Paris Review* has been published by The Paris Review Foundation, Inc., a not-for-profit 501(c)(3) organization.

The Paris Review is available in digital form to libraries worldwide in selected academic databases exclusively from EBSCO Publishing. Libraries can contact EBSCO at 1-800-653-2726 for details. For more information on *The Paris Review* or to subscribe, please visit: www.theparisreview.org.

Contributors

Keith Newlin is Professor and Chair of the Department of English at the University of North Carolina Wilmington. He is the author or editor of ten books, and his recent work includes *Hamlin Garland: A Life* (2008) and, as editor, *A Summer to Be: A Memoir by the Daughter of Hamlin Garland* (2008), *A Theodore Dreiser Encyclopedia* (2003), and two reprints of books by Hamlin Garland. At present he is the coeditor of *Studies in American Naturalism*, distributed by the University of Nebraska Press.

Stanley Archer was a Professor in the English Department at Texas A&M University.

Petrina Crockford lives and writes in Colorado.

Matthew J. Bolton is Professor of English at Loyola School in New York City, where he also serves as Dean of Students. He received his doctor of philosophy degree in English from the Graduate Center of the City University of New York (CUNY) in 2005. His dissertation at the university was titled "Transcending the Self in Robert Browning and T. S. Eliot." Prior to attaining his Ph.D. at CUNY, he also earned a master of philosophy degree in English (2004) and a master of science degree in English education (2001). His undergraduate work was done at the State University of New York at Binghamton, where he studied English literature.

Jennifer Banach is a writer and independent scholar who lives in Connecticut. She has served as the contributing editor of *Bloom's Guides: Heart of Darkness* (2009) and *Bloom's Guides: The Glass Menagerie* (2007) and is the author of *Bloom's How to Write About Tennessee Williams* (2009) and *Understanding Norman Mailer* (2010). She has also composed teaching guides to international literature for Random House's Academic Resources division and has contributed to numerous literary reference books for academic publishers on topics ranging from Romanticism to contemporary literature. Her work has appeared in academic and popular venues alike; her fiction and nonfiction have appeared under the *Esquire* banner. She is a member of the Association of Literary Scholars and Critics.

Lorie Watkins Fulton is Assistant Professor of Literature at William Carey University. She teaches undergraduate and graduate classes in American literature, and her research interests include southern literature, African American literature, and American modernism. Her current project is a book-length manuscript that examines William Faulkner's political critique of the Cavalier myth in his late fiction. She has published essays in journals such as *The Faulkner Journal*, *The Hemingway Review*, *Southern Studies*, *African American Review*, *Mississippi Quarterly*, *Southern Literary Journal*, and *Modern Philology*.

Laurence W. Mazzeno is President Emeritus of Alvernia University, Reading, Pennsylvania. He is the author of nine books, including *The Dickens Industry*, *Tennyson: The Critical Legacy*, and the forthcoming *Jane Austen: Two Centuries of Criticism*. He is a former editor and current member of the editorial board for *Nineteenth-*

Century Prose. A frequent contributor to reference books and encyclopedias, he has also written extensively for popular periodicals and online journals.

Carlos Baker was the Woodrow Wilson Professor of Literature at Princeton University. His books on Shelley and Hemingway have been influential in defining the fields of study on those authors. He wrote and edited numerous volumes of fiction and nonfiction, including *Shelley's Major Poetry: The Fabric of a Vision* (1948), *Hemingway: The Writer as Artist* (1952), *Forty Years of Pulitzer Prizes* (1957), *Hemingway and His Critics: An International Anthology* (1961), *Ernest Hemingway: Critiques of Four Major Novels* (1962), *Coleridge: Poetry and Prose* (1965), *Modern American Usage: A Guide* (with Jacques Barzun, 1966), *Ernest Hemingway: A Life Story* (1969), *Ernest Hemingway: Selected Letters, 1917-1961* (1981), *Echoing Green: Romanticism, Modernism, and the Phenomena of Transference in Poetry* (1984), and *Emerson Among the Eccentrics: A Group Portrait* (1996).

Mark Spilka is Professor Emeritus of English and Comparative Literature at Brown University, where he served as editor of *Novel: A Forum on Fiction*. His books include *Love Ethic of D. H. Lawrence* (1955), *Dickens and Kafka* (1963), *D. H. Lawrence: A Collection of Critical Essays* (1963), *Virginia Woolf's Quarrel with Grieving* (1980), *Hemingway's Quarrel with Androgyny* (1990), and *Eight Lessons in Love: A Domestic Violence Reader* (1997).

Dewey Ganzel is Emeritus Professor of English at Oberlin College, Ohio. He is the author of *Fortune and Men's Eyes: The Career of John Payne Collier* (1982) and *Mark Twain Abroad: The Cruise of the Quaker City* (1968). His essays have appeared in such journals as *Modern Fiction Studies*, *Journal of Modern Literature*, *American Literature*, and *Sewanee Review*.

Delbert E. Wylder was Professor of English at Murray State University, where he served as the department chair and founded the university's creative-writing program. Over the course of his career, he also founded the Western Literature Association, was a founding editor of *Western American Literature*, and authored several books, including *Emerson Hough* (1981) and *Hemingway's Heroes* (1969).

Donald T. Torchiana was Professor of English at Northwestern University. An internationally recognized scholar of Irish literature whose books include *Backgrounds for Joyce's "Dubliners"* (1986), *W. B. Yeats and Georgian Ireland* (1966), and *Among School Children and the Education of the Irish Spirit* (1965), he also published a number of articles on American writers such as Faulkner and Hemingway.

Scott Donaldson is Emeritus Professor of English at the College of William and Mary, where he taught for more than twenty-five years. A leading literary biographer of twentieth-century American authors, his books include *John Cheever: A Biography* (1988), *Fool for Love: F. Scott Fitzgerald* (1983), and *By Force of Will: The Life and Art of Ernest Hemingway* (1977). He has served on the board of the Hemingway Foundation/Society and also as the organization's president from 2000 to 2002. His most recent work is *Fitzgerald and Hemingway: Works and Days* (2009).

Sibbie O'Sullivan is Senior Lecturer in the University Honors Program at the University of Maryland as well as a poet, playwright, and short-story writer. Her latest work includes *Little Wheel* (2005), a CD of poems; *The Body* (2004), a play; and a nonfiction piece, "Out of the Loop," which Robert Atwan, editor of *The Best American Essays 2001*, selected as a notable essay of the year. She is currently at work on the libretto for a John Stephens opera titled *The Devil in the Flesh*.

Ira Elliott is Assistant Professor of the Humanities at the Cooper Union for the Advancement of Science and Art. He earned his Ph.D. from CUNY Graduate School with a dissertation titled "Hemingway Unbound: Reading a Modernist Subjectivity" and has published in the *Journal of Modern Literature, LIT: Literature Interpretation Theory*, and *American Literature*.

Jeremy Kaye is a doctoral candidate and lecturer at the University of California, Riverside. His work has appeared in *The Hemingway Review* and the *Journal of Popular Culture*.

Donald A. Daiker is Emeritus Professor of English at Miami University, where he teaches composition, American literature, and short stories. Specializing in the works of Ernest Hemingway, he has contributed to *The Hemingway Review*. He has also published nine books on the subjects of composition, literature, and the art of writing, the most recent being *Composition in the 21st Century: Rereading the Past, Rewriting the Future* (2003).

Dana Fore is a lecturer for the University Writing Program at the University of California, Davis. He earned his Ph.D. from Davis in 2005 with a dissertation titled "Masculinity, Disability, and the Literature of Bodies on Display."

Acknowledgments _____

"Ernest Hemingway" by Stanley Archer. From *Cyclopedia of World Authors, Fourth Revised Edition*. Copyright © 2004 by Salem Press, Inc. Reprinted with permission of Salem Press.

"The *Paris Review* Perspective" by Petrina Crockford. Copyright © 2011 by Petrina Crockford. Special appreciation goes to Christopher Cox, Nathaniel Rich, and David Wallace-Wells, editors at *The Paris Review*.

"The Wastelanders" by Carlos Baker. From *Hemingway: The Writer as Artist* (1952), pp. 75-93. Copyright © 1952 by Princeton University Press, 1956 2nd Edition, 1980 renewed in author's name. Reprinted by permission of Princeton University Press.

"The Death of Love in *The Sun Also Rises*" by Mark Spilka. From *Twelve Original Essays on Great American Novels* (1958), pp. 238-256, edited by Charles Shapiro. Copyright © 1958 by Wayne State University Press. Reprinted with the permission of Wayne State University Press.

"*Cabestro* and *Vaquilla*: The Symbolic Structure of *The Sun Also Rises*" by Dewey Ganzel. From the *Sewanee Review* 76, no. 1 (Winter 1968): 26-48. Copyright © 1968 by the *Sewanee Review*. Reprinted with the permission of the editor.

"*The Sun Also Rises*: The Wounded Anti-Hero" by Delbert E. Wylder. From *Hemingway's Heroes* (1969), pp. 31-65. Copyright © 1969 by The University of New Mexico Press. Reprinted with permission of The University of New Mexico Press.

"*The Sun Also Rises*: A Reconsideration" by Donald T. Torchiana. From *Fitzgerald/ Hemingway Annual 1969*, pp. 77-103. Copyright © 1970 by Bruccoli Clark Layman. Reprinted with permission of Bruccoli Clark Layman.

"Hemingway's Morality of Compensation" by Scott Donaldson. From *American Literature* 43, no. 3 (1971): 399-420. Copyright © 1971 by Duke University Press. All rights reserved. Used by permission of the publisher.

"Love and Friendship/Man and Woman in *The Sun Also Rises*" by Sibbie O'Sullivan. From *Arizona Quarterly* 44, no. 2 (1988): 76-97. Copyright © 1988 by University of Arizona. Reprinted with permission of University of Arizona.

"Performance Art: Jake Barnes and 'Masculine' Signification in *The Sun Also Rises*" by Ira Elliott. From *American Literature* 67, no. 1 (March 1995): 77-94. Copyright © 1995 by Duke University Press. All rights reserved. Used by permission of the publisher.

"Reading Around Jake's Narration: Brett Ashley and *The Sun Also Rises*" by Lorie Watkins Fulton. From *The Hemingway Review* 24, no. 1 (Fall 2004): 61-80. Copyright © 2004 by the Hemingway Society. All rights reserved. Reprinted with permission of the Hemingway Society.

"The 'Whine' of Jewish Manhood: Rereading Hemingway's Anti-Semitism, Reimagining Robert Cohn" by Jeremy Kaye. From *The Hemingway Review* 25, no. 2 (Spring 2006): 44-60. Copyright © 2006 by the Hemingway Society. All rights reserved. Reprinted with permission of the Hemingway Society.

"The Pedagogy of *The Sun Also Rises*" by Donald A. Daiker. From *The Hemingway Review* 27, no. 1 (Fall 2007): 74-88. Copyright © 2007 by the Hemingway Society. All rights reserved. Reprinted with permission of the Hemingway Society.

"Life Unworthy of Life? Masculinity, Disability, and Guilt in *The Sun Also Rises*" by Dana Fore. From *The Hemingway Review* 26, no. 2 (Spring 2007): 74-88. Copyright © 2007 by the Hemingway Society. All rights reserved. Reprinted with permission of the Hemingway Society.

Across the River and into the Trees (Hemingway), 13, 54, 223
Adams, Richard P., 70
Alcoholism, 9, 103, 117, 211, 214, 237, 246, 294
Allen, Mary, 72
Anderson, Sherwood, 12, 24, 32, 88, 90, 161, 182
Androgyny, 37, 46, 74, 111, 135, 230, 234, 249, 266, 268, 332
Anti-Semitism, 78, 108, 240, 278, 291, 294, 311
As I Lay Dying (Faulkner), 51
Ashley, Brett (*The Sun Also Rises*), 9, 18, 59, 106, 133, 153, 166, 216, 232, 335; androgyny, 41, 111, 135, 249; and Jake Barnes, 103, 110, 118, 137, 143, 160, 168, 198, 227, 234, 245, 265, 272, 284, 319, 324, 338; and Mike Campbell, 104, 213; as Circe figure, 69, 99, 139, 274, 279; and Robert Cohn, 103, 129, 241, 307; critical responses, 69, 72, 270; and religion, 100, 281; and Pedro Romero, 104, 119, 136, 162, 282, 323

Baker, Carlos, 69, 76, 164, 175, 209, 217, 240, 297, 311, 334
Baker, Sheridan, 176
Balassi, William, 5
Baldwin, Marc, 77
Barlowe, Jamie, 72, 291
Barnes, Jake (*The Sun Also Rises*), 5, 18, 23, 28, 68, 93, 186, 194, 204, 250; and Brett Ashley, 99, 110, 120, 168, 198, 227, 271, 319, 325; and bullfighting, 156, 315, 337; and Robert Cohn, 38, 167, 232, 297;

and Bill Gorton, 94, 209, 263, 340; impotence, 42, 107, 146, 258, 285, 333; as narrator, 59, 108, 145, 161, 271, 297, 301; as newspaperman, 145, 207; and religion, 100, 138, 187; and Pedro Romero, 119, 286; and sports, 112
"Battler, The" (Hemingway), 237
Belmonte, Juan (*The Sun Also Rises*), 156, 164, 218, 323, 336
Benson, Jackson J., 70
Berman, Ronald, 78, 308
Biblical allusions, 46, 94, 147, 167, 176, 180
"Big Two-Hearted River" (Hemingway), 4, 113
Bill Gorton. *See* Gorton, Bill
Blackmore, David, 340
Bloom, Harold, 72
Blotner, Joseph, 52
Bourke, Joanna, 331, 341
Boxing, 38, 59, 108, 112, 116, 128, 166, 180, 210, 302, 315
Boyarin, Daniel, 295
Brenner, Gerry, 48, 73, 283, 290
Brett Ashley. *See* Ashley, Brett
British Blondes, 229
Brodkin, Karen, 299, 311
Broer, Lawrence R., 327
Bryfonski, Dedria, 79
Bullfighting, 5, 44, 71, 115, 119, 123, 155, 160, 164, 176, 185, 194, 218, 248, 262, 286, 305, 315, 337
Butler, Judith, 250

Campbell, Mike (*The Sun Also Rises*), 9, 43, 103, 106, 115, 213, 279, 323
Canby, Henry Seidel, 171

Castration, 46, 147, 271, 295, 304

Catholicism, 100, 114, 138, 158, 181, 186, 208, 280, 335

Chase, Cleveland, 67

Clyne, Frances (*The Sun Also Rises*), 42, 109, 127, 160, 207, 212, 232

Code hero, 68, 116, 290

Cohn, Robert (*The Sun Also Rises*), 9, 31, 38, 58, 78, 106, 108, 115, 128, 159, 180, 183, 196, 211, 232, 272, 282, 294, 301, 315; and Brett Ashley, 96, 103, 141, 241, 275, 307; and Jake Barnes, 61, 125, 162, 167; and Pedro Romero, 132

Comley, Nancy R., 74, 290, 328

Conrad, Joseph, 177

Count Mippipopolous. *See* Mippipopolous, Count

Cowley, Malcolm, 17, 51, 205

Curnutt, Kirk, 78

Davidson, Arnold, 77, 252, 265

Davidson, Cathy, 77, 252, 265

Death in the Afternoon (Hemingway), 34, 49, 57, 123, 132, 138, 149, 185, 195, 249, 328

DeFazio, Albert J., III, 78

Dollimore, Jonathan, 252, 258

Donaldson, Scott, 71, 271, 291, 297

Doody, Terrence, 315

Eby, Carl P., 74, 304, 327, 332

Eliot, T. S., 70, 98, 107, 177

Elliott, Ira, 75, 332

Fantina, Richard, 75, 309

Farewell to Arms, A (Hemingway), 13, 88, 111, 170, 203, 223, 249

Farrell, James T., 67, 203

Faulkner, William, 24, 49

Femininity, 41, 135, 229, 251

Fiedler, Leslie, 69, 177, 270, 275, 294

Fishing, 96, 113, 149, 181, 220, 261, 281, 340

Fitzgerald, F. Scott, 8, 30, 33, 87, 146, 177, 206, 230, 300, 312

Fleming, Robert E., 266, 327

For Whom the Bell Tolls (Hemingway), 13, 18, 29, 54, 100, 268

Forter, Greg, 47

Frances Clyne. *See* Clyne, Frances

Frederic Henry. *See* Henry, Frederic

Freedman, Jonathan, 294

Friedman, Melvin, 71

Friendship, 45, 142, 149, 197, 212, 227, 234, 238, 245, 287

Fruscione, Joseph, 57, 63

Fulton, Lorie Watkins, 73

Gandal, Keith, 78

Ganzel, Dewey, 176, 195, 327

Garden of Eden, The (Hemingway), 14, 249, 266, 269

Gender roles, 37, 73, 232, 236, 250, 256

Georgette (*The Sun Also Rises*), 42, 110, 178, 207, 233, 253, 276, 291

Gibson Girl, 230

Gilman, Sander, 300

Gladstein, Mimi Reisel, 270, 275, 328

Gorman, Herbert, 67

Gorton, Bill (*The Sun Also Rises*), 60, 94, 106, 112, 130, 157, 209, 341, 344; and Jake Barnes, 238, 261, 339; and Mike Campbell, 214

Grace under pressure, 13, 68, 125

Great Gatsby, The (Fitzgerald), 66, 146, 269, 295, 300

Green Hills of Africa (Hemingway), 179, 183, 222

Griffin, Peter, 267

Harris. *See* Wilson-Harris
Harry Morgan. *See* Morgan, Harry
Hays, Peter L., 79
Hemingway, Ernest; and Sherwood
    Anderson, 12, 24, 32, 88, 161, 182;
    and anti-Semitism, 78, 294, 311; on
    Joseph Conrad, 177; and William
    Faulkner, 49; and F. Scott Fitzgerald,
    10, 30, 87, 146, 206, 312; iceberg
    theory, 14, 49, 278; marriages, 13,
    222; Nobel Prize, 13, 54; in Paris, 3,
    12, 23, 28, 77, 206; and Ezra Pound,
    24, 29; writing career, 4, 12; writing
    style, 7, 14, 18, 36, 47, 49, 66, 98,
    278; on writing *The Sun Also Rises*,
    7, 87
Hemingway code, 68, 77, 116, 203,
    290
Hemingway hero, 12, 17, 68, 108, 116,
    147, 199, 290
Henry, Frederic (*A Farewell to Arms*),
    13, 29, 223, 269
Homoeroticism, 73, 261, 304, 336,
    340
Homosexuality, 45, 75, 111, 135,
    173, 179, 183, 207, 216, 234,
    237, 249, 257, 264, 332, 340
Hook, Andrew, 76
Hotchner, A. E., 181
Hovey, Richard B., 70
Howells, William Dean, 229

If I Forget Thee, Jerusalem (Faulkner),
    57
Impotence, 40, 46, 107, 125, 137,
    146, 175, 227, 237, 258, 263,
    285, 301, 333, 343
In Our Time (Hemingway), 3, 12
Islands in the Stream (Hemingway),
    14, 18, 249
Itzkovitz, Daniel, 303

Jake Barnes. *See* Barnes, Jake
James, Henry, 27, 263
James, William, 148
Jewishness, 38, 59, 78, 160, 211, 240,
    291, 294, 306, 311, 315
Jordan, Robert (*For Whom the Bell
    Tolls*), 13, 18, 29, 193, 224, 268
Juan Belmonte. *See* Belmonte, Juan

Karl, Frederick R., 62
Kennedy, J. Gerald, 31, 77
"Killers, The" (Hemingway), 171, 310
Kriegel, Leonard, 335
Kumar, Sukrita Paul, 285

Lady Brett Ashley. *See* Ashley, Brett
Larson, Kelli, 65
Lawrence, D. H., 108, 261
Lewis, Robert W., 69, 167
Littell, Robert, 89
Lockridge, Ernest, 327
Loeb, Harold, 4, 58, 105, 182, 211, 311
Lost generation, 12, 17, 65, 91, 99, 171,
    181, 184, 246, 269
Lynn, Kenneth S., 59, 76, 261, 269, 311

McHaney, Thomas L., 62
Martin, Wendy, 73, 261, 281, 287, 290
Masculinity, 38, 43, 46, 74, 135, 173,
    236, 251, 259, 295, 302, 308, 333,
    341
Maurois, André, 67
Mellow, James R., 76, 266, 331
Messent, Peter, 77
Meyer Wolfsheim. *See* Wolfsheim,
    Meyer
Meyers, Jeffrey, 63, 249, 297, 334
Meyerson, Robert E., 310
Michaels, Walter Benn, 299, 302
Mieli, Mario, 262
Mike Campbell. *See* Campbell, Mike